SEX, DRUGS & ROCK 'n' ROLL

Toby Miller
General Editor

Vol. 30

The Popular Culture and Everyday Life series
is part of the Peter Lang Media and Communication list.
Every volume is peer reviewed and meets
the highest quality standards for content and production.

PETER LANG
New York • Bern • Frankfurt • Berlin
Brussels • Vienna • Oxford • Warsaw

DOUGLAS BRODE

SEX, DRUGS & ROCK 'n' ROLL

The Evolution of an American Youth Culture

PETER LANG
New York • Bern • Frankfurt • Berlin
Brussels • Vienna • Oxford • Warsaw

Library of Congress Cataloging-in-Publication Data
Brode, Douglas.
Sex, drugs & rock 'n' roll: the evolution of an American youth culture / Douglas Brode.
pages cm. — (Popular culture and everyday life; vol. 30)
Includes bibliographical references and index.
1. Youth—Sexual behavior—United States—History.
2. Teens—Sexual behavior—United States—History.
3. Youth—Drug use—United States—History.
4. Teens—Drug use—United States—History.
5. Youth—United States—Social conditions—History.
6. Teens—United States—Social conditions—History.
I. Title. II. Title: Sex, drugs and rock 'n' roll.
HQ27.B685   3305.2350973—dc23   2014043805
ISBN 978-1-4331-2887-5 (hardcover)
ISBN 978-1-4331-2886-8 (paperback)
ISBN 978-1-4539-1506-6 (e-book)
ISSN 1529-2428

Bibliographic information published by **Die Deutsche Nationalbibliothek.**
Die Deutsche Nationalbibliothek lists this publication in the "Deutsche
Nationalbibliografie"; detailed bibliographic data are available
on the Internet at http://dnb.d-nb.de/.

Cover image by Dan Zollinger

© 2015 Peter Lang Publishing, Inc., New York
29 Broadway, 18th floor, New York, NY 10006
www.peterlang.com

Printed in the United States of America

ACKNOWLEDGMENTS

With great thanks to my son Shane Johnson Brode, for his endless hard work and great judgment in helping me pick the precisely appropriate images for this volume. And to Eileen Dykeman, who gave so much of her time to proofreading and going over my text with the finest of fine-tooth combs ever imagined in order to eliminate any possible glitch, however small. And with great appreciation to Tony and the entire team at the Copy Center on Stone Oak Parkway in San Antonio, Texas, for all their time, help, and support.

DEDICATION

To:
JOSEPH AGOSTINELLO

the greatest football coach and mentor any 1950s teenager
could have hoped for

and

the graduating class of 1961 Patchogue High School
who shared with me the joys and sorrows of being among
America's first youth culture

All photographs/stills included in this volume belong to the author.
Sole responsibility for using them rests with the author.

CONTENTS

THE POLITICS OF NOSTALGIA: Film historian Richard Schickel coined that term in 1968 to describe a strain in American entertainment allowing the mass-audience to sentimentally recall a past era, however unpleasant in its reality, as some bygone golden age of happier days; while George Lucas did not initiate romanticization of the late-1950s/early 1960s, *American Graffiti* (Ron Howard, Cindy Williams) crystalized that already potent trend. (Courtesy: Lucasfilm/The Coppola Company/Universal).

Prologue

TWIXT TWELVE AND TWENTY

The First American Teenagers

"Yeah, yeah, yeah, I go to swingin' school.
The cats are hip and the chicks are cool."

—Bobby Rydell, *Because They're Young*, 1960

During the second week of September 1955, between ten and fifteen million young Americans, the vast majority twelve years old, embarked on the first-stage of their post-childhood lives. The previous spring, they had graduated from grade schools in large cities and small towns across the industrial northeast, the strictly-segregated south, a largely rural southwest, wide-open prairies across the Midwest, and the isolated, in many ways insular northern tier. They entered larger middle- and junior-high schools that collected such teenagers, as they would soon be known. Unbeknownst to them, these youngsters formed a virtual tidal wave: baby-boomers, born during the middle of World War II. Many were the offspring of men and women who married shortly after meeting so as to respectably engage in sex before servicemen were shipped overseas.[1] Never before in the country's social history had such a vast number simultaneously showed up for the second phase of their educations. School systems across the country were unprepared and overwhelmed.[2] Less obvious was that a Sea Change in morals, mores, and manners would shortly occur. Or that the movies they chose to watch and music they listened to would hence-forth reflect and derive from these new kids on the block.

Most shared a common core: what we now refer to as popular culture. At the time, there was no real consciousness of this being anything other than appealing, insignificant experiences. One key innovation was that a large num-ber had grown up watching television.[3] Until a year previous, the TV set in a living-room was a status symbol.[4] An antenna on the initial home in a neigh-borhood to boast one indicated an affluent household. Here was, until those ugly things proliferated, the great signifier of belonging to a new abundance and affluence which, like the advent of mainstream TV, essentially began in 1948. Following a postwar recession, the American economy had boomed.[5] With each passing year, the price of a TV set plummeted. Likewise, the qual-ity with which TVs were turned out (assembly-line style, like cars in Detroit) diminished. Early on, The Tube was encased in oak consoles, with faux antique doors that could be opened when a family chose to turn on the set. By 1955, the year that television went viral, new models were tinny, cheap-looking. More significantly, they would be turned on at the beginning of each day, off again at bed-time. That hour stretched ever later, thanks to late-night talk shows and old movies.[6] If two years earlier, kids begged to be admitted into a TV-owning household to watch *Howdy Doody* or its less-remembered competition—*Rootie Kazootie, Kukla, Fran, and Ollie, The Magic Cottage*—with the child residing there, now TVs were accessible for all but the poorest. Owing to the limited number of channels, more often than not everybody watched the same shows. A great number of these became central to people's lives.[7] There was of course *I Love Lucy* on Monday and, later, on Wednesdays, Walt Disney's first hour-long show. The Davy Crockett Craze dominated these kids' waking hours during the latter part of 1954 and throughout the winter of 1955. Only three episodes were produced during that first season, broadcast between Dec. 15, 1954 and February 23, 1955. Yet kids were entranced; mesmerized even.[8]

For earlier generations, radio created a sense of community within families who listened devotedly to their favorite shows. TV, however, exerted a hyp-notic effect without precedent. A nightly entertainment buffet included old films, a video mosaic of Hollywood history. Also, serious live drama, inexpen-sive children's programming, situation comedy, quiz shows, ancient cartoons, and something innovative called 'the news.' Theatrical newsreels like *The March of Time* soon disappeared, rendered irrelevant.[9] Why watch a week-old summary when, for a similarly-paced fifteen minutes, up-to-date news appeared on TV nightly? Key details were picked up from the Talking Heads by children, playing on the floor while waiting for *Crusader Rabbit* to begin. Swarthy, angry Sen. Joseph McCarthy frightened some of them even more than the villains on *Superman*. Kids knew a Red Scare existed but left that for grown-ups to deal with. The war in Korea, which for reasons that they could not comprehend was referred to as a "conflict," played nightly until its indecisive end in 1953.[10]

*

That sense of indecisiveness came to define life in those times. The Fifties would not be thought of as the 'Happy Days' until the early 1970s. Then, a mythic vision of the past was created via that TV show, movies like *American Graffiti* (George Lucas, 1973), and onstage the Broadway play *Grease*. Happiness, when that decade is less romantically considered, had not been the reality for most Americans in an era when the Cold War cast a mushroom shaped shadow over the quietude of daily lives. In one film, *The Atomic City* (Jerry Hopper, 1952), Gene Barry received top billing as a physicist working in Los Alamos. The focus remained on this man's ten-year-old son (Lee Aaker). The child upsets his father by asking questions about what will happen when the atomic war comes. His dad tries to get the lad to change the phrasing to "if." While the boy promises to do so, he keeps forgetting. Most kids who caught this B item at a Saturday matinee couldn't boast a parent who worked in the atomic industry. Like the film's child hero, many had gradually become convinced, owing to nuke drills, that end of days was nigh. Many were exposed to the educational short *Duck and Cover* (Anthony Rizzo, 1951) in which a Disney-like turtle assured kids survival was possible, offering hints how to do so. The advice was so patently absurd (like holding a piece of paper over one's head) children laughed out loud. A few lived in house-holds featuring well-stocked bomb shelters in the basement.[11] None of those precautions, however well-intended, convinced the first generation of atomic-age children they were likely to reach the age of 21. They'd seen such science-fiction flicks as *The Beast from 20,000 Fathoms* (Eugene Lourie, 1953), *Them!* (Gordon Douglas, 1954), and *Godzilla, King of the Monsters!* (Terry Morse, Ishiro Honda, 1955) in which radiation releases prehistoric creatures, such diversions speaking to our worst collective fears.[12] Happy days? For David Halberstam, "it was a mean time."[13] Not on the surface. During the Eisenhower era, life ebbed and flowed as if all was right with the world.

Still, underneath that uneasy calm . . .

A few sage observers had early on seen this coming. Some expressed it in what was then largely considered escapism: The Movies. In 1943, Alfred

Hitchcock (1899–1980) collaborated on *Shadow of a Doubt* with Thornton Wilder (1897–1975). The latter's beloved play *Our Town* (1938) had idealized life in middle-America during the pre-World War II years. Like most stage productions, the 1940 film directed by Sam Wood was shot on a studio back lot; the sort of quasi-realistic, semi-stylized approach employed for the Andy Hardy series starring Mickey Rooney as a 1930s predecessor to the '50s teenager. With *Shadow of a Doubt,* Hitch broke with tradition. He shot in an actual California town, Santa Rosa, for realistic verisimilitude.[14] Despite Wilder's participation, this project played as a rejection of everything *Our Town* said about such a "Grovers Corners" place. The heroine, Charlie Newton (Teresa Wright), a sixteen-year-old, offers an early incarnation of the typical teenager soon to emerge. A thriller plot has this wide-eyed waif dealing with her once beloved Uncle Charlie (Joseph Cotton), openly posing as a phony aristocrat though secretly an American Jack the Ripper. In one of the film's remarkable set-pieces, Charlie Oakley confronts Young Charlie:

> What do you know, really? You're just an ordinary little girl, living in an ordinary little town. You wake up every morning of your life and you know perfectly well that there's nothing in the world to trouble you. You go through your ordinary little day. And at night, you sleep your untroubled ordinary little sleep, filled with peaceful stupid dreams . . . You live in a dream. You're a sleepwalker, blind. How do you know what the world is like? Do you know the world is a foul sty? . . . The world's a hell. What does it matter what happens in it? Wake up, Charlie. Use your wits. *Learn something!*[15]

What Uncle Charlie wants Young Charlie to learn is his philosophy. In a nutshell, nihilism: everything adds up to nothing; life is without rhyme, reason, meaning. Uncle Charlie is the shape of things to come. He is The Fifties—"mean," dark, threatening; a virtual cesspool of horrors churning below a genteel exterior— before that decade even began. In an era when virtually everyone was absorbed with the war, most Americans had no time for soul-searching. There was right and there was wrong. Hitler was wrong. In fighting what Gen. Eisenhower called our Crusade in Europe,[16] we instantaneously became white knights. *Shadow of a Doubt* is the only Forties movie in which WWII doesn't seem to exist.

But there is a more terrible truth here. Young Charlie, the small-town girl par excellence, knows on some instinctual level that things were not precisely right *before* Uncle Charlie stepped off that train. "We just sort of go along and nothing happens," she muses early on. "We're in a terrible rut. What's going to be our future?" As in Shakespeare's vision of Hamlet's Elsinore, peasants bound about as if nothing is wrong while a few troubled souls secretly admit deep fears: Something's rotten in the state of Denmark. And in the then-contemporary U.S.

(a)   (b)

(c)   (d)

YOUTHFUL IMAGES OF A NEW ERA: (a) Mamie Van Doren delights in her record collection (courtesy: Universal); (b) all-American boys (Jon Voight, center) relax after football practice in *Out of It* (courtesy: Pressman-Williams/United Artists); (c) a typical suburban teen (Sandra Dee) has her wish for her own phone granted (courtesy: Universal); (d) despite Pre-World War I period trappings (the film mostly takes place in 1915), James Dean and Julie Harris embody the angst of young love in a manner that spoke directly to Fifties teens in *East of Eden* (courtesy: Warner Bros.)

when World War II ended, rather than a wonderful new world order, the grim Cold War began. For a seminal film of that time, *The Best Years of Our Lives* (William Wyler, 1946), screenwriters Robert Sherwood and MacKinlay Kantor intended their title as ironic. While the boys were overseas, everything altered, if subtly. On return, the effect was akin to a *Twilight Zone* (1959–1964) episode in which some astronaut descends to find the surface of life the same, its essence changed in a slightly surreal manner. He can't place what's wrong. Something, though, clearly is. To blend Wilder with Thomas Wolfe, veterans discovered you can't go home again to Our Town. Hollywood expressed this sensibility via the noir style, anticipated by Hitchcock. Confused, angry anti-heroes (an earlier notion of simple, pure good-guys no longer existed) dutifully walked the mean streets of what once seemed great metropolises. Such places had degenerated into asphalt jungles during our idealistic if, as things turned out, naïve overseas quest to save the world.

Noir titles indicated a gnawing sense of disillusion with the way things were: *Somewhere in the Night* (Joseph L. Mankiewicz, 1945), *The Big Sleep* (Howard Hawks, 1946) *Out of the Past* (Jacques Tourneur, 1947), *Nightmare Alley* (Edmund Goulding, 1947), *White Heat* (Raoul Walsh, 1948). Though 1955's teenagers had been too young to experience such dreary visions during their theatrical releases, TV venues such as the legendary *Million Dollar Movie* now showcased such films.[17] Impressionable youth absorbed such images of a world gone sour and, in time, insane, absurd. Hitchcock captured the tenor of those times with *Rear Window* (1954), expanded from a short work of pulp-fiction by Cornell Woolrich.[18] The film offered a color-noir with a vivid tableau of diverse residents in a lower-Manhattan housing complex. These people never acknowledge, much less speak to, one another. In addition to the expected thriller plot, Hitch's film offered an oblique commentary on an emergent way of living (or existing) in which the neighborly attitudes of Main Street, U.S.A. were all at once gone.

A term would be coined to describe this sorry state of affairs: The Lonely Crowd, introduced in a 1950 book by sociologist David Riesman and several colleagues.[19] They noted, with due concern, that centuries of an American sense of ongoing community, which had reached its peak during World War II, suddenly gave way to an alternative in which people sealed themselves off and apart in invisible cocoons. Not even the old standby of sending boys off to combat helped. A decade after what author James Jones defined as "The Last Good War"[20] ended, the first bad one, Korea, set the pace for Vietnam and Iraq. Regrettably, Hitchcock had been point-on. Uncle Charlie didn't bring a waking nightmare to Santa Rosa, aka Grovers Corners. It had been there all along, waiting for a catalyst to rip open this dark underbelly of life on Main Street, U.S.A.

*

Notably, there are no blacks on view in Santa Rosa. Nor were there any in *Our Town*. A few household servants, perhaps, living on the far edges of society; some porters for the railroad. Though no warning sign is on view to let visitors know, Grovers Corners existed for Anglos only. Such prejudice was not reserved for African Americans. Italians, Greeks, Jews, the Irish . . . a Polish lower-working class are mentioned briefly in Wilder's play, though never included in the drama. However rich the vocabulary of residents, the term 'integration' remains unknown. But during World War II, President Harry Truman followed up on the late President Roosevelt's desire to alter that. By 1944, the military had belatedly become racially diverse.[21] When the overseas war concluded, a battle for Civil Rights at home began. If their parents felt vaguely threatened by such figures as Dr. Martin Luther King, a large number of teenagers were intrigued. Some wanted to get involved. A few actually did, joining in marches, protests, discussions.[22]

This was a time of change, drastic change. No one felt the waves of transition more than baby boomers, caught in the middle between past and future.[23] Though big cities and small towns still existed, something new had, in addition to TV, swept the land. Ever more kids were raised in suburbia. William J. Levitt (1907–1994) in 1946 had created a housing development near Hempstead, Long Island, bearing his name: Levittown.[24] Rich and poor weren't welcome; suburbia was a middle-class undertaking. Houses went for $5,000 each, the top price a bread-winner earning $3,000 a year could handle. Though Levitt was Jewish, God's chosen people were not particularly welcome. Blacks? Verboten! Not that Levitt was a racist. Rather, he fancied himself a hard-nosed businessman, grasping that the vast majority of working class whites whom his suburban dream spoke to weren't ready for ethnic neighbors, even in the industrialized northeast.[25]

At any rate, "It was Bill Levitt who first brought (Henry) Ford's techniques of mass production (and assembly line construction) to housing."[26] Similar buildings were according to Paul Goldberger

> social creations more than architectural ones—they turned the single detached single-family house from a distant dream to a real possibility for ever more Americans who, in previous decades, would likely have dwelled in an apartment or at best rent a small house.[27]

Levitt hailed his cookie-cutter creations as a last bastion against the Reds: "No man who owns his own house and lot can be a communist," he insisted.[28]

Others perceived the innovation as a mass invite to conventionalism and conformity. "Little houses made of ticky-tacky," Malvina Reynolds noted, "and they all look just the same."[29]

Suburban life, when eventually dramatized, would come in for harsh scrutiny. *No Down Payment* (Martin Ritt, 1957) revealed the frustration of men who worked white and blue collar jobs to try and pay for (always they were 'in the hole') a vaguely unsatisfying lifestyle. As a result, many among them nightly drowned their difficulties in cocktails. Unsatisfied wives (though many couldn't precisely explain *why*) also drank during daytime. *No Down Payment*, set during the early fifties, depicted people who were raising eight- or nine-year-olds. By that decade's mid-point, such kids would become The First American Teenagers. People between the ages of twelve and twenty have always existed; never, though, had they been posited as a unique sub-division of society. A popular singer, Pat Boone, penned *Twixt Twelve and Twenty*,[30] the first attempt to understand what made "today's" young people different from previous kids.

*

For clearly they *were* unique. All young people have to deal with problems; these had to deal with original problems. One, which would come to be called The Generation Gap,[31] had to do with an ever-increasing strain between teenagers and their parents. This included not only those troublesome youths soon branded as juvenile delinquents,[32] but also "nice kids" who came to question everything around them. In part, this occurred because they had more leisure time than ever. The era of sweat-shops in cities, or a dawn-to-dusk days spent farming in rural areas ceased to be—or at least no longer constituted the norm.[33] Some teenagers had jobs, though few were required to turn that money over to the family, often the case in the nineteenth century. Youth had money, including "weekly allowances" (often generous) for those whose families were relatively well-off. Cold cash made them attractive to advertisers who, for the first time in social history, began catering to a Youth Market.

Yet another unique element of then-contemporary youth was their status as the first raised under the auspices of Dr. Benjamin Spock (1903–1998). In his influential 1946 book *Baby and Child Care* (throughout the 1950s, only the Bible sold more copies), Spock combined pediatrics with psychology, the latter then coming into its own.[34] He persuaded parents (in particular, moms) to listen to children as never before in hopes of understanding and supporting them as individuals; as well as to empower youth by allowing kids to make their own choices, an entirely new concept. Spock's supporters argued such an enlightened approach would inspire a greater sense of self-worth. Detractors saw a danger in creating a generation of spoiled brats, each such child coming to always expect instantaneous gratification.

To a degree, youth's problems had to do with Madison Avenue. Though advertising and public relations firms located on the fabled boulevard between New York City's Park and Fifth Avenues had been hawking pretty much every imaginable object since at least 1911,[35] TV emerged as a highhanded hucksters' impossible dream come true. As compared to casual, occasional radio listening in the past, the citizenry was held spellbound by this emergent medium. An old-fashioned talk-fest after dinner, or playing board-games like Monopoly, drastically diminished. Watching TV, most people remained mum until a commercial break. If the advertisement contained a clever sales pitch, folks remained quiet. As a host of new products poured onto the market, advertisers came up with catchy jingles and eye-popping visuals, virtually brainwashing viewers into buying. That included kids. Maypo, a maple flavored cereal, had been a moderately successful product in Vermont since 1953. The company launched a blitz of TV spots, conceived/written by Mad Avenue Maven George Cois, with clever animation by John Hubley. The spots featured a Dennis the Menace type brat, dwarfed by a huge cowboy hat, screaming at his harried mother: "I want my Maypo!" Without any firm idea what this product might be, children aped the cartoon character in their homes. In no time, Maypo became a bestselling national brand-name.[36]

Without anyone realizing it, the old-fashioned idea of capitalism at its best (producing the finest quality product, netting a handy profit by selling this to anyone in need of the item) gave way to consumerism: Take an utterly unnecessary, even worthless commodity, then convince the public they absolutely could not live without such an ersatz item—Rube Goldberg contraptions for the masses. Actual consumption following such a purchase must necessarily fail to live up to expectations, now called 'hype.' The more the public was drawn into such an empty relationship with ubiquitous products, the less fulfilled their lives. If grown-ups shrugged and accepted this as their lot in life, teens began to simmer, seethe, swear to themselves they wouldn't end up just like their parents, secretly fearing that they would.

Constantly, Mom and Pop tried to buy themselves into happiness by spending rather than, as in the past, saving. Then again, why save for a future ever less likely to exist when an atomic war would shortly end everything?

An ever increasing part of the population attempted to spend their way into oblivion. Assembly lines processed a homogenization of the once diverse culture. In Detroit, where this approach had been perfected, Henry Ford's traditional (and all at once dated) idea of turning out cars that would last an owner a lifetime gave way to "planned obsolescence."[37] New automobiles from General Motors and their competitors, including the ill-fated Edsel, were designed to fall apart in three years, precisely when owners would want a new model to keep up with neighbors. Even hamburgers fell prey to this ploy: in 1948, Dick and Maurice McDonald developed the concept of Fast Food. Via a process that turned out miniscule overcooked burgers in a shorter time than diners could handle orders, the brothers were able to sell each for 15 cents, served with a side of fries for an additional dime.[38] Success proved so great that a chain emerged, knocking older eating establishments out of business as the Golden Arches became an icon. So too were the Holiday Inns[39] which, beginning in 1951, were built by entrepreneur named Kemmons Wilson (1913–2003). These offered a standardized sameness and safety as opposed to haphazard Motor Courts, soon to be savagely depicted in Hitchock's dark-comedy *Psycho* (1960).

Now that almost everyone could afford some brand of car, and up-to-date highways were being constructed nationwide, the logical move was to ally America's developing auto-culture with already existing consumerism. In 1953, Eugene Ferkauf (1921–2012), already the owner of five popular discount stores in the New York City area, created out of his individual genius for marketing the first shopping mall. Every conceivable product could now be brought into close quarters, stores no longer spread out as in organically developed cities. A wide variety of outlets could be crowded together, under a synthetically designed umbrella; also, as near to customers' suburban homes as possible. E.J. Korvette removed the old necessity of a long drive downtown.[40] Besides, many people didn't enjoy going there anymore. Suburbanites might not admit to prejudices but they were keenly aware cities they'd deserted were filling up with ethnics, including many African Americans, recently relocated from the south. In truth, the arrival of ethnics hastened the Anglo flight to the suburbs, even if in the northeast few would openly admit that.

This migration occurred when it did for a reason. Before 1945, though white Southerners treated blacks abominably, they also feared any desertion by a cheap labor force for cotton farming. Stories, handed down from one generation to the next within African American families, recall furtive attempts to slip aboard trains heading north in the middle of the night only to encounter armed rednecks waiting to deter them.[41] Then, technology intervened. Mechanized cotton pickers could achieve in a day the equivalent results of fifty laborers. Combine harvesters could reap, thresh and winnow simultaneously. Innovations like these flooded the market in 1946.[42] Immediately, a long-standing attitude reversed itself. Blacks were not only allowed to leave but encouraged to do so. The migration that had begun as an ongoing trickle upward into such areas as Harlem and Detroit transformed into a steady flow, then a great river. During the late 1940s and early 1950s, more than five million African Americans relocated in northern tiers.[43] Downtowns, deserted by newly-affluent Anglos, provided homes for the rapidly incoming population. In time, these would be referred to as, somewhat condescendingly, ghettos.[44] And, later still (and far more politely), black communities. Shopping centers picked up the slack in downtown sales, a fact that could not be denied after Christmas 1954. Sales at Korvettes leaped to $2 million and, the following holiday season, to $28 mill.[45] The very idea of shopping in America entered a new era, part of the emergent zeitgeist.

What did such people purchase to enhance their lives? For, as writer Poppy Cannon noted, "Never before has so much been available to so many of us as now!"[46] Golf clubs were a favorite choice for many wives who wanted their spouses to enjoy the same sport as Ike; this was now a trendy way for 'guys' to spend a weekend afternoon. Husbands bought for their wives new models of Frigidaires, produced by Westinghouse,[47] hawked on TV by Betty Furness. Such state-of-the-art refrigerators had enough space to store plenty of frozen food, including newly-created TV dinners.[48] Other appliances ran the gamut from automated can-openers to dishwashers and home laundry units, all offered up as wonderful enhancements, freeing the modern housewife's hours for fun and meaningful activities. Yet, as Betty Friedan would point out in the early 1960s, a remarkable number of upscale women sank into the despair of watching afternoon soap-operas as a form of vicarious living while downing one cocktail after another.[49]

(a)   (b)

(c)   (d)

GROWING UP WITH TELEVISION: (a) Children of the early 1950s discovered inter-active media with *Winky Dink and You* (courtesy: CBS/Barry & Enright Prods.); (b) unaware of any Generation Gap, old-timers Tommy and Jimmy Dorsey introduced Elvis on *Stage Show* (courtesy; Jackie Gleason Prods./CBS); (c) dispelling the myth that rock 'n' roll was synony-mous with delinquency, Dick Clark hosted clean-cut kids on *American Bandstand* (courtesy: WFIL Philadelphia/ABC/Dick Clark Prods.); (d) 'Girl in the Cage' Lada Edmund, Jr. reigned as uncrowned queen of Go-Go dancers on *Hulabaloo* throughout the mid-Sixties. (courtesy: NBC; Gary Smith Prods.).

*

As to kids, what to buy them? Easy to answer! Davy Crockett items: trading cards, plastic forts, buckskin jackets, picture books, toy guns, and a recording of that enormously popular show's theme song, moving up to Number One on *Billboard*'s Top Ten.[50] Likely, such a purchase would be a 78-rpm recording, similar to their parents' favorites: Patti Page, Frank Sinatra. The family gathered around the living-room phono to listen as Bill Hayes sang verse after verse, beginning with "Born on a mountain top in Tennessee. . . ." A precious few opted instead for a newer venue, still in the experimental stage: the 45 rpm. RCA had long hoped to create a compact, durable disc. During the Depression, no market existed for new items. During the war, more pressing issues dominated any communications experimentation. On April 2, 1949, *Billboard* carried an advertisement for the thinner, small, unbreakable disc.

New phonographs designed to play such items were likewise smaller. Mass production allowed them to be sold at a cheaper price than the more formidable older models. For reasons unknown, the public didn't at once embrace this device. When prices for TV sets finally plummeted and older phonographs were discarded to make room for them, the small console model player became popular (1953–1955). These also made nice Christmas gifts for the kids. At once, young people took to listening to "their" music in their rooms, a seemingly unimportant undertaking that actually led to the overhaul of child-parent relations. A year later, one of the most asked-for presents for holidays/birthdays was a phone of one's own, further sealing off teenagers, who could talk endlessly with one another and, better still, avoid doing so with grown-ups altogether.

Six months after kids received copies of the Crockett ballad on 78 they began to purchase their own 45s. These were cheaper—priced at 79 rather than 99 cents—as such, more affordable. The question was, what records to buy? That would be determined for them by the radio, as the market success of low-cost phonographs was shortly followed by the first low-cost/lightweight models. Early in 1947, Bell Laboratories began experimenting with replacing vacuum tubes, previously necessary for amplification, with "transistors."[51] A solid state amplifier allowed for smaller radios. Texas Instruments offered such a model in mid-1954. A more sophisticated version, the Regency TR-1, arrived in stores in early November—like the 45 rpm in time for holiday shopping. An advertising blitz increased demand. Shortly, teens carried their own radios around wherever they went. While TV usurped center stage in the typical living-room, youth excused themselves. TV programming that their moms and dads preferred—*Life Begins at Eighty, Arthur Godfrey and His Friends, See*

It Now—struck them as boring. Upstairs, they became masters of their own domain. Flipping the radio dial, initially to locate some station playing "Davy Crockett," twelve-year-olds discovered something else entirely.

On April 12, 1954, a Texas-based rhythm 'n' blues band, Bill Haley and his Comets, recorded a number written by Max C. Freedman and James E. Myers, "Rock Around the Clock."[52] The Comets were not the first to offer a version. One month earlier, Sonny Dae and His Knights committed the number to American Hot Wax in a peppy if less definitive cut. Decca, a minor label hoping to become a major, had for years been releasing 'jump music.' During the war, servicemen and their girlfriends desired to dance more wildly than popular mellow music of the Tommy Dorsey band had allowed for. Decca now released Haley's cut into the market as one more Rockabilly song, these being increasingly popular in the Deep South during those postwar years.[53] This genre (though no one yet thought about it in such lofty terms) revitalized the old mountain music, revved up a notch for the ever more popular electric guitar. That instrument, introduced as early as the mid-1920s by George Beauchamp, had been perfected in 1946 when Les Paul (1915–2009) designed the first Solid Body model.[54] The 'new sound' would achieve ever more popularity thanks to emergent talents including Junior Doyle, Zeb Turner, Carl Perkins, the Maddox Bros. and Rose, Jerry Lee Lewis and, shortly, the young Elvis Presley. As thrilled fans noted, "They played hillbilly music but it sounded red hot. They played real loud for that time, too."[55] A then-young grand-daddy of roadhouse, Hank Williams (Sr.) (1923–1953), won a huge following via his contributions, causing this performer to be considered by some music historians as the original avatar of what soon came to be called rock 'n' roll.[56]

During this process, one of the crudest forms of indigenous American music would be updated for the 20th century's latter half. Bluegrass melodies, an Ozarks twang, New Orleans gospel, Beale St. 12-bar blues, Nashville country and progressive drumming from Beat musicians in the north were filtered through a tape-echo chamber, this adding an appropriately eerie cutting-edge quality. Such sounds rolled along with the rockin' Big Beat of hard metallic-sounding guitars. That term, "rockin'," derived from a tonal-edge and intense drive in an emerging nouveau folk-music for the atomic age. Seemingly as innocuous as what giddy "be-bop hepcats" had embraced during the war, no one could have guessed that shortly such music would become the source of hysterical national controversy. Or that some of rock's loudest critics would be onetime hepcats from a decade earlier who now railed at the music of choice of their hipster teenagers.[57]

Haley's recording enjoyed local, then regional popularity. Initially, no disc jockey in such big cities as New York or Los Angeles would play it. Eddie Fisher, Doris Day, and the Lettermen momentarily remained the top pop stars. Had it not been for a coming-together of unrelated forces, the musical form known as rock 'n' roll might have never made itself felt. Aware of the ever larger African American population currently living in the urban northeast, a radio station in each such city played the music of choice for such a target audience.[58] This even occurred in the South, where Dewey Phillips' *Red, Hot and Blue* show on WHBQ gradually developed a following among young whites as well as blacks. As a result, such "race music" artists as Louis Jordan, Arthur Crudup, Ike Turner, Big Mama Thornton, Big Joe Turner, Fats Domino, Chuck Berry and Bo Diddley were appreciated by a bi-racial (or more impressive still *non*-racial) listenership. "Political boss Ed Crump might keep the streets and schools and public buildings segregated, but at night Dewey Phillips integrated the airwaves."[59] In Cleveland, Alan Freed (1921–1965), broadcast *The Moondog Show* on a "superstation" which featured a 50,000-watt clear-channel broadcast.[60] This meant listeners across the Midwest could enjoy the same songs not on different outlets but one, organized by a single force. Freed, a onetime New Yorker with a wiseguy attitude, had the profound impact of transforming scattered teenagers into America's original youth community.

In late winter/early spring of 1955, kids happened on "Honey Love," "Crying in the Chapel," "Maybelline," "Hound Dog," "Ain't That a Shame," and "Shake, Rattle and Roll." Overwhelmed best describes their reaction. Yet many felt themselves to be outsiders: allowed to listen in on other people's music. Then came July 9, 1955. At the moment when "Crockett" fell out of the Top Ten, "Rock Around the Clock," circulating regionally for the better part of a year, hit the national charts. When kids ran out to buy 45s of this example of white rhythm 'n' blues, the record soared to Number One. For some time, down in Memphis Sam Phillips (1923–2003) of Sun Records had, in his own words, been searching for "some white boy who could sing the black music" and "make me millions" thanks to the impact of such a crossover.[61] At this time, he discovered Elvis Presley, soon to be crowned King of Rock 'n' Roll. However short-lived Haley's stardom (he lacked charisma), he yet remained the man for the moment. When kids convened at schools a month later, Coonskin Caps tucked away or tossed aside, there was something else to talk about. "Did you hear that song?"

When discussion of "Rock Around the Clock" abated, they spoke of something else that had of late caught their interest. Second only to music were The Movies. At age twelve, most kids still spent Friday evenings with their parents, watching one of 1954's big studio releases: the gaudy musical *There's No Business Like Show Business* (Walter Lang) with Marilyn Monroe, the edge-of-your seat thriller *Dial M For Murder* (Alfred Hitchcock), the strange Western *Johnny Guitar* (Nicholas Ray), the original airport saga *The High and the Mighty* (William A. Wellman) with John Wayne, and the sword-and-sandals epic *Demetrius and the Gladiators* (Delmer Daves). One film, Irving Berlin's *White Christmas* (Michael Curtiz), ended that year on a melancholic note. As former servicemen, Bing Crosby and Danny Kaye come to realize their current affluent lives do not satisfy them. They long for "the good ol' days" of World War II. Dads in the audience likewise felt such a nostalgia, wondering why and how their longed-for return home had led to something other than the best years of their lives. Young people also crowded into Saturday matinees, mostly Westerns with Audie Murphy, low-budget horror and sci-fi films, and silly comedies starring Jerry Lewis. Then, in March of 1955, many witnessed a movie that altered their lives.

Since the decade's early days, Elia Kazan (1909–2003) had been hoping to star the era's greatest Method actors, Marlon Brando and Montgomery Clift, in a screen adaptation of John Steinbeck's domestic epic *East of Eden*.[62] For various reasons, mostly scheduling problems, that project had not come to fruition. Over the years, Marlon and Monty had grown too long in the tooth to convincingly play the teenage brothers, Cal and Aron, both in love with a girl, Abra; also coming to blows over their ongoing competition for emotional response from a cold, distant father, Adam. Finally, Kazan recast the piece with a pair of unknowns, James Dean and Richard Davalos. Julie Harris played the girl, Raymond Massey the family patriarch. The film had its New York premiere on April 10, 1955. By mid-March, a roadshow edition reached middle America. Kids who attended with parents or on their own were, to coin a phrase, blown away by what took place onscreen. Despite the pre-World War I setting, this film spoke directly to *them*. Detailed historical trappings aside, here was by implication a movie about what it meant to be young and confused during the 1950s: The Generation Gap at its most intense, superb storytelling about young people who had been treated to an enviably upscale lifestyle but felt lost yet could not understand why. In a nutshell, rebels without a cause, at least any obvious one. This was "their movie." And their star. Needy, surly, vulnerable, outraged, sad-eyed, remote, soul-searching; rebellious, angry, apologetic; hungry for love but unable to express such emotions in words; desperately longing for a friend, managing to self-destructively ruin any chances for such salvation; sexy if vaguely androgy-nous . . . James Dean came across as a contemporary Hamlet without a Horatio to nourish the sweet prince.

Overnight, Dean "came to symbolize the belief of the youth of that era that because they were young, they were misunderstood."[63] As he once supposedly told friend/fellow actor Dennis Hopper: "I want to take Marlon Brando (in *The Wild One*, Lazlo Benedict, 1953) shouting, 'Fuck you!' and Montgomery Clift (in *A Place in the Sun*, George Stevens, 1951), crying 'Please somebody love me!' and crush them together into a single character."[64] Hanging out on the school-grounds before or after class during in early September, 1955, teens excitedly spoke of *East of Eden* and "Rock Around the Clock." They were thrilled to learn Dean would next appear in a modern drama, allowing him to directly address the issues of contemporary teenage-hood. Anticipating the late October release of *Rebel Without a Cause* (Nicholas Ray), kids were stunned to learn on September 30 that Dean had died while driving his Porsche at devastating speeds. If "live fast, die young" had not yet emerged as a mantra, it did now.

*

Teenagers lost their great idol moments after discovering him. In mourn-ing, they also hungered for a replacement. Where to find one? And who out there could fill the bill? The answer came from the least likely of venues: TV, increasingly mundane in their minds. Incredibly, on their parents' favorite live broadcast of old-fashioned music. Jimmy and Tommy Dorsey had set their famed bickering aside to co-host *Stage Show*. When CBS realized that their devoted following was made up largely of older folks, network executives sug-gested including fresh-faced performers in hopes kids would watch, too. But there were so many to choose from! Gene Vincent, Eddie Cochran, Buddy Holly. . . . Yet one stood out, a cavorting hillbilly who drove crowds wild when appearing in person throughout the South. Importantly, RCA Records had won Elvis Presley away from Memphis' small Sun label. Despite their ner-vousness of breaking with tradition, the company wanted in on the money to be made from Big Beat. Elvis would be either first or one of the first of these marginalized performers to be marketed by a major corporation.

In the entertainment industry, power recognizes power. RCA would release their first Elvis album on March 13, 1956. What if the rising star were to perform a month and a half of appearances on the Dorsey show, beginning before that date to hype the 33 1/3 long-playing album, continuing after it reached record stores? Not only would sales soar; so would the show's ratings. On January 28, 1956, Elvis stepped on stage, before live cameras, shrieking out a number while swiveling his hips in the style of a member of some rural religious cult. Adults were shocked, if not yet outraged. Initially, the vulgarity struck them as comedic. Any hostility came later, when the grinning star would be labeled a menace to society by self-appointed moralists looking for someone specific to blame for those vast, complex changes overcoming the social structure.

Kids, on the other hand, were as mesmerized as they'd been by Dean.

The beloved comic Jackie Gleason once described Elvis as "Marlon Brando with a guitar."[65] More correctly, Elvis was James Dean carrying that instrument. Elvis combined Dean's movie-star charisma with the sound offered by Haley. Shortly, Presley signed a Hollywood contract. After several false starts, 20th Century Fox announced he would be added to the cast of a B Western, "The Reno Brothers," to be released shortly before Thanksgiving 1956. By the time that film reached theatres, it had been retitled *Love Me Tender* (Robert D. Webb) to emphasize Elvis' presence.

A New Music was about to be incorporated into The Movies. When that happened, a true youth cult—simmering for several years—roared into a full, rich, and undeniable existence. In time, its attitudes would take over all of American popular culture for everyone, regardless of biological age.

· 1 ·

TOWARD A NEW AMERICAN CINEMA

Three Films That Altered Everything

> "Youth unto itself rebels,
> None else being near."
>
> —William Shakespeare, *Romeo and Juliet* (1591)

Soon after the creation of a commercial film industry in and around Hollywood during the early 1910s, The Movies offered a sense of community among constituencies with far-flung backgrounds and significant regional distinctions. People might experience radically different educational upbringings at school and attend houses of worship offering drastically different visions of the cosmos. Many hailed from Old World origins that deeply distrusted one another. Even when it came to music on the radio or via records, differing sounds appealed to local tastes. Yet when families anywhere in America set off for the local movie theatre they unknowingly experienced what might be considered a normalization process. Owing to the Production Code, accepted by studio heads as a self-censoring device in the early 1930s to stave off outside interference,[1] films that arrived in theatres from the established studios (which up until the late 1940s often owned movie-going venues) was required to pass a litmus test, insuring no one would be offended by what was shown. Parents could rest assured that even those rare films designed to not only entertain but address serious issues wouldn't offend. Most products were calculated to appeal to all age groups, reaping larger financial rewards. As a result, any typical film had to perform a constant juggling act, each sequence capturing the interest of varied audience sectors, including middle-aged, the elderly, youth, even toddlers.

No franchise so ably represented this elaborate, in time formalized (for those who produced them), ritualized (as to consumers) showmanship than The Andy Hardy films during the fifteen-film series' nine-year run 1937–1946). The first, A Family Affair (George B. Seitz), had been based on an already quaint play by Aurania Rouverol called Skidding (1928). This mild divertissement dealt with an upper-middle-class family during the 1920s economic boom. MGM's film, shot at the height of the Great Depression, offered less a romanticized version of contemporary life than an idealization of something which, if it ever existed, was gone. Judge Hardy (Lionel Barrymore, later Lewis Stone), and his demure/domestic wife (Spring Byington, replaced by Fay Holden) initially provided the focus. Their son (Mickey Rooney) eventually assumed that position as made clear by the final title, Love Laughs at Andy Hardy (Willis Goldbeck, 1946). Rooney was 25, his character of indeterminate age. Here, Andy might be thought of as a prelude to The First American Teenager: more independent than previously, driving his own jalopy, intensely pursuing girls while also dancing to a notably bigger beat than a few years before.

> The Hardy cycle represented what Michael Wood identified as the essential structure of the industry in its great days: settled financiers on the East Coast were investing in uprooted adventurers on the West Coast because of their supposed expertise on the subject of what the Middle West really wanted. The movies did not describe or explore America, they invented it, dreamed up an America all their own, and persuaded us to share the dream. (italics mine)[2]

The box-office failure of a belated follow-up, Andy Hardy Comes Home (Howard W. Koch, 1958), illustrated how completely Hollywood had lost touch with any national common chord, if such a concept ever did exist outside of the popular imagination—this largely a construct of Hollywood. Though the studios continued to churn out ever-less-successful projects, unwilling (perhaps unable) to spot the hand-writing on the wall, during the 1950s any solidarity between geographical areas and successive generations diminished. More grown-ups chose to remain home, watching TV, except perhaps on the weekend when a Technicolor musical or ancient-world-spectacle beckoned. Little children could now get their fill of cartoons every afternoon on the small screen. That left an ever more sizable chunk of the citizenry, ten million teens at the decade's beginning, over fifteen million at its close, all in search of 'their' outlet. TV seemed too homogenized, in particular shows like *Ozzie and Harriet* and *Father Knows Best,* which offered white-bread images of how juveniles ought to behave in contrast to the way contemporary youth did.

In response, a New American Cinema evolved. No one planned it or oversaw its development, at least not in the beginning. Here was an entirely organic process that happened because it had to.

*

The irony as to the first 1950s Youth Cult Movie is that it was conceived, created, and distributed as a serious work for adults. *The Wild One* (Laslo Benedict, 1953) was produced by Stanley Kramer (1913–2001), among those Hollywood postwar filmmakers who grasped that in a re-aligned America, movies conveying liberal social consciousness would be required to address emerging issues.[3] These included *Home of the Brave* (Mark Robson, 1949), offering an in-its-time radical argument in favor of integration, and *High Noon* (Fred Zinnemann, 1952), employing traditional Western settings for a thinly-disguised attack on McCarthyism. Such films set the pace for the era's Message Movie: didactic (sometimes overly so), preaching a moderate form of progressive ideology in hopes of altering the public's attitudes. When studios like Columbia initially balked for fear of possible controversy, which might cost them at the box-office, Kramer formed an independent company and allowed United Artists to release such personal statements. When most such films were financially successful, The Majors followed suit.

The Wild One's evolution began with a factual occurrence. In 1947, various motorcyclists converged on the small town of Hollister, CA during the Fourth of July weekend. Their general rowdiness was reported by local journalists. Editors at *Life*, always in search of some strong story, saw a speck of blood here that might be nurtured into a journalistic pecking-party. The July 21, 1947 issue transformed 'The Hollister Riot' (no such thing ever occurred) into a national issue, setting the pace for much New Journalism to follow: making rather than reporting the news.[4] Actual photos were too mild so *Life* dispatched professionals to the scene where what had been nothing more than minor mischief was restaged/recreated. Stunt men performed dangerous cycle-stunts for the cameras; these were then printed and received by a naïve public as 'proof' of youthful chaos penetrating middle-class enclaves. To sell more magazines at this moment an ongoing postwar myth had been invented. In the public consciousness if not reality, hordes of bikers wildly tore down public highways. Suburban types (i.e., the magazine's readership) were forewarned of an oncoming danger that existed nowhere but in the media-created American psyche.

Fiction writer Frank Rooney employed the occurrence as inspiration for an even more exaggerated short story, "The Cyclists' Raid," published in *Harper's* (January 1951), later included in an anthology, *The Best American Short Stories of 1952*. On the lookout for relevant/temporal material, producer Kramer optioned the piece and assigned John Paxton to do a screenplay. Shooting this ever more overblown tale of contemporary outlawry was assigned to director Benedict, whose memorable visuals would further heighten a vivid over-the-top contemporary drama. These bikers were, at least onscreen, presented as throwbacks to bandits of the Billy the Kid variety, terrorizing an adult community (tellingly, there are few if any young people living in the movie's village) with no Pat Garrett to walk down the dusty street and halt a supposedly mounting menace.

Such a comparison to the Old West and Hollywood Westerns is not insignificant. The opening features Johnny Strabler (Marlon Brando) and his gang on a far horizon, riding directly toward the camera eye. They parallel the Miller gang during *High Noon*'s title sequence, cycles now contemporary equivalents of horses from period pictures. One member of Johnny's gang, the Black Rebels, wears a Union Civil War campaign cap. A prominent figure in the opposing gang, led by Chino (Lee Marvin) and called The Beetles (likely the source of the British band's name),[5] wears an animal-skin cap of the type associated with mountain men. What shapes up in the small-town ('Carbonville') recalls gunfighters taking over Hadleyville in *High Noon*. One distinction is telling. Instead of Gary Cooper as no-nonsense Will Kane, the modern lawman (Robert Keith) is a sniveling weakling. Our once-strong frontier male hero has, as the Russians were then loudly claiming, given way to a culture of decadent affluence, America and older Americans now spineless.[6]

As to narrative structure, *The Wild One* might be thought of as *High Noon*'s inverse. There, meek townsfolk hide away in fear as bad guys strut about until Marshal Kane alone faces down free-living (i.e., libertarian) elements. In *The Wild One*, Ray Teal plays a restaurant owner who delights in money being spread about by "the visitors," begging neighbors to tolerate increasing violence so as to keep cash registers ringing. Though John Wayne never attacked this film as communist propaganda (as he did *High Noon*),[7] he might well have, since the capitalists' greed serves as the root of all evil. In opposition to *High Noon*'s conclusion, here Keith's 20th century authority figure hides away in his office while the townspeople, finally angered, head off on a witch hunt of the type that marked all aspects of the early 1950s. Wrong-headedly, they choose Johnny who, alone among the bikers, attempted to maintain order.

As to the star, Rebecca Bell-Metereau has written that the film "established Marlon Brando (1924–2004) as an icon of rebellion."[8] That is not precisely true. Unlike James Dean, who actively sought Youth Icon status, Brando recoiled at such a possibility.[9] Brute Stanley Kowalski in *A Streetcar Named Desire* (Elia Kazan, 1951), quick-thinking Mark Antony in Shakespeare's *Julius Caesar* (Joseph L. Mankiewicz, 1953), confused Terry Malloy in *On the Waterfront* (Kazan, 1954), world-conqueror Napoleon in *Désirée* (Henry Koster, 1954), the easygoing Manhattan playboy Sky (Bat) Masterson in the musical *Guys and Dolls* (Mankiewicz, 1955), and a quick-witted Asian in *Teahouse of the August Moon* (Daniel Mann, 1956) all, like Johnny, appealed to Brando as diverse character leads. As a Method actor, schooled by legendary teacher Lee Strasberg,[10] Brando disappeared into one after the other rather than like the aforementioned Wayne and other Old Hollywood stars imposing an ongoing persona on a long succession of roles. Another observer, Jon Lewis, comes closer to the truth in noting that "*The Wild One* was widely viewed as a celebration of the very outlaw behavior it purportedly condemned."[11] Offered as a cautionary fable for adults who ought to avoid such possible events, the young people attending *The Wild One* cheered the mild biker-boy Johnny and, in some cases, applauded Marvin's Chino, based on real-life cycle legend Willie Forkner. *The Wild One*'s warnings about a potential menace were sidetracked as existing cyclists became poseurs, modeling themselves on Johnny as to clothing choices and exaggerated mannerisms. More than 2,000 years ago, Aristotle argued that art imitates life. In our own time, the equation often turns the other way around.

(a)   (b)

(c)   (d)

THE RIOT THAT NEVER WAS: (a) Though Marlon Brando perceived 'Johnny' as a challenging character role, the public accepted his black-leather biker-boy as a popular and enduring icon; (b) Johnny (Brando, second from left) and gang members cast their male gazes at a female rebel (Yvonne Doughty) though male-bonding dominates the drama; (c) Chino (Lee Marvin) and Johnny (Brando) rumble in the streets; in the actual incident, little if any violence occurred; (d) bad-boy Brando finds himself fascinated and repelled by the old-fashioned values of a small-town girl (Mary Murphy).

(All images, courtesy: The Stanley Kramer Company/Columbia Pictures).

Kramer enabled this misreading (or alternative interpretation) via an ill-advised prologue: "This . . . story . . . could never take place in most towns. But it did in this one." To the contrary, the whole point of the piece is that this *could* happen in *anywhere* in America. The film's Carbonville is *High Noon's* Hadleyville, Grovers Corners from *Our Town*, also Carvel, California: that calm, cheery enclave where the Hardy Family resides, its placid surface and Anglo inhabitants shocked as something radical arrives. This helps explain the reoccurrence of a single word nearly two dozen times: *Crazy!* One of the bikers goes by that nickname. Johnny employs the word as his mantra, the stock answer to everything anyone says. Even the demure town-girl Kathie (Mary Murphy), at first horrified, then intoxicated by the emergent chaos, picks up this term. She surrenders at mid-movie to its nihilism: a sense that the world has gone mad. And, of course, it recently had: the postwar-era delivered a gnawing sense of imminent annihilation owing to the Bomb; a mistrust of neighbors due to the Red Scare; a fear that if we didn't hurriedly invade outer space, extra-terrestrials would arrive owing to flying-saucer sightings that began in 1947.[12] Overnight, crazy became the New Normal.

The film is rightly recalled for choice dialogue. When Kathie asks Johnny where his friends are headed, the biker replies: "You are *too* square! You don't go *anywhere*. You just *go!*" Better yet:

GIRL: Hey, Johnny! What are you rebelling against?

JOHNNY: What've you got?

The main theme, even title for *Rebel Without a Cause*, has here been set in cement. Another element further developed in that upcoming film will be sexuality, more specifically the issue of masculinity. At one point, macho Johnny rescues Kathie from reveling bikers, whizzing out of town into the wide-open spaces. She's behind him on the bike, holding on for dear life. Momentarily, they appear as Lancelot and Guinevere in some pre-Raphaelite painting. When alone in a local Avalon-like refuge, Johnny attempts to forcefully impose himself on her. Kathie, too exhausted to fight back, tells him to go ahead, have "his way." Immediately, Johnny nervously distances himself from her. An epiphany occurs as Kathie realizes she's no longer afraid of (or attracted to) him: "*You*'re afraid of *me!*" At once, she transforms from powerless to all-powerful.

By implication, then, *The Wild One* is about the male's desire for and fear of the (eternal) female. This is particularly true considering the look on Johnny's face when Kathie speaks the above; clearly, she has struck a chord. The macho posturer remains at best only half-conscious of his concerns about women. Earlier, Johnny rejected the over-sexed, openly available Britches (Yvonne Doughty) to pursue this obvious virgin. His only alternative is a swift

retreat into the male group, rendered by context as an obliquely homosexual choice. Hints that gayness seethes under the cyclists' tough-guy strutting
about run rampant. "I *love* ya, Johnny," Chino admits on three occasions. This
refrain helps explain their brutal fist-fight as a socially acceptable alternative to what they may secretly wish to experience with one another's bodies.
Meanwhile, gang members pursue local girls. The females initially feign lack
of interest, then giddily succumb. The biker-boys respond by becoming so
obnoxious that the females, truly uncomfortable now, depart. The cyclists
appear less disappointed than relieved. They shrug, turn away, and dance with
one another, appearing more at ease. One diminutive biker employs a rag-
mop as a wig, slipping into affectations of femininity which cause the others to half-kiddingly (if *only* half!) fight over him. Johnny appears supremely
comfortable in their company; alone with Kathie, he withdraws into himself,
needing to be mothered.

This shifting of power, particularly in terms of homosexual and heterosexual desire/alignment/commitment, is represented by the continual transference of a real object that in context transforms into a symbol, and a phallic
one at that: The trophy one of the Rebels steals from a legitimate cycle rally
and slips to Johnny. By its very nature, the upright pointed object represents
supremacy of a male order; by achieving it falsely, also receiving it from the
most overtly effeminate gang member, *The Wild One* implies that Johnny's
macho behavior is play-acting, particularly when he allows the trophy to hang
low around his waist. Soon this becomes the property of Chino; whether he
takes it off Johnny's bike or one of his lackeys does, we do not know. With
Chino's admitted "love" for Johnny already acknowledged, Johnny's defeat of
Chino and reclaiming the trophy represent his reassertion of his masculinity
(or a show of such), temporarily stolen. When Johnny attempts to give the
trophy to Kathie, the virgin—not comfortable accepting his phallus in the
flesh or symbolically—rejects it/him. Following the traumatic if accidental
killing of an elderly bystander with its tragic implication of patricide, Johnny
finally convinces Kathie to take the object. They exchange smiles, suggesting
Johnny has at least initiated a process of normalization. Though he is not yet
able to commit to such a serious-minded young woman (he rides off alone in
the final shot, one final Western-genre visual echo), it's worth noting that he
is now no longer a part of the black-leather male community. Johnny's journey, inward as well as outward, has only begun. Johnny recalls Alan Ladd in
one of the decade's memorable Westerns, *Shane* (George Stevens, 1953), lost
and lonely if undefeated, just beginning his search for self.

*

Sexual politics, subtly dramatized rather than openly acknowledged, also underlines *Rebel Without a Cause* (Nicholas Ray, 1955). Here another (if notably different) youth (James Dean) finds himself caught between an adoring male (Sal Mineo) and an initially stand-offish female (Natalie Wood). Germination began with a book of that title published in 1944 by psychiatrist Robert M. Linder (1914–1956), subtitled "The Hypnoanalysis of a Criminal Psychopath," which had nothing to do with postwar juvenile delinquency as a social issue. Linder chronicled one particular criminal's violent acts, tracing his stet behavior to examples of childhood trauma. This served as a significant case study at a time when analysis remained a mysterious process to the public. Warner Bros. optioned the piece but attempts to create a film along the lines of the later *Three Faces of Eve* (Nunnally Johnson, 1957) failed to coalesce. Following the success of *The Wild One*, studio executives wondered if Linder's title might be drawn out of the mothballs. Iconoclastic director Nicholas Ray (1911–1979), who since his directorial premiere *They Live by Night* (1949) associated himself with issues of postwar youth,[13] expressed interest. Ray decided to sidestep superficial imitation of *The Wild One* by focusing on well -to-do rather than marginal youth. As a result, the title took on an altered if more relevant issue: Why are some teenagers miserable when they have plenty of money?

Without stating the answer outright (as Kramer might have less subtly done), Ray—collaborating with writers Stewart Stern and Irving Shulman— allowed viewers to draw their own conclusions. The film's three case studies— Jim Stark (Dean), Judy (Wood), and Plato (Mineo)—illustrate an existing triad of problems facing contemporary suburban youth. Jim's father (Jim Backus) is a weakling, dominated by his wife (Ann Doran). At one point Mr. Stark dons her apron, visually diminishing his masculinity. "Stand up!" Jim screams as his father grovels over a spilled food-tray. Not surprisingly, Jim turns to a strong-armed police-social worker, Ray (Ed Platt). Earlier, the former marine knocked the boy around when attacked. An autobiographical figure for the director, Ray parallels the sheriff (Jay C. Flippin) in *The Wild One* who finally arrived to restore order, much to Johnny's relief. As a common link between the working-class youth and this affluent counterpart, each boy craves the strict order that his chaotic behavior flies in the face of. Both desperately long for a physically powerful yet emotionally wise father-figure.

AND YOU THINK YOUR FIRST DAY OF HIGH SCHOOL WENT BADLY? (a) Jimbo (James Dean) finds himself involved in a switch-blade fight; (b) participates in a chickie-race hosted by a local beauty (Natalie Wood); (c) almost kills his father (Jim Backus); (d) and finally finds his true family as part of an alternative youth culture (with Sal Mineo, far right). (All images, courtesy: Warner Bros.)

As to the other leads, Judy lives in a seemingly well-ordered home in which all amenities (dinner at a precise hour, etc.) are observed in a traditional if an empty manner. Her problem has to do with an emotionally remote father (William Hopper) who can't deal with his sixteen-year-old's ripening sexuality. Judy needs affection and guidance more than ever. He—fascinated if horrified by her budding beauty—turns his attentions to her non-threatening little brother. The crisis occurs when Judy tries to show affection by kissing him, twice. The first time, he waves her away. Upon her bestowing a second kiss, the man becomes hysterical, slapping Judy, blaming her for his own unacceptable and barely-repressed desires. She as a result runs into the night, joining a group of peers who also, for varying reasons, need to escape stultify-ing homes. Plato fills in the third possibility: his father has deserted the family; his absent mother leaves this boy-child in the care of a well-intentioned maid (Marietta Canty); she is the most positive and sympathetic adult on view other than Ray. Desperate to find some surrogate for the father-role, Plato—the puppy-like boy who shoots actual puppies in an act that objectifies his suicidal impulses—attaches himself to Jim, the school's new arrival.

Shortly, though, it becomes clear Plato's emotional response to Jim is not entirely paternal or fraternal. From the moment they are brought together at a police station during a lengthy opening sequence, Plato considers Jim with what, to borrow from Laura Mulvey,[14] might be termed The Homosexual Male Gaze. While most of the fictional boys who appear here likely have pictures of pretty female stars posted inside school lockers, Plato's adored image is of Alan Ladd, a handsome actor whose complex sexuality has on more than one occasion been considered.[15] Plato considers Jim as Jim does Judy, and as she does Buzz (Corey Allen), local leader of the black-leather-jacket/blue-jeans/cowboy-booted crowd. These are local boys who have seen *The Wild One* and imitate its characters to achieve a sense of identity, some semblance of com-munity neither their parents nor teachers provide. They consider themselves to be individualists though, as in *The Wild One*, the similarity of costumes implies an alternative conformity. If Johnny was a bit of a poseur, these are self-styled carbon copies of what may not have been the real deal to begin with. Most significantly, these relatively rich kids are determined to spite not only their own parents but their class by assuming vestiges of lower classes, particularly from the deep South and old West.

However much they, along with the focal triad, dominate the film's run-ning time, it's clear when everyone arrives for school that at least ninety per-cent of these teens are obviously well-adjusted. The majority are in a good mood, sporting attractive, socially acceptable fashions. The film, as Ray con-ceived it (if not necessarily how the movie would be received) isn't about the majority of modern youth, relatively happy, but rather a small if significant minority. The question raised was not why most contemporary teens are 'reb-els without a cause' (they weren't) but why a few, those that garner headlines, are so angry when they clearly do not want for anything tangible. Simply put, why are they rebels, and what is The Cause?

Obviously, there's that unsatisfying suburban lifestyle, depicted in sharp (even exaggerated) detail. Also parents, particularly fathers, present and weak (Jim's and Judy's), non-existent (Plato's), or brutal and insensitive. The latter is the case with Moose (Jack Grinnage), whose hard-edged dad plans to whip the boy for getting in trouble rather than listening to his son, something all the film's parents have a problem with. (It's significant that at the end, Jim and Mr. Stark are for the first time engaged in meaningful conversation.) Moose's situation echoes Johnny in *The Wild One* who, when beaten to a pulp by the Main-Sreeters, defiantly shouted: "My old man could hit harder than *that!*" There is another cause, however, that exists at the heart of *Rebel*. The film's first act concludes as students visit the Griffith Observatory. A scientist (Ian Wolf) illustrates, with state-of-the-art projection equipment, how our earth emerged out of nothingness, and the manner in which, in due time, it will return to non-existence. "We will disappear into the blankness and void from which we came," he states in a chillingly calm voice that sends Plato leaping under his chair in horror, even silencing unruly gang members. "The earth will not be missed," obscurity our fate. Afterwards, the kids go crazy—that key term for life in the fifties, particularly the young, who witness such stuff rather than the faith-based education of their parents—by engaging in destructive behavior (slashing car tires), entering into switch-blade fights.

At the movie's precise mid-point, they head up to a high cliff. There, Jim and Buzz engage in a Chickie Race: driving stolen cars to "the edge," as Buzz refers to the long drop into the ocean. Presented with a nihilistic world-view, they have little choice but to respond in kind. Why wait around for the end of the world, rendering them powerless, when they can empower themselves by bringing it about on their own terms? How important that the film concludes at the observatory. Or that Plato, perhaps sensing his own imminent demise, fearfully cries: "Jim, do you think the end of the world will come at night-time?" Jim's reply is significant: "No. At dawn." That is when this movie concludes, as a day-worker (director Ray) arrives to begin a new day in this cyclic drama that, however contemporary, adheres to classical unities of time and place. Even as the film's auteur imposes on his 'radical' work such an ongoing template of ancient tragedy, so do the film's teens seek for some semblance of order to dispel encroaching chaos.

Much of *Rebel*'s power derives from a surprisingly conservative treatment of a revolutionary issue, an irony that would come to dominate youth-oriented films at least until the decade's end. Importantly, such films were made for youth by grown-ups.[16] The kids' bad behavior is, by implication, a call for help, an insistence on being seen and heard in a way they would not be were these misfits to, like the vast majority of youth, remain home at nights, watching white-bread TV. They rebel as part of a Marxist dialectic, though none has ever likely to have heard that term. The "rebels" are actually reactionaries, desperate for frontier values that have recently disappeared. What Jim wants—needs!—is for his father to stand up and truly "be a man." He means this in a macho sense that may not qualify as politically correct in our day. (At one point, Jim wishes out loud for his dad to punch his mother.) Jim shamefully considers his financially successful father an abject failure as a man, particularly in sharp contrast to the rugged foil provided by Ray, who beats Jimbo. At the end, though, father and son do reconcile. While the dad makes an effort to live up to his son's expectations, the teenager experiences his own epiphany. He tried, in a fatherly manner, to save Plato and failed miserably. How can he now condemn his own father when he himself has clearly proven a disaster at fulfilling that role?

An ancient Greek sensibility is omnipresent, shades of *Oedipus Rex* on view. "Do you want to *kill* your own *father?*" Jim's mother (Ann Doran) howled, Jocasta-like. Jim himself cannot decide whether he wants to seduce Judy while they are isolated in an abandoned mansion or beg her to mother him. He lays his head in her lap like a boy-child with an earth mother, though they are the same age. This creates a conflict with Plato, who at one point fires a gun at Jim. Plato attempts to kill his youthful surrogate-dad owing to a sense of betrayal owing to Jim's clear, if confused, love for Judy, resulting in a homo-erotic vs. heterosexual tug of war not unlike that in *The Wild One*. As to *Rebel*, it's worth noting that Ray, a bisexual, was according to his own admission simultaneously involved with Dean, Wood, and Mineo.[17] Resultant onscreen tumult may best be seen as an artistic objectification of Ray's own inner sexual demons, organically infused in the work during the complicated process of filmmaking.

Not surprisingly, then, a transference (not of guilt, as in the films of Hitchcock, but love and loyalty) occurs even as it did in *The Wild One*. Here we encounter a double-McGuffin. In the title sequence and visual prologue, a drunken Jim falls down on a Los Angeles street where he pathetically attempts to care for an abandoned furry toy monkey. Like a dutiful parent, Jim covers the mechanical creature with a torn sheet of newspaper to serve as the security blanket he wishes some sympathetic passer-by would wrap around him. In the police station, Jim notices Judy dropping her make-up compact and secretly grabs it. He saw that Judy impulsively clicked it open, then snapped the object closed like some steel vagina. This will be returned to her at mid-movie. "Hey, Judy," Jim asks, forcing her to peer into the mirror, "want to see a *monkey?*" With that line, the objects merge. Back in her possession, Judy will flick the compact open and closed when fantasizing about "being with" Jim rather than Buzz. In a rare close-up, Ray magnifies the compact, his Cinemascope image employed to blow this intimate object up to epic propor-tion. For Judy, the character presumably still a virgin (like the female lead in *The Wild One*) despite Judy's faux-performance of worldliness, this is as much a female's coming-of-age story as, for Jim, it is a boy's version.

At the end, when the film concludes with a gunfight that recalls the Western genre underlining so many important youth films, Judy holds the compact close, as she hopes to now hold Jim. Even as Alan Ladd, drawn into this film's sensibility via Plato's adored pin-up, shook hands with Jean Arthur during their final scene together in *Shane* (George Stevens, 1953) rather than kiss her (the Old Hollywood conventional finale), Jim finally says: "Dad, this is Judy. She's my *friend*." Lover and/or mother; either, both, neither. The bond of a true friendship is what such kids want most; its absence, and the abyss that has replaced any meaning in their lives, is the root cause of their seem-ingly inexplicable acts of rebellion. Lest we forget, Shane spent that entire film attempting to reverse a generalized notion of him as a coward after back-ing down from a bar-room confrontation with a rude cowboy (Ben Johnson). Jim's worst fear is to be thought of as "chicken." This causes a boy who wants to avoid trouble to become involved in just that as a result of peer pressure. Perhaps this explains why, when this author asked Dennis Hopper, who plays Goon in *Rebel* and became a close friend of its doomed actor/star, to describe James Dean, Hopper considered the question, then replied: "James Dean . . . was . . . Alan Ladd in *Shane*."[18]

*

The archives at MGM list the official release date for *Blackboard Jungle* (Richard Brooks) as March 25, 1955, seven months before Warners distrib-uted *Rebel*. That film arrived at some theatres on October 27, less than a month following Dean's death in a traffic accident (9/30/1955). In some areas, *Blackboard Jungle* wasn't screened until early 1956, owing to an inci-dent which reportedly occurred at the premiere. When "Rock Around the Clock" by Bill Haley and the Comets appeared over the opening credits, kids in attendance went wild. They danced in the aisles and, according to at least one source, tore up seats.[19] A revisionist view suggests such information was as overly exaggerated as that concerning a "cyclists' riot" several years earlier. Others guess that the *Blackboard Jungle* incident may have been a press agent's gimmick: kids were hired to dance on cue, their "spontaneous" actions later enhanced to create box-office interest among the young. Whatever the truth, many markets were afraid to book *Blackboard Jungle* until the controversy died down. As a result for a considerable number of viewers the second-produced film in the triad was the last to be seen. More significant: alone among them, it was the only film in the triad to actually include rock 'n' roll.

(a)   (b)

(c)   (d)

JUVENILE DELINQUENCY, REALITY OR MYTH?: (a) New teacher 'Dadier' (Glenn Ford) confronts the reality of street kids on his first day at work; (b) Dadier survives by isolating the worst (Vic Morrow, left) and best (Sidney Poitier, right) among the tough youths; (c) while the classroom riot sequence was accurate to such situations, *Blackboard Jungle* never establishes how rare such disruptive elements actually were in the 1950s; (d) Dadier must rely on war-time skills to survive after a student attempts to kill him with a hard ball.
(All images, courtesy: Metro-Goldwyn-Mayer)

If the presence of that rock anthem (a modest hit before the movie promoted it, a major one after) had a great deal to do with the reception of
Brooks's (1912–1992) movie as a youth-targeted piece (some would argue
this had *everything* to do with it), the work had always been planned as an
adult-oriented feature. Richard Dadier (Glenn Ford), the lead, is an early-
middle-aged man, a married World War II vet who attended college on
the G.I. Bill and now wants to teach. The character first appeared in a
1954 novel by Evan Hunter (1926–2005), its theme the stress involved in
attempting to educate that portion of society many authorial figures deem
to be un-educatable. Book and film do touch on the supposed "epidemic" of
juvenile delinquency during the immediate postwar era.[20] Other than a few
minor details—choices in clothing and phrasing in the book, less so music as
rock 'n' roll was not yet popular during the period (1951–1952) in which the
novel takes place—these could be slum kids from any era. There is little difference between them and those in Sidney Kingsley's 1935 play *Dead End* or
Warner Bros. film version (William Wyler, 1937). Hunter addressed ongoing,
even universal issues first, temporal elements secondarily, as did Brooks when
penning his screenplay.

For economy's sake, Brooks simplified Hunter's sprawling epic about a
middle-class man attempting to accomplish something in a slum school. The
movie instead offers Manichean dualities for several supporting characters,
adult and juvenile. One older teacher (Louis Calhern) is reduced from the
book's three-dimensional figure to a ranting hard-liner who believes teens
must be beaten into submission. In contrast, there's a newcomer (Richard
Kiley) hoping to reach troubled souls. Likewise, there are two 'wheels' (fifties
slang for the Big Wheel): a nasty, violence-prone creep (Vic Morrow) and a
wholesome loner (Sidney Poitier). Dadier grasps that to succeed he must isolate and polarize them, manipulating sheep-like students into rejecting their
gang leader in favor of the salvageable youth. That the good kid is African
American draws from Civil Rights cinema appearing onscreen simultaneously
with Youth Movies.[21] Poitier (1927–) had previously appeared in *Cry, The
Beloved Country* (Zoltan Korda, 1951), from Alan Paton's novel with its plea
for African nationalism and would soon star in *The Defiant Ones* (Kramer,
1958), the centerpiece of Message Moviemaking. Such reduction of the book's
richer verisimilitude levelled any sense of an all-encompassing expose to the
simplistics of a modern morality play. Even as the teens must choose between
these two potential leaders, Dadier is pushed to embrace the one or the other
of his own potential role models among teachers.

Also, *Blackboard Jungle* set into place a new genre in which a well-intentioned teacher overcomes teen resistance, winning kids over to his values, in the process making decent citizens of them. A dozen years later, a 1960s version featured Poitier in the teacher's role, attempting to enlighten English punks in *To Sir, With Love* (James Clavell, 1967). Though such stuff makes for crowd-pleasing entertainment, more than a few academics condemn such narratives. In the latter film, Poitier "reaches" kids in his English class by throwing the textbook away and teaching them how to make a salad. In *Blackboard Jungle*, the all-boy class is delighted when Ford/Dadier shows cartoons to spark interest in discussing ideas. Another department member rightly questions whether he is doing the job he's paid for: Help them read more effectively. In neither movie do we have a sense that, once the salad is devoured, the cartoon enjoyed, there will be any carry-over to the actual task at hand: increased literacy.

More immediate in impact than the two previously discussed films, *Blackboard Jungle* proves less honest than either. In them, even the worst sort of trouble-makers—Johnny, Buzz—were allowed a sense of humanity via a motive for questionable behavior. Those rebels *do*, as it turns out, have causes. No so Artie West, the bad-ass played by Morrow. Artie's fate (he's dragged off with his closest confederate to reform school or, more likely considering a truck-hijacking, prison) goes against the grain of progressive thinking in the Kramer movie. There, adult audiences learned that Johnny could, and should, be understood. His path to rehabilitation, we know from the final shot, has begun. If Kramer's work assumed a 1950s liberal position, Brooks's pushes in the opposite direction. No matter how dedicated the teacher may be, some souls can't be saved and we had damn well better accept that. Isolate them, remove them, sacrifice the few so the many may survive. Ford's Dadier ("Daddy-O!" to hipster kids) says so, his other kids eventually agreeing, helping with the exorcism of Artie from their midst. Dadier assumes a moral stance somewhere between the extremes of fellow teachers, neither completely cynical nor naively idealistic at the conclusion.

During the final sequence, when Artie West pulls a switchblade on 'The Teach,' he's hopped up on drugs, this stated by Miller (Poitier). Such a drug reference would have been impossible less than a year earlier owing to the censorship restrictions. *Blackboard Jungle* must be commended for including a mixed student body in terms of race: Miller is African American, West Irish, also Italian (Dan Terranova), Puerto Rican (Rafael Campos), and Jewish (Paul Mazursky). Yet the most important innovation was the rock 'n' roll record with which the film opens and closes. This was a last minute addition; varied stories ranged from the possibility that the director caught the tune on the radio and was inspired to add "Rock Around the Clock" as a musical kicker to the possibility that actor Ford heard his son Peter playing the disc and brought it to the studio.[22] Either way, this film likely would have, without the song that became an anthem, been seen by a decent-sized crowd of young adults, few kids picking up on it, its youth-cult film status never happening.

That said, its inclusion may have done more of a disservice to The New Music than has heretofore been noted. By all reports, Ford's teenage son was a well-adjusted boy. Though the offspring of a movie star, Peter—like the vast majority of young people who had recently fallen in love with rural Rockabilly and urban rhythm 'n' blues—was a wholesome kid. We observe just such boys and girls onscreen when Dadier visits another school. From math and science labs to shop classes, glee club practice to the athletic field, civil and social duties to genial kidding around, here are well mannered, nicely behaved, ever-respectful teenagers. They are as exaggerated cartoon-like depictions of good kids as those in Mr. Dadier's class are of 'the other sort.' The point is, those nice kids do not listen to rock 'n' roll, at least not in this movie. Yet as Ford's own son made clear, nice young people *did* listen in everyday life. Rock 'n' roll had become youth's music of choice, not specifically those who lived on the edge. This helps explain why most parents and/or teachers didn't initially express any objection to it. How different was this from their own swing and be-bop? Not much, particularly considering WWII vets and their short-skirted girlfriends dancing like giddy maniacs as evidenced on film in *Buck Privates Come Home* (Charles Barton, 1947).

Then, along came *Blackboard Jungle* and everything changed. Not only does the film feature bad kids jiving to the Haley song (boys dancing not with girls but other boys, briefly continuing that notion of a homoerotic element in exclusively male gangs) while the good ones will have none of it. One memorable moment occurs when Kiley's well-intentioned, hopelessly naïve teacher brings his precious/priceless collection of jazz and swing records to school in hopes of making teenagers sense a similarity between music and math. Not unexpectedly, Artie West leads the worst kids in an orgy of destruction, breaking every disc, reducing the teacher to tears and, thereafter, provoking his hasty resignation. For adults who caught the film, that sequence offered a revelation. They had come to be educated about the teaching profession; instead, they learned something about rock 'n' roll, whether or not this was true outside the film's context. Here was the music of a generation of new barbarians:

those who wished to destroy the music these adults adored, and their world as well. They had to be stopped. The first step: despite one band's insistence that "rock 'n' roll was here to stay," rock 'n' roll must go. At once!

Almost overnight, an indigenous form of evolving music transformed in the adult imagination from a harmless diversion for all kids into an abiding threat. Nice teens whose moms and dads bought them 45 r.p.m.s only months earlier were shocked when parents changed their minds. Here was something dark and dangerous, this rock 'n' roll. They now knew this, or thought they knew. Certainly, such parents believed. And something had to be done about it. No matter that the music was as innocuous as Ragtime or The Blues had been in their eras, appealing to youthful giddiness. This was different! Of course, it wasn't. But if perception is reality, that was the perception beginning late in 1955. As a result, films that included rock 'n' roll could not do so neutrally. Instead, they had to defend it, leading to an entire subgenre of Youth Movies.

· 2 ·

SHAKE, RATTLE AND ROCK

The Big Beat on the Big Screen

"Rock 'n' roll is here to stay.
It will never die.
It'll never go away,
Though I don't know why."
—Danny (Rapp) and the Juniors, 1958

For teenagers who swarmed into theatres on March 21, 1956 to catch the first film specifically tailored for them, a sense of déjà vu set in as the opening credits rolled, accompanied by "Rock Around the Clock," precisely as in *Blackboard Jungle*. What followed, though, disappointed the target audience: A conventional romance involving forty-ish band manager Steve Hollis (Johnny Johnston) and Corinne Talbot (Alix Talton), a mature musical agent. Together, Steve believes, they can propel Bill Haley and the Comets to superstardom. Cautious, she prefers to stick with fast-fading Big Bands. Melodramatic complications ensue as Steve falls in love with a dancer, Lisa (Lisa Gaye), whose wild gyrations accompany the band's performances; Corinne, who covets Steve, seethes. As Lisa has just turned 22, there are no lead teen characters in what was over-hyped as the first 1950s Youth Film.

Reasons for this were multitude. *Rock Around the Clock* (Fred F. Sears) was the product of a major studio, Columbia. Headed up by Harry Cohn

(1891–1958), released two years before his passing, here was an old man's notion of what a youth-exploitation flick should be. Involved in the production of such important A-movies as *Picnic* (Joshua Logan, 1955), Cohn allowed his B-movie specialist Sam Katzman (1901–1973) to produce. During the 1940s, his bread-and-butter flicks were black-and-white quickies: the studio-bound *Jungle Jim* African-adventure series, a seemingly endless string of Bowery Boys comedies, small Westerns starring the likes of Tom Tyler. Now, television offered such stuff for free so such second-features had to present something else. Director Sears was 43, the same age as the movie's male lead. Robert E. Kent and James B. Gordon's storyline chronicled the mainstream's discovery of rock, though the details presented here are fictional. When Steve can no longer secure bookings for swing acts, the adult public now being more interested in small jazz combos, he fortuitously stops off in a small town. There, Steve notices local young people adore a rockabilly band. The Comets are mechanics and farm boys, picking up extra bucks by performing Saturday night gigs. Learning that disc jockey Alan Freed (1921–1965) mounts large rock 'n' roll Jamborees, Steve comes up with the idea of televising such an event. Overnight, rock 'n' roll becomes a coast-to-coast phenomenon.

Other than Haley and other rock 'n' roll acts like Freddie Bell and his Bellboys, even the music is square. When Steve and Lisa engage in a (mild) romantic beach scene, the background tune is the love theme from *From Here to Eternity* (Fred Zinnemann, 1953). Any danger of teens tearing up theatre-seats had more to do with frustration than inspiration. Tony Martinez's Latin combo performs the precise sort of music teenagers had come to *Rock Around the Clock* to escape. Vocals/instrumentals performed by Haley's boys save the day, members wearing their signature outfits: plaid jackets and black bow ties. As if by magic, they had somehow stumbled upon on white Southern rock: ages-old hillbilly, powered by a bigger beat more in tune with the hard-driving tempo of the times. Making clear that rock wasn't an aberration but a logical extension of where pop music had long been headed are The Platters. Their sophisticated, on-the-edge-of-sentimentality delivery of numbers like "My One and Only You" makes clear these African American performers have merely updated the enchantingly mellow sounds of such predecessors as The Mills Brothers and the Ink Spots. In the film, the only adults who have a problem with rock are elderly matrons who also detest the mambo and cha-cha.

That was indeed the case when *Rock Around the Clock* was written during the waning months of 1955, then shot in January.[1] The fallout from *Blackboard Jungle* had just begun, so it didn't strike the avatars of this piece to include a controversy as it didn't yet exist. When the film premiered three months later, *Rock Around the Clock* appeared hopelessly outdated owing to its mild presentation of what had become incendiary. To comprehend the sudden turnabout, it's necessary to recall that this tempest in a teacup was preceded by other situations involving adult fear as to the impact of popular culture on kids. Most obviously was a scandal involving comic books. These seemingly ephemeral forerunners to the more respectable graphic novel of today received the lion's share of blame for an increase in juvenile delinquency. In the decade following the war, the rate of youth crime doubled.[2] In *1,000,000 Delinquents*, Benjamin Fine, a respected social commentator, warned that this must be considered "a national epidemic" which, if not "checked," would "go on spreading and contaminate many good cells in our society."[3] Though this Pulitzer-prize winner was too savvy to denounce any one thing as the root of evil, many who read his book simplistically demanded just such a scapegoat.

The United States Congress, finding itself under pressure, held hearings in 1953. Middle-aged or elderly white men in expensive suits turned their wrath on a handy suspect, comics. The vendetta might have never moved in this direction were it not for the 1954 publication of *Seduction of the Innocent* by Fredric Wertham. In it, he insisted that horror and war comics allowed "criminally or sexually abnormal ideas" to infect the minds of previously healthy children.[4] The most damaging claim was that comics likely had "detrimental and delinquency-producing effects on the emotionally normal"[5] teenager. That, of course, was patently absurd, as any senior citizen of today who has never in his or her life committed a crime can attest to, despite a youthful addiction to *Mad*. Whether violent fantasies can feed already diseased minds—young, middle-aged, or old—remains another issue, relevant still in this age of violent video-games. Still, there has never been a shred of evidence to suggest exposure to media materials might corrupt anyone not inclined to dangerous behavior. Movies, which had also become more violent and sexual during the postwar years, were likewise scrutinized by Washington.[6] Lurid elements appeared in film noirs that appealed to adults, while such sordid paperback novels as Mickey Spillane's Mike Hammer series were exclusively sold to grown-ups. Nonetheless, someone or something had to be blamed for the juvenile delinquency "epidemic." With the new Comics Code supposedly doing its job (wholesome as well as troublesome teenage boys wept when Catwoman disappeared from D.C.'s *Batman*), youthful crime failed to diminish. Yet *another* scapegoat was needed. Citizens ignored Paramount's exec Frank Freeman when he claimed the problem resulted from "the foundation

of our way of life—the (postwar suburban) home—and divorces and drinking."[7] This idea, already proposed by *Rebel*, was not what they wanted to hear.
Denial set in, and adult anger was redirected toward rock 'n' roll.

(a)

(b)

REAL AND REEL: In 1956, the rock musical hit movie screens. (a) *Rock Around the Clock*
(Fred F. Sears) featured Bill Haley and the Comets performing the title song (courtesy: Clover
Prods./Columbia); *Rock, Pretty Baby* starred Rod McKuen (fourth from left) and John Saxon
(center, with guitar) as fictional musicians who form the first 'garage band' ever to appear in an
American film. (courtesy: Universal International).

Despite its flaws, *Rock Around the Clock,* which had been budgeted at a tight $300,000, quadrupled its cost in box-office earnings.[8] A follow-up was hurriedly thrown together. Katzman and company came up with *Don't Knock the Rock* (Sears, 1957), released Dec. 14, 1956 to capitalize on teens' Christmas vacation. Though this film did address the by-then widespread controversy (as the title announces), screenwriter Kent once more focused on an adult male hero: Arnie Haines (Alan Dale), a pop star who has successfully made a crossover to rock. Pushed to the edge of exhaustion by his money-mad manager (Alan Freed), Arnie heads home to the village of Mellondale for the summer in hopes of spending quality time with his easygoing mom and pop. But the mayor, aware of a developing witch-hunt, states that "rock 'n' roll is for morons," proclaiming Arnie persona non grata in his hometown. With adults, that is; the kids adore him, as they do other acts such as Little Richard and The Treniers. An obvious improvement over *Rock Around the Clock* is that this follow-up contains only Big Beat performers, other than Dale himself.[9]

This was the first film to depict the Generation Gap as to music. Grown-ups support the mayor, insisting they won't tolerate rock 'n' roll which "impacts on the morality of our young people." The central conflict involves a mother-daughter rift. A journalist (Fay Baker) mindlessly joins the crusade to blame Big Beat for juvenile delinquency while her bright offspring (Patricia Hardy) insists the contemporary sound is only "a symptom of (youth) analyzing themselves." Though the film takes the kids' side, its message appears aimed at an adult viewer. The paradox is that few (if any) grown-ups would go to see such a film. At a dance where Haley and the Comets perform, teenagers remain remarkably well-behaved, at least until an underage blonde nymphet (Jana Lund) makes a scene to spite Arnie, who has spurned her advances. In time, the truth unfolds; the WASPish journalist is won over, retracting everything she previously claimed. Rock is revealed to be no different from the Charleston, itself at least a tad controversial when so many of these grown-ups were young and fully embraced that sound.

Freed reveals this to the older generation when he and some local kids stage "The Pageant of Art and Culture." Rock is demonstrated to have naturally developed from preceding musical forms, like them reflecting the mood of any particular era. Also notable, the filmmakers sincerely attempt to depict integration, suggested in the previous film. Though all the teenage dancers in *Rock Around the Clock* were white bread (at the time, a mixed-race group would have kept the film from bookings anywhere in the South, causing

Columbia to lose money), several African American acts were integrated into the show. That's taken a step further here. When Little Richard performs "Tutti Fruitti," two black dancers assume center stage to display current dance steps. Likely they are intended to be perceived as professionals, brought along with the company, though that's never stated. Though the white kids do not share the dance floor with them, waiting until these performers finish, Freed had at least taken a small step in the right direction.

This may have had a great deal to do with Freed's destruction two years later. Officially, he was excised from the music industry owing to acceptance of Payola, money from record companies in exchange for air-time on his popular radio and TV shows.[10] Teenagers loved Freed, who "became one of them, the kids, on their side as opposed to their parents, the first grown-up who understood them and what they wanted."[11] Like most pioneers in any endeavor, that left him open to become a sacrificial lamb. There was never any doubt Freed had indeed accepted bribes. That practice was widespread throughout the unregulated industry of the time; it would have been a greater surprise had he not. This man's avid support of not only white rockers like Haley but also African American talent including Chuck Berry had outraged racists, not only in the Deep South. Most suburbanites everywhere advocated an anti-integrationist agenda.[12] Now, their kids were dancing to what was openly denounced by powerful adults: "rock 'n' roll inflames and excites (white) youth like jungle tom-toms" complained the Rev. John Carroll of Boston.[13] An industry publication, *Music Journal,* insisted rock 'n' roll threatened to destroy mainstream values of white teenagers owing to its "throwback to jungle rhythms."[14] Though jazz likewise derived from African American sounds, as did such other relatively non-controversial musical forms as be-bop and the blues, bigots now

> objected to its racial background and content, even claiming that rock 'n' roll was a plot jointly sponsored by the Kremlin and the NAACP . . . to tear down the barriers of segregation and bring about sexual promiscuity, inter-marriage, and a decline in the morals of young whites.[15]

Considering the generalized witch-hunting mentality of the Fifties, it's hardly surprising that racists, fearful of an alliance between Jews and blacks, perceived Freed as an Hebraic Pied Piper, ready to lead naïve kids off to enjoy "jungle music" by Freed's friend Berry. Freed would be thrown to the wolves while squeaky-clean Dick Clark, also brought before a committee on similar charges, survived. In a notable irony, the sole film in which Freed played himself as a lead rather than in a supporting capacity, *Mister Rock and Roll* (Charles Dubin, 1957–58), hit theatres at precisely the moment when this early advocate of rock began his sad, swift decline.

Not, however, before insuring that The Big Beat (this the title of his brief-lived Manhattan-based Saturday night show) would continue. The film that most effectively portrays Freed as "a visionary champion of racial equality who almost singlehandedly transformed America's musical taste"[16] was *Rock, Rock, Rock!* (Will Price, 1956). An indie flick, it lacked the slickness of production values that Columbia studios endowed on even its minorleague projects. From today's perspective, the movie's technical clunkiness seems endearing, part and parcel of its unique identity as a cultural artifact. Importantly, *Rock, Rock, Rock!* abandons the established/annoying pattern of a middle-aged male as the focus. Tuesday Weld (thirteen when *Rock, Rock, Rock!* was filmed) is Dori Graham, a typical 1950s teenager. As this film was shot before the controversy, this rock 'n' roll addict also adores her parents. Dori's free time is spent at the malt shop. Enjoying ice-cream sodas and burgers, she reveals no sense that rock 'n' roll has had a negative impact on her personality. Her boyfriend Tommy (Teddy Randazzo) is an aspiring rock 'n' roller yet anything but a rebel. Well-mannered, Tommy presages the ultra-clean-cut crooners like Frankie Avalon, soon to be promoted by Dick Clark on his *American Bandstand* late-afternoon TV show. Here, Freed hosts such a dance-cavalcade, allowing Tommy to make an appearance as a local-talent guest. Before Tommy gets his big shot, the movie-goer is treated to such stars as The Moonglows, Frankie Lymon and the Teenagers, and Chuck Berry.

Freed brings black talent to white kids watching at home in suburban living-rooms. But as this film pre-dates any mass-hysteria, in context there is no concern on the part of Dori's parents. Mr. Graham (Jack Collins) initially appears unmoved though not offended by first-wave rock 'n' roll. He reads a newspaper while Dori and her friend (Jacqueline Kerr) groove to the music. Then, Mr. Graham gets into it, boogie-ing along with the girls with no hint of the negative parental reaction soon to come. As for Freed, he remains a distant figure, a mentor of young talent and friend to kids, meeting them at a high-school sock hop. Here, he insists they study hard and obey their parents. Released one month before *Blackboard Jungle*, the film posits rock 'n' roll as the music of the country's good teenagers.

At one point, a wholesome Frankie Lymon sings his anthem:

Life is what you make it.
It all depends on *you*.
I know, I know, I know:
Because I'm *not* a juvenile delinquent!

Shortly thereafter, one film vividly captured the momentary madness of a mainstream backlash. In *Shake, Rattle, and Rock* (Edward L. Cahn, 1956), Groucho Marx's long-time foil, society dame Margaret Dumont, sets out to jail an agreeable TV show host (Mike Connors) for bringing Fats Domino and Big Joe Turner into suburban living-rooms. *Shake, Rattle, and Rock* hit theatres in November 1956, as the faux fury over rock reached its crescendo, then swiftly died down. Less than a month later another film presented the post-controversy situation while also establishing a subgenre in which nice kids create a band, appearing not very different from Mickey Rooney and Judy Garland in the 1940s. In Rock, Pretty Baby (Richard Bartlett, 1956), the kids are John Saxon, the Marlon Brando of 1950s Youth Movies, as the band-leader, with former Disney child-star Luanna Patten his solid-as-a-rock (no pun intended) girlfriend. She, the most interesting character on view, supports her steady guy's desire for a musical career while keeping him on an even keel with his parents and other band-members, played by such diverse film actors as *Rebel's* Sal Mineo and future pop-poet Rod McKuen in Rock, Pretty Baby (Richard Bartlett, 1956).

Patten's character, like those earlier played by Lisa Gaye and Patricia Hardy, offers a telling portrait of an emergent young American woman, able to balance career ambitions with personal agendas. As for Saxon's hero, the conflict with his father (*Rebel's* Edward Platt) has little to do with rock 'n' roll per se. The dad wants his boy to, like him, continue on to a university, becoming a medical professional. What irks him is the boy's burning desire to be a musician, though jazz, pop, swing or big band would also be intolerable. Mom (Fay Wray) proves understanding as to the needs of both men in her life, the idea of adult women as more enlightened than their male counterparts also a recurring device in youth films. They have a lovely home (an adorable kid sister, called Twinky, is played by Shelley Fabares), with no hint of juvenile delinquency. That's true too of the sequel, *Summer Love* (Charles F. Haas, 1958), in which the band plays to the delight of adults as well as teens.

This star-on-the-rise syndrome would motor the early Elvis oeuvre once he moved past the B Western limits of *Love Me Tender*. Elvis's second film, *Loving*

You (Hal Kanter, 1957), borrows its plot from earlier rock cheapies, though this Paramount release is in color. Press agent Glenda Markel (Lizabeth Scott) happens upon a rockabilly performer, Deke Rivers (Presley), in a small town. By exploiting Deke's popularity with teens on a national level she may catapult herself and her partner (Wendell Corey) into the big time. Raw capitalists, they plan to market Deke and the New Music, but prove to be false parental figures who would corrupt his pure sound for their own (not his) financial gain. Rushing to Deke's rescue is a girl (Dolores Hart) who resembles earlier characters played by Gaye, Hardy, and Patten: An adoring and dedicated if also wise girl-woman of his own age, she alone understands Deke's talent must be slowly nurtured. At this time, Col. Tom Parker (1909–1997), Elvis's manager, regularly turned down offers for roles in such prestigious films as *Rio Bravo* (Howard Hawks, 1959) and *West Side Story* (Robert Wise, 1961), convincing Elvis to instead appear in ever less ambitious musicals.[17] These were more likely to make a fast, fat profit, particularly when proceeds from the soundtrack recordings were added. Though the precise details in *Loving You* are fictional, they do parallel Presley's life, and that of other young rock stars. The Establishment, after initially rejecting them, rapidly reversed course, attempting to homogenize those wonderfully raunchy elements which had initially attracted the teenagers.

Later that year, *Jailhouse Rock* (Richard Thorpe, 1957) reiterated the struggling rock 'n' roller plot while offering a major innovation. Here Vince Everett is torn between an even more obvious stand-in for Col. Parker, Hunk Houghton (Mickey Shaughnessy) and another ambitious though moral young woman (Judy Tyler as Peggy) who wants to make money but share it fairly with her client. She insists he remain true to his hillbilly roots rather than allow wolf-like adults to simultaneously capitalize on the boy's raw talent while corrupting its essence. What sets this film apart is a sequence in which former jailbird Vince performs the title sequence for the TV cameras. Choreographer Alex Romero originally planned on staging this number in the manner of a traditional MGM dance routine of the Gene Kelly/Fred Astaire variety.[18] Elvis' attempts to follow Romero's patterns proved disastrous; everything spontaneous (and best) about his iconoclastic gyrations evaporated. Elvis (like Vince in the film) told Romero, "Man, it's not *me*." Knowing nothing of rock 'n' roll, Romero listened to Elvis' records, then, asked: "Would you show me what you do on stage?" Romero explained to Elvis that he planned to "take what you do and work it into the routine, and it's going to be you, what you normally feel comfortable doing, but I'm going to choreograph it."[19]

SELLING THE BIG BEAT: (a) The first true rock-exploitation flick was advertised via images of the 'new' music in tandem with emergent dance styles (courtesy: Sam Katzman Prods./ Clover Pictures/Columbia); (b) the role of rockers was diminished to focus on Hollywood's new blonde bombshell (courtesy: 20th Century-Fox); (c) the myth that rockers were also delinquents was furthered in poster art for Elvis's fourth feature (courtesy: Hal Wallis Prods./Paramount); (d) distributors mixed Youth Sub-Genres, combining rock 'n' roll with Hot-Rod films (courtesy: American International Pictures); (e) edgy rock flicks were turned out on miniscule budgets by indie producers (courtesy: Fairway); (f) The Twist Craze rounded out the first wave of rock movies (courtesy: (Paramount).

This resulted in a perfect marriage of Hollywood dance musicals and the uninhibited rhythms of rock. From that moment, rock 'n' roll would no longer be marginalized as a sidelight of the movie musical, becoming the essence of the form. Elvis' next film, *King Creole* (Michael Curtiz, 1958), had Presley singing not only rock 'n' roll but pop, jazz, even Creole/Cajun tunes deriving from the New Orleans setting. At that moment, rock was integrated into mainstream popular music.

In addition to films in which Elvis more or less played himself, another release fictionalized his meteoric rise. Shortly after the advent of Elvis, Golden Age TV writer Paul Monash set to work on a scenario revealing the manner in which manager Parker not only turned a small-town boy into a star but manipulated his client's life. This became "The Singin' Idol," a one-hour live dramatic presentation on *Kraft Theatre* (1/30/1957). The teleplay received strong reviews, appealing to an adult audience owing to its mature treatment of the subject matter. In an intriguing irony, one song, "Teenage Crush," became a hit for Tommy Sands, who played Elvis-like Virgil Walker. 20th Century-Fox optioned the script, then set about reducing the impact by re-imagining it as yet another exploitation item for teens, *Sing, Boy, Sing* (Henry Ephron, 1958), with the Machiavellian manager played by Fred Clark on TV here enacted by Edmond O'Brien. What little of the original impact that came across in Claude Binyon's milder screenplay (now focusing on Virgil's loneliness rather than adult exploitation) seemed as old hat in mid-1958 as it had been mindblowing early in 1957. "Teenage Crush" was gone; as a previous hit, the song was considered an oldie that might date the piece. In place of raw rockabilly the film offered up puerile pop. One saving grace is actor Nick Adams as a weak-minded rube who becomes Virgil's only friend. In actuality, Adams played that role with Elvis himself.[20]

*

Until Elvis entered the military on March 24, 1958, immediately becoming an all-American boy, an aura of controversy had surrounded him. A foil had been presented by Pat Boone (1934–), who rated Number Two in record sales, second only to Presley. As clean-cut and ever-smiling as Presley appeared funky and surly, Boone claimed descent from the American pioneer Daniel Boone. This wholesome performer starred in a trio of teen musicals, in color with bright lighting. *Bernardine* (Henry Levin, 1957) had Boone and his malt-shop pals imagine the title dream girl. *April Love* (Levin, 1957) featured a backwoods romance between Boone and Shirley Jones. In *Mardi Gras* (Edmund Goulding, 1958) Boone played a military-school cadet who wins a date with a movie star (Christine Carrere). Meanwhile, the weekly *Pat Boone Chevy Show* on ABC (1957–1960) allowed for an alteration between pop standards and youth-oriented songs. With any controversy a dim memory, teen stars could now play lead roles, the case with Elvis-lookalike Fabian in *Hound-Dog Man* (Don Siegel, 1959). Also, supporting parts in big pictures, Fabian again in *North to Alaska* (Henry Hathaway, 1960) which was headlined by John Wayne, Capucine, and Ernie Kovacs. Frankie Avalon joined Wayne that year for *The Alamo. Rich Nelson worked with Wayne in Rio Bravo (Howard Hawks, 1959).*

Not that Hollywood was yet finished with rock 'n' roll films about adults. The first major studio project to include Big Beat performers, 20th Century-Fox's *The Girl Can't Help It* (Frank Tashlin, 1956), features Tom Ewell as Tom Miller, another agent/manager who can't procure bookings for his jazz bands now that rock has arrived. He's given a final shot at making "moola" when gang boss 'Fats' Murdock (Edmond O'Brien) hires Tom to promote a blonde, Jerry Jordan (Jayne Mansfield). Since her singing voice is anything but conventional, 'Fats' believes The Big Beat, which allows kids to scream their lungs out, is the way to go. *The Girl Can't Help It* rates as a one-of-a-kind movie. Though the budget was big enough to allow for color photography and Widescreen, everything about it oozes exploitation. Mansfield incarnates a caricature of Marilyn Monroe's early dumb blonde roles that actress played, for example, in *The Seven Year Itch* (Billy Wilder, 1955). The studio hired Tashlin (1913–1972), unique among directors in that he'd begun his career in anima-tion at Warner Bros. and Columbia. The eccentric director's breakneck-paced Looney Tunes "used all kinds of camera angles, montages, and pan shots, ver-tical and horizontal"[21] to create a world that did not, like Disney films, offer imitations of reality. Tashlin's cartoons *insisted* on their artificiality as the basis for their sophistication as well as silliness. That may explain why *The Girl Can't Help It* opens in small-screen and black-and-white. Actor Ewell destroys any cinematic equivalent to live theatre's proscenium arch by directly address-ing the movie-going audience while persuading them to shift perspectives to color and CinemaScope. As with the Merrie Melodies, Tashlin's live-action films self-consciously reveal themselves to be movies rather than attempt to hide this fact from the audience.

Tashlin's live-action films, including several with Jerry Lewis, are often described as living cartoons,[22] an approach Mansfield was more than able to embody. One sequence has her strut down a city street (shot in the studio to enhance a demarcation with reality) in a tight black dress, carrying a pair of milk bottles tight against her chest. Males standing about go mad. All the while, Little Richard's semi-crazed rendition of the title tune enhances a sense of parody carried over to the film's rock acts (Eddie Cochran, Gene Vincent, Fats Domino, and Eddie Fontaine). Each performs not as in a Columbia exploitation flick (at face value), but rather burlesquing himself. Despite its in-your-face vulgarity, *The Girl Can't Help It* rated as one of the year's box-office hits with teens *and* adults. Some rock aficionados may resent the manner in which Ewell, in a tux, affecting disdain, opens the film by snobbishly speaking about youth's music. That the film itself condescends toward The Big Beat is belied by an understanding of the era in which this film was released. Middlebrow TV talk show hosts, notably Steve Allen (1921–2000), had taken to openly displaying contempt for what they failed to understand. On a 1957 broadcast, Allen recited in a stentorian tone the lyrics for "Be-Bop-a-Lula" to laughter from his adult live audience. Tashlin was not satirizing rock 'n' roll so much as Allen's pseudo-sophistication.[23]

Also significant is rock's contextualizing within the movie's mis-en-scene. Though the title sequence features young people dancing to The Big Beat (wholesome kids, doing so politely), from that point there are no teenagers on view until the final Prom Night episode. As Tom escorts Jerry from one adult-oriented night club to the next, the groups playing include the Platters and The Treniers. Though adults who have arrived to catch these acts do not jump up and dance, they obviously relish such performances. Moreover, rock 'n' roll acts are alternated with top-level jazz stars Abbey Lincoln, Ray Anthony, and Julie London. Such an approach works here as it did not in *Rock Around the Clock*. There the two styles, haphazardly mixed, clashed. In a more ambitious context, they balance beautifully. The theme Freed insisted on now comes across, if in a less didactic manner: there is no old music as opposed to new music, only great music, genre less significant than an individual's talent and the essential quality of any single piece of work.

Perhaps the final example of a Youth Film with an adult star was *Let's Rock* (Harry Foster, 1958). Julius La Rosa, a crooner who enjoyed some popularity on TV's *The Arthur Godfrey Show,* appears as Tommy Adane, a faded pop-star not unlike himself. Tommy glumly watches teen talent (The Tyrones) on a Freed/Clark type program. That, his agent insists, is "what the kids are looking for today." Booked onto such a show (Wink Martindale plays the host) to promote his new single, Tommy realizes that teens could care less. In contrast to Tommy's dead-on-arrival ballad, and to reveal the music today's youth enjoys, there's a cross-cut to Paul Anka singing "I'm Still Waiting for You." But this too is a ballad! Moreover, the music, lyrics, and tone are almost identical to those performed by Tommy. In truth, teenagers did not turn their backs on ballads, enjoying slow-dancing as much as their parents had. The problem for any La Rosa-like crooner is not that they fail to offer rock, rather that they are early-middle-aged, Anka (playing Anka) sixteen. "How many ballads are there on the Top Ten?" Tommy's agent sighs. Actually, most of the songs on the Top Ten when this film was released *were* ballads: "It's All in the Game" (Tommy Edwards), "Since I Don't Have You" (The Skyliners), "Sixteen Candles" (The Crests), "It's Only Make Believe" (Conway Twitty), "To Know Him is to Love Him" (The Teddy Bears), "Come Softly to Me" (The Fleetwoods), and "Tears on My Pillow" (Little Anthony and the Imperials). Every other song played on *American Bandstand* was a ballad. This was the case at sock-hops in high-school gymnasiums all across the country.

Only Chuck Berry could claim:

It's got to be rock 'n' roll music
If you wanna dance with me!

Truth be told, the term "rock 'n' roll" no longer referred only to hard-driving Rockabilly or intense rhythm 'n' blues, now encompassing all music, ballads included, played by young artists for young listeners. A belated acceptance of rock in the late 1950s by major companies (Capitol, Dot, R.C.A, etc.) had much to do with cost efficiency. As the agent in *Let's Rock* points out, records featuring a three or four instrument band (drums, electric guitar and piano required; bass-guitar optional) could sell two million discs to teenagers. More mature performers, insisting on an expensive 48 person orchestra (with strings), likely would 'move' 250,000 records to mature purchasers. Sinatra fans continued to buy his records but now preferred those 33 1/3 r.p.m. long-playing albums. A persistent myth insists that with the advent of Big Beat, popular music curled up and died, rock knocking pop off the charts. The reality was far more complex. In 1957, the greatest year for early rock, the fifteen most successful hits included four by Elvis Presley, "Too Much," "All Shook Up," "Teddy Bear," and "Jailhouse Rock." Others of that ilk were "Party Doll" (Buddy Knox), "That'll Be the Day" (The Crickets), and "Wake Up, Little Susie" (The Everly Brothers) for a total of seven. The other eight—the *majority* of top hits—were pop. Pat Boone—wholesome, mature, married—had two, the up-tempo "Love Letters in the Sand" and the soft, gentle "April Love." Tab Hunter, a movie idol, performed "Young Love." Crooner Perry Como, a hold-over from the 1940s, scored with the easygoing "Round and Round." Another

(a) (b)

(c) (d)

THE BIG BEAT ON THE BIG SCREEN: (a) Rock 'n' roll's first authentic genius, Louis Jordan, incarnates every rabid racist's worst nightmare by introducing "swing music" to a white woman; (b) hundreds of teens (and a few curious adults) line up to see Elvis on the big screen for the first time; (c) Rock 'n' roll finally integrated into a pre-existing movie musical format in *Jailhouse Rock* (Metro-Goldwyn-Mayer); (d) Alan Freed was among those progressive D.J.s who integrated the airwaves.

clean-cut type, Jimmie Rodgers (wholesome if with a country twang) broke through with "Honeycomb." Sam Cooke, who likely would have become a Sammy Davis type Vegas headliner were his life not cut short, offered up the year's best ballad, "You Send Me." Another slot belonged to Paul Anka, performing his own composition, the romantic ballad "Diana." The only woman who won a spot on the charts was Debbie Reynolds, with "Tammy." Despite the long-held rumor that the once popular *Your Hit Parade* Saturday night musical on NBC came to a close because its middle-aged stars couldn't adjust to rock, there were more than enough old-fashioned hits to fill that half-hour. The series was cancelled because CBS owned Saturday night with its top-rated *Have Gun, Will Travel* and *Gunsmoke*: Westerns were now all the rage on TV.

Let's Rock ends with the lie to end all lies. La Rosa gives up on ballads and the kids go mad for him. Actually, he appears ridiculous attempting to perform to The Big Beat. Nothing turned teens off more than watching some over-the-hill (in their minds) 30-year-old trying to get down and boogie, explaining why *Let's Rock* was the first youth-music movie to lose money. Kids likewise failed to show up for *Senior Prom* (David Lowell Rich, 1958) in which jazz great Louis Prima likewise tried to perform Big Beat without success. Besides, the function of rock 'n' roll exploitation flicks—dishing out The New Music onscreen fast and furiously for that initial audience—ceased to exist. A major company, Paramount, was ready to now incorporate rock 'n' roll into a relatively expensive and ambitious film, the aforementioned *King Creole*. Based on an adult novel by Harold Robbins, directed by the genius who had helmed *The Sea Hawk* (1940), *Yankee Doodle Dandy* (1942) and *Casablanca* (1942), co-starring such top talent as Walter Matthau and Carolyn Jones in support of Elvis, rock 'n' roll had survived a faux controversy and effectively navigated its pop-culture journey from marginal to mainstream.

*

If *Let's Rock* can be considered the last such film, isolating the first proves more difficult. Some music/movie historians bestow that honor on break-through films featuring Louis Jordan (1908–1975). Though relatively popular during the 1930s and early forties, Jordan's career surged during the postwar era. Then, his unique contribution—Jordan transformed Big Band "swing" into rhythm 'n' blues "jump"—no longer appeared ahead of, rather for, the times. Jordan's 1946 recording of "Let the Good Times Roll" caused this good-natured/self-parodying singer to be crowned "King of the Jukebox." His discs simultaneously won top spots on African American "race music" charts and *Billboard*'s Anglo-oriented Top Ten. Certainly, other black stars preceded Jordan as to crossover appeal, Nat "King" Cole, Duke Ellington, and Count Basie among them. Yet they had achieved such status by "singing white"; integrating into the musical world, offering color-blind pop. Jordan paved the way for Chuck Berry, Little Richard, Bo Diddley and James Brown, who won over white audiences without down-playing their ethnic identities in their popular art.[24]

Likewise Jordan's films played not only in race-movie-going venues but also (a major breakthrough) at middlebrow theatres as an ever more tolerant and accepting public wanted to see as well as hear their pop idol. In 1946, Astor Pictures released *Beware* (Bud Pollard). A decade before Elvis' arrival, here was a musical movie that brought an early form of rhythm 'n' blues to a mixed audience. The film opens with a dazzlingly edited sequence, cutting from close-ups of Jordan's Decca 78 r.p.m. releases like "Is You Is or Is You Ain't My Baby" (1944) to long-shots of the marquee atop New York's fabled Paramount Theatre, circling down to where huge (and notably integrated) crowds await this star's arrival. *Beware*, its title a warning to America's racists, served as a precedent for early rock 'n' roll exploitation films with performers playing themselves, mythologizing their pop ascendency. One song, "Long Legged Lizzie," reveals Jordan's genius, enhancing jazz and blues with a more prominent rhythm section. Newly popular electric guitars are on view, as they are in *Reet, Petite and Gone* (William Forest Crouch, 1946). As Rudy Toombs noted, this follow-up film set the pace for a youth-oriented performer to break with (borrowing from Marshall McLuhan) pop-jazz's long-standing tradition of a "cool" tradition (Bing Crosby, Frank Sinatra, Perry Como) by daring to be openly "hot."[25]

Sadly if not surprisingly, Jordan's stardom quickly came to a close at that moment when the musical trail he blazed became settled by other, younger pretenders to the King of Rock 'n' Roll throne. Jordan gave way to sudden superstars closer in age to kids who overnight embraced such sounds that had been a long time in coming. Shortly, the Big Beat concert film appeared with *Rock 'n' Roll Revue* (Joseph Kohn, 1955), produced by African American entrepreneur Ben Frye. He had just then completed a 13-episode TV series, *Show Time at the Apollo*. The show brought legendary black artists to a largely white suburban audience. Despite the feature film's title, showcased acts ran the gamut from genius-level conventional performers such as Duke Ellington, Lionel Hampton, and Nat "King" Cole to breakaway acts including Louie Bellson, Little Buck, and Joe Turner. The remarkable pop-rock songstress Dinah Washington neatly bridged any gap. Shot in Harlem with Willie Bryant as host, this presentation of talent proved unexpectedly popular, not only with an exclusively black movie-going audience but crossovers from the Anglo community. Frye immediately rushed into production a more ambitious follow-up. *Rhythm-and-Blues Revue* (Kohn, 1955). This pageant-like piece provided an unpretentious peek at rock 'n' roll's relationship to the history of American popular music.

In fact, such a sound and accompanying dance movements dated back to the war years. *The Fighting Seabees* (Edward Ludwig, 1944), concerning Americans stationed in the South Pacific, featured a mid-movie sequence in which servicemen and nurses steal a little time-out from the rigors of war. Knowing that many will not long survive, they tear up the floor as the jazz ensemble playing Big Band music slips into a precedent of The Big Beat. Star John Wayne gets down and dirty, boogying with Adele Mara. At the insistence of presidents Roosevelt and Truman, the armed services were integrated during WWII. It only made sense a musical (and dance) integration would reflect in pop culture such a major social undertaking. Onscreen mixing of black and white performers would see the light in 1956. Shot at year's end, *Rock, Baby, Rock It* (Murray Douglas Sporup, 1957), with its paper-thin plot about mobsters attempting to muscle in on Dallas' music scene, became infamous for incompetence as to technique. Yet any such defects emerge as testaments to the authenticity of this no-budget opus: the first known project by, for, and about young people who salute their own music, without interference from adult producers. Even at the height of racial animosity in the Lone Star State, Johnny Carroll (with the Hot Rocks) could comfortably share a stage with Roscoe Gordon and the Red Tops. A conventional product, *The Big Beat* (Will Cowan, 1957) focused on young adult Joe Randall (William Reynolds) who hopes to save his middle-aged dad's floundering record business by lining up rock acts. The film relies on the already outdated approach of balancing older acts (Harry James, George Shearing, Gogi Grant) with newcomers. The latter include Fats Domino, The Del Vikings, and the Dominos. Rapid-fire cutting between white (The Four Aces) and black (The Mills Brothers) performers visually challenges any previously presumed color line.

Over the next several years, movies of varying quality heightened the ability of rock to conquer racism. *Jamboree* (Max J. Rosenberg, Milton Subotsky, 1957) featured one more man-eating music biz dominatrix (Kay Medford) manipulating a pair of wholesome young singers (Paul Carr and Freda Holloway, the latter's voice dubbed by Connie Francis) by breaking up their duo (and a budding romance) to make more money, selling them as single performers. Anglo artist Carl Perkins ("Glad All Over") and African American star Joe Williams ("I Don't Like You No More") are treated as equals off- and on-stage. *Go, Johnny, Go* (Paul Landres, 1958), Freed's final film, had the disc jockey facilitate a mentoring by partner Chuck Berry of a white-bread kid (Jimmy Clanton). *Juke Box Rhythm* (Arthur Dreifus, 1959), a late arrival from Sam Katzman at Columbia, told a silly Cinderella story in which a visiting princess (Jo Morrow) falls for an American singing star (Jack Jones). Notable is that Jones' middle-of-the-road pop-star shared center-stage with the incomparable Johnny Otis doing "Willie and the Hand Jive."

*

If the early 'defense of rock 'n' roll' film genre began with Alan Freed, this movement would conclude with Dick Clark in 1960. In *Because They're Young* (Paul Wendkos, 1960), Clark played a dedicated high-school teacher. At mid-movie, there's a dance at Harrison High. Guitarist Duane Eddy and vocalist Jimmy Darren perform live. The kids, all of them nice and normal, gather around the stars and listen respectfully. Though some hoods show up, rock 'n' roll music doesn't accompany them—only the good teens. The sequence plays like an answer to the opposite situation in *Blackboard Jungle*, four years and a seeming eternity earlier. Rock had come into its own as youthful mainstream music. But as numerous late 1950s J.D. movies make clear, the transition was slow and difficult.

· 3 ·

BAD BOYS, DANGEROUS DOLLS

The Juvenile Delinquent on Film

"He's a rebel and he'll never be any good.
He's a rebel 'cause he never does what he should.
But just because he doesn't do what everybody else does
That's no reason why I can't give him all my love."
—Gene Pitney (writer); The Crystals (performers), 1962

By 1960, many of *Rebel*'s innovations from five years earlier had long degenerated into tiresome clichés. That year, an indie company produced what may be the final 1950s style J.D. opus, *High School Caesar* (O'Dale Ireland). The Buzz character, or Wheel, here assumes central focus. Matt (John Ashley) dresses in black leather, blue jeans, and cowboy boots. His cronies turn their shirt-collars up to express their generalized arrogance. Matt runs a protection racket, beating up kids who refuse to pay. They steal and sell upcoming tests, fix the student election so Matt will become president, and drive expensive cars. Matt has a Judy-like girlfriend (Daria Massey) whom he treats as a trophy. Artless in presentation, *Caesar* does contain some value as a cultural artifact. The first half takes place almost exclusively in school; *Rebel* allowed us no sense as to what transpired there. We can guess, though, that Buzz, like Matt, took the opposite approach of *Blackboard Jungle*'s Artie West, with his contemptuous hostility toward the faculty. Matt sucks up, conning adults into believing he's a nice boy. As with other 1950s juvenile-crime films, a common thread serves as connective tissue: problems arise from parents who are not around to talk to their kids. Matt falls to pieces when he receives an allowance check without a note, much like Plato in *Rebel*. As a talisman (if one that will bring about Matt's fall), the confused boy clings to a gold coin, the only gift his father gave him with sincere feeling. The leader of the pack in public, Matt, a cry-baby at heart, weeps when alone in his room.

As to music, the introduction of Matt's gang is accompanied by jazz. This continues as they work over an innocent kid. Shortly, the story moves to an afternoon dance in the school, where all the non-hoods are pleasantly performing the lindy-hop to mild rock 'n' roll. Matt and his lackey (Steve Stevens), an effeminate youth, choose to remain on the sidelines. Briefly, Matt's companion attempts to dance with the gang-leader; Matt appears more relaxed than he does later, hitting a dance floor with his girl. A homo-eroticism as to highly formalized costuming and ritualized movements goes with the grain of previous 1950s youth-crime films. However modest the pro-duction, here is proof that rock and delinquency had been successfully sepa-rated in the public consciousness. In large measure, this had been achieved by Dick Clark, whose weekday live TV show *American Bandstand* featured only well-mannered kids dancing to the Big Beat. Nonetheless, for a five year period, juvenile delinquency and rock 'n' roll had been all but inseparable in late 1950s Youth Movies.

*

The first postwar J.D. film may well have been *Bad Boy* (Kurt Neumann, 1949). In it, the initial onscreen example of a juvenile delinquent was por-trayed by the most significant real-life hero of recent years. Audie L. Murphy (1925–1971), a self-confessed "rural runt" from a poverty-stricken home in Texas farm and cattle country,[1] joined the army and went on to win, among other international distinctions, the Congressional Medal of Honor. Murphy's boyish good looks made him a candidate for movie stardom. He was approached by independent producer Paul Short to play the title role in a project financed by a Texas theatre chain with ties to worthy causes. Variety Clubs International helped fund Boy's Ranch, a rehabilitation center for trou-bled youth. A movie focusing on its workings under the leadership of 'Coach' Marshall Brown (played by Lloyd Nolan) would be showcased in Variety Clubs' theatres and hopefully win nationwide distribution, all profits chan-neled back into the Ranch. Hollywood's Allied Artists agreed to co-produce;

Short and his partners insisted only that the lead be played by an authentic Texan. Enter Audie.

Danny, as Nolan's voice-over announces, was "no Bowery Boy"; i.e, no throwback to big-city troublemakers that had always been on view in life and on film. Robert Hardy Anderson's script establishes that here we encounter a new sort of youth problem, deriving from emergent difficulties in our world. The intro continues: "Clean-cut; from your own neighborhood . . . or mine." Danny is Jim Stark in embryo, a rebel without a (seeming) cause. Acting as a psychiatrist, a relatively new kind of medical hero for the era's walking wounded, Brown sets out to discover the root of Danny's "issue," then begin a hoped-for cure. Others insist that Danny is a "hopeless case." Brown echoes the famed Father E.J. Flanagan (1886–1948), founder of Boy's Town, who claimed: "There is no bad boy!" Here, Brown states: "I don't believe there are any hopeless boys, only hopeless people who grow hopeless about them."

In time, Brown discovers that current unacceptable behavior derives from a seemingly decent, if in truth dysfunctional, home. No child, claims Brown as the first screen representation of 1950s liberal idealism, is ever born this way. That point of view would come under harsh scrutiny during the upcoming decade, *Blackboard Jungle* offering an opposing point of view (See Ch. 1). In fact, a schizophrenic aura divides 1950s films on the J.D. issue. The liberal approach is well-expressed here: at birth, Danny was neutral. Experience, not biology, determined who he would become. "Somewhere, some-time, something happened to this boy that made him the way he is . . . ." Once Danny's obsession with his late mother and hatred for an aloof stepfather are acknowledged, he becomes a candidate for recovery. At the conclusion, Mrs. Brown (Jane Wyatt) accompanies the former J.D. back to their ranch after an understanding judge allows Danny a reprieve. "Let's go *home*," his new mother-figure sweetly says. The root of modern youth's problems, or so the era's progressive films would have us believe, is the lack of a scrupulously strict yet emotionally warm home environment. *Bad Boy* exists to disprove its title.

Immediately, a backlash set in. *The Bad Seed* first appeared as a novel by William March in 1954 and adapted into a play by Pulitzer-prize winner Maxwell Anderson (1888–1959) one year later. In 1956, *The Bad Seed* reached the screen from Warner Bros, directed by Mervyn LeRoy. Arriving in theatres in-between *Rebel* and *Blackboard Jungle*, this domestic thriller seemed a respite from serious troubled youth movies dominating Hollywood product. Here was an edge-of-your-seat exercise in suspense that might've been directed by Hitchcock. The focus is on an upper-middle-class wife/mother (Nancy Kelly) who devoutly spends much time with Rhoda (Patty McCormick), her eight-year-old: Smart, obedient, pretty, well-mannered, utterly charming. Until, that is, a series of circumstances, at first seemingly unrelated including the apparently accidental death of a neighborhood child, forces the mom to break through her shield of denial, realizing Rhoda is a serial murderess. The distinction between play and movie is that in the original, the mother dies from a self-inflicted gunshot wound while her child sets out to continue killing. Owing to the Production Code, the mom survives while the girl explodes when struck by lightning, deus-ex-machina style.

In retrospect, the title offers a plea to reconsider the liberal approach to youthful crime. *The Bad Seed* provided a fighting document for the right, embracing *Blackboard Jungle*'s message: There are those among the young who cannot be cured or re-integrated into the main. These bad seeds, Artie West the most infamous, must be kept locked away from the community-at-large or they will destroy it from within. *Bad Boy* and *Rebel* insist nurture can overcome nature; *Blackboard Jungle* and *The Bad Seed* alternately argue that nature will always win out—that even the best possible social system (the mom in *The Bad Seed* comes close to perfection) will prove helpless when people are confronted with one of nature's (i.e., biology's) mistakes.

Still, how could such fine folks, their blood-line "pure," have produced a monster? In a sudden twist, the mother learns from her dad (Paul Fix) that she herself was adopted, her own mother a notorious serial-killer. That trait, which didn't reassert itself in her case, has returned with a vengeance in the girl. No amount of kindness, discipline, attention, or other quality of life could have prevented what happened. DNA is destiny. Or so the film says.

*

Whereas *Bad Boy* and *The Bad Seed* deal with problem children from "nice" neighborhoods, the other side of the 1950s J.D. film focused on young people trapped in depraved situations. Again, the broader meaning of a term taken from hipster-youth's jive-talk has resonance: "Crazy!" In the ambitious *Crime in the Streets* (Donald Siegel, 1956), a gang member (Mark Rydell) employs that word as his personal mantra, unconsciously expressing the general acceptance by chaotic rebels of a world gone mad. Slum kids may have in the past (and past films) lashed out in anger at their roles as have-nots in life. Now, youth in general, including those high on the 'have' list, share a common complaint as canonized by *Rebel's* observatory scene. *City Across the River* (Maxwell Shane, 1949) served as predecessor of all 1950s slum-gang flicks, based on a best-seller from 1946 entitled *The Amboy Dukes*, by Irving Shulman (1913–1995). Among the first to grasp that slum crime was assuming an ever-angrier aura, Shulman capsulized such a vision in a work that pushed boundaries for descriptions of violence and sexuality. Much material in *The Amboy Dukes* was too ripe for presentation by a slow-to-change Hollywood. Though the project was toned down, diminishing its potential to disturb, something of Shulman's vision did come across in this sad tale of one such boy, Frank Cusack (Luis Van Rooten), member of a Brooklyn street gang.

The plot involves Frank's marginal role in the killing of a teacher by two other Brooklyn gang members. The none-too-subtle message is that biology had nothing to do with his behavior, Frank's environment is held responsible. He desperately wants (and at moments does try) to escape, though always some trick of fate pulls him back. As in other works, the script insists that often-absent parents may be responsible for contemporary youth crime. Shulman gave this a unique spin: Frank's Mom (Thelma Ritter) is gone all day at work, the boy left alone and lonely. The mother holds down her jobs not out of economic necessity but to stash away enough funds so Frank can leave. Her well-intentioned plan backfires. Then again, for Mrs. Cusack to stay at home would likewise doom Frank to remain owing to a lack of funds for higher education. The grim truth this movie professes: Not only is there no escape for a Frank Cusack; there is no conceivable solution to the problem, even when parents do everything they can.

Among the supporting roles in *The Amboy Dukes*, none stood out more vividly than Mitchell Wolf, played in the film by Tony Curtis (1925–2010). Critics took note of his surly appearance and greasy demeanor, as did the public. Young Elvis Presley created for himself a persona directly modeled on Curtis in this film.[2] When pressured to come up with a sequel, Shulman chose Mitchell Wolf as protagonist. The novel *Cry Tough* (1949) follows Wolf's release from prison and attempts to return to the neighborhood without being sucked back into criminal activity. One might have expected Universal to snap this up as a Curtis vehicle. For whatever reasons, that did not happen. It would take the better part of a decade for *Cry Tough* to reach the screen.

WALK ON THE WILD SIDE: (a) Real-life war hero Audie Murphy incarnated the post-war era's first psychologically disturbed bad boy (courtesy: Paul Short Prods./Allied Artists); (b) James Dean combined the neediness of Montgomery Clift with the arrogance of Marlon Brando (courtesy: Warner Bros.; (c) Johnny Nash played a young African American rebel with many causes, all racially oriented, in *Take a Giant Step* (courtesy: Hecht-Hill-Lancaster/UA); (d) the lowest level of street crime provided the focus for the highest level of Hollywood's popular art in *West Side Story* with George Chakiris (third from left) and Russ Tamblyn (eighth from left) as rival gang leaders. (courtesy: Mirisch/Beta/United Artists).

During that period, a new aspect of street crime developed in Brooklyn, The Bronx, and New York's East Harlem (previously referred to as Italian Harlem, soon to be called Spanish Harlem). This three-block square area, centered about 110th St. in District 11, witnessed a wave of new immigrants from Puerto Rico. As early as 1917, Puerto Ricans were considered U.S. citizens without enjoying full benefits after passage of the Jones-Shafroth Act. A continual trickling-in gave way, during World War II, to many who hoped to find jobs vacated by those New Yorkers now overseas. During the early 1950s, the cost of plane tickets were lower, flights more affordable for an ever larger number of people. "The Great Migration" began. By 1950, well over 30,000 Puerto Ricans resettled in New York per year.[3] Hostilities developed between youthful members of this ethnic group and those descended from Polish immigrants. Such tension was suggested in *Blackboard Jungle* between the characters played by Rafael Campos and Vic Morrow, though that element was played down there.

Such conflict did exist, and begged to be dramatized. Broadway offered a dazzling vision of the street wars with the groundbreaking musical *West Side Story* (1957). An inspired collaboration including Arthur Laurents (book), Leonard Bernstein (music), Stephen Sondheim (lyrics), and Jerome Robbins (choreography) led to high popular art derived from lowly social problems. Though the equally majestic film would not appear for four years, Hollywood powers-that-be attempted to bring this uniquely 1950s variation on youth gangs to the screen. When *Cry Tough* (Paul Stanley) finally appeared in 1959, the Jewish gang was transformed into a Puerto Rican community; the character of Mitchell Wolf, now called Miguel Estrada, was played by John Saxon, an Italian American. (The studio insisted it had no Puerto Rican stars.) *Cry Tough* features a paradoxical combination of exploitation elements (sensuous photography of Saxon and his young bride, Linda Cristal, in bed; over-the-top performances for adult gangsters not unlike those on TV's *The Untouchables* of 1959–1963—in-your-face violence), such moments interspersed with what appears to have been a sincere desire to bring a serious issue to national awareness.

Earlier arrivals (including Joseph Calleia as the lead's father) in the barrio, like residents in other ethnic areas, tried to forge an honest life. Always, they were aware that the criminal minority targets them as easy prey. Any such honest ambitions Miguel harbors are dashed as he realizes that to make headway, he must not only tolerate the presence of but join with the local adult crime boss (Joe De Santis). Other than several overly-obvious studio shots, *Cry Tough* does convince as kitchen-sink drama, bolstered by a film-noir aura. Impressive about Harry Kleiner's script is its insistence on positing the barrio's criminal element, young and adult, as a small minority. Their violent acts overshadow the decency of hard-working immigrants who maintain religious values and cultural traditions as a bulwark of old-fashioned order against the encroaching contemporary chaos. As one adult points out to Saxon's anti-hero, this minority's current experiences repeat, in an ongoing continuum, what earlier arrivals—Italians, Irish, Jews, the Polish, etc.—faced. Work hard, go slow, achieve the American Dream gradually and, sadly, likely not for oneself but the next generation. That, or live fast, die young, but reap the temporary benefits of criminal activity for immediate gratification. Tragically, the latter too often wins out, as it does here for the ill-fated lead.

Just such a vision would permeate John Frankenheimer's *The Young Savages* (1961), based on a 1959 novel *A Matter of Conviction* by Evan Hunter. If Hunter's *Blackboard Jungle* launched the urban-youth crime genre, here was that film's bookend, returning to delinquency in poverty-stricken areas while expanding the one aspect that Hunter's previous work all but ignored, racial animosity between longtime residents (in this case Italian) and newly arrived Puerto Ricans. The film opens as three members of the Thunderbirds gang cross over from their own neighborhood to adjoining Puerto Rican territory, employing switch-blades to kill a blind fifteen-year-old (Jose Perez). The setting's ultra-realism is visually countered by a series of odd yet satisfying angles, cut together in swift montage, allowing the film's audience to experience the killing as it subjectively must have felt for those involved. As one gang member chooses to employ the word "Crazy!" we assume here is yet another vivid depiction of senseless violence in a now mad world.

Yet as Assistant D.A. Bell (Burt Lancaster) investigates before representing the state in an upcoming trial, a strikingly different set of circumstances unfolds. Far from an innocent, hapless victim, the deceased, Roberto Escalante, was murdered not in an act of madness but righteous (if hardly rightful) vengeance. The seemingly sweet blind boy was a leader of the equally violent Puerto Rican gang The Horsemen. Escalante planned a deadly invasion of the Italians' neighborhood. He also pimped out his fifteen-year-old sister. While such revelations hardly justify what the Thunderbirds did, they allow Bell to grasp this wasn't, in today's terminology, a hate crime, perpetrated on the most vulnerable member of the Puerto Rican community by boys who were racists. Rather, the assault was, from their point of view, what Hunter implied in his original title: a matter of conviction, a point of honor according to their values.

Bell, whom we learn was born in Italian Harlem, originally named Bellini, serves as an autobiographical figure for novelist Hunter (1926–2005). A native of that area, Hunter was born Salvatore Albert Lombino. In *Blackboard Jungle* he came down on the conservative side of the equation, hard-cases like Artie West were considered beyond hope. Clearly, the Evan Hunter who drama-tized that cautionary fable is not the authorial voice we here encounter. The parallel to Artie West, Arthur Reardon (John Davis Chandler), must indeed be sent to prison. And he is. Now, though, that figure is no two-dimensional image of evil but a carefully-constructed person with complicated motives for his unacceptable behavior. The hope is that prison will not simply cage this beast but transform him, through psychoanalysis, into a functional human being. Another youth (Neil Nephew), who doesn't possess the intelligence to tell right from wrong, is not sent to prison but an institution for the crimi-nally insane. The one boy (Stanley Kristien) who didn't stab the victim, only trailing the others out of peer pressure, will attend reform school. In each case, punishment fits the crime in a liberal manner that views the overall situation as complex, a notable change from *Blackboard Jungle*.

If Hunter has grown as an artist, his transformation has its fictional objec-tive correlative in Bell's journey. Initially, he seeks the death penalty, rugged individualism his modus operandi. Bell overcame his environment; if he did, then so could any of these boys. At mid-movie, Bell begins to doubt that, partly owing to pressure from Bell's upscale Anglo wife (Dina Merrill). She here represents an abiding liberal-consciousness that helps win Bell over, especially when the protagonist realizes he may have married this woman less out of love than as part of a semi-conscious perception of the princess-like figure as Aryan goddess, a necessary trophy on his journey toward assimilation into the mainstream. Another step occurs when he hears the mother (Shelley Winters) of the non-lethal Italian gang-member explain that:

> I always heard that a kid got in trouble because he didn't have love. I loved Danny more than anything. You thank God that you didn't have to raise your kid on the streets.

As in many previous films, environment must be considered the culprit. Now, however, two environments—the neighborhood and the home—are con-trasted. However loving the mother clearly is, that may not be enough to override overwhelming poverty and a desperate hunger to fit in with others of one's age. At least the mother's positive influence balances, if not cancels out, the negativity of street survival. Who then ought to be held responsible? Adults, certainly, though less parents of poor kids than wealthy outsiders like the D.A. (Edward Andrews) who hopes that a harsh conviction will propel him to the governorship as an anti-crime activist (no matter what actually happened); a yellow-journalism tabloid that wants to simplify the issue into a Manichean victim/victimizers situation to sell papers; even Bell himself, whose traditional values about right and wrong gradually dissipate, allowing a progressive to emerge. When the slain boy's mom complains she feels justice was not achieved because all three didn't go the electric chair, a changed Bell takes a mature view: "A lot of people killed your son, Mrs. Escalante." Among them, this current Bell condemns the previous Bell.

*

Three years earlier, Frankenheimer had made his film directorial debut with *The Young Stranger* (1957). Robert Dozier's script had its germination on Golden Age TV ("Deal a Blow"; *Climax*, 8/25/1955), also directed by Frankenheimer. The story, set in upscale Beverly Hills, starred James MacArthur as Hal, accused of juvenile delinquency, and Whit Bissell as his adult accuser. In the theatrical version, James Daly played a TV writer-producer, clearly an autobiographical figure for Dozier. He's stunned to learn that his always agreeable son was dragged down to police headquarters. There, a tough sergeant (James Gregory) plans to throw the book at this "typical" example of a bad boy. No question, young Hal punched a movie theatre manager. But the adults make the mistake (a recurring one in youth films) of refusing to listen to his side of the story. Hal's future (he's college-bound) could be endangered by a criminal record. Gradually, the truth will out: Hal punched the man not because he'd been tossed out of the theatre for mild goofing around, only after the manager stopped the boy from leaving—physically attacking Hal with the assistance of his assistant.

Despite an overly neat, unconvincingly happy ending, *The Young Stranger* owns a unique status as the only film of its time to suggest that America's supposed epidemic of juvenile crime may have been as mythic as the concurrent fear that communists were taking over the country. Pulitzer-prize winner Benjamin Fine announced in *1,000,000 Delinquents* that between 1945 and 1953, youth crime increased nearly 50%,[4] employing the term "epidemic" for the first time.[5] F.B.I. director J. Edgar Hoover vowed to make suppression of this "plague of youthful lawlessness" a top priority.[6] In time, historian Charles Gilbert noted that while there might be a germ of truth to the fast spreading rumor, "public impression of the severity of this problem was . . . exaggerated."[7] Stephen Tropiano has suggested that the reason for this may have been "the lack of a uniform definition" of juvenile delinquency.[8]

Young people have always illegally drunk beer, become rowdy at Saturday night movies, and driven too fast in cars. However, during the 1930s and 1940s, such transgressions were not taken too seriously by adults who believed this to be normal enough. Rather than book boys and girls on major charges including "hooliganism," policemen tended to report such scuffles to parents, who were expected to solve the problem. Also, there was little solid data then as to youthful crime. Information gathering had not begun in any scientific manner; youth crime did not exist as a concept. The U.S. had more important things to worry about, what with the Depression, then World War II. Now that things had quieted down, the media creating a perception of crimes uniquely perpetrated by youth and social research now a science, a mythic vision of widespread juvenile crime emerged. As to more severe cases that did exist, newspapers that published headlines such as "TEENS WHO KILL FOR THRILLS"[9] failed to take into account that twenty years earlier, Bonnie Parker and Clyde Barrow did precisely that. The difference was, no one had in the 1930s isolated the issue of "youth" (this was simply a crime) as being responsible, even if the perpetrators did happen to be young.

In *The Young Stranger*, we encounter a teen who couldn't appear more normal, and whose worst sin is putting his shoes up on a theatre seat, then speaking glibly to an authority figure. Apparently, the manager has read *1,000,000 Delinquents* and, as a result, was itching for one such kid to dare and enter his business. As a result he over-reacts, creating a major issue (and criminal situation) where none existed. Youth crime may have largely been a form of mass hysteria that existed more in the minds of those who read and believed the overblown accounts. How interesting that the TV version appeared on August 21, 1955, two months before *Rebel's* release. This project served as a warning against buying into that film's myth. *Rebel's* long day's journey into night and another day's beginning includes a switch-blade fight, a deadly chickie race, and a zip-gun shootout. The Frankenheimer-Dozier collaborations offered an anti-mythic view of the majority (*Rebel* dealt with a minority) of "contemporary kids." Fascinatingly, James Gregory's character provides a direct parallel to Edward Platt in *Rebel*, if here that judicious authority figure gives way to such an ideal mentor's nightmare opposite. The danger, *The Young Stranger* insists, was not what youth was about to do to adults but what witch-hunting adults might do to youth.

*

The bad boys more than met their match in films about female delinquents. A minor indie film, as intriguing subject-wise as it is technically incompetent, created the prototype for the postwar bad girl. *Delinquent Daughters* (Albert Herman, 1944) focused on a once-prim high-schooler (June Carlson) who takes to driving around in hot-rods, gulping down alcohol, and dancing in abandonment at a juke-joint. Eventually, she participates in criminal activity. Arthur St. Claire's script for this PRC quickie was among the first to argue that parents must be blamed for whatever their offspring do. Assuming more "progressive" attitudes, allowing teenagers greater freedom, America's moms and pops had unintentionally created the current social situation.

Though Marilyn Monroe (1926–1962) is generally recalled as the adult Dumb Blonde of 20th Century-Fox Technicolor extravaganzas, the woman born Norma Jean Baker early on set the pace for upcoming bad girls. In *Clash by Night* (Fritz Lang, 1952) she played a naughty nymphet in trouble after becoming involved with an unsavory older man. That same year, Marilyn enacted a seemingly sweet babysitter with schizoid tendencies in *Don't Bother to Knock* (Roy Ward Baker). This prototype would be continued by other actresses. In *The Violent Years* (William B. Morgan, 1956), scripted by Edward Wood, Jr. (1924–1978), liberal enlightenment is expressed by an understanding adult. "No child is inherently bad," a stern if considerate judge (I. Stanford Jolley) tells the parents (Barbara Weeks, Arthur Millan) of an 18-year-old (Jean Moorhead) about to be sent away for, among other things, first-degree murder. In flashback, the teen's double life is documented: demure girl-next-door type in their conventional home, black-leather clad leader of an all-girl gang by night. Their crimes include knocking over service-stations for loose change (though they hardly need the money) and preying on young couples in lovers' lane. At one point, the foursome engage in vandalism at the bequest of the communist party. By containing the Red Scare within a youth-crime film, *The Violent Years* reinforces what many grown-ups believed and feared: all that had gone wrong with their neat little world was part of a vast inter-connected plot by powerful forces aligned against them. The Commies, comic books, youth crime, rock 'n' roll, *Shock Theatre*, motorcycles. . . .

The judge continues: "Adults create the community that kids learn from." In flashback, we witness the home situation as Paula and her mother pass one another in the living room.

PAULA: Mom? Got a minute to talk? It's rather important.
MOTHER: Good gracious, no! I'm an hour late already. "Charity First" . . .

(a)   (b)

(c)   (d)

(e)   (f)

BAD GIRLS COME IN ALL SHAPES, ALL SIZES: (a) before achieving superstar status, Marilyn Monroe played a teenager with a hankering for bad-boy Keith Andes in *Clash By Night* (courtesy RKO Radio Pictures); (b) wholesome-looking Tuesday Weld draws post-*Psycho* Anthony Perkins into a web of murder in *Pretty Poison* (courtesy 20th Century Fox); (c) The "bad girl's bad girl" Jana Lund lights up in the girls' room between classes in *High School Hellcats* (courtesy: American International Pictures); (d) Sandra Harrison becomes the American cinema's first-ever vampire with fangs following experimentations by an adult scientist in *Blood of Dracula* (courtesy: A.I.P.) (e) Tura Satana kicks male butt in the Drive In classic *Faster, Pussycat! Kill! Kill!* (Russ Meyer, 1965; courtesy: EVE Prods.); (f) well-mannered child Patty McCormick secretly murders other neighborhood kids in *The Bad Seed* (courtesy: Warner Bros.)

However well-intentioned, it's all the parents' fault. Though never expressed in words, Paula's motive for juvenile delinquency was born of desperation for attention from her dad. As a newspaper editor, he's constantly at the office, overseeing stories about youth crime. What better way to get him involved with his daughter than become an element in the syndrome that consumes his time? As *The Violent Years* nears its finale, the tone turns strident, shrill. A return to old-time religion is the only answer, we are informed. Though there's no observatory sequence here, these kids have, one way or another, come in contact with a nihilistic world-view. This is expressed in a constant refrain: "So what?" After the pregnant/jailed daughter dies in childbirth (if the term over-the-top didn't already exist it would have to be created to describe an Ed Wood screenplay) the mom realizes her great mistake: "It's a strong, hard lesson we've been taught." The dad adds: "We must now look forward, using the past as a pattern of judgment for the future." 'We' means not only he and his wife but all parents in the audience . . . if any showed up.

For like other youth-exploitation flicks, *The Violent Years* preached to the converted. That would hold true two years later with *High School Hellcats* (Edward L. Bernd, 1958), produced by James H. Nicholson and Samuel Arkoff for their emergent American International Pictures. The lead, Joyce Martin (Yvonne Lime), another wholesome-looking blonde, recalls Paula in *The Violent Years*. Offering an unofficial prequel to that film, this narrative chronicles Joyce's seduction (considering the intense lesbian implications, that term provides a double-edged sword) into joining a similar girl gang. Joyce's status as new girl in school recalls Jimbo in *Rebel*, reviving the all-important "fitting in" theme. For a female Jim Stark, it's as important to be seen as "not chicken." A shop-lifting initiation, organized by a female Buzz (Jana Lund), substitutes for the chickie-run. If Jimbo inadvertently insulted the establishment by stepping on the school crest, Joyce is tricked into wearing slacks, incurring a teacher's wrath.

That character, Trudy Davis (Rhoda Williams), combines elements of Edward Platt's Ray in *Rebel* and Margaret Hays' female teacher in *Blackboard Jungle*—the faculty member who insisted that "there are no bad teens" to cynical male colleagues. Here, Miss Davis is the one adult who listens and cares, and to whom the girls, all but the most extreme (Jana Lund here, like Vic Morrow in *Blackboard Jungle*, being beyond help) can go to when peer pressure or family interference becomes too tough and a mentor is required. She appears to be recently graduated from college and not much older than her students, providing a bridge between kids and parents. A teacher of Health and Physical Education, Miss Davis unofficially employs her position to discuss Sex Education in a way that's not patronizing to "boy crazy" girls. Yet other than Joyce, who strikes up a gentle romance with a notably good boy (Brett Halsey), the gang girls show no serious interest in men. Boys are so many props, the necessary "dates" for parties and the like, much as girls were to the black-leather boys in male-oriented J.D. films. In *High School Hellcats*, at a "wild party" (tame by today's standards), the female J.D.s casually exchange partners. On the other hand, each girl's commitment to the female clique is essential to her sense of identity. After Lund's leader is murdered, we learn that another gang member did this out of jealousy, fearing newcomer Joyce had usurped her place. "She made me her flunky," the knife-wielding girl screams while attempting to stab the heroine, "and then *you* came around and I saw that she *wanted* you more than me."

Why are these bad girls, like bad boys in parallel projects, so dedicated to one another? "A home away from home," they say of their midnight meetings in an abandoned theatre, this film's equivalent to *Rebel's* old mansion. Such an alternative becomes necessary when one's actual home no longer "works" as it is supposed to. Joyce Martin is played as a combination of *Rebel's* Jimbo and Judy; scenes in her upper-middle-class abode (a house is not a home, at least not always; never in late 1950s J.D. films) appear carbon copies of the earlier movie's confrontations. Dialogue echoes what only a few years previously seemed so fresh is now, owing to repetition in inferior films, overly familiar:

FATHER: Can't get her to do anything right anymore. And the way she dresses!
            The tight sweaters, too much lipstick . . .

Still, such words serve as a testament—whether contained in a classic or one of its corny imitations—of what did gnaw away at many (if not most, certainly not all) first-wave American teens. As one gang girl states (a bit too overtly to be believed): "If we had the right kind of home, we wouldn't have to go looking for another one." She speaks not of superficial amenities (their parents buy these girls everything) but essential old-fashioned values that failed to survive the postwar migration from small towns and large cities to sprawling suburbs. Far from the radical statements many kids (and a few adults) came to such movies in anticipation of, here were—sordid subject matter aside—pleas for a return to a more traditional lifestyle. As with *Rebel*, *High School Hellcats* concludes with a hopeful, relatively happy ending: The parents realize the mistake of being emotionally aloof. They embrace the kids, willing to try and make things better. Joyce Martin, the female Jim Stark, is anything but "bad"; only lost, confused, lonely, a juvenile forced into delinquent behavior as a desperate means of getting attention. Within a decade, a plethora of such films—*So Young So Bad* (Bernard Vorhaus, Edgar G. Ulmer, 1950), *Teenage Bad Girl* (Herbert Wilcox, 1956), *Rumble on the Docks* (Fred F. Sears, 1956), *The Delinquents* (Robert Altman, 1957), *Cry Baby Killer* (Jus Addiss, 1958, which introduced Jack Nicholson), *Juvenile Jungle* (William Witney, 1958), *The Rebel Set* (Gene Fowler, Jr., 1959), *So Evil, So Young* (Godfrey Grayson, 1961), among others—became so repetitious as to characters, situations, and themes that the youth audience, which initially crowded into theatres, lost interest. Among the overlooked were intelligent films that attempted to communicate youthful problems in a way that would become accessible to grown-ups. *Teenage Rebel* (Edmund Goulding, 1956) was the ridiculous retitle of a sensitive Broadway play, *A Roomful of Roses*, by Edith R. Somner. The piece concerned an upscale mother (Ginger Rogers) who welcomes into her home her distraught daughter (Betty Lou Keim). The girl, having been living with her dad (Michael Rennie), never successfully adjusted to her parents' divorce. No rebelliousness of an exploitive nature is on view, only serious miscommunication of the sort that makes for intelligent social drama. *The Unguarded Moment* (Harry Keller, 1956) offered a highly thoughtful expansion on *Blackboard Jungle*'s sequence in which the considerate female teacher is almost raped by an over-sexed student. Here, Esther Williams and John Saxon assume the roles. In *Blackboard Jungle*, the would-be rapist was a nameless monster, lurking in the shadows. Here both the young male and his intended victim are delineated as complex people.

*

On rare occasion, a genre piece would appear that revealed the possibilities when ambitious, talented filmmakers were enlisted. More often than not, these were penned by Reginald Rose (1920–2002), the Golden Age of Television writer whose adult scripts included *12 Angry Men*, both the live TV play and 1957 film. Early in 1956 Rose's drama *Dino* appeared on *Studio One in Hollywood* (1/2/1956) with Sal Mineo as a troubled Italian teenager, Ralph Meeker playing a social worker who penetrates his hard shell. Unfortunately, a film version by Thomas Carr was rushed into production, Mineo repeating his role, the adult part assumed by Brian Keith, to cash in on the play's strong reviews. Released half a year later, the film failed to match the original's power. More impressive was yet another film adaptation of a Rose TV play, *Crime in the Streets*, which opened in theatres June 10, 1956. The TV version had aired on March 8, 1955, more or less simultaneously with initial screenings of *Blackboard Jungle*. For the film, a strong and inventive director, Donald Siegel, successfully translated the material from small screen to large.

Even the title suggests a companion piece to *Blackboard Jungle*, as does the presence of Dan Terranova in both films as a gang member. The political philosophies of the two could not be more at variance. Frankie Dane, this film's gang leader (played by future director John Cassavetes in the TV and film versions), has much in common with Artie West. So deeply mired was Artie in his criminal psychosis that Richard Dadier's microcosmic class-room experiences a catharsis as the bad egg is exorcised. The opposite occurs here, progressive thinking is the underlying attitude. The mentor, a social worker (James Whitmore), insists that Frankie Dane not be thrown to the wolves. Dane's criminal activity, we discover, derives not from bad DNA but a horrific past. Frankie's dad whipped him when Frankie was still a child. As a result, he can't stand to be touched. Frankie sets out to kill a witness able to identify a gang member in court. He does not so much because of the friend's legal actions than as a result of having been abused as a child, creating a parallel to the upscale J.D. drama *The Young Stranger*. The script allows Frankie a moment of self-searching angst that, had *Blackboard Jungle* been willing to follow Artie West home, his character might have offered:

> Look at this place! Open your eyes and have a look at this *hole* I live in. I have a hole in my shirt. Who did it to me? I'm sittin, waitin' to get even. And when I find him, I'm gonna spill his brains into the gutter.

As Burt Lancaster's character pointed out in *The Young Savages*, everyone is guilty for allowing such a situation to occur. Though Frankie's dad deserted the family, there are hints he did so only after discovering his wife flirting with other men. Nonetheless, she (Virginia Gregg) is portrayed in a sympathetic light. "How can I be at the restaurant and home both?" the exhausted waitress wails. Whitmore's do-gooder acknowledges she's right about that, though a neighbor simplistically tries to blame the parents. Finally, that long-standing cliché is being challenged. Rose stretches his story into Biblical dimensions when Frankie considers killing his beloved kid brother (Peter J. Votrian) after the innocent child threatens to inform on him to the police. This Cain and Abel element stops short of tragedy, allowing Rose to make his point: Yes, even the Artie Wests/Frankie Danes can be salvaged, if only society decides that such a crusade is worth the effort and expense.

*

The decline, then disappearance of the late 1950s J.D. movie occurred for numerous reasons, not the least of them that the decade came to a close. The Second Wave of American teenagers who emerged in 1960–1961 had their own problems, necessitating a new sort of film to dramatically deal with their issues. Also, the genre had received a satiric jibe in the summer of 1957 when Jerry Lewis played a nice boy mistaken for a youthful thug, with Darren McGavin his police counselor in *The Delicate Delinquent* (Don McGuire). Richard Bakalyan, who enacted the lead troublemaker earlier that year in *The Delinquents*, appeared as Artie, a comedic reference to *Blackboard Jungle's* Artie West. As George Bernard Shaw long ago noted, a joke is an epitaph on an emotion. Having laughed at stereotypes, few moviegoers—young or adult—could ever take them seriously again.

Ultimately, though, the be-all and end-all occurred on October 18, 1961, when *West Side Story* (Robert Wise) opened in Super-Panavision splendor. The brilliance of the now-four-year-old play was retained even as Wise opened the piece up to its possibilities for cinema, most notably in the still-awe-inspiring first sequence: the camera-eye glides across Manhattan, finally isolating a rough neighborhood where gang war erupts. The plot, which borrows from Shakespeare's *Romeo and Juliet*, in summary sounds like so many exploitation films, including *This Rebel Breed* (Richard L. Bare, William Rowland, 1960), also featuring Rita Moreno. Yet *West Side Story* reached considerably higher artistic heights—stretching beyond the best in upper-middle-brow entertainment to achieve permanent status as a popular classic. Here's a case study as to how talent and ambition can transform what, before the Broadway version's premiere in 1957, had been perceived by many as material unworthy for serious consideration. *West Side Story* was recognized as a masterpiece, one appealing to audiences of all ages. Though its music was not rock per se, Big Beat elements (as well as a Latin melodies) were integrated into the more conventional elements of musical drama. At one point during production, Presley was considered for the male lead, the hope being that Bobby Darin, Paul Anka and other talented rock 'n' rollers might also appear. Though such casting didn't occur, the idea remains intact. An Oscar sweep in early April 1962, including Best Picture of the Year, made clear films featuring switch-blade rumbles could now play top venues, rather than as in the past automatically being relegated to the lowly grind-house circuit.

Or, in the postwar era, its popular outdoor counterpart, the Drive In.

·4·

I LOST IT AT THE DRIVE IN MOVIE

An All-American Outdoor Grindhouse

"I'm all alone
At the drive in movie.
It's a feelin' that ain't too groovy
Watchin' werewolves without you."
—Danny, after being dumped by Sandy, in *Grease*,
the original stage play (Jim Jacobs and Warren Casey)

Late in 1968, *Targets* premiered on the Drive In circuit. In due time, *Targets* would, pan-cinema style, be screened in the nation's art houses. One of many young hopeful future filmmakers then performing various chores for A.I.P, co-writer/director Peter Bogdanovich (1939–) had been given the go-ahead to make any film he wanted. The only requirements: The budget could not exceed a tight $125,000, while the script must include a role for the horror star Boris Karloff, who owed producer Roger Corman two days' work. Bogdanovich was also required to include a 15-minute segment from a previous Karloff thriller, *The Terror* (Corman, 1963), to round out the upcoming film's running time (financing allowed for a mere 75 minutes of new footage) to ninety minutes. A devotee of Universal monster movies from the 1930s, Bogdanovich was inspired to mount a mini-tribute to the gifted actor so essential to their appeal. In keeping with the Corman/AIP aesthetic, the first-time auteur also hoped to address a highly contemporary issue: The increasing amount of violence in society, which apparently began with the JFK assassination. Bogdanovich drew on two seemingly unrelated incidents. On April 25, 1965 Michael Andrew Clark, a desperate teenager, abused by his father, seized a rifle, climbed a hill overlooking California's Highway 101, and fired randomly at passing cars. On August 1, 1966, Charles Whitman, a Vietnam vet and young family man, murdered his wife and mother, then climbed high on a tower at the University of Texas, Austin. There, he randomly shot at those below. These incidents had caused people in general, and the press in particular, to ask if, following the brief promise of a glorious New Frontier, America was degenerating into a redo of the untamed wild West.

Bogdanovich collapsed the two real-life people into a fictional figure (Tim O'Kelley) who repeats those key actions, afterwards crawling up into the screen of a run-down Drive In theatre. From there, he's able to randomly kill teenagers who arrive after dark to see the latest bloody horror flick; Baron Orloff (Karloff) has arrived in person to host the premiere before retiring, at age eighty, from acting. Even as killings occur onscreen, and characters in the movie (within the movie) writhe in anguish, the youthful assassin simultaneously fires, sending some hapless victim into convulsions as horrific as those contained in the gruesome 'entertainment.' Orloff, who gradually grasps what's taking place, realizes that his old-fashioned brand of make-believe violence has been dwarfed by the incursion of real violence into everyday life. The film, distributed shortly after the assassinations of Martin Luther King and Robert Kennedy, proved agonizingly appropriate for the moment. In retrospect, rarely has the give-and-take relationship between The Movies and real-life, as well as the manner in which each reflects the other, been so persuasively dramatized. Considering that this film, designed to be shown in Drive Ins, occurs at one, here is a deconstructive and self-referencing movie that might be thought of as the uber Drive In flick.

*

Outdoor movies had proven popular with the public before the first gas-powered cars were manufactured in France by Panhard & Levassor circa 1891 as residents of Hawaii gathered in open-air areas to watch crude flickers.[1]

Such open-air picture shows spread to the U.S.; known as Airdromes, these were walk-ins, surrounded by fences but without ceilings. Patrons sat on benches.[2] No one would have yet thought to accommodate cars; automobiles were still a plaything for the rich. Gradually, they become a middle-class possibility after Henry Ford's assembly-line began mass-producing the Model T in Michigan in 1908. By this time, movies had replaced Vaudeville as mainstream America's favorite entertainment. If by 1927 an estimated 90 per cent of the public attended The Movies,[3] a mere 7 per cent owned cars. Though a whopping 15 million had been produced and sold, this must be contextualized within the population, 119,000,000.[4] Still, with ever more cars on the road, gas and service stations proliferated. What Time's Henry Luce would hail as The American Century had opened.[5]

Clearly, our "society and attitude changed, and at the center of this transformation were the car and the movie."[6] The Drive In first appeared in New Jersey on June 6, 1933, ushering in a summer season when those with leisure time and a little money (the Depression aside, such folks did exist) were eager to employ autos they'd purchased during better days to search for low-cost fun. Richard M. Holinshead, Jr. (1900–1975), who serviced cars for a living and spent his free time at the movies, had experienced an epiphany: Combine those evolving American obsessions. "The hybridization of these two novelties brought about a tremendous change in the country,"[7] including an ever more casual attitude about 'going out' for an evening. No longer did a couple need to pay a baby-sitter; bring the kids. Specific smoking sections at indoor theatres weren't necessary with families cocooned in their cars. Restrictions on talking no longer applied. The Drive In provided a new type of entertainment paradoxically combining elements both public and private.

This trend quickly spread. California's first Drive In opened at the intersection of Pico and Westwood later that year. Horn-like projectors for sound gave way to individual in-car speakers while ramps were designed to make it easier for patrons to see the screen over the top of the car in front of their own. The disastrous economics of the 1930s and focus on international survival during the war years left little room for business expansion, this swiftly returning with the advent of postwar affluence. Alfred P. Sloan, Chairman of the Board for General Motors, determined that the timing was right to re-posit cars as a necessity rather than a luxury.[8] Where better for a family to show off their new model than at the Drive In? Initially family-friendly, outdoor theatre venues featured double-bills of recent hit films along with charming chestnuts from the past. But as more teenagers came to own hot-rods (see Ch. 12), allowance money burning holes in their pockets, and escape from parents a high priority, it was only natural that entrepreneurs would cater to this crowd. Before long, rural Drive Ins replaced the old downtown Grindhouse as the primary source for unsavory escape.

*

Among the most popular fare were the girls-in-prison pictures. The predecessor was *Caged* (John Cromwell, 1950), a serious expose from Warner Bros. Eleanor Parker starred as a girl wrongfully sent away; Hope Emerson played a sadistic matron (implicitly and, at times, explicitly lesbian). Lee Patrick was a bad girl in conflict with the heroine as to status "inside." Better than anticipated box-office suggested to Hollywood's powers-that-be that this film's success had less to do with sincere social consciousness than lurid fascination with edgy material. Cheap-jack imitations flooded the market, garish advertising often promising more than a film actually provided. Already in the process of churning out J.D. bad-girl flicks, American International was quick to recognize a gold mine. Their first, *Reform School Girl* (Edward Bernds, 1957), presented as a prequel to *High School Hellcats* (from the same director): a sensationalized portrayal of the life awaiting girls who refuse to stay home and watch *The Danny Thomas Show* with parents. The title character, Donna (Gloria Castillo), initially appears a nice teen, guilty only of being in the wrong place at the wrong time. Her seemingly clean-cut date (Edward Byrnes) has not only stolen the car they cruise in but, while speeding, kills a pedestrian. Donna is wrongly tried and convicted as an accomplice (this borrowed from *Caged*) and shipped off to the State Reformatory for Troubled Young Women. As a foil, writer-director Bernds employs another *Caged* plot-device that would soon serve him well in *High School Hellcats*: good-girl inmate Donna meets a truly bad-to-the-bone brat (Yvette Vickers), she reminiscent of Yvonne Daughty's 'Britches' in *The Wild One*. She attempts to do Donna in with scissors, allowing for a cat-fight between blonde heroine and brunette bad girl, immortalized in the poster. A relatively happy ending is achieved, thanks to another *Rebel*-Ray figure. Ross Ford is here the understanding male who believes in Donna's innocence. As this would become a recurring device, girls-in-prison movies might be perceived as anti-feminist. A few male predators would appear but most adult male authority figures were fatherly. Any women in charge exploit the girls, while little sisterhood is seen behind bars, the women battling one another for survival.

The box-office returns attested to the Youth market savvy of Samuel Z. Arkoff (1918–2001), a former lawyer, and his partner James Nicholson (1916–1972), who entered The Biz as a theatre manager.[9] With innocent heroines plunged into an abyss they neither wanted nor deserved, such teen prison pictures spoke to a fear (or perhaps invented it) on the part of every good girl who arrived for a Drive In date beside her boyfriend in his Wheels and secretly worried while watching: there but for the grace of God go I. That premise would reappear in Untamed Youth (Howard W. Koch, 1957), from Aubrey Schenck, released by Warner Bros. (Now everyone wanted in on the lucrative market.) As to the already discussed issue of juvenile delinquency and rock 'n' roll, Untamed Youth was the first prison picture to incorporate the New Music into such New Movies. Mamie Van Doren (see Chapter Five) is the first female to perform a Big Beat number ("Oobala Baby") onscreen. Also on view is early rock star Eddie Cochran, performing "Cottonpicker" while playing the wondrously-named Bong. The good girl, wrongly perceived by corrupt adults as bad, Jane (Lori Nelson), is hitchhiking cross-country with her sister (Van Doren) in hopes of making it in Hollywood. When they mistakenly go skinny-dipping in a pond, the girls are sentenced by a stern female judge (Lauren Tuttle) to serve time. The work farm is run by a local entrepreneur (John Russell), an exploitive male. He lords it over the girls, while seducing the decent if naïve judge, whom he's dating, that wants to help his "wards." When exposed as a menace, Untamed Youth turns out to be the rare female prison picture that does offer something of a proto-feminist sensibility. The lady judge performs an about-face, siding with the girls, freeing them, and imprisoning the man.

The money earned by such cheap-jack items convinced Warner to make their own such films. House of Women (Crane Wilbur, 1962) featured two well-respected actresses, Ida Lupino as the innocent prisoner (the star way too old for her part) and Constance Ford as the matron/sadist. Neither a true expose nor an effectively lurid exploitation item, this big studio's self-conscious attempt at a compromise satisfied no one and failed to show a profit. The genre swiftly fell out of favor, in part because the Production Code kept filmmakers (even indies) from depicting the graphic sex and violence that the target audience for such fare craved. When, in 1967, a ratings system appeared, the new freedom of the screen allowed female prison flicks to return in a relatively uncensored form. Philippines-lensed trash-cinema entries included Women in Cages (Gerardo de Leon, 1971) and The Big Bird Cage (Jack Hill, 1972), the latter starring Pam Grier. One of the best, Jackson County Jail (Michael Miller,

1976) featured 1960s starlet Yvette Mimieux as the latest innocent waif to be wrongly arrested. In the meantime, A.I.P. and its competitors focused on other Youth subgenres that were precisely right for what could, and would, succeed at that time.

*

An inter-related pair of possibilities that readjusted time-tested clichés for America's initial youth culture were horror and sci-fi, as well as innovative combinations of the two. The first such entry was the best. *I Was a Teenage Werewolf* (Gene Fowler, Jr., 1957) took as its template Universal's monster-movie *The Wolfman* (George Waggner, 1941). In that, Lon Chaney (Jr.) played Larry Talbolt, a normal man who, bitten by werewolf Bela Lugosi, becomes one himself. Modern teenagers were aware of this decade-and-a-half old chestnut as Universal had recently released 52 of their famed horror/sci-fi films to TV under the umbrella of *Shock* (aka, *Shock Theatre*).[10] Teens, bored to tears by most of what played on TV, stayed up late to watch legendary monstrosities. Writer-producer Herman Cohen (1925–2002), a onetime assistant theatre manager in Detroit, had found work in Hollywood with Poverty Row outfits including Realart, churning out B Westerns and horror flicks like *Bride of the Gorilla* (Curt Siodmak, 1951) with Chaney. Despite the middle-aged actors, Cohen grasped that teenagers were the likely viewers so he wisely readjusted the genre for them.

(a)

(b)

(c)

(d)

A 20ᵗʰ CENTURY ENTERTAINMENT FORM: (a) Outdoor 'walk-in' theatres were in operation before most people owned cars; (b) initially, Drive Ins catered to young-adult couples; (c) shortly, teenagers happened upon the perfect place to slip away together; (d) a young woman marvels at Art Nouveau/Deco architectural stylings for a soon-to-open Drive In.

Cohen's script combined the outcast teenager of *Rebel Without a Cause* with the fantastical-thriller trope. At miniscule Sunset productions, Cohen raised $100,000, picking actors already associated with Youth Films. Michael Landon, as a high school pariah, had portrayed a J.D. in *These Wilder Years* (Ray Rowland, 1956). Yvonne (Fedderson) Lime had appeared in *Untamed Youth*, shortly starring in *Dragstrip Riot* (David Bradley, 1958) and *High School Hellcats*. Perhaps most important was the choice of Whit Bissell for the psychiatrist assigned to help the confused lead. Instead, he transforms the hapless boy into the title figure. Earlier that year, Bissell played the insensitive adult in *The Young Stranger*. Cohen was aware too that owing to ongoing development of ever more mighty weapons of mass destruction and the intense race for space, our country had become obsessed with, yet fearful of, science. Also, psychiatry in actuality (and in popular cinema) was now widespread, if still controversial with the public. How right were Cohen's instincts, then, to eliminate *The Wolfman*'s conventional approach of having the hapless anti-hero bitten by a werewolf. This teenager turns into such a deadly creature owing to an aloof and highly-educated adult, a parallel to the observatory's coldly-threatening astronomer in *Rebel*.

Sensing commercial potential, Arkoff and Nicholson at A.I.P. picked up distribution rights. The film netted more than $2 million, multiplying its negligible negative cost by more than twenty. Not surprisingly, the majors set about imitating *Teenage Werewolf*'s formula, though not even A.I.P. would ever recapture its macabre appeal. Having 'Teenage' in the title certainly hadn't hurt. *Teenage Zombies* (Jerry Warren, 1957), *Teenage Caveman* (Corman, 1958), and *Teenagers From Outer Space* (Tom Graeff, 1959) followed in rapid succession, each a tad less successful than the previous. Missing from these titles: the "I Was a . . . .," which had added an immediacy between the isolated teen-hero and an equally lonely boy in some theatre. A.I.P.'s immediate follow-up, *I Was a Teenage Frankenstein* (Herbert L. Strock, 1957), brought back Bissell in an identical role (Gary Conway, the victimized boy). But the film proved so dull and unengaging, word-of-mouth spread rapidly among teens and the film fizzled.

No one sequence in *I Was a Teenage Werewolf* so mesmerized its audience as much as the gymnasium incident, featured prominently in advertising. Hopped-up on whatever it is the evil adult has shot through the boy's veins (possibly an early metaphor for drugs, pushed on vulnerable teens by predatory grown-ups), Tony Rivers wanders into the school gym. There, a girl (Dawn Richard), in a jet-black leotard emphasizing her remarkable figure, sweats as she exercises on equipment. Watching her movements, Tony's animal instincts overcome his social consciousness. In psychiatric terms that teenagers in attendance had likely never heard, Tony's ID takes precedence over his Super-Ego even as his Ego fights to force dark desires down. In a fit of horror-movie hysteria not unlike the one in which Chaney chased down a beautiful girl under the spell of moonlight madness, if more graphic and unsettling, Tony loses control and pounces on her, simultaneously attempting to rape and murder his victim. Tony serves as an objective-correlative for every troubled teenage boy harboring deep-seated, long-repressed psycho-sexual issues. Raging hormones provide this horror film's realistic subtext, even as the ugliness which overcomes Tony's face might be thought of as a symbolic means of dealing with extreme acne.[11]

Rendering the sequence more unsettling still is that the "ordinary" teenage-girl was portrayed by *Playboy*'s Centerfold model from the May 1957 issue. Though teen boys weren't supposed to be able to get their hands on copies of that magazine, they of course did. Word had spread like wildfire that dream-girl Dawn Richard would, in this upcoming movie, play the victim. The implications hardly qualify as what we refer to as politically correct today. Still, the sequence—and film containing it—objectified something fearsome and fearful, the hormone-driven edge of hysteria within every teen boy, here vividly portrayed as would not have been allowed in a realistic film of that era though possible in mere "escapist" thrillers.

Another subgenre of horror/sci-fi allowed filmmakers to deal with another current concern. The rash of U.F.O. sightings, which began in the late 1940s,[12] suggested a subject for financial exploitation. Flying-saucer movies proliferated. Initially, this resulted in such first-rate films as *The Thing From Another World* (Christian Nyby, Howard Hawks, 1951) and *The Day the Earth Stood Still* (Robert Wise, 1951), such classics soon supplanted by program pictures like *It Came From Outer Space* (Jack Arnold, 1953) and ultra-low budgeters including *Robot Monster* (Phil Tucker, 1953). One minor masterpiece, *Invaders from Mars* (William Cameron Menzies, 1953), proved successful because the invasion was portrayed from a child's point of view, kids associating with Jimmy Hunt's character. Now, those children were teenagers, ripe for exploitation. *The Blob* (Irvin S. Yeaworth, Jr., 1958) offered an odd combination of old Hollywood craftsmanship and indie savvy. European-born Yeaworth (1926–2004), a resident of Pennsylvania, had shot a youth-exploitation film, *The Flaming Teen-Age*, 1956), while earning his bread-and-butter by producing industrial/educational movies. Kay Linaker (1913–2008), *The Blob*'s screenwriter, had graduated New York University and would become a film professor at Keene State College, New Hampshire. The 'star,' Steve McQueen, was then being hyped as the next big thing, shooting this low-budget item before going to work on his successful TV Western *Wanted: Dead or Alive* (1958–1961).

Shot in and around Valley Forge, PA, *The Blob*, initially budgeted at $120,000 but coming in under-budget $10,000 less, grossed a whopping $4 million during its initial run. McQueen's youthful cult following helped.

So did color and widescreen, this the first indie youth-horror item to feature such amenities. Best of all, the monster (a hunk of shimmering purple Jello) was never clearly seen. Since no zipper ran down the back of the monster's costume (this was the case with *Robot Monster*), the horror did not dissipate. Finally, a nifty pop-rock song by Burt Bacharach, recorded by The Four Blobs (singer Bernie Knee performing the number "Beware of the blob . . ." five times, mixing them together in the studio). During the weeks preceding the premiere, a 45 r.p.m. was circulated to radio stations across the country. Airplay turned this into a hit, popularity of the goofy song with teens increasing their anticipation for the film.

Though 27 at the time of shooting, McQueen portrayed a typical teen also named Steve. He and his girlfriend (Aneta Corsaut) spot a meteor-like UFO descending one Saturday night while necking in a local lovers' lane. The narrative concerns attempts by them, plus several other hot-roddin', drag-racin', rock 'n' rollin' teens (wild but hardly delinquents) to convince the area's adults an invasion has begun. The premise is pure Boy Who Cried Wolf: Teenagers have told so many whoppers that no one believes anything they say. Understandably, this science-fiction item struck a chord owing to visions that teens in attendance held as to themselves and their marginalization by adults. Steve less resembles the lonely Jim Stark in *Rebel* or the hostile Artie West in *Blackboard Jungle* than Hal in *The Young Stranger*, well-behaved though a target for derision by adults owing to his age. When at *The Blob's* conclusion the kids are proven correct and they volunteer to help fight this gooey/deadly thing, the movie suggests such a healing process might occur in life as well. The Generation Gap can be bridged, if only adults will (as realistic films had already insisted) *listen* to teenagers.

As with all memorable horror films, there's a stand-out sequence. At the midpoint, Steve determines to round up other kids from his high school. Knowingly, he heads to the Capitol Theatre (located in nearby Phoenixville PA), as most kids will be there, watching the latest horror flicks. They are; the problem is, the blob has slipped in as well, up into the second floor projection booth. In a prototype for advanced film theories such as reflexivity[13] and deconstruction,[14] teenagers watching *The Blob* merge with those appearing in *The Blob*. The film-within-the-film halts, yet the screen-within-the-screen occupies the entire screen(s). Our perception is their perception. We are them; they, us. Kids in theatres turned to see if indeed there had been a rip and the show would necessarily be halted, even as onscreen teens do when the image cuts back to them. In those rectangular open windows from which a movie is projected, the blob oozes out into the auditorium. We hear screams from onscreen teens running from the blob and actual teens watching *The Blob* mix. At that moment, post-modern cinema was born.

*

Though most such movies were geared to teenage boys, producers were aware that nearly half the young moviegoers were female. Similar films were designed in which the heroine did not merely follow a boyfriend around but assumed center stage. The best, *I Married a Monster From Outer Space* (Gene Fowler, Jr., 1958), employed the personal approach from Fowler's *I Was a Teenage Werewolf*. Gloria Talbott (1931–2000), a brunette whose ethereal beauty qualified her as a cult-movie queen, plays Marge Bradley, twenty-one, her teen years having just ended. Marge is engaged to likable Bill Farrell (Tom Tryon). The two plan to settle down in the suburbs; what Marge doesn't know is that her soon-to-be spouse's body has been possessed by an alien. Something's clearly wrong, however, as Marge notices that Bill has become remote, aloof, distanced. Worse (and here Louis Vittes's script stretched P.C. boundaries) is that their off-screen sex-life doesn't satisfy her.

When *I Married a Monster* was released, the assumption remained in place that "good girls" (Marge included) remained virgins until marriage. Though such thinking would shortly be challenged (see Ch. 7), these were the Eisenhower years, a young audience expected to bring to the theatre basic values supposedly shared by society-at-large. Here's another example of the youth-oriented horror film working on a metaphoric level. Marge represents a projection in two years of most teen-girls watching alongside current boy-friends/potential husbands. *I Married a Monster* offers a nightmare-scenario of what marriage likely will bring: frustration, gnawing melancholy, deep disappointment in sexual as well as emotional coupling with the supposed 'dream guy' of a year or two earlier. A girl's greatest fear was that, in life as well as in this fantasy, she might marry a monster from outer-space—if only in the symbolic sense that men are from Mars, women from Venus.

One year earlier, the hauntingly beautiful Talbott had appeared in a film that did cast her as a teen. In *The Daughter of Dr. Jekyll* (Edgar G. Ulmer, 1957) she plays a naïve virgin whose father was the infamous scientist. Though a gothic castle substitutes for suburbia, here is a modern fairytale for adolescents with Talbott as the audience surrogate. Her character is mentored by a (supposedly) kindly adult (Arthur Shields). Yet the girl wonders if she might, at night, become a werewolf/vampire. In a plot stolen/borrowed from Universal's earlier *She-Wolf of London* (Jean Yarbrough, 1946), the heroine eventually realizes her grown-up mentor is the monster. However shoddy the film's production values, at least one critic has argued that implied by the proceedings is "a critically significant text within the melodramatic crisis of female identity in the 1950s."[15] Even the lowliest of pulp films may contain considerable value as pop-culture artifacts, so many distorted fun-house mirrors that, any phantasmagoria aside, reflect reality.

Here again we encounter what Hollywood refers to as the Money Shot, an intense sequence employed to sell a motion-picture via some irresistible moment. In the form of a werewolf, Shields's character wanders into the mist-strewn night; as he does, this film's female point of view evaporates, the following sequence being photographed from his male gaze. He peeks in a window, spotting an attractive woman (Marjorie Stapp) in the process of dressing for an evening out. The clothing she dons is provocatively sleazy, identifying her not only as to gender but class, also sexual experience; she is not, like the demure heroine, a virgin. The phone rings; she picks it up, hearing about a monster on the loose. Even as that monster closes in, she laughs sarcastically at the warning—until realizing what's there, and that she is about to die. Pacing is deliberate as Shields, in thick make-up, closes in, allowing the audience time to savor her fear—and to anticipate her death throes even as the monster does. By her demeanor, choice of clothing, and intention of a sensuous night, the film, Puritanical in its morality if not as to the graphicness of this deeply disturbing (if, for viewers of the time, undeniably arousing) moment, implies that she deserves precisely what she gets. Her sexuality renders her complicit in the brutal act. She was, as the saying went, asking for it—the very sort of prejudicial, unfair assumption that has been challenged by enlightened people in our own time.

Such a cheap thrill would be provided by numerous genre films. In *The Monster That Challenged the World* (Arnold Laven, 1957), word spreads in a beach community that giant mollusks are attacking people at night. One beautiful girl (Barbara Darrow) laughs at warnings from her mother, if in a notably less sarcastic manner than *Daughter*'s victim. Soon she becomes the creature's prey while walking along the surf, wearing a notably provocative bathing suit. Also in a bathing suit—a bikini this time around, as these are the Sixties—(see Ch. 6) is Tina (Marilyn Clarke), the unabashed flirt who becomes first victim to an atomic-radiation monster in *The Horror of Party Beach* (Del Tenney, 1964). As compared to good kids frolicking in the surf, Tina knocks down alcohol and incites a fist-fight between two would-be boyfriends. It comes as no surprise when, in a snooty mood, she swims off onto some rocks and is ripped to shreds by a Thing. Here are cautionary fables, warning teen girls they ought not to be too independent; also masturbatory fantasies for geek guys who, unable to get a date with girls who look like this, associated their own acne-laden faces with such male monsters, these films providing a cinematic release for frustration and deep-seated anger.

Another actress, Sandra Harrison, headlined *Blood of Dracula* (Herbert L. Strock, 1957), A.I.P.'s inevitable attempt to create a female equivalent to *Teenage Werewolf* and *Teenage Frankenstein*. Here, sci-fi is fused with the girls-behind-bars motif as yet another virgin, misperceived as a J.D., finds herself in reform school. A butch matron (Louise Lewis) secretly desires to harness the atom for evil purposes. Inevitably, Harrison's Nancy Perkins wanders by night, employing her fangs (the first time such a device was employed in an English-language horror film) to tear apart her female schoolmates and intrigued males. Serious analysis may be something of a stretch, yet this minor entry can be read as a metaphor for the manner in which an inexperienced 1950s girl might turn violent at the slightest touch, however innocent, owing to fears instilled by educational and religious institutions concerning a female's physical fulfillment. Certainly, that is the theme of another, more artistic film on the subject, *Repulsion* (Roman Polanski, 1965) starring the young Catherine Deneuve.

*

(a)   (b)

(c)   (d)

RE-IMAGINING SCI-FI FOR THE YOUTH MARKET: (a) As early as 1953, Hollywood sensed the need to narrate horror flicks from a child's point of view with *Invaders From Mars* (courtesy: Alperson Prods./20th Century Fox); (b) once wide-eyed boys transformed into horny teenagers about to morph into hormonal monsters in *I Was a Teenage Werewolf* (courtesy: Sunset Prods./AIP); (c) good kids come to the rescue of disbelieving adults in *The Blob* (courtesy: Fairview-Tonylyn Prods./Paramount); (d) a 1950s virgin-bride experiences post-wedding trauma rather than the expected bliss in *I Married a Monster From Outer Space* (courtesy: Paramount).

Exploitation filmmakers made some miscalculations, none greater than a feeble attempt to reignite the early rock 'n' roll controversy via a pair of remakes, *Twist Around the Clock* (Oscar Rudolph, 1961) and *Don't Knock the Twist* (Rudolph, 1962). Neither caught on with Second Wave teenagers, now in high school, despite the presence of Chubby Checker, a leading exponent of the dance craze, in each. Reasons were obvious. The twist could be seen daily, for free, performed on *American Bandstand*, and no one apparently objected. More significant, as Eisenhower left office and John Kennedy moved into the White House, youth became an object of envy and desire for adults rather than disdain. Stay forever young, Bob Dylan would shortly suggest. The public was ahead of him; everyone wanted to be, or at least look, and act, young. This included the Jet Set, whose activities were noted by *Vogue*. When Sybil Burton, estranged wife of the British movie star Richard Burton and a top Manhattan Beautiful People trend-setter, danced at The Peppermint Lounge to the beat of Joey Dee & The Starliters, the Twist caught on everywhere, and with everyone. People young or old didn't need to see a film about twisting around the clock as they were doing so. No one had to be told to *not* knock the Twist since no one knocked it. *Hey, Let's Twist* (Greg Garrison, 1961) fared a bit better, thanks to footage of the Peppermint Lounge.

Columbia Pictures released the two Chubby Checker vehicles, but executives at A.I.P. were apparently too savvy to believe that lightning would strike twice. Arkoff and Nicholson had moved on, adapting to color for horror after noting the success of England's Hammer films with American audiences. *The Curse of Frankenstein* (Terence Fisher, 1957) and *Horror of Dracula* (Fisher, 1958) had proven popular with post-*Shock Theatre* teens who anticipated new renderings of the old tales, now starring Peter Cushing and Christopher Lee. At once, A.I.P.'s genius-in-residence Roger Corman (1926–) set to work on a series of Edgar Allan Poe adaptations, most starring Vincent Price. Upscale, if only in comparison to A.I.P.'s previous offerings, these films actually won praise from critics owing to their eerie Gothic sets; strikingly surreal use of color, both muted and garish; and smart scripts by Richard Matheson and Charles Beaumont—both veteran writers from *The Twilight Zone* (1959–1965). The first two, *House of Usher* (1960) and *The Pit and the Pendulum* (1961), set the pace story-wise: a young man (Mark Damon/John Kerr), supposedly a teenager though played by a mature actor, makes a perilous journey to a haunted palace where a strange, dark haired beauty (Myrna Fahey, Barbara Steele) has fallen under the spell of Price's megalomaniac, played in a Grand Guignol style. The trope of youth-menaced-by-adults had not yet worn thin, at least not when re-imagined for a new decade.

*

In truth, most youth-horror items were as terrible as their titles: *Cult of the Cobra* (Francis D. Lyon, 1955) with Faith Domergue, *Attack of the Puppet People* (Bert L. Gordon, 1958) with June Kenney, *The House on Haunted Hill* (William Castle, 1959) with Carol Ohmart, *The Wasp Woman* (Roger Corman, 1960) with Susan Cabot, and *Blood Feast* (Herschel Gordon Lewis, 1963) featuring *Playboy*'s Connie Mason. When the names of these works didn't deter teens from giddily seeking out such stuff, parents and teachers shook their heads in sorrow. Here, they sighed, was proof apparent that, as actor Paul Lynde would howl in the Broadway and film versions of *Bye Bye Birdie*: "What's the matter with kids today?" They'd opted for rock 'n' roll over easy-listening standards by Perry Como, Andy Williams and Jerry Vale. Now, they apparently didn't realize these exploitation items were, in a word, awful. And they were just that, at least according to the aesthetic standards of adults. But such approaches to entertainment (or art) are nothing if not subjective. Devouring music and movies the previous generation found reprehensible constitutes an act of revolution, culturally speaking. Good taste, or what had been accepted by the middleclass majority (i.e., suburbanites) as that, could be considered bad if perceived from a different (i.e., youth) angle. Things change; values alter along with them. That holds true with popular cinema. Perhaps the kids of the 1950s sensed the tip of an iceberg in what would come to be called (and studied as) popular culture, parents being hopelessly mired in fast-fading standards. Those who held Frank Sinatra's voice up as an ideal were likely offended by early Elvis's Rockabilly. That doesn't necessarily mean either is inferior to the other, only that 'art' or 'junk' depends on any one evaluator's point of view.

Two films would call into question that very concept of good taste. First to appear was *Plan 9 from Outer Space* (Ed Wood, 1959). The writer-director (1924–1978), had not been college-educated and hailed from a small city in upstate New York where his father had worked for the post office. The mom dressed up her son in girl's clothing during the day for amusement. Following a stint in the Marines, Wood headed for Hollywood. Miniscule-budget films included *Glen or Glenda* (1953), originally titled "I Changed My Sex," based on the case of Christine Jorgensen (1926–1989), the first man to undergo such a medical process. In *Plan 9*, initially called *Grave Robbers from Outer*

Space, Wood assembled an eclectic cast: Tor Johnson, an immense, inarticulate professional wrestler; Vampira (Maila Nurmi), Los Angeles' *Shock Theatre* hostess; Bela Lugosi, famed for Universal's *Dracula* (Todd Browning, 1931); he died four days into the shoot. Wood talked his chiropractor, Tom Mason, into yanking a cape over his head and standing in for Lugosi (whom he did not resemble). Not surprisingly, the story makes no sense. Actors can be seen banging into the scenery, which visibly shakes. To claim that the performances are over-the-top understates the situation. For special effects, Wood dangled paper plates on strings in hopes they might be passed off as flying saucers. The dialogue literally defies description; lines spoken in *The Mole People* (Virgil Vogel, 1956) sound in comparison like Shakespeare.

If a beloved Hollywood legend is to be believed, *The Little Shop of Horrors* (Roger Corman, 1960) was completed in less than three days on a budget of $30,000. Corman and writer Charles B. Griffith had just wrapped *A Bucket of Blood* (1959), shot for $50,000 over five days, on sets left over from *Diary of a High School Bride* (Burt Topper, 1959), which cost $80,000, filmed over a seven-day stretch. A.I.P. had given Corman a go-ahead to make *A Bucket of Blood* at an unimaginably small sum. When he somehow pulled that off, Corman wondered if he might immediately outdo himself over the following weekend.[16] Griffith wrote the script on Friday evening, filming commenced that night, and the wrap party took place late Sunday. The story concerns Seymour (Jonathan Haze), a goofy schnook in love with Audrey (Jackie Joseph). Unfortunately, he creates a human-eating plant that begs: "Feed me!" Jack Nicholson appears as a masochist who visits a dentist's office, begging: "No novocain—I want the pain!" Corman, who had collaborated with Arkoff and James Nicholson for some time, came to this film with a life's journey notably different than Wood's. Born to the wife of an affluent Detroit engineer, Corman moved with his family to California and attended Beverly Hills High. He studied at Stanford University, also at Oxford. Before involvement with low-budget filmmaking, Corman had worked at 20th Century-Fox where he played a hand (uncredited) in creating a classic, *The Gunfighter* (Henry King, 1950) starring Gregory Peck.

Plan 9 From Outer Space and *Little Shop of Horrors* were laughable, though that's not necessarily meant as a criticism. Teens, expecting something frightening, found themselves giggling, then roaring wildly at the humor, intended or not; most likely *not* in the case of Wood's film, very much so with Corman's. Both paid off the target audience, if not in the manner anticipated. Still, a pay-off is a pay-off. Perhaps owing to that distinction between horror and humor, these films refused to recede in the memory of those who caught them. When Drive In managers took to booking "Dusk to Dawn" shows, featuring five or six films, *Plan 9* and *Little Shop*, recycled, showed up regularly. Compared to such negligible films as *Frankenstein 1970* (Howard W. Koch, 1958) starring the perennial nymphet Jana Lund or *The Monster of Piedras Blancas* (Irvin Berwith, 1959) with former stripper Jeanne Carmen, a veteran of *Untamed Youth*, these two features continued to exert box-office appeal long after the initial runs. Word spread in any region among what had become the youth community when either (or, better still, both) would be on the bill. Initially, the Drive In staff was stunned when car-loads of kids created traffic jams on back roads leading toward the theatre. Grasping from their clientele precisely why such a sizable turn-out occurred, managers would rebook both several months later, and the syndrome repeated itself.

In time, phrases had to be invented to describe such a phenomenon. These included cult films[17] and guilty pleasures,[18] so bad they were good— if in a radically redefined definition of the term 'good.' The appeal of such alternative cinema stretched beyond the greaser crowd. College-bound kids, whose parents believed they should be interested in more lofty stuff, likewise indulged. When in the early Sixties teenagers moved on to higher education, they surprised adults by not leaving their taste for low-brow cinema (or for that matter rock 'n' roll) at home. When *Plan 9* or *Little Shop* appeared on late-night TV, fraternity brothers would gather around to watch, calling out the dialogue in unison. It may be impossible to ascertain whether Susan Sontag (1933–2004) saw either. It seems a safe bet, however, that this radical author of *Against Interpretation*[19] indulged in both. In "The Politics of Camp" (1964) she excited and outraged the high-brow art world by insisting what in the 20th century's first half was dismissed as "kitsch"—popular art of an exaggerated mode, including pink flamingo lawn ornaments and Carmen Miranda musicals—might be worthy of reconsideration. What had been written off as appealing only to lowbrow tastes might actually be the most significant cultural items of their time—Superman comic books and rococo furniture included. Sontag's division of "naïve camp" (vulgar objects of pop consumption that do not know they are vulgar) as compared to "deliberate camp" (purposefully bad; winking at the audience to reveal this) describes Wood's *Plan 9* (apparently, he believed he'd been making a great film) and Corman's *Little Shop* (knowing it was impossible to create anything of 'quality' in the time available, the director purposefully burlesqued the very sort of movie his title promised). These concepts would become ever more significant in the mid-to-late 1960s, when Andy Warhol's renderings of tomato soup cans and Roy Lichtenstein's poster-sized blow-ups of Sunday funnies panels dominated self-consciously vulgar pop art that challenged modernist tastes left over from the 1950s.[20]

The Movies arrived at such a sensibility early on. This explains why those aforementioned films by Wood and Corman, initially relegated to the grindhouse and Drive Ins, would in time be revived at stellar art-houses and prestigious cosmopolitan museums for retrospectives. Even as Italian opera and Shakespearean theatre, each considered vulgar in its era, eventually triumphed, emerging as key cultural artifacts while what had been considered lofty and respectable work fell by the wayside, so did the once-disparaged junk cinema in the reign supreme. Indeed, *Little Shop* would eventually be transformed into a semi-edgy off-Broadway play (1982), which was brought to London's West End (1963) as a legitimate show, reaching the screen in the form of a mainstream-movie (Frank Oz, 1986), and in time Broadway (2003). The very title of Quentin Tarantino's *Pulp Fiction* (1994) announced eventual enshrinement of once-outrageous pop culture within the mainstream venues of mall theatres. As early as 1972, the title of John Waters's *Pink Flamingos* indicated such collapsing of cultures by suggesting a grindhouse mentality was not all that far from the era's art house, where his own iconoclastic films found a home. Essentially, everything that had been disparaged by people of taste (i.e., middle-brow standards) before 1955 was heralded as divinely decadent following 1970. It comes as no great surprise, then, that in Tarantino's *Pulp Fiction*, the retro-1950s diner/club features a blonde hostess who impersonates that era's queen of sleaze, Mamie Van Doren.

· 5 ·

THE TRAMP IS A LADY

Mamie Van Doren and the Meaning of Life

> "She loves the free-flown wind in her hair;
> Life without care.
> She's broke, but it's ok . . .
> That's why the lady is a tramp."
> —Lorenz Hart, *Babes in Arms*, 1937

In Woody Allen's science-fiction comedy classic *Sleeper* (1973), hero Miles Monroe wakes up in a dystopian future. There, he learns everything he's ever been told (and, without question, believed) was good for him is, in fact, bad. And vice-versa:

Dr. Melik: This morning for breakfast, (Miles) requested something called 'wheat germ, organic honey and tiger's milk.'

Dr Aragon: Oh, yes. Those were the 'charmed' substances that some years ago were (chuckling) thought to contain life-preserving qualities.

Dr. Melik: You mean there was no deep fat? No steak or cream pies or . . . hot fudge?

Dr. Aragon: *Those* were thought to be *un*healthy! Precisely the *opposite* of what we now know to be true.[1]

Screenwriter Allen's above interchange between these two scientists of tomorrow focuses on foods. While such a reversal may not prove true as to diet, it does seem the case with popular culture. Teenagers growing up in the Fifties (the *real* 1950s, not the sentimentalized version of TV's *Happy Days*) learned that mass entertainment falls into two distinct categories: That which should be consumed and that which shouldn't.

In 1957, every real-life equivalent of Ron Howard as Richie Cunningham knew the structure by age twelve: read good comics from Dell, not the sexy-violent E.C. editions. At age fifteen, pick up a respectable book by James Michener, not some desultory trash by Mickey Spillane. Subscribe to *Boy's Life*, stay away from *Mad*. When older, purchase *Life*, avoid *Men's Adventures*. Pat Boone? Okay. Chuck Berry? God forbid! For a movie, catch *Around the World in 80 Days* (Michael Anderson, 1956). Don't go near that Grindhouse on the edge of town where they show the low-budget *Teaserama* (Irving Klaw, 1955) with bad girl Bettie Page and Nudies like *The Amoral Mr. Teas* (Russ Meyer, 1959).

If you should be exposed? Stop, or you'll go blind.

For mature actresses, you couldn't do better than anything starring Jennifer Jones, who won the Oscar for a religious film: *The Song of St. Bernadette* (Henry King, 1943). Blondes? Doris Day: Highly acceptable. Marilyn Monroe was to be avoided until she cleaned up her act, abandoning the fishnets with crimson shoes from *River of No Return* ((Otto Preminger, 1954) for haute couture in *The Prince and The Showgirl* (Laurence Olivier, 1957). Take a giant step down from Marilyn and there's her over-ripe imitator, Jayne Mansfield. No one rates lower than that queen of mammary madness[2] on the cultural radar.

Oh, but *wait!* Indeed, one did: the peripatetic blonde so far down on Tinseltown's Z list that, in comparison, Mansfield appeared innocuous. The platinum queen of sleaze cinema, Mamie Van Doren (1931–), popularizer of the "bullet Bra" and skimpy bikini bathing suits. (see Ch. 6) Legend had it that Mansfield reveled in being Monroe as much as Marilyn hated being Marilyn. People forgot to mention that Mamie Van Doren loved being Mamie. That was the secret to both her success and survival. As of this writing, she remains the longest-living icon from an era that gave us Elvis, Jack Kerouac, Arthur Miller, Rod Serling, Dwight D. Eisenhower, Sandra Dee, Joseph McCarthy, James Dean, Little Richard, Grace Kelly, Ed Wood, Ed Sullivan, and Fess Parker as 'Davy Crockett.' If Mamie once existed at the rock bottom of 1950s kitsch, she reigns supreme in our post-Tarantino America, when it's that bottom, not the top, we most warmly recall from the good (or bad) old days. The diner sequence in *Pulp Fiction* offers homages to Marilyn and Mansfield as well, but it's the Mamie lookalike who stands out for kitsch-addicted audiences.

*

It wasn't always that way. Born Joan Olander on Feb. 6, 1931 in Rowena, South Dakota, of solid Scandinavian stock, the future Queen of Sleaze Cinema won a contract at Howard Hughes's R.K.O. Studios at age fifteen.[3] She initially seemed destined for a conventional career as a shapely but innocent natural blonde of the type Oscar-winner Ingrid Bergman played. Early pin-up shots suggest this was how her agents planned to market Mamie: Sexy but sweet. Illustrator Alberto Vargas caught that aspect of her while employing M.V.D. as a model for an *Esquire* cover. Modest Studio program pictures like *The Second Greatest Sex* (George Marshall, 1955) cast her as a clean-cut type in this country-musical updating of Aristophanes's *Lysistrata*. Already, though, Mamie hungered to play the bad blonde, if in upscale projects. Her first major disappointment occurred when Ado Annie in *Oklahoma!* (Fred Zinnemann, 1955) went to Gloria Grahame. Still, success is the best revenge. Shortly, Mamie cornered the market on such parts, if in less than lofty projects.

In life, Mamie had already broken the hearts of boxer Jack Dempsey, crooner Eddie Fisher, playboy Nicky Hilton and jazz bandleader Ray Anthony.[4] The latter, she briefly married; they had a son, Perry, in 1956. Earlier, Mamie had been hitched (to Jack Newman, a businessman) only to realize she preferred an independent if never solitary lifestyle. If this were to be her lot in life, why shouldn't Van Doren do much the same thing on celluloid? Like all artists, in every medium, M.V.D. would express herself through the work. Her timing proved precisely right as the youth film had just then come into existence. Over at Universal studios, someone thought up the idea of a female version of the male-oriented juvenile delinquent melodramas. The first:—*Running Wild* (Abner Biberman, 1955)—was about tough cops trying to handle one more J.D. street-gang.

In her autobiography *Playing the Field*, Van Doren admitted an initial reluctance to take a step down from conventional fare such as *His Kind of Woman* (John Farrow, 1951), a California-set noir starring Robert Mitchum. (The title referred not to Mamie but Jane Russell.)[5] Nonetheless, while breaking into what would eventually come to be called The Twist before Biberman's camera, Mamie would confess: "I discovered how exciting rock 'n' roll" could be.[6] Shortly, she was seen tearing down Sunset Boulevard on the back of James Dean's motorcycle while, career-wise, searching for yet another teen-oriented movie. As to the latter, she had little choice: Universal, which under the auspices of mogul Ed Muhl had convinced M.V.D. to "go bad" onscreen, dropped her contract when she gave birth.[7] In their view, motherhood was the province of clean-cut female stars. A swinging chick (and shortly single mother), both in due time to be seen as significant staples of liberation, was not, to put it mildly, the order of the day. Mamie found herself an indie performer as a result of male hypocrisy, L.A. style.

*

American pop culture undergoes a constant and relentless shaking-out process. As a result, many entertainment and art objects that seem likely to last forever are forgotten before their eras wane. To the contrary, a considerable amount of work that seemed silly, unimportant, and innocuous turns out to have lasting appeal. If anyone had dared claim in 1955 that half a century hence, Sloan Wilson's upper-middle-brow bestseller *The Man in the Gray Flannel Suit* might be gone from libraries or bookstores while Grace Metalious's much-reviled novel *Peyton Place* would become the subject of doctoral theses in literature, they would have been scoffed at as fools. Yet that is precisely what happened. Today's high culture is yesterday's low culture plus time. The late pin-up queen Bettie Page, when tracked down by reporters during her final years in southwestern obscurity, asked in bewilderment: "Why *now*?"[8] During her brief heyday, the girl who wanted more than anything to be a movie star could not even get into those low-budget quickies Mamie headlined. Today, Page's image appears on as many products as James Dean, Monroe, and Elvis—all of whom likewise passed the test of time.

Others did not. Take the aforementioned Jennifer Jones, particularly in comparison to Mamie. The two worked more or less simultaneously. Jones appeared in high-profile projects such as the upscale interracial romance *Love Is a Many Splendored Thing* (Henry King, 1955), a middlebrow biography of a leading poetess in *The Barretts of Wimpole Street* (Sidney Franklin, 1957), and the Scott Fitzgerald adaptation *Tender Is the Night* (King, 1962). Considered instantaneous classics in their time, all are ignored and/or forgotten today. Not so as to Mamie's humble output. The crime-thriller *Guns, Girls and Gangsters* (Edward L. Cahn, 1959), a tawdry police saga *Vice Raid* (Cahn, 1960), and the low-budget sci-fi entry *The Navy vs. the Night Monsters* (Michael A. Hoey, 1966) boast large, loyal followings.

Kitsch or camp—perhaps a bit of both?—they offered pleasure way back then. And still do today, for Mamie's considerable cult of avid followers.

Jones's *Song of Bernadette* rarely shows up on Turner Classic Movies other than at Christmas or Easter because so few people want to watch it. *High School Confidential!* has become a staple of their late night 'TCM Underground,' reserved for indie movies that helped shape our contemporary point-of-view. Schlock from the late 1950s was summarily dismissed as being devoid of any underlying meaning upon initial appearance. From a post-modernist perspective, such films rate as subversive art. Whether that was in any way intentional seems not to matter. In the end, it's all about what's actually up there onscreen. Small companies grinding out Mamie Van Doren movies did not necessarily set out to break rules. They simply didn't know any better, couldn't afford anything more. France's Wunderkind Jean-Luc Godard, viewing such shock exploitation items, was inspired to create his 'innovative' *Breathless* (1960) in homage; that seminal film brought grindhouse conventions to the art-house circuit.

However paradoxically, incompetence and genius are often difficult to tell apart. That certainly had been the case with the paintings of Vincent Van Gogh, condescended to until his death as impossibly bad, enshrined as the greatest 19th century artist ever since. More often than not, judgments from an era's aesthetic Establishment prove subjective and temporal. Lest we forget, Jack Kerouac was laughed at by the literati as a "typist, not a writer."[9] Then-adored 'serious' authors are mostly forgotten today. Do any books by such middle- to upper-middle brow figures as Sloan Wilson, Frank Yerby, John Hersey, A.J. Cronin, John O'Hara, James Gould Cozzens, or Frances Parkinson Keyes remain in print? *On The Road* has not only sold spectacularly since 1957 but, every bit as significant, has come to be seen as an American masterpiece: the 1950s equivalent of Scott Fitzgerald's *The Great Gatsby* (1925), one of those rare novels that, in its specific story, by implication captures the high, wide and broad essence of its entire era.

*

To reverse a once-popular cliché, behind every great woman there stands a great man. In Mamie's case, that would be Albert Zugsmith (1910–1993), a journalist turned producer who first worked with Mamie on a tidy adult Western, *Star in the Dust* (Charles F. Haas, 1956). She played a comparable part to Grace Kelly's Anglo goddess four years earlier in *High Noon* (Fred Zinnemann, 1952). Mamie still remained ambitious for mainstream stardom. Zugsmith had produced a variety of projects including several classics of their genres: *Written on the Wind* (Douglas Sirk, 1956), a deliciously overwrought upscale melodrama; *The Incredible Shrinking Man* (Jack Arnold, 1957), among the best of the 1950s science fiction films; and *Touch of Evil* (Orson Welles, 1958), a top-drawer noir. Sensing that Universal lacked the freewheeling creative spirit which he required, her 'Zuggy' switched studios.[10] At MGM, the top brass decided it was time to set aside their classy image and speak to that new Youth Audience. Zugsmith, executives guessed, was their man.

What Von Sternberg had been to Dietrich, Zugsmith would become for M.V.D.: the filmmaker who aided an upcoming star in the perfection of her onscreen iconography. In truth, Mamie had already appeared in her second teen-exploitation flick, *Untamed Youth*, for producer Howard Koch. (See Ch. 3.) She hit it off with her co-star, rocker Eddie Cochran. Likewise, Mamie grew ever more aware that her husband Anthony desperately clung to a past musical style. "I (was) one of the first actresses to be identified with rock 'n' roll," Mamie later recalled.[11] Jayne Mansfield preceded Mamie with *The Girl Can't Help It*, afterwards unwisely distancing herself from such stuff—hoping like M.M. to climb the ladder to high status. Mansfield failed miserably. Mamie? She knew a good thing when she heard it.

Thus began Mamie's hottest career period as one release followed another: *Born Reckless* (Andrew Bennin, 1958), a more mainstream item about rodeo-riders and their women, *The Big Operator* (Charles F. Haas,1959), with Mickey Rooney as a corrupt union boss, and *The Beat Generation* (Haas, 1959), a crude/cheap exploitation of the social movement. Way too cheesy for most moviegoers, they established Mamie as an early cult queen.[12] Personally, Mamie had already fallen into disgrace. When Doris Day learned that she was contractually required to appear in a film with her (*Teacher's Pet*; George Seaton, 1958), the female lead wouldn't acknowledge the scene-stealer's presence on the set. Day went so far as to request that the shooting schedule be arranged so they would never meet.[13] Doris was typecast as her usual goody-two-shoes type, opposite Clark Gable; Mamie played a temptress who tries to win him away.

As for Mamie's junk movies, parents warned their offspring that to attend them was tantamount to becoming one of "those hoods" in *Blackboard Jungle* (1956). Hungry to work even as these J.D. films fell out of favor, Mamie journeyed to Italy to shoot the first Giallo (garish Italian horror in a Hitchcock mode), *The Beautiful Legs of Sabrina* (Camille Mastrocinque, 1959). She had already usurped Marilyn's early tawdry image in *The Girl in Black Stockings* (Howard W. Koch, 1957), decades before MTV divas from Cher and Madonna to Christina Aguilera and Lady Gaga joyously imitated the declasse/verboten fashion-statements Van Doren dared to embody: Fish-nets stockings, black-leather jackets, bullet-bras, slinky-satin and bikini bathing-suits.

Then one day (December 31, 1959 to be precise) the 1950s (which some believed would go on forever) ended. Unlike many other youth stars, stuck in that decade's groove, Mamie was just getting going. The first wave of American teenagers, those who had entered junior high in the fall of 1955, prepared to set off for college. Mamie made the move first, co-starring with Tuesday Weld and Brigitte Bardot's kid sister Mijanou in *Sex Kittens Go to College* (1960). Zuggy directed this time around; country-rocker Conway Twitty played a preppie-hipster! This would become a definitive *objet d'art* in the Van Doren *oeuvre*. Zugsmith's camp classic embodied every mom and pop's worst fears: Mamie at her wildest, rock 'n' roll at its rawest.

Appearing at the new decade's very onset, *Sex Kittens* actually encapsulated the 1950s. Or at least middle-America's fear and loathing, here painted in surreal strokes: a virtual apotheosis of an era's junk culture that, by watching, freed young people to move on to Jack Kennedy, James Bond, Bob Dylan and The Beatles. For here was college as every high school boy desperately dreamed it might be . . .

*

In the 21ˢᵗ century, our so-called mainstream no longer rates as white bread. "We have met the enemy," Walt Kelly noted half a century ago, "and he is *us!*"[14] Mamie, of course, did not singlehandedly create such a cultural revolution. If any one person can be credited with that, it was Elvis. Yet more than any other actress, Mamie understood on some instinctual level the shape of things to come. Film historian Steve Sullivan has described her embrace of a then-emergent musical style:

> Recall that when Mamie cast her lot with rock 'n' roll in 1957, there was a genuine risk involved. Many ministers, redneck DJs, and self-appointed moralists were condemning the music as sinful, staging record-burning parties and pressuring corporate sponsors not to support this heathen symbol. Even though many of those censors were hardly likely to be Mamie Van Doren fans, in any event studio execs had to be nervous about one of their stars being linked to such a controversial new force.[15]

By embracing rock before it was culturally correct to do so, Mamie's mainstream career crashed. Once having cut an album of rock songs, she could not go home again to respectable genres she'd once appeared in: the John Wayne action vehicle *Jet Pilot* (Josef von Sternberg, 1950); a giddy M.O.R. musical *Two Tickets to Broadway* (James V. Kern, 1951); the costume film *Yankee Pasha* (Joseph Pevney, 1954) as a harem girl—all respectable releases from major studios of the type in which Jennifer Jones then flourished. Yet in a recent edition of Leonard Maltin's *Movie Guide*, Jones isn't indexed among old-time stars such as Bette Davis, Joan Crawford or Barbara Stanwyck.[16] Few denizens of the 21ˢᵗ century, including many film students, recall her name. Mamie? Bring up The Blonde and eyes widen. She was sleazy *and* slutty; she had it all, back when those terms—today offered as admiration in an age of ballsy female rock-stars like Beyonce—were still considered negatives.

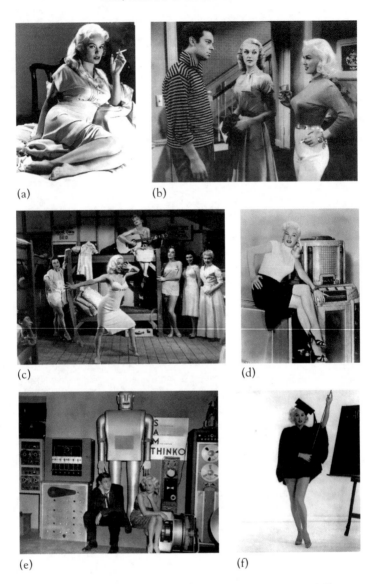

(a)   (b)

(c)   (d)

(e)   (f)

ONCE IN LOVE WITH MAMIE: (a) Studio photographers purposefully capture Mamie in a style recalling sordid cover illustrations for cheap pulp-fiction paperbacks, then called Bus Station books (courtesy: Universal); (b) teen Russ Tamblyn (right) ponders whether to 'give it up' to a classy teacher (Jan Sterling, center) or his nymphomaniac Auntie Mamie in *High School Confidential!* (courtesy: Zugsmith Prods./M.G.M.); (c) Mamie instructs fellow bad girls how to strut their stuff to a rock n' roll beat in *Untamed Youth* (courtesy: Warner Bros.) (d) and revels in her *declasse* image as a juke-joint girl (Courtesy: Universal); (e) a post-feminist before modern feminism had even been born, Mamie reveals that girl-power derives from beauty conjoined with brains (courtesy: Zugsmith Prods.); (f) Marty Milner pensively joined Mamie for a film originally to have been titled "The Beauty and the Robot" (courtesy: Allied Artists).

Even as *High School Confidential!* and *Sex Kittens Go to College* entertained kids on a Drive In double bill, *BUtterfield 8* (Daniel Mann, 1960) played to adults in upscale theatres. The film was released in stereo-sound and full-color widescreen. Mamie's? Black-and-white, with tinny music that reverberated over the outdoor-theatre receivers. Yet *BUtterfield 8* was, like any of Mamie's outings, all about sex. And, significantly, sex from a woman's perspective: Liz Taylor played a high-priced call-girl, in love with a married client (Laurence Harvey). When he refuses to leave his wife for her, Liz's character drives her sports car over a cliff in the manner of Bette Davis in *Dangerous* (Alfred E. Green, 1935), who there fatalistically plowed into a tree—like dozens of other ill-fated femmes from the golden age of three-handkerchief weepers.

In the 21st century's second decade, *BUtterfield 8* seems irrelevant to anyone other than diehard movie buffs. The still-in-effect Production Code insisted that any woman who sexually transgresses, however sympathetic, must pay with her life; on the other hand, a cheating male can go home and be forgiven after proper penance. No matter how cosmeticized *BUtterfield 8* may have been with its aura of big-studio gloss, this high-profile product does not in any way challenge the double standard that, today, strikes most everyone in America as offensive. Choosing to be charitable, we might forgive the film its anti-feminist slant as *it wasn't their fault—they didn't know any better back then.* After all, this was three years before Betty Friedan's *The Feminine Mystique* reached bookstores.

Always, though, there are artists who think outside the box. Tip-of-the-iceberg types offer hints as to what will in time be accepted into society and the pop culture that reflects it. In Hollywood, such people worked outside the mainstream. The good news was that maverick movies didn't need to follow Production Code guidelines that reined in The Majors. So the ideology contained in them, dismissed as vulgar then, might in retrospect be seen as far-seeing. No greater contrast could be drawn than between the outdated antique *BUtterfield 8* and *Sex Kittens Go to College*, released the same year. Ignore its shoddy production values and Zugsmith's film offers a proto-feminist point of view.

*

In it, Mamie plays scientist Dr. Mathilda West (a reference to Mae?), selected by a university's computer as the new head of a department. Upon arrival, everyone on campus stares in disbelief at a platinum blonde, cleavage displayed in *outre* clothing never before seen on this staid campus. Most faculty and staff, men and women, believe a terrible mistake has been made. No matter if her brain is as brilliant as their computer insists. They can't allow someone who looks like this to remain. Would she please be gracious enough to leave . . . at once?

Her answer is no. West qualifies for the job in terms of her intelligence and academic record. That's all that ought to matter. If others have a problem with her appearance, it's their worry. She does her work well, refusing to apologize. In her mind, there's nothing to apologize for. She's the pioneer for those female professors of today who choose to wear blue jeans and black leather, giddily flaunting tattoos that only male truck drivers and hard-edged sailors sported a half-century ago.

More than one married man, believing West's "look" allows an indication of her morality, attempts to get her into bed. She's not interested in being some man's toy, no matter how rich or powerful. Eventually it's revealed West previously worked as a stripper. She doesn't deny it. Coming from poverty, yet early on sensing the quality of her mind, West made a hard/cold decision to temporarily employ her body so as to earn enough money to complete an education, including a Ph.D. If that might be troublesome to Second Wave feminists, always uncomfortable with "the objectification of the sexualized female body,"[17] it doesn't constitute a problem for post-feminist women of the 21st century, who demand equality with men while flaunting their sex appeal.[18] Considering West's intents and results, her stripping didn't represent the exploitation of women by men but precisely the opposite. She did what she had to do to get here, playing down (rather than up) to men's childish fantasies.

Now, of course, she could afford more expensive clothing. That's not her way. She dresses in the manner that she does *not* because she doesn't know better but because she's grown to like it. And will not relinquish a style that, as an individual, she still enjoys, however much this flies in the face of convention. West does not give in; *they* must change. Incredibly, they do!

Mamie's character in *Sex Kittens* might be thought of as Taylor's from B*Utterfield* 8 turned upside down, inside out, and backwards. Liz's retro-woman always wanted to live off her body, if in a supposedly acceptable means of doing so: high fashion modeling. Showing herself off as manqué was an end, not a means, until Liz allowed a man to become central in her life. Still, her character apparently doesn't enjoy sex. Mamie's West loves sex, though she will not live in bondage (literal or figurative) to any man. With a sad whine, Liz apologized to everyone for what she'd degenerated into, then roared off into the sunset . . . (Ugh!) Mamie? She slaps her small but strong fists against those curvaceous hips, belligerently challenging anyone, male or female, to dare question the necessary journey by which she re-invented her life . . . and did so for the better.

Liz embodied then. Mamie? *Now.*

That helps explain why the young people of today laugh out loud if they should happen upon B*Utterfield* 8 and boo at the end. *Sex Kittens*, they adore—laughing *with* it, cheering the finale. They admire what the film has to say about the role of women in society, however unlikely producer Zugsmith had such ambitions in mind. No matter. Always, in entertainment and art, it's the work (not the motive behind it) that matters most.

*

Initially, Fifties youth films propagandized against the New Morality that began with Elvis' first TV appearances in 1954. In Mamie's movies, criticism gave way to celebration. One sequence in *Sex Kittens* has her lecturing students on the joys of *mis*-behaving, this the most daring such onscreen moment since Mae West undermined a rural school while working as a substitute teacher in *My Little Chickadee* (Edward Cline, 1940). To the old educational adage about growing up to be good boys and girls, Mae rolled her eyes, sashaying across the schoolroom, cackling: "Propaganda!" Instead of guiding Tuesday Weld away from casual sex with cute co-eds like Marty Milner, Mamie here seduces the boy herself. Mamie is Mae West taken to a nightmare scenario of edginess even as the Fifties segued into the Sixties.

In an earlier era, West was driven out of Hollywood by moralists who still had the power to destroy careers, always targeting women unapologetic as to their naughtiness. Jean Harlow, who embodied the blonde mystique two decades before Mamie, could be forgiven her sins as, at the end of any movie, she fell to her knees, begging the male lead (more often than not Gable) to marry her. In *The Misfits* (John Huston, 1961), Marilyn did the same, and with the same star. Not Mamie, not even for Gable (in *Teacher's Pet*). Though she may, like Norma Jean, have grown up wanting to become Harlow,[19] Mamie in fact emulated Mae—using men, onscreen and in actuality, the way they traditionally used women (for lust rather than love), walking away when done. Mae paid a price for being ahead of her day and in studio pics. Mamie arrived in the right place at the right time, if not to be accepted by the status-quo than at least as an avatar for change.

By 1955, the tide had begun to turn. *Playboy* appeared at mid-decade, offering an early glimpse of the Swingin' Sixties in which sex and sin would no longer necessarily be perceived as bound together. Its first celebrity nude, Marilyn, hadn't given Hugh Hefner permission to print earlier nude photos. When M.V.D. shortly appeared in the buff, she did so willingly. And enthusiastically. It was her choice, as a woman, as a person, as an individual. Truth be told, Mamie, not Marilyn, was the female who altered everything. At the conclusion of each of her junk movies, Mamie flicked a figurative finger at mainstream morality. She was bad. To the bone. What's more, she *liked* being precisely that, onscreen and off, as the pulp tabloids of those days eagerly reported.[20]

Most significant, Mamie never compromised. Elvis copped out by cleaning up his act, swiftly arcing from the bad boy of *Jailhouse Rock* to the secular saint of *Kid Galahad*. In so doing, he lost his youth-cult status. Mamie chose to never remove her black-leather jacket. Though Elvis and Mamie dated,[21] he avoided co-starring with her for fear she might taint his new image. Yet Jerry Lee Lewis, once and future king of pure redneck Rockabilly, cheerfully joined her for *High School Confidential!* Like Lewis, M.V.D. hadn't embraced a 1950s youth phenomenon to cash in on rock's popularity, then move on to bigger, supposedly better things. She had committed. That was that.

As author Sullivan put it:

> Far from being just another of the Hollywood blondes, Mamie was unique in ways that remain important from today's perspective. Where Marilyn was deeply ambivalent about her bombshell image and Jayne frequently tried to renounce it even while carrying the image further, Mamie reveled in her sex-symbol persona with no regrets or excuses. While her two contemporaries were traditional in their musical and pop culture tastes, Mamie . . . was to be indelibly stamped into the pop-culture psyche as the definitive "bad girl" who served as the irresistible recruiting agent for juvenile delinquency.[22]

In *Teacher's Pet*, Mamie solidified this persona by singing a quasi-autobiographical number, "The Girl Who Invented Rock 'n' Roll." A few years later, MGM lost interest in the waning early-rock scene. Zugsmith and Mamie headed over to *declasse* Allied Artists for *Sex Kittens* (originally to have been titled *The Beauty and the Robot*), then back to Universal for *The Private Lives of Adam and Eve* (Zugsmith, 1960), one of the first films to be described as "so bad it's good" by fans. Having invented rock 'n' roll (or at least solidifying its essence), M.V.D. then inspired Susan Sontag's eventual creation of camp.

*

During the mid-sixties, college students crowded around frat house TVs to watch *Adam and Eve* on late night TV even as they did *Plan 9* and *Little Shop*. Some would call out lines of dialogue as, a generation later, another wave of hipster youth would for *The Rocky Horror Picture Show* (Jim Sharman, 1975). Throughout the 1960s, Mamie remained alive and well on late-night TV. Her career was another matter. *College Confidential* (Zugsmith, 1960), a surprise flop, bookended the success of *High School Confidential!* a year earlier. What would have seemed a likely M.V.D. role in *Platinum High School* (Charles Haas, 1960) went to perennial starlet Terry Moore. The following year, Famous Artists ceased representing Mamie.

With no films in the offing, she developed a live stage show, premiering at the Chi-Chi Club in Palm Springs. Next came a dinner theatre stint in *Wildcat*, an obscure musical, at the Meadowbrook Theatre in New Jersey. There was but one further step downward: a no-budget nudie called *Three Nuts in Search of a Bolt* (1963) for producer-writer-director Tommy Noonan. Mamie wasn't the first to go this route; Jayne had previously appeared in *Promises! Promises!* (King Donovan, 1963) opposite Noonan, the male star of each.

As for the battle of the blondes, Jayne and Mamie finally co-starred in 1966's *Hillbillys* (sic) *in a Haunted House* (Jean Yarbrough, 1967), a country comedy that mainly played the rural South. One night, the two faded glamour girls, according to a long-lived Show Biz legend, joined one another in a run-down bar for cognac and conversation. The now busted busty bombshells shared watered drinks and salty tears. Both knew the era of the platinum blonde had passed. All at once everyone was agog over the waif look: Twiggy in fashion, Mia Farrow on the screen. Or their opposite, those athletic-looking Amazons Ursula Andress and Raquel Welch. "You know," Mamie told Jayne, "Marilyn was the lucky one"[23] referring to Monroe's 1962 death. Shortly, Jayne died in a car crash while traveling from a minor late night live-gig to a TV performance on some small-city local show.

Not Mamie. She survived to experience the youth cult of the late 1960s. Overnight the free love she, a decade ahead of everyone else, had dared popularize became the norm. One might guess Mamie would look kindly on such rebelliousness. One would be wrong. As the country veered left, her politics turned right. Instead of joining the heated protest against our involvement in Southeast Asia, Van Doren offered her services as a volunteer performer, taking whatever risks necessary to cheer up troops at the front. If that sounds surprising, it's consistent. When France's Brigitte Bardot was informed that the hippie girls who appeared in porn films claimed her as their inspiration, she all but spit in anger. Bebe insisted that what Linda Lovelace and Marilyn Chambers did was obscene, compared to her subtle (conservative, by 1970s standards) sensuality. Elvis, whose gyrations initiated the youth movement and was once condemned as the centerpiece of a vast communist plot to destroy America's morality via rock 'n' roll, paid a surprise visit to President Richard Nixon, who had once condemned Elvis. Presley requested special/ secret permission to help the Feds wipe out student radicals. Kerouac, who immortalized 1950s style rebellion, condemned long-hairs who idolized him and, inspired by Jack's greatest book, headed out on the road.

If that sounds crazy, note that John Dos Passos, fire-brand author of the 1930s Red-tinted *U.S.A.* trilogy, would support Republican Barry Goldwater's presidential bid in '64. Actor-director Dennis Hopper, whose *Easy Rider* (1969) *had* incarnated late-1960s radicalism, supported Ronald Reagan in his 1980 run for the White House. So did Bob Dylan. More often than one might guess, yesterday's wildest radical turns out to be tomorrow's most severe reactionary.

*

In 1975, at the height of popular interest in the modern Women's Movement, Martha Saxton wrote:

> Women's history, unlike men's, is also the history of sex. If a woman transcends her sexual identity, it is with difficulty and cause for endless comment. If she doesn't, no one is surprised. A woman who capitalizes on it, on the other hand, is used or ridiculed.[24]

As for Marilyn and Jayne, no matter how hard either worked to be taken "seriously" as an actress, each (like Mamie) experienced a career more predicated on "sex and publicity" than "talent."[25] But if written off as the least significant of the fifties' blondes, how different Mamie now appears. Marilyn and Jayne had dutifully "mastered a high child's voice and a number of squeals and coos"; each

> was a demonstration of what to do and how to do it, when female sexuality was a come-on, a taste, a broken promise. Take a good look, (each) said, but don't touch. (They) taught lessons in artifice, enticement, and hypocrisy.[26]

Not Mamie. There was nothing "little-girlish" about her. And no broken promise. When in *High School Confidential!* she comes on to a teenage boy,

Mamie means precisely what she says. This is no fun flirtation of the Monroe/ Mansfield order, rather hard, cold seduction of the type that older women enact, without hesitation or embarrassment, in today's world and in today's movies. Could they do so if Mamie hadn't paved the way? The bridge between then and now was erected by Mamie Van Doren. To a degree, she *was* the bridge, for better or worse, depending on one's chosen ground in our ongoing culture wars.

Mamie's image can be written off as anti-feminist only if one accepts the now-dated standard of Una Stannard with her Second Wave Feminism notion of The Beauty Trap.[27] Today's *post*-feminist women perceive things differently—combining the Feminist's once radical, now mainstream insistence on absolute equality with a rejection of de-glamorization to avoid being labeled a Sex Object. Today's woman, powerful yet gorgeous, is far more likely to be perceived as a Sexual Being—the basic problem (then and now) not having to do with "sexiness" but "objectification." Beauty, so re-configured, rates as one more employable tool on the road to independence and success.

Beginning in the late 1960s, "It was no longer a choice between marrying or (bra) burning. No one had to do either. This wave of sexual honesty deprived Jayne of a persona"[28] even as it legitimized Mamie's in-your-face toughness that scorned any "lisping" or "purring."[29] If like Marilyn "Jayne was never in charge"[30], Mamie was never *not* in charge, whether we consider her screen characters or her off-screen life.

*

More than any other blonde goddess of her era, Mamie Van Doren was ridiculed. Yet she was the only one who would never allow herself to be used. Not by studios, as evidenced by Mamie's open rebellion against their stifling restrictions. And not by the men in her life. Monroe desperately attempted to become (or at least pass for) normal (whatever that means) by assuming the route of a sequential monogamist—marrying a variety of men, famous and unknown. Ultimately, she was used by every guy except the first, ironically the only who offered Norma Jean a semblance of the housewife lifestyle she claimed to covet yet felt smothered by. Mansfield was exploited by 20th Century-Fox, which created her as their alternative to abiding superstar Marilyn only to dump Jayne the moment that Monroe agreed to obey company rules in exchange for better roles.[31] Jayne's own attempt to deal with the opposite sex was to cling to a difficult marriage with Mickey ("Mr. Universe") Hargitay while involving herself in endless illicit affairs.[32] M.V.D., if her claims in the 1987 autobiography are to be believed, walked out on any man who became abusive. And despite a long line of lovers, she turned down such attractive men as James Dean, Warren Beatty, and Frank Sinatra. Why? Because she happened to be married at the time and always took her vows seriously.

The woman who onscreen symbolized slutishness embodied in her daily life the opposite of what that term implies. In this case, the onscreen Tramp was in real life the real lady. At least, though, with the acknowledgment of The Three Blondes in *Pulp Fiction*'s dancin' at the diner sequence, the spirit and legacy of Mamie has re-surfaced. The title of her hit single "The Girl Who Invented Rock and Roll" may have been a gross exaggeration. What can't be denied is more startling and more revealing: Mamie invented *us*.

As *Sleeper*'s Dr. Aragon put it, All those things once believed to be bad for us turned out to be good: Blue jeans, black leather, cowboy boots; comic books, rock 'n' roll.

And, most particularly, the films of Mamie Van Doren—a daring pioneer who, among other achievements, rated as the first Hollywood actress to model a bikini onscreen, doing so back when this still suggested sleaziness rather than a wholesomeness that the swimsuit would, by the mid-1960s, come to symbolize.

· 6 ·

SURF/SEX/SAND/SPIES

The Battles of Bikini Beach

"Surfing expresses . . . a pure yearning for a visceral, physical contact with the natural world."
—Bruce Jenkins, *North Shore Chronicles*, 2005

The bombings of Hiroshima (08/06/1945) and Nagasaki (08/09/1945) brought to a close our war in the Pacific while ushering in the Atomic age. A notable test occurred on July 1, 1946, at remote Bikini Atoll. Among those aware that a brave new world had dawned was French designer Louis Réard (1897–1984), who earlier realized conventional swimsuits no longer satisfied daring young *Parisiennes*. Inspired by the bomb test, he announced on July 5 at the Piscine Molitor fashion-show that his equally explosive swimsuit would appropriately be called The Bikini.[1] Even in Gay Paree, this "scandalous" item created a furor. Réard grasped that no professional model would display herself in something so skimpy.[2] Micheline Bernardini, a Casino de Paris nude performer, did the honors. Critics complained that civilization would be threatened by a fashion item recalling the ancient pagans. An appreciative minority argued that the Bikini came into being because it had to; the world was ready for something shocking in fashion even as it reeled from spectacular scientific innovation. The international press, ever hungry for new fodder, turned Réard's event into a "media sensation."[3]

If models were initially wary, chic Gallic women living in the breezy climes of St. Tropez embraced The Bikini wholeheartedly. As Brigitte Bardot (1934–)

shortly rose to fame, she took to wearing this swimsuit that projected the natural casualness of her lifestyle on and off-screen. *The Lighthouse Keeper's Daughter* (Willy Rozier, 1952) was retitled *The Girl in the Bikini* to emphasize the association of this female from the upper strata of society with the suit. Momentarily, the Bikini asserted that women who donned it accepted the postwar liberalism as to manners and mores. But as to America? Serendipitously, a seemingly unrelated event paved the way for eventual acceptance. In 1943, while shortages of materials remained a serious issue, the government requested that women's swimwear be reduced by ten percent, "removing first the skirt panel on a one-piece garment," and "then the midriff too."[4] For reasons relating to "austerity"[5] a woman could claim that she was not a show-off, rather a patriot.

By the mid-fifties, daring American actresses, Mamie Van Doren the most prominent, modeled Bikinis in fashion spreads for men's magazines. Others, considered far classier—Joan Collins, Suzy Parker—followed suit, leading to legitimization. In 1959, Cole of California marketed the first Bikini for sale in the U.S. On many beaches, women who dared wear one were arrested. But when teen-idol Brian Hyland performed "Itsy Bitsy Teenie Weenie Yellow Polka Dot Bikini" a year later, the humorous lyrics (at the end it's revealed the girl is nine years old) helped America adjust. Shortly, even nice girls could wear one. In the early 1960s, the epitome of female innocence was defined by two women: Sandra Dee (1942–2005) and Annette Funicello (1942–2010). If they were to don Bikinis, the swimsuit's acceptance was assured.

*

A key predecessor to the beach film, shot simultaneously with the Bikini's arrival in U.S. stores, contains daring two-piece outfits. In *Gidget* (Paul Wendkos, 1959) the focus was less on swimsuits than the surf and a sport imported in the early 20th century from Hawaii. Young people, fed up with the world around them and looking to drop out, did not necessarily have to go the way of the Beat Generation (see Ch. 11), mostly glum types who haunted cellar clubs. An alternative appeared among sun worshippers since surf culture also included a search for some elusive truth. These were Dharma Beach Bums, practicing a sport that derived from mythological ideas about engaging in athletic endeavors to achieve transcendence. Surfers claimed to reach another level, the mind left behind as the unconscious body reached for pure spirituality. Even as there were weekend Beats who dressed the part in Greenwich Village coffee clubs, so were there part-time surfers: high-school kids wanting in on the action. Serious surfers would have nothing to do with such hobbyists, at least not unless they could prove themselves as truly dedicated.

One young woman who did win over the cult was Kathy Kohner (1941–), daughter of mid-level L.A. screenwriter Fred Kohner. To escape the every-day hell that is high school, the diminutive girl headed out to Malibu beach, becoming fascinated with the surf culture then developing.[6] Stories which she ecstatically related to her father inspired him to turn them into a teen-oriented novel. Gidget sold more than 500,000 copies, resulting in a Hollywood option. Beneath the gloss of Columbia's colorful surf-and-sand shenanigans, the film projected serious concerns about postwar youth. Francie is "a teenage tomboy" at odds "with her teenage friends"[7] Francie is a young person of the postwar era who has received all the expected benefits of affluence yet experiences vague malaise. Also, proto-feminist elements appear in the narrative. The 'Girl Midget' sets out to be accepted by an all-male group, not as yet another pretty hanger-on but as one of the guys. Initially the butt of jokes, she wins them over by proving she's their equal. The book's subtitle: "Little Girl with Big Ideas." If a telling comment on its time, Gidget does also look forward to the future.

The most interesting character is not Francie (Dee) or her boyfriend Moondoggie (James Darren) but Big Kahoona (Cliff Robertson). Fourteen-year-old Francie becomes so emotionally distraught owing to her on-again/off-again romance that she corners the thirty-year-old Big Kahuna and attempts to seduce him. Though this doesn't happen, owing to censorial restrictions, it's clear that Kahuna might well have taken advantage of the situation if it weren't for his awareness that Francie only hopes to make Moondoggie jeal-ous. In this frolic of a film, he offers a rare insightful peek into the dedicated surf bum. On a technical level, Gidget employed blue-screen technique for the benefit of actors who couldn't surf. Such an approach would be continued throughout the Beach Party saga. Unnoticed at the time, this would serve as a source for condescending laughter in the late Sixties, when more realistic shooting-styles provided a foil to obvious in-studio devices. With the advent of the Nostalgia Movement (see Epilogue), this ceased to seem intrusive, rather a charming bit of deconstruction. When employed in a beach reunion film Back to the Beach (Lydall Hobbs, 1987), viewers laughed with knowing good humor. A now purposeful and self-conscious employment brought back warm memories of a simpler age. Or, at least, what in 1987 people wanted to believe 1963 had been like.

Perhaps unintentionally, Gidget also introduced a gay subtext that would continue through the genre. "If bikini-clad beauties are your cup of tea," Tom Lisanti pointed out in Hollywood Surf and Beach Movies: The First Wave, 1959–1969, "you are out of luck."[8] However, "beefcake" is plentiful enough that the film rates as

a boy watcher's dream. Numerous scenes of the shirtless young men riding the waves
are featured. So much flesh is on display that there is a boy for every taste from rugged
and virile Cliff Robertson to boyish and smooth James Darren.[9]

Shortly, the genre would shift toward a focus on young women in ever skimpier suits. Yet young men would remain plentiful, soon pumping up the beefcake. Lisanti's description makes clear that a homosexual audience, however
closeted, could derive visual pleasure, as did young female ticket-buyers.

In addition to a female coming-of-age story, *Gidget* does make "a sincere
effort to capture the surfer culture of the time albeit toned down for a movie
audience"[10]—that is, movie audiences of 1959. That could not be said of the
next step in the genre's evolution, *Where the Boys Are* (Henry Levin, 1960),
about students attending spring break in Florida. Like *Gidget*, it assumes a
female point of view. One of the four central characters, played by Yvette
Mimieux, does sport a bikini. She had already donned one for a less prestigious junk movie, *Platinum High School* (Charles Haas, 1960). Whereas there
the Bikini posited Yvette as an innocent child of nature, in the bigger MGM
opus she's 'the bad girl' owing to her casual surrendering of her virginity. (See
Ch. 7). A mid-1950s value system is imposed on an early 1960s studio film.
Shortly, such a stigma would be removed, the bikini in the following decade
coming to symbolize, incredibly, chastity.

One year later, *Blue Hawaii* (Norman Taurog, 1961) would return to surfing as the story's focus. Chad Gates (Elvis Presley) is, like Elvis himself, a
returning serviceman, collapsing the person into the persona. However wholesome, Chad does experience The Generation Gap. His well-to-do mother
(Angela Lansbury) wishes to smother Chad with her love while drawing him
into the family business. Chad would prefer to live as a surf bum. In an intriguing plea for racial intermarriage, Chad plans to settle down with a native
Hawaiian, Maile (Joan Blackman). Also, he prefers the company of natives
(his "brothers") to his parents' expensively suited friends. Chad is willing to
work, but for himself. The Bikini makes a notable appearance. Chad's gift to
Maile is a two-piece he's brought back from France, allowing us to perceive the
barely-there shreds of cotton as representational of the first suit to penetrate
American culture. While Maile does look remarkable in it, *Blue Hawaii* offers
opportunity for equality in observation of the body beautiful. Elvis, looking
fit in a tight swim-suit, provided a prime object for gazing by straight women
or gay men. While critic Laura Mulvey may identify a 'male gaze' angled only
at women, in truth all audiences—male, female; gay, straight—seek out visual
pleasure in films, this being essential to the cinema's unique appeal.

FULL CYCLE FOR A SWIMSUIT: (a) Brigitte Bardot dared pioneer the atomic age fashion statement(courtesy: Sport Film); (b) Hollywood gradually embraced the bikini if initially holding it in reserve for mature spy girls like Ursula Andress (courtesy: United Artists); (c) gradually, wholesome teens like Yvette Mimieux displayed ever more of themselves (courtesy: M.G.M.); (d) during the late 1960s, the bikini connected with Hippie fashions, here modeled by Salli Sachse (courtesy: A.I.P.); (e) owing to feminism's disdain for female body display as "objectification," even sex symbols like Farrah Fawcett avoided the suit during the 1970s (courtesy: ABC-TV); (f) post-feminist women such as Jessica Alba returned to the bikini as empowering and liberating. (courtesy: Columbia/Mandalay/MGM).

*

Other precursors were oriented around adult characters: observing with fascination and consternation the near-nakedness of modern teens, wondering/fearing whether this aspect of contemporary youth might be accompanied by practice of free love. In *The Marriage-Go-Round* (Walter Lang, 1961), adapted by Leslie Stevens from his 1958 play, a college professor (James Mason) shares a genteel life with an equally well-educated wife (Susan Hayward). Their middle-aged Eden is interrupted by the arrival of a transfer student from Sweden (Julie Newmar). As the film is set near a college campus, young people are plentiful. Mostly, they remain in the background, except for one scene in which Newmar joins some muscular boys at a swimming pool. Their shenanigans pick up on previous ones in *Gidget* and the motel's pool sequences in *Where the Boys Are*. Despite her glorious physique, Newmar doesn't wear a Bikini. This was a 20th Century Fox 'major' release. The producers likely feared their mainstream audience might be shocked.

The girl makes no bones about her intent to seduce this man. Her goal is not, as in most comedies of the *Pillow Talk* (Michael Gordon, 1959) era, sex itself. She neither hungers for such satisfaction nor is she repulsed by it; she has no compulsions whatsoever about sex and will casually enjoy the act as a means to achieve what she wants: a child. "I *vant* your *genes!*" Newmar tells Mason. His brains combined with her body ought to produce perfection. At mid-movie, Newmar gleefully explains her plan to the wife of her male prey. "You're very sick in the head," Hayward's character sighs. Innocuous as the film may be, such a line, spoken and received at face value rather than with irony, may reveal more than the writer intended. Free love, then widely ascribed to the Swedish, strikes academics of the time as perverse. That would shortly change.

The shift occurred in *I'll Take Sweden* (Fred de Cordova, 1965). Two generations of American men—Bob Hope and Frankie Avalon—bridge any Generation Gap by traveling together to that country where both fall in love with its freedom of physical display and playful attitude toward sex. By mid-decade, American girls would (to a degree as a result of such films) come to believe it was possible to be clean-cut yet sexually active. Such a sensibility would not, though, be forwarded by the Beach films, despite the centrality of the Bikini. The first, *Beach Party* (William Asher, 1963), picked up on the view expressed in *Marriage-Go-Round*. Co-producer Sam Arkoff later claimed he got the idea for this exploitation item while in Italy in 1962, watching a comedy about an older man becoming obsessed with bikini-beach girls, perhaps *Crazy Desire* (Luciano Salce, 1962). *Beach Party*'s structure likewise concerns a mature male, Prof. Robert Sutwell (Robert Cummings) and his female assistant,

Marianne (Dorothy Malone) who peek at California's young people stripped down to the basics, including Frankie Avalon as Frankie and Annette Funicello as Dolores "Dee Dee." The adults rent a beach house, he planning to chronicle the antics of high-schoolers so that he can write an anthropological treatise about these non-violent young savages. The distinction from *The Marriage-Go-Round* is that at the end, rather than reject the kids' back-to-nature attitude, adults embrace it. Sutwell has never recognized that Marianne adores him and a romance finally blossoms. This might be thought of as the first Sixties Youth film to propose the upcoming Woodstock theory: "Teach your parents well."[11] When Sutwell learns to surf, he and Marianne also enjoy rock 'n' roll played by Dick Dale and the Dell-Tones at Big Daddy's; here are representative adults who, in the Sixties, became infatuated with the Youth Culture.

Here, an equivalent to Julie Newmar's Swedish émigré is Eva Six as a Hungarian Amazon. She sets her sights on Frankie; she too is rejected, as will be similar foreign females, femme fatales all, who appear in the sequels. In *Muscle Beach Party* (William Asher, 1964), a similar role is played by Luciana Paluzzi as a European contessa, Juliana. *Pajama Party* (Don Weis, 1964) has yet another Swedish girl, Helga (Bobbi Shaw), her European attitudes on sex portrayed as dangerous to our value system, notably marriage. The European-ness of such girls conveys a sense of xenophobia: an abiding fear of foreigners who throw the American mating system off-balance. The "sick" stigma Hayward's educated American woman placed on such thinking would not abate until the Sixties' second half. Meanwhile, an abiding conservatism, "Fortress America" in a social and cultural rather than military attitude, remained in place.

Paradoxically, *Beach Party* films project a morality that contrasts with the skimpy swimsuits on view. Conservative values are set in place from the first, as Dee Dee makes clear to friend Rhonda (Valora Noland) that she won't consider sex with Frankie before marriage. One sequence parallels Dee's attempted seduction of Robertson in *Gidget*; Dee Dee, exasperated with Frankie's frustration and roving eye for "available" girls, sets her sights on older man Sutwell. He, like The Big Kahoona, understands her motives and sends her back to Frankie, virginity intact. Annette is the only girl in the first film *not* in a bikini, wearing an old-fashioned suit that covers her navel. According to Hollywood legend, this has to do with a promise Annette made to her mentor Walt Disney who implored his former Mouseketeer not to wear revealing outfits.[12] Annette's stunning white two-piece represented a compromise between what Uncle Walt wanted and what AIP needed. The concern was not entirely without warrant; "AIP received flak from puritanical groups all over the country."[13] More than 200 socially conservative newspapers "had to airbrush out the belly button (in the film's advertisement) to appease their readers."[14] Arkoff marveled at this lingering Victorianism: "Just as though some evil lurked in the belly button."[15]

It's worth noting, though, that as the series continued, Annette's bathing suits became ever skimpier. In *Muscle Beach Party*, her navel is, if inadvertently, revealed. With each film the supposed "no navel clause" diminished. Importantly, Annette's clean-cut reputation did not suffer. She remained the Virgin goddess and, for a foil, the filmmakers recast Valora Nolan as Animal, a believer in free love. In comparison to role model Dee Dee, Animal offers a cautionary figure—a cartoonish variation on Mimieux's ill-fated non-virgin in *Where the Boys Are*. Lory Patrick plays an identical character in *Surf Party* (Maury Dexter, 1964). The impact was considerable: For the first time, the realization dawned on the American populace that cultural conservatism and moral conservatism might not necessarily go hand in hand. The epiphany: a woman's freedom for sexual display didn't imply that she also embraced freedom of sex. When worn by Annette, the once taboo bikini became a symbol of sexual chastity. Sandra Dee likewise left her Gidget-era one-piece behind to wear something more daring in *Take Her, She's Mine* (Henry Koster, 1963). The swimsuit that had, when worn by Bardot, symbolized the coming Sexual Revolution now was re-posited to represent resistance to that movement. In an age when ever more Hollywood stars were willing to pose nude for *Playboy*, Carol Lynley doing so in 1965 after reaching the legal age of 21, young women who refused to doff their bikinis could now, if with a certain irony, be perceived as old-fashioned, if in a necessary rewrite of what that term had meant. When female nudity appeared in mainstream films beginning in 1967, the Bikini Beach movies came to seem charmingly antiquated, the suit itself having undergone re-signification owing to an ever-changing social context.

Perhaps by accident, writer Lou Rusoff came up with several plot points that transformed a quickie-flick shot for $350,000.00 into a box-office bonanza. Following *Beach Party*'s August 7, 1963 release, it netted more than $4 million in profits.[16] He focused not on the true surf culture that *Gidget* had at least attempted to represent but the weekend surf crowd. Partly owing to *Gidget's* popularity, a reclusive coterie of drop-outs observed with growing anger as their lifestyle transformed into a youth craze. Frankie, Dee Dee and other focal teens arrive on the beach for a two-week vacation. After that, they'll return to school and jobs. Meanwhile, Rusoff dropped one element from *Gidget*, the constant movement from kids at play to their home lives. There are no parents on view here, nor are they mentioned. Likely, this had been the case to keep costs low. Whatever the motive, such removal from reality proved essential to their success. Here was a modern Never-Never Land. If kids nationwide could not like the onscreen teens visit this fabled if non-existent world, they could share in its youth-utopia for two hours of vicarious experience.

Another key element was nostalgia. The Fifties had been haunted by many icons; the first, Brando as Johnny in *The Wild One*. A decade later, that menacing image had withered. *Beach Party* included Eric Von Zipper (Harvey Lembeck) and his Rat Pack, with character actor Lembeck providing a point-on imitation of Brando, freeing viewers to giggle at what had once concerned them. Von Zipper and his gang appear as escapees from a half-forgotten past, slipping through a time tunnel, their dark demeanor comically contrasting with the bright sunshine.

Perhaps most significant was the casting of Annette in a role originally offered to Sandra Dee. *Gidget* (the film, not the novel) had continued the long standing notion that Aryan girls were good girls. Such a belief-system, a holdover from nineteenth-century values, had entered films at their initiation with D.W. Griffith's "Golden girls" (i.e., Anglo virgins until marriage): Lillian Gish, Mary Pickford, Mae Marsh.[17] Latinos and other ethnics, in Hollywood films (mainstream and exploitation), played Vamp-temptresses in contrast to the whitebread ideal, be she upper-class (Grace Kelly) or clean-cut middle-class (Doris Day). Dee had been posited as a teen version of the latter. Disney broke new ground when, between 1955–1958, he posited Annette as the Girl Next Door on *The Mickey Mouse Club*, challenging the cliché. Now, by starring Avalon rather than a Troy Donahue type as the male lead, Arkoff and Nicholson picked up on Disney's innovation, carrying the banner of ethnic equality into the Sixties—a decade that would be all but defined by The Movement.

Sadly, there are no African Americans in *Beach Party*. That was due to AIP's recruiting young performers (Salli Sachse, Patty Chandler) off the beaches, notably Malibu. Soon, though, Stevie Wonder was integrated as a musical guest in *Beach Blanket Bingo* (Asher, 1965), the approach Dick Clark had taken to include ever more African Americans on TV's *Bandstand*. The sequel, *Muscle Beach Party*, introduced a new element. Believing that Von Zipper's gang had been milked dry (they would be missed and return), screen-writer/co-producer Robert Dillon added a group of body-builders as comedic antagonists. In comparison to the Rat Pack, the musclemen are all male. Likewise, they show no interest (as Von Zipper did) in stealing away surf-girls. However simplistic and incorrect, during the early 1960s a myth held that body-builders were homosexuals. Musclemen were, in the pre-Arnold Schwarzenegger era, perceived as narcissists who did not pump up to impress females but themselves and perhaps other men.[18] Gayness further developed in *Beach Party* films when Tommy Kirk (1941–), a gay actor, replaced Avalon as Annette's love interest in *Pajama Party*. As was the case with Rock Hudson in *Pillow Talk*, here was a gay man playing a straight man who as part of the plot pretends to be a gay man.

Gender-bending would become a major element (and, as such, an issue) in the non-AIP *Beach Ball* (Lennie Weinrib, 1965). Two beach boys (Don Edmonds and Robert Logan) don women's clothing to slip away from the police, later forced to sing as a duet to maintain their cover. If the latter recalls Bing Crosby and Danny Kaye subbing for Rosemary Clooney and Vera-Ellen in *White Christmas* (Michael Curtiz, 1954), the former draws on memories of Jack Lemmon and Tony Curtis in *Some Like It Hot* (Billy Wilder, 1959). Again, this is situated within the context of 'harmless' entertainment, mostly taken that way by audiences of the day. More recently, Gay Studies insists on a close inspection of such images (no matter how humble any particular film) to fully grasp the manner in which subversive elements enter mainstream discourse.[19]

As in the previous films, ideas concerning gender are indeed bent. Since the viewer (however middle-of-the-road) is already invested in the male leads, any laughter elicited is not *at* the characters' expense but *with* them. Elvis disguises himself as a girl for similar purposes in *Girl Happy* (Boris Sagal, 1965), as would the frat boys in *The Girls on the Beach* (William N. Witney, 1965). In *Winter a-Go-Go* (Richard Benedict, 1965), Bob Kanter's character is played as openly gay. The experience of watching such a film is to remove the long-perceived sense of threat associated with gender transgression. Despite heterosexual men's warm memories of beach babes in bikinis, these films also forwarded a gay agenda in an altering and evolving America.

The third series entry, *Bikini Beach* (Asher, 1964), brought adults back in the form of Harvey Huntington Honeywagon (Keenan Wynn), a land-developer who plans to push young people off the beach, then build a retire-ment home for seniors. This device by writers Asher, Dillon and Leo Townsend implies a growing realization that the tenor of the times had changed since President Kennedy's assassination (11/22/1963). Any belief that enlightened adults would willingly support youthful endeavors like The Peace Corps was replaced by an intensifying sense of resentment. The mid-1950s Generation Gap came bounding back if in a more openly hostile form. No longer would kids challenge only parents and teachers but the adult-governed social-structure at large. "Don't trust anyone over 30!,"[20] the youth mantra of the late 1960s, is never verbalized here. But its sensibility motors the movie. In *Under the Yum Yum Tree* (David Swift, 1963), Jack Lemmon plays a middle-aged landlord who leers at (and attempts to seduce) bikini-clad girls by the pool. Earlier films with similar subjects, including *Bachelor in Paradise* (Jack Arnold, 1961) starring Bob Hope, posited such a male as an enviable role model; now, he's The Big Bad Wolf—not a character to be laughed with but at. Kids on view are, like those in *Beach Party*, portrayed as healthy in their more open attitudes about physicality and, in time perhaps, sexuality as well.

(a)　　　　　　　　　　　　　　　　(b)

(c)　　　　　　　　　　　　　　　　(d)

ON THE BEACH: (a) the innocent fun of early of surf cinema: *Gidget* with Sandra Dee was shot before the Bikini had become acceptable (courtesy: Columbia Pictures); (b) a two-piece, much less a bikini, remained a rarity in 1960's *Where the Boys Are* (Paula Prentiss, Dolores Hart, Yvette Mimieux, Connie Francis)/(courtesy: MGM); (c) Elvis added male beefcake to female pulchritude in his Hawaiian-lensed beach musicals (courtesy: Paramount); (d) Queen of the Beach Annette Funicello is the most covered-up girl in sight (courtesy: American International Pictures).

An odd but in retrospect less than outrageous relationship would develop between the beach films and another entertainment innovation of the early 1960s, the spy thriller. The first James Bond vehicle, *Dr. No* (Terence Young, 1963) opened in theatres a month and a half before the premiere of *Beach Party*, likewise including Bikinis. Ursula Andress' iconic appearance, rising up from the surf in a stunning white suit, introduced the item on an adult actress. Intriguingly, Luciana Paluzzi appeared as a bad girl in both *Muscle Beach Party* and *Thunderball* (Terence Young, 1965). Beverly Adams, a co-star in *How to Stuff a Wild Bikini* and *Winter a-Go-Go*, played Lovey Kravezit, Dean Martin's whacky assistant, in the Matt Helm spy series. Donna Michelle, *Playboy*'s Playmate of the Year, 1964, decorated the screen in *Beach Blanket Bingo* and the low-budget Bond take-off *Agent for H.A.R.M.* (Gerd Oswald, 1966). Arkoff and Nicholson came up with the idea of collapsing the two genres in *Dr. Goldfoot and the Bikini Machine* (Norman Taurog, 1965). The title figure (Vincent Price) caricatures the Bond villain from *Goldfinger* (Guy Hamilton, 1964). His beautiful minions, robots who kill men (but never have sex with them!), are played by beach party regulars: Susan Hart, Patty Chandler, Mary Hughes, Loree Holmes, Sue Hamilton, and Laura (daughter of Jim) Nicholson. Avalon is the surf-bum performing Bond-like service to defeat the forces of evil.

Never having appeared in a generic beach film per se, Ann-Margret did navigate from poolside with Elvis in *Viva Las Vegas* (George Sidney, 1964) to assisting Martin as Helm in *Murderer's Row* (Henry Levin, 1966). In *Out of Sight* (Lennie Weinrib, 1966), a would-be Bond (Jonathan Daly) arrives on the beach to discover three wholesome-looking Bunnies-in-bikinis— Scuba (Wende Wagner), Wipeout (Maggie Thrett), and Tuff Bod (Deanna Lund)—are paid assassins for the evil network FLUSH. Each beauty seemingly attempts to seduce the faux-agent, always planning to keep her virginity intact (and remain a "good-girl"), however casual she may be about killing. Tuff Bod marvels at the ecstasy she'll experience by inflicting death when sex is expected, insisting that she'll be a virgin still on her wedding night. Patty Chandler, "wholesome" in the AIP series, giddily said of her role in the spy thriller *The Million Eyes of Su-Maru* (Lindsay Shonteff, 1967): "For the first time in my life, I get to play—a killer!"[21] *Su-Maru* starred Shirley Eaton as pulp-fiction author Sax Rohmer's female equivalent to Dr. Fu Manchu. Previously, Eaton played the bikini babe who gets gilded in *Goldfinger*. Salli Sachse, a Beach Party regular, is one more clean-cut "slaygirl" while Avalon portrays a beach boy traveling world-wide as a teenage secret agent. In

Catalina Caper (Lee Sholem, 1967), Tommy Kirk is a scuba-obsessed college student who battles a criminal conspiracy. His bikini-clad girlfriend (Venita Wolf) is more than willing to help him waste bad guys but has no intention of allowing Kirk's character to go "all the way" until they are married.

*

Conversely, another element to emerge was a hint of proto-feminist thinking. In 1963, Betty Friedan's *The Feminine Mystique* was published, challenging the limited roles of women in our society while ushering in Second Wave Feminism. The book was largely read by intellectuals and academics of the type Susan Hayward played in *The Marriage-Go-Round*. Such ideas, though, did trickle down in college classrooms and other forums to the mainstream. *Beach Blanket Bingo* has Dee Dee repeating *Gidget*'s proto-feminist paradigm by standing up to Frankie's outrageous insistence that sky-diving is too difficult and dangerous for a woman. This might have been mere happenstance were it not for Frankie's chauvinistic rant that women belong in the kitchen, the very place which Friedan insisted females had a right to abandon. Leslie Gore didn't sing her feminist Declaration of Independence "You Don't Own Me" in *The Girls on the Beach* though her presence emphasized that theme: sorority girls cease depending on their boyfriends, banding together to achieve their goals. A similar trope occurs in *Wild Wild Winter* (Lennie Weinrib, 1966). Several ski bunnies, hardly averse to wearing bikinis on ice-clad slopes, tire of endless boys with embarrassing come-on lines, admitting to each other the sisterhood they share is more significant than superficial relationships with males. *One Way Wahine* (William O. Brown, 1965) presents a strong individual (Joy Harmon) who purchases a one-way ticket to Hawaii, where she plans to begin a new life for herself, men a non-issue. An early Hollywood feminist filmmaker, Stephanie Rothman, in *It's a Bikini World* (1967) undercut early beach film views of women as sexual objects by revealing that, beyond their visual/physical allure, these were smart, skillful women, eager to prove themselves in "a man's world."

If that sounds radical, the genre's ongoing conservatism can be documented via the line-up of Old Hollywood stars. A listing rivals the roll call of ships and heroes at the opening of Homer's *Iliad*: Peter Lorre, Buddy Hackett (*Muscle Beach Party*), Boris Karloff (*Bikini Beach*), Buster Keaton, Dorothy Lamour, Dorothy Kilgallen, Elsa Lanchester (*Pajama Party*), Keaton, Earl Wilson (*Beach Blanket Bingo*), Keaton, Mickey Rooney, Brian Donlevy (*How to Stuff a Wild Bikini*, Asher, 1965), Keaton, Karloff, Basil Rathbone and Patsy

Kelly (*The Ghost in the Invisible Bikini*), and Gary Merrill and James Gregory in the non-AIP *Clambake* (Arthur Nadel, 1967). *For Those Who Think Young* (Leslie H. Martinson, 1964), a slick if empty attempt by Frank Sinatra's production company to cash in on AIP's gold mine while furthering the career of daughter Nancy, included Anna Lee, Jack LaRue, Allen Jenkins, Robert Armstrong, George Raft, and Roger Smith. Unlike the "angry youth" movies that preceded Beach diversions and yet another set of anti-Establishment items to follow, the beach romps revived timeworn clichés for an era in which more skin could be revealed but basic values remained unchallenged. Like Elvis's vehicles, including *Girl Happy* (Boris Sagal, 1965), these were musicals—rehashes of the type that swimming star/sex symbol Esther Williams once appeared in, only with bare midriffs. Some were directed by old Hollywood hands; *Pajama Party* by Don Weis, who guided Donald O'Connor and Debbie Reynolds through their studio song 'n' dance item *I Love Melvin* (1953). When *Look* printed a cover story about Beach Musicals, in 1964, the genre ceased to be even mildly edgy, as did the once controversial Bikini bathing-suit.

Perhaps that served as the germination point for a swift demise. Many high-schoolers who once flocked to *Beach Party* were now off at college, their interests altered. A third wave of American youth would, during the late 1960s, turn their backs on not only Old Hollywood films but supposed youth-movies that embraced traditional values. Also, AIP made so many sequels so quickly that any peekaboo appeal at getting to see Bikinis onscreen lost its ability to allure. Other indie companies churned out similar if often inferior products: *Surf Party* (Maury Dexter, 1964), *Beach Ball* (Lennie Weinrib, 1965), *The Beach Girls and the Monster* (Jon Hall, 1965), *Daytona Beach Weekend* (Bob Welborn, 1965), *The Girls on the Beach* (Willia N. Witney, 1965), *A Swingin' Summer* (Robert Sparr, 1965), and *Wild on the Beach* (Dexter, 1965). More than one genre fan saw too many clinkers and simply gave up. Also, times had so altered that the attitudes embodied by beach films seemed antiquated. Bikini-clad virgins frugging on the beach appeared silly when at the next theatre over sophisticated hippie-chicks did so as a prelude to an orgy in *The Day the Fish Came Out* (Michael Cacoyannis, 1967).

People are rarely willing to pay for what they can get for free. When *Beach Party* premiered, ecstatically wild dancing or the up-to-the-minute sound of acts like the Beach Boys were nowhere to be found on TV. ABC's *Shindig* premiered on Sept. 16, 1964. NBC's *Hullabaloo* followed suit on Jan. 12, 1965. Many of the emergent rock 'n' roll acts that had exclusively been seen in Beach Movies suddenly appeared on a weekly basis. As for the dancing, Lada

Edmund (Jr.), a beach babe in For *Those Who Think Young*, became The Girl in the Cage. Another surf-and-sand veteran, Carole Shelyne, would similarly perform on *Shindig* from 1964–1966. If Bikinis were not yet on view on TV (in the mid-Sixties Barbara Eden was infamously required to conceal her belly button in *I Dream of Jeannie* (NBC; 1965–1970), that too would alter when *Rowan & Martin's Laugh-In* (NBC; 1968–1973) debuted. Goldie Hawn, Judy Carne, and others gleefully danced in such swimsuits. The Beach Genre might be seen as a casualty of its own swift-spreading success.

*

That freed filmmakers to abandon the Bikini in favor of a return to the basics: i.e., surfing. The first such project, *Ride the Wild Surf* (Don Taylor, 1964), had originally been intended as a co-starring vehicle for Jan (William Berry) and Dean (Ormsby Torrence), the first surf-style musicians to achieve a number one mainstream hit with "Surf City" (1963). Their roles were eventually played by Peter Brown and Tab Hunter, though the duo did sing the title song over the closing-credits. Along with Fabian, male and female stars (Barbara Eden, Shelley Fabares, and Susan Hart) were encouraged to play their roles realistically to capture an actual surfer's desire to simultaneously conquer and surrender to nature, in the form of a great wave. Legendary surfers like Mickey Dora and Greg Noll had appeared in *Beach Party* films strictly to 'make some bread.' Their efforts here, photographed by gifted Joseph Biroc, conveyed in a way AIP had not the combination of physicality and spirituality that mutely speak to a surfer's soul. Much of the drama is over-wrought, in writing and performance. Yet that hardly diminishes our visual education about sportsmen who did follow the sun, not only on vacations or weekends.

But the best was yet to come. If AIP's final beach films *How To Stuff a Wild Bikini* and *The Ghost in the Invisible Bikini*, as well as latter rip-offs like *It's a Bikini World*, failed to find an audience, a documentary created as a labor of love went on to become the surprise commercial (and critical) hit of 1966. Bruce Brown (1937–) had been shooting surf movies since his 16 mm non-theatrical *Slippery When Wet* (1959). This he would show at lectures on a sport he adored. With five more such projects under his belt, Brown came up with the idea of a movie that would appeal equally to diehard surfers and mainstream audiences. Brown raised enough cash to shoot a gonzo reality flick. He followed two California-based surfers, Robert August, a top student, and Mike Hynson, a wiseguy pretty boy, around the world:

I've always felt that an endless summer would be the ultimate for a surfer. It's really simple to cross the equator during our winter and find summer in the Southern Hemisphere. I thought how lovely just to travel around the world following summer . . . [22]

Here were Kerouac's Subterraneans, rising up from their cellar clubs yet still searching for a Great Truth always receding on the horizon. The film's imagery, as well as Brown's voice-over, conveys an understanding of the sport of surfing in a way no previous movie had. Despite beautiful settings and bodies on display, a surfer experiences a subtle flirtation with death, most notably when daring the legendary waves on Oahu's North Shore. Knowledge of one's vulnerability only added to each surfer's sense of existing as an individual among a *cognoscenti* who grasp that the elusive Perfect Wave is a sought-after ideal, always pursued, never encountered, yet the only route to transcendence. Brown articulated the "surfer mentality: You just work if you have to. I work 2 ½ years, and I'll go surf 2 ½ years. Then I'll be even."[23] If there can be no conclusion to a quixotic quest, The Big One always occurring on the next beach over, any joy is inherent in the journey: a noble if doomed attempt to achieve Nirvana.

*

By the late Sixties, America's mood had not bounced back from the emotional and spiritual depression following President Kennedy's death. If anything, the national spirit further soured. The Civil Rights Movement underwent an ugly turn when three activists were murdered in Mississippi during the summer of 1964. Ghetto-burnings occurred in major cities; abroad, the Vietnam War escalated, ever more young people called up to serve in a conflict that appeared less comprehensible than Korea. During spring 1968, Dr. Martin Luther King was assassinated (4/4/1968), then Sen. Robert Kennedy (6/6/1968). Clearly, the JFK killing hadn't been some grotesque aberration but, apparently, the New Normal in an ever more violent society. Surf cinema could not survive intact; if it were to continue, the films must take on a more conflicted tone. In *Lord Love a Duck* (George Axelrod, 1966), Tuesday Weld satirized the kind of bikini beach girls Sandra Dee once played at face value. *Don't Make Waves* (Alexander Mackendrick, 1967), from Ira Wallach's *Muscle Beach*, crystalized the death of idealism as one aging would-be surf bum (Tony Curtis) falls in love with a bikini-clad beach bunny (Sharon Tate) only to grasp, once he beds her, the person is nothing like her glamorous persona. *The Sweet Ride* (Harvey Hart, 1968) portrayed three aging surfers (Tony Franciosa, Michael Sarrazin, Bob Denver) not as free-living rebels but pathetic life-losers, unable to commit to women and build mature, meaningful relationships. Though not a genre film, *Out of It* (Paul Williams, 1969) offered a Long Island beach sequence between a high school football star (Jon Voight) and the local blonde teen-queen (Lada Edmund, Jr.) in which he complains that the good times (i.e., Happy Days) are over; he and others like him are about to be drafted.

Finally, *The Arousers* (Curtis Hanson, 1972) provided an epilogue to the Beach cycle. This low-budget horror film stars Tab Hunter as Eddie, a hand-some, sandy-haired 'hunk.' He hangs around surfer spots and, older now, men-tors young boys as to the ways of women. In this, he seems not so different from Big Kahuna in *Gidget* or, perhaps, an older version of Steamer, Hunter's character in *Ride the Wild Surf*. Young beach bunnies come on to him but he rejects their advances. From the opening sequences, however, we sense some-thing's 'off.' This is a slasher film set on the beach, not another romantic com-edy. Losing control, Eddie pushes a girl away, causing her to be killed. Initially, Eddie appears guilt-ridden, then realizes the experience provided him with an incredible release. A surfer second-cousin to Norman Bates in *Psycho* (Alfred Hitchcock, 1960), Eddie strikes up relationships with other sexually frank girls, murdering rather than satisfying them when the moment of sexual truth arrives.

During the decade and a half since *Gidget,* the virgin as role model for women had all but disappeared. By the early 1970s, good girls could not only display their bodies in Bikinis but also share them with men. Here we discover the root of Eddie's problem and motoring of his murders. Eddie can't deal with the new paradigm. Unable to cope with the end of a dichotomization of women, "good" and "bad" based on a female's degree of sexual experience, he strikes out blindly against girls who for him represent a sensibility that goes against the grain of everything he lived by in the early 1960s. "Is it me?" the first confused girl/victim asks, moments before her demise. No! it's *him;* his inability to adjust to a changing world. As to this, he might be seen as signi-fier of an entire generation of men, Eddie's acts of violence representing their simmering, if of course less explosive, resentment.

Simply, the beach genre could not co-exist with a return, however par-adoxical, to what Brigitte Bardot had engendered a decade and a half ear-lier: the Bikini as symbol for a women's freedom to display her body,but also to legitimize the female body relevance for personal sexual satisfaction. For too long, surf 'n' sand had served as a conduit for Songs of Innocence. By 1965 popular culture necessarily began to embrace actual experiences of the type Bebe in Europe, Van Doren in the U.S., had demanded. The Sexual Revolution, in a state of evolution since the World War II years, now over-took America. And, with it, the Hollywood product.

· 7 ·

THE LAST AMERICAN VIRGIN

Sandra Dee and The Sexual Revolution

"If it feels good, do it."
—Aleister Crowley, 1904

The germination of a New Morality[1] began shortly after the turn of the century, increased following the First World War, then exploded immediately
after World War II. *Sexual Behavior in the Human Male* (1950) by researcher
Alfred Kinsey (1894–1956) revealed "the vast difference between American
sexual behavior (that) the society wanted to believe existed and American
sexual practices as they" did exist.[2] Adultery proved to be common among
married males; 80% of interviewees admitted to having cheated. Kinsey's
follow-up, *Sexual Behavior in the Human Female* (1953), sold 250,000+ copies.
The publication insisted that, far from being disgusted by the thought of
sex, normal women were obsessed with it. While lingering Victorian standards insisted that "good" women must rise above such primitive instincts,[3]
Margaret Sanger (1879–1966) renewed her life-long crusade for birth control
with financial backing from Katharine McCormick. These pioneers defied
existing Comstock Laws[4] and the Catholic Church, challenging a 19th century ethic that sex should not be a source of pleasure, rather a despised chore;
evil yet necessary to produce children; i.e., original sin. Dr. 'Goody' Pincus

(1903–1967) offered his biological skills and, on June 23, 1960, the FDA awarded a seal of approval to the first oral contraceptive, available to married women for the purpose of limiting the number of children. Swiftly, the Pill was embraced by single females as well.[5]

Several key films illustrated the obvious need for a saner, safer approach to sexuality. *Peyton Place* (Mark Robson, 1957), like the 1956 novel by Grace Metalious, reasserted the accuracy of Kinsey's reports. Based on the author's observations of life in a New England small town, this domestic epic opens in the calm-before-the-storm preceding WWII. Top-billing went to Lana Turner as Constance Mackenzie, a single mother dedicated to daughter Allison (Diane Varsi). This teenager emerges as the focal character thanks to a voice-over narrative, her middle-class coming-of-age story paralleled with that of Selena Cross (Hope Lange), who hails from the wrong side of the tracks. Selena's stepfather (Arthur Kennedy), an abusive alcoholic, isn't unaware of the girl's maturing body, raping her, she in self-defense kills him. Allison will be accused of engaging in sex with a virginal lad (Russ Tamblyn) though their supposed nude swimming incident remained "innocent." Another classmate, Betty Anderson (Terry Moore), faces hurdles in marrying a rich boy (Barry Coe) as his father (Leon Ames) objects. This owes less to class standing than Betty's 'bad reputation' (she's a non-virgin). Despite melodramatic indulgences, the film achieves its aim: Kinsey-like revealing that behind the façade of every seemingly nice, normal community, sexual repression simmers.

Essentially, 'Peyton Place' was *Our Town*'s "Grovers' Corners" with its dark underbelly at last exposed. In this context, Allison, Selena, and Betty served as templates for distinct types of females taking shape in the modern world. Betty is the 'easy girl,' hardly a new concept. The difference is that following Rodney Harrington's death, grieving widow Betty wins over his dad, who gradually comes to understand that a non-virgin-before-marriage isn't necessarily a bad person. Selena, who seeks an abortion, is portrayed as a sympathetic girl driven to the brink by circumstances not of her making. Allison, whose sexual relations aren't dramatized, presents an early example of a 'normal' girl morphing into womanhood. Setting a career in publishing above any relations with men, Allison offers a precursor of the feminist-era woman. (See Ch. 8.)

For teens in the audience, the pivotal sequence occurs as Constance joins high-school principal Rossi (Lee Philips) for coffee. A born-again virgin, Connie is attracted to the man but terrified of sex, even in the context of potential marriage. This owes to her previous affair with a married man, which produced Allison. When Constance returns home to discover Allison's party guests necking with the lights low, she explodes. This new generation believe themselves to be behaving well, as none indulges in intercourse. They're as shocked by Constance's reaction as she is to what, in her view, is a virtual orgy. Though the term Generation Gap isn't employed, *Peyton Place* was one of the first films to posit onscreen that rapidly developing divide between old and new.

Four years later, another movie addressed sexual issues via a period piece setting. *Splendor in the Grass* (Elia Kazan, 1961), set in the late 1920s, can be read as an unofficial prequel to *Peyton Place*. Clearly, it's a superior work: an artistic milestone attesting to the skills of its creators and emergence during the 1960s of a New Hollywood. William Inge wrote the screenplay; his previous work included the play *Bus Stop* (1955) and its movie adaptation (1956). Though a major release from Warner Bros., Hollywood honchos were aware that more than two-thirds of the nation's moviegoers were between the ages of twelve and twenty-five.[6] As a result, Natalie Wood as Deanie Loomis and Warren Beatty (in his film debut) as Bud Stamper become the dramatic focus.

"HEY! YOU CAN'T SAY THAT IN A MOVIE!" Maggie McNamara drops a verbal bomb when she dares to use the word "Virgin" in front of William Holden and David Niven in the otherwise tame and notably old-fashioned *The Moon Is Blue*.

SCENES FROM THE SEXUAL REVOLUTION, WAVE ONE: (a) innocent/virginal teens (Russ Tamblyn, Diane Varsi) inadvertently create a scandal by slipping into the woods in *Peyton Place* (courtesy: Jerry Wald Prods./20th Century-Fox); (b) an in-love couple (Warren Beatty, Natalie Wood) try to discern how far is "too far" in *Splendor in the Grass* (courtesy: Newton/NBI/Warner Bros.); (c) wholesome kids (Troy Donahue, Sandra Dee) face the reality of pregnancy in *A Summer Place* (courtesy: Warner Bros.) (d) a college prof (James Mason) becomes the target of a Swedish exchange student (Julie Newmar) in *The Marriage-Go-Round* (courtesy: Daystar/20th Century-Fox); (e) casual sex ceased to be a 'no-no' once James Bond (Sean Connery) and golden girl Shirley Eaton hit the sack in *Goldfinger* (courtesy: Eon Prods./ UA); (f) Pollyanna grows up as former Disney star Hayley Mills adjusts to la dolce vita in *Take a Girl Like You* (1970); (courtesy: Albion/Columbia).

Inge (1913–1973) drew upon his earlier theatre-work and the ongoing obsessions that drove him to suicide at age 60. Deanie's desire, at her mother's prodding, to marry up on the social scale—they are respectable middle-class, whereas Bud is the son of a local (Kansas) mill owner (Pat Hingle)—recalls Kim Novak in *Picnic* (Joshua Logan, 1955). The mental problems that nearly destroy Deanie, who seems stable enough initially, echoes *Dark at the Top of the Stairs* (Delbert Mann, 1960) with Shirley Knight. As in *Peyton Place*, the problem here is sexual repression dating back to Puritan ideals. A double standard, never admitted publicly, allowed the male to secretly satisfy animal "appetites," leading to dichotomization of women as 'good' (virgins) or 'bad' (non-virgins).[7] In the film, Bud's father suggests his boy enjoy himself on the sly with the town slut (Jan Norris) to take the pressure off Deanie, of whom he approves, until marriage. When confused Bud adheres to such disastrous advice, a domestic tragedy results; the well-matched young people marry others ill-suited for them. If there is any hint of optimism at the end, this exists in the implied hope that, in the future, there might yet be a better way. After all, things do change.

That process served as subject matter for *A Summer Place* (Delmer Daves, 1959), with its storyline contemporary. Like the majority of pre-1960 "important" productions, the focus—at least initially—is on adults, primarily the female lead, Sylvia (Dorothy McGuire). Like Deanie, Sylvia hails from a solid family. She was careful to remain a virgin despite love for a poor boy, Ken (Richard Egan). Owing to pressure from another ambitious mother, Sylvia instead married wealthy Bart (Arthur Kennedy). They now share his mansion on Pine Island, Maine, along with teenage son Johnny (Troy Donahue). Their problem: Bart (like Mr. Stamper) has surrendered to alcoholism and his money is gone. To make a go of it, they rent out rooms in their frayed genteel palace. Who should arrive but Ken, now a self-made millionaire. Also, Ken's frigid wife Helen (Constance Ford) and their daughter Molly (Sandra Dee). Even as Sylvia and Ken slip into a long-repressed affair, the kids strike up a summer romance. One poignant scene occurs after Johnny and Molly take a sailing trip during which their sloop overturns. Innocently, the two spend the night together. But when they are discovered the next day, Helen coldly insists that a doctor inspect her daughter to ascertain that Molly is still "pure." In the aftermath, a humiliated Molly becomes so distraught that she, like Deanie with Bud, throws herself at Johnny. The difference here: two generations later he rejects dichotomization as to women. Molly remains a good girl in his eyes even after they make love and she becomes pregnant. Youth's values, in society and on film, have altered.

*

An irony exists in that Sandra Dee's first major role in a big movie casts her as a good girl who gets pregnant. In her highly popular 'Tammy' films, Dee came to represent a teen version of Doris Day, that mature star simultaneously thought of as the "professional virgin" in grown-up sex-comedies.[8] By decade's end, in the play *Grease!* (1969), black-leather jacketed bad girl Rizzo mocks the blonde good girl: "Hey, look at me. I'm Sandra Dee! Loaded with virginity!" In *Tammy Tell Me True* (Harry Keller, 1961) the spirited country girl heads off to college where she becomes romantically (though not sexually) involved with her teacher (John Gavin); in *Tammy and the Doctor* (Harry Keller, 1963), this occurs with an equally handsome surgeon (Peter Fonda). In time, Dee would become so closely associated with Tammy Tyree, it comes as a surprise to many that she did not originate that character. The 1960s franchise had begun in the late 1950s; the first, *Tammy and the Bachelor* (Joseph Peveny, 1957), expressing the abiding sensibility of that decade. Tammy, who according to the narrative recently turned 16, was played by 27-year-old Debbie Reynolds. Cid Ricketts Sumner's novel *Tammy Out of Time* presented child-woman Tambrey as a barefoot girl in blue jeans, living far from the madding crowd. Tammy's home is a houseboat on the Mississippi River; she shares that hillbilly abode with Grandpa Dinwitty (Walter Brennan). Peter Brent (Leslie Nielsen), a young Louisiana plantation owner, crashes his plane nearby; the swamp denizens rescue him. A genuine affection develops between Peter and Tammy, despite his engagement to Barbara (Mala Powers), a pseudo-sophisticated social-climber back in cynical civilization.

The film's unexpected box-office success happily surprised execs at Universal. Shot for $700,000, *Tammy* brought in over $3 million in ticket sales, ranking it among the Top Ten hits of 1957.[9] Tammy comes across as a second cousin to Daisy Mae in Al Capp's *Li'l Abner* comics as Tammy also oozes backwoods sensuousness. Yet she embodies a neo-Victorian value system, which says much about late 1950s girls who identified with her. Early on, Peter swims nearly naked with Tammy, *Blue Lagoon* style, without attempting to take advantage. He appreciates her combination of open sensuality and radical innocence. Later, at his home, they curl up on a bed. Yet it never occurs to Peter to impose himself on her before marriage. As Marjorie Rosen later remarked about Dee's Tammy:

> While she presented the most passive, fluttery pink-and-white-ribbons perfection, her ample mouth recalled the petulance of an adolescent Bardot. By scaling down this image of feline sexuality for the nubile high-school set, Dee wove the transition

between the fifties' naivete and the sixties nymphet, exhibiting a provocative self-awareness, almost a fear of her own sexuality, which in view of the decade's moral expectations, was sensible.[10]

*

Though the Nymphet has always been associated with the 1960s, the first such film, *Baby Doll* (Elia Kazan), debuted in 1956. Earlier, Kazan and author Tennessee Williams had challenged the Production Code with *A Streetcar Named Desire*. However concerned the play (1947) and later film (1951) were with sexuality, their drama focused on adults. Not so *Baby Doll*. A wily Southerner (Eli Wallach) enacts cruel revenge on a neighbor (Karl Malden) whom he believes cheated him. Wallach's Loki-like character sets out to compromise the virginity of his enemy's child-bride (Carroll Baker). Baby Doll lolls around in a cradle-like bed in sensuous lingerie, impatiently await-ing legal age before their bond can be consummated. In truth, she hardly appears aghast as to an early immoral tryst. This dark comedy presented a true enigma; an adults-only film about a girl-child, set in the sleaziest of situations, nonetheless a work that could only be appreciated by the most sophisticated viewer.

In its original conception, the Nymphet element had been a side light. During the shoot, Kazan realized Baker's writhing about might create a sen-sation and heightened this aspect.[11] A poster in theatre lobbies depicted the blonde sucking her thumb, like some unaware infant. This proved arousing and disturbing to potential moviegoers. The image, shortly an icon, set off a national debate. The Roman Catholic Church denounced the film while *Time* insisted that *Baby Doll* was "the dirtiest American-made motion pic-ture that had ever been legally exhibited."[12] Years later, Wallach would shake his head in bemusement: "What the hell was the furor all about?"[13] If it was 'about' anything, the sparks flared owing to the notion that an existing atti-tude about girls—they ought to remain virgins until marriage—had been called into question for the first time in a mainstream film. Five years earlier Maggie MacNamara dared speak the forbidden 'v' word in *The Moon Is Blue* (Otto Preminger, 1953). Yet she did so only to defend such status. Whether or not Baby Doll was conquered proved a moot point. She neither feared nor felt guilty about that possibility; here was the heart of all outrage.

Baby Doll would be followed by *Bonjour Tristesse* (Otto Preminger, 1958) in which sophisticate David Niven's romance with a mature woman (Deborah Kerr) is menaced by his worldly-beyond-her-years daughter (Jean Seberg) who harbors Electra-like feelings. During the 1960s, everything blew wide open. In *The Last Sunset* (Robert Aldrich, 1961), cowboy Kirk Douglas purposefully walks to his death in a gunfight after realizing the underage blonde (Carol Lynley) he's just bedded is his daughter from a previous tryst. "How," advertisements asked a year later, "did they ever make a movie out of *Lolita?*" This referred to the Stanley Kubrick film of Vladimir Nabokov's acclaimed novel. In truth, 'they' did not. Nabokov's Dolores Haze hadn't been an overdeveloped teenager but a skinny 12-year-old child; Humbert Humbert a serial molester targeting the tyke. In so doing, the book's Humbert repeats a similar action from his past. In the film, Lo, as played by 14-year-old Sue Lyon, is a 15-year-old-girl/woman: first glimpsed by Humbert luxuriating in a bikini, flashing this recently arrived man (James Mason) a come-hither look. This Humbert has seemingly never before been attracted to a younger woman. Then again, this is no normal teen, rather the Nymphet of Sixties' Cinema incarnate: fifteen or sixteen, going on 21; one moment flirtatious, the next coy, then demure.

Earlier, *Claudelle Inglish* (Gordon Douglas, 1961) had depicted the process by which a 1950s-style Sandra Dee might transform into a 1960s Lyon/Lolita. As in Erskine Caldwell's novel, here is one more cautionary fable as to what might befall the good-est of good girls (i.e., the most virginal) should she slip even once. The title character (Diane McBain), a Georgia teen, adores a handsome farm boy (Chad Everett). Their pastoral existence ends when he's drafted. On their final night, he promises to marry Claudelle upon return. The vulnerable girl "gives in." Shortly, her devotion is shattered by a "Dear Claudelle" letter. When word leaks out, other hillbillies who previously coveted Claudelle as a potential bride now only want to take her out on the sly for sex. The onetime innocent turns into a cold-hearted Nymphet. In a bizarre conclusion, Claudelle dies by shotgun blast from a crazed dad whose son was destroyed by their dalliances, qualifying Claudelle as the first onscreen victim of the then-emergent Sexual Revolution.

THE NYMPHET COMES OF AGE: (a) France's Bardot created a revolutionary screen prototype, the under-age sexpot, in such films as *Come Dance With Me* (courtesy: Francis Cosne/ Kingsley International/Union Films); (b) Carroll Baker brought the nymphet to U.S. screens in *Baby Doll* (courtesy: Newtown Prods./Warner Bros.) (c) Jean Seberg incarnated an innocent-looking waif who still plays with dolls while plotting a murder in *Bonjour, Tristesse* (courtesy: Wheel Prods./Columbia); (d) Sue Lyon combined the still-controversial Bikini with a Pretty Baby archetype in *Lolita* (courtesy: MGM); (e) Terry Southern's radical rewrite of *Candide* introduced Ewa Aulin as 'Candy' (courtesy: ABC/Corona); (f) Joy Harmon combines the Nymphet icon in tandem with American car culture in *Cool Hand Luke* (Jalem/Warner Bros.)

France's Brigitte Bardot had introduced the archetype of a wide-eyed underage beauty who lays waste to men and boys alike in the art-house import *And God Created Woman* (Roger Vadim, 1956). Most Nymphets were blonde: Beverly Adland in *Cuban Rebel Girls* (Errol Flynn, 1959); Jenny Maxwell in *Blue Hawaii* (1961); Yvette Mimieux in *Toys in the Attic* (George Roy Hill, 1963); Leslie Parrish in *The Manchurian Candidate* (John Frankenheimer, 1963)) Teri Hope in *Fun in Acapulco* (Richard Thorpe, 1963), Andrea Dromm in *The Russians Are Coming, The Russians Are Coming* (Norman Jewison, 1966); Janet Landgard in *The Swimmer* (Frank Perry, 1968) and Tuesday Weld in *Pretty Poison* (Noel Black, 1968) and *I Walk the Line* (John Frankenheimer, 1970). Many were English: Sarah Miles in *Term of Trial* (Peter Glenville, 1962); Susannah York in *Tom Jones* (Tony Richardson, 1963), Hayley Mills in *Gypsy Girl* (John Mills, 1965), Judy Geeson in *To Sir, With Love* (James Clavell, 1967), and Sue George in *All Neat in Black Stockings* (Christopher Morahan, 1969). Occasionally, there might be a brunette: Stephanie Powers in *Experiment in Terror* (Blake Edwards, 1963), Pamela Tiffin in *Harper* (Jack Smight, 1966). Raven-haired Brigid Bazlen played Salome as a Biblical-era Go-Go dancer in *King of Kings* (Nicholas Ray, 1961). Or redhead: Ann-Margret in *Bus Riley's Back in Town* (Harvey Hart, 1965).

Perhaps the definitive Nymphet appears in *Cool Hand Luke* (Stuart Rosenberg, 1967), detailing life on a deep-South chain-gang. One hot day, while Luke (Paul Newman) and others slave away repairing a road, a blonde (Joy Harmon), identified only as The Girl, drives up, parks in their line of vision, and sets about washing her car. Purposefully, she sloshes herself with soapy water. A cruel glint in her eyes and overt body language make clear that she takes pleasure in so torturing the men. "She don't know what she's doing," one mutters. "She knows *exactly* what she's doing!" Luke replies. We encounter what Laura Mulvey would eventually label as 'the male gaze,'[14] if in context presented from an anti-feminist point of view: men stare at women not because it's in their nature to do so but because women demand it.

This Sixties cycle reached an apex with *Candy* (Christian Marquand, 1968), based on Terry Southern's notorious "naughty" novel. The book was considered un-filmable when published in 1958. The shattering of the Production Code in 1967 by *Bonnie and Clyde* and *The Graduate* altered that. A big-studio (Columbia) major release (Cinerama), *Candy* featured male superstars (Marlon Brando and Richard Burton among them) in cameos and was distributed as a Christmas holiday release, adding insult to injury for conservatives who saw this as an assault on their traditional values. Candy (played by Ewa Aulin, a

17-year-old Scandinavian beauty-contest winner) emerges as a variation on Voltaire's *Candide* (1759), giddily wandering from one precarious experience to the next, here all of a sexual nature. What distinguishes *Candy* from previous Nymphet movies is the casual manner in which "sex-capades" are portrayed. Some of the men Candy meets apparently "score" while others do not. Blithely, Candy rolls about in the semi-nude. Her virginity is shed as swiftly as her miniskirts and chic outfits. There is no guilt after any such encounter.

*

If at the decade's opening Sandra Dee offered a transitional figure between 1950s naïfs and 1960s nymphets, Ann-Margret (1943–) seized on that notion and ran with it. On Broadway, in the 1960 production of *Bye Bye Birdie*, Susan Watson played Kim MacAfrey, typical mid-American teen, as a undeveloped girl, precisely what the play called for. When Kim accepts boyfriend Hugo's pin, she sets about planning their future. Kim sings "How Lucky to be a Woman (Like Me)." Watson's performance elicited the response producers had hoped for: laughter owing to the irony of a teensy girl-child expressing such cynical sentiments:

> To have one job to do:
> Pick out a boy and change him
> Into the man you want him to be.
> How lucky to be a woman like *me*.[15]

Three years later, Ann-Margret performed that number in the film by George Sidney, any irony absent. A well-developed young woman of 20, Ann-Margret mouthed the song while performing a striptease, rolling about on her bed. While critics considered this a betrayal of the source, another perspective insists that this alteration was necessary, considering the time lag between stage and film versions. Watson had played a typical 1958 teen, the year in which the play was set; Ann-Margret, an equally vivid representative of the Second Wave of teens who reached sixteen in 1963, the film's year of release, also its time period.

All the same, Ann-Margret's Kim is a virgin. If previously there had been a clear-cut dichotomy—a girl was either wild on and off the dance floor, like Mamie Van Doren, or shy, virginal, and demure, Sandra-Dee style—Ann-Margret combined elements of each. Her persona: the virgin-slut, a wild-child as Terpsichore if a hold-out when in some boy's arms. There had been a precedent for all that was about to alter onscreen and off: *Because They're Young* (Paul Wendkos, 1960) offered a half-hearted defense of Ann (Tuesday Weld), a decent, ambitious (she hopes to be an actress) high-school girl who "slipped" once with a bad boy, Griff (Michael Callan). Ann keeps her secret, aspiring to be the girlfriend of a good boy, Buddy (Warren Berlinger), who has no notion of Ann's previous mis-step. The film transforms Ann into a heroine, particularly when she publicly reveals her non-virginal status to rescue Buddy from an unfair charge of assaulting Griff. All the same, the film doesn't let us know if Bud and Ann will make a go of it; their chances are shaky at best. All of this is contrasted with the foil of Jim (Doug McClure) and Ricky (Roberta Shore), she posited as role-model. In his sexual hunger (Jim here resembles *Splendor*'s Bud Stamper) Ricky, like Deanie, insists they not "go all the way." In comparison, Ann is a cautionary figure.

One film caricatured Virgin-mania, the cult of marriage, and the Nymphet obsession. In *Double Trouble* (Norman Taurog, 1967), Elvis Presley drives madly about Europe in hopes of finding some country that will allow him to marry an underage girl (Annette Day) he's gone mad for.

*

Meanwhile, what a teenage boy hoped for once he held a girl in his arms had altered drastically during the past three years, largely as a result of *Playboy*. When the first issue of that once-daring publication hit the streets of Chicago in December 1953, Hugh Hefner (1929–) hoped to sell a decent number of the 70,000 issues he'd barely financed. These would, with a little luck, be purchased by males over 21. Thanks to the inclusion of several nude photographs of Marilyn Monroe, now a superstar though a hungry model when she had posed in the buff for Tom Kelly, *Playboy*'s first issue sold out. Within a year, the magazine had not only become a success but impacted the tenor of its times. Rather than being, like sleazy girly books of the past, sold under the counter, *Playboy* was displayed alongside mainstream publications. The young women who followed Monroe as "Playmates of the Month" did not convey a dark Bettie Paige edginess but embodied The Girl Next Door, if now with her clothes off. Hef's column, "The Playboy Philosophy," insisted that a hedonistic lifestyle was preferable to an outmoded (if it had ever actually been viable) Victorian code. In less than five years, this monthly had, for millions of American men, reversed long-held values.

The first film to openly portray Hefner's new sensibility was *The Tender Trap* (Charles Walters, 1955). As Charlie Reader, Frank Sinatra embodies the *Playboy* ideal. He's a well-to-do bachelor, 'entertaining' a quartet of diverse beauties in his lavish apartment. Then he meets an actress (Debbie Reynolds). Reader hopes to draw her into his stable of sleek race-horse-like playmates.

Though hardly oblivious to his charms, she'll date but not sleep with him; not until he marries her. She may be the last American virgin; take her or leave her. Eventually, he agrees. This initial stage of the Sexual Revolution freed men to play around but failed to challenge the stigma that a woman who engaged in such activity must be ruled out for a serious relationship.

As the Sixties dawned, something happened which even Hefner had not likely foreseen. In half a decade, *Playboy* became so mainstream that ever younger men were exposed to it. By 1961, even as that First Wave of American teen-agers entered college, many moms and pops purchased a subscription for their boys. Sinatra in *The Tender Trap* would be joined onscreen by younger versions of The Playboy. Pop singer Bobby Darin (1936–1973), hyped as a Frank Sinatra for the rock 'n' roll generation, brought a younger equivalent of Charlie Reader to the screen: The wiseguy pseudo-sophisticate who scores with lots of girls. However, he like an earlier generation of men still hungers for a virgin bride, the major difference being that the Pill had rendered such status ever rarer. In *Come September* (Robert Mulligan, 1961), Darin played out this roundelay with Sandra Dee, shortly to become Mrs. Darin in real-life. In *State Fair* (Jose Ferrer, 1962), an updating of the 1945 Richard Rodgers-Oscar Hammerstein II musical, with Pamela Tiffin embodying the virgin (as a wistful farm girl). As this was a new decade, geared to a new generation of moviegoers, something significant occurs that was *not* included in *The Tender Trap*. The Dee and Tiffin characters each, at their respective movie's mid-points, appear on the edge of "giving in." A new possibility appeared on cinematic and social horizons: good girls, as Tiffin states outright, are *not* angels, existing on some higher moral level than the seducible females. They experience the same pangs of desire. The difference is, they must still continue to try and live up to the Victorian ideal, less because their basic values tell them to than that they're smart enough to grasp this is a survival tactic for any young woman still hoping for marriage. Two years later, such a paradigm still remained, if in its final throes. *For Those Who Think Young* (Leslie L. Martinson, 1964) had Tiffin, as a West Coast college girl, winning a rich handsome playboy (James Darren) solely because she alone resisted his charms.

As often occurs, less respectable movies had already suggested that this was an outdated approach. *College Confidential* (Albert Zugsmith, 1960) features Steve Allen as a Kinsey-like sociology prof who, while conducting a sex sur-vey, realizes that most of his female students have secretively surrendered their virginity. As the Pill was accessed by ever younger women in actuality, the onscreen image of the all-American-girl necessarily altered. The extent of this sea change can be understood by comparing two ensemble films from the early 1960s. In *Where the Boys Are* (Henry Levin, 1960), four Chicago college-girls (Dolores Hart, Paula Prentiss, Connie Francis, Yvette Mimieux) head to Florida's Daytona Beach for spring break. Products of their times, all are intent on meeting eligible guys with marriage in mind. We have the impression that they are all virgins. One (Hart) is wooed by a slick playboy (George Hamilton). When she refuses to bed him, he initially dumps her to pursue easy conquests. In time, he (not surprisingly) returns to propose marriage. Their happily-ever-after ending contrasts with the cautionary fable involving Mimieux, who quickly gives in to a boy. He loses interest; as a result, she has a nervous breakdown, madly wandering down a late-night highway in a floridly overwrought scene.

Three years later, the same director featured Hart (in her final screen appearance) in *Come Fly With Me* (1963). She here plays a virtual redo of her *Where the Boys Are* character, now a little older, working as an international airline stewardess. The one thing that has not changed for her or the other focal girls (Pamela Tiffin, Lois Nettleton) is that marriage remains their aim. Glamorous careers are perceived only as a temporary stop-gap in that direction and a means of meeting eligible men (particularly those flying First Class). The distinction is that female virginity no longer constitutes an issue, not for the girls nor for the men they come into contact with. At one point, Hart's character spends the night with a handsome European (Karl Boehm). The film neglects to tell us whether or not they engage in sex. The point: *it doesn't matter*—not in terms of whether he might later be willing to marry her. She may or may not have been a virgin before that night. It doesn't seem likely, true for both her girlfriends. In the post-pill era, the assumption on the part of young men is that most girls aren't. What had been the signifier of purity and innocence for millennia had overnight become irrelevant.

*

How the mainstream value system altered so quickly can be best understood by considering another influential magazine. Premiering in 1886, *Cosmopolitan* had been created as a guide for young women of high quality who wished to live by ladylike standards of the day. With its firm sense of the do's and don'ts, this monthly guide to respectability as wife and mother reached its height of popularity during the mid-1950s. Then, the emergent suburban lifestyle led to wild rumors of everything from wife-swapping to sordid affairs. Motor courts, established along every highway as a low-priced alternative to old-fashioned downtown hotels, were reputed to be hotbeds for mid-afternoon trysts. By the early 1960s, things had altered so radially in such a short time that the publishers of *Cosmpolitan* sensed a complete makeover was necessary if their magazine was to survive,[16] their uptight readership having given way to a generation of girls on the go. Helen Gurley Brown (1922–2012), whose *Sex and the Single Girl* (1962) announced that in the age of the Pill, females claimed the right to sexual liberation, became editor-in-chief. An publication that had been founded during the anti-erotic Victorian-era (1837–1901) now offered advice on how to achieve satisfying orgasms.

(a)

(b)

WHAT A DIFFERENCE A DECADE MAKES!: (a) In 1954, three over-25 women (virgins or pretending to be) head for Europe to meet men, matrimony on their minds (courtesy: 20th Century-Fox); (b) in 1964, their counterparts (non-virgins or pretending to be) follow a similar route in search of sex without lasting commitments (courtesy: (20th Century-Fox).

The difference a decade can make becomes clear when considering two different versions of the same story (by John H. Secondari), directed by filmmaker Jean Negulesco. *Three Coins in the Fountain* (1954) and *The Pleasure Seekers* (1964) concern attractive females (Dorothy McGuire, Maggie McNamara, Jean Peters in the original; Pamela Tiffin, Carol Lynley, Ann-Margret in the remake) working and romancing in Europe (Rome; Madrid). All similarity ends there. In 1954, they are, self-consciously, young *women*: smart, sensible, serious-minded despite their lighter sides. In 1964: goofy, giddy *girls*; silly, irresponsible. In 1954, all are assumed to be virgins; the one who apparently isn't hopes that news won't get around. In 1964, it's assumed they are experienced. The sole virgin (Tiffin) begs the others not to let anyone know. The 1954 trio approach male prey subtly; in 1964, they are cougar-like, coming on strong; Ann-Margret's character is aggressive. One basic 1954 rule is that if a woman becomes involved with a married man, she'll be destroyed. In 1964, Lynley's brief affair with her boss (Brian Keith) is presented as a valuable learning experience. In 1954, a girl who sleeps with a man before marriage learns the hard way he'll want nothing to do with her thereafter. In 1964, only by entering into a whirl-wind romance with an attractive doctor (André Lawrence) does Ann-Margret conquer and win him.

In its time, this polished piece of fluff-entertainment paved the way for a more artistically ambitious work, *The Graduate* (Mike Nichols, 1967). With its explicitness (always rendered in an artistic manner) this breakthrough masterwork challenged the still-in-effect Production Code, which had to be abandoned in favor of the first Ratings System. Benjamin Braddock (Dustin Hoffman) becomes involved with an older married woman (Anne Bancroft). In time he leaves that affair to pursue a serious relationship with a sweet girl (Katharine Ross). Here, the irony is that she, Elaine Robinson, is the mature woman's daughter. Importantly, the girl is posited as an innocent owing to her attitudes and values. Whether Elaine is or is not a virgin is never mentioned. It isn't an issue; not for Benjamin, other men who hope to marry her, the target audience, or even, so far as we can tell, her parents. What happened in college is Elaine's business. *The Graduate* is rightly regarded as a milestone, not only for such stylistic innovations as soaring cinematography by Robert Surtees, working under the influence of Nouvelle Vogue imports like *Jules and Jim* (Francois Truffaut, 1961). Such films had played on the American art-house circuit, where aspiring youngish film directors like Nichols and Francis Coppola witnessed, absorbed, and stored away such devices.

Coppola, who had been laboring on such Drive In items as *Dementia 13* (1963) for producer Corman, had the previous year provided what might be considered the first salvo (critically acclaimed if less commercial than *The Graduate*) in the development of revolutionary filmmaking. *You're a Big Boy Now* (1966) incorporated then-contemporary music by folk-rock group The Lovin' Spoonful, with songs specifically written for the film by John Sebastian, in anticipation of *The Graduate*'s contributions by Simon and Garfunkel. Importantly, this movie, based on a novel by David Benedictus, dealt with a notably less-exploited but equally important concern of The Sexual Revolution: The male virgin, that sad-eyed boy for whom the excitement in the air since *Playboy*'s first issue hit the stands apparently exists for everyone but him. Peter Kastner, a Canadian actor who had starred in Canada's most notable youth film, *Nobody Waved Goodbye* (Don Owen, 1965), played Bernard Chanticleer, an intellectual youth who accomplishes his job at the New York City Public Library by whizzing around its corridors on roller-skates. Having recently moved into his own apartment, Bernard hopes to lose his virginity with a Go-Go dream-girl (Elizabeth Hartman). He fails to see that his everyday co-worker Amy (Karen Black) is more suited to his desires, needs, tastes. Here was the first U.S.-lensed film to honestly deal with the all-too-common problem of premature ejaculation and its horrors for a sexually confused young male.

Bernard's foil is one more accomplished playboy type, Tony Bill, subbing for George Hamilton. Overwhelmed by the neon-nightlife around him, Bernard momentarily appears a predecessor to Travis Bickle (Robert De Niro) in *Taxi Driver* (Martin Scorsese, 1976). Were it not for a series of circumstances that allow Bernard to achieve a happy coupling with Amy, he might well have found himself standing before the mirror, muttering: "You talkin' to me?" And, perhaps, even headed out to achieve with a gun what he has been unable to do with his penis, sex and violence becoming horrifically intermingled. Similarly-themed movies soon appeared: *The First Time* (James Neilson) with Wes Stern; *The Sterile Cuckoo* (Alan J. Pakula) with Wendell Burton; *Last Summer* (Frank Perry) with Bruce Davison; and *Out of It* (Paul Williams) with Barry Gordon. The proliferation made clear that Hollywood continued to recognize how all-important the teen audience had become.

*

Not surprisingly, this led to a string of synthetic projects that aped the style of *You're a Big Boy Now* and *The Graduate* without conveying similar substance. The most outrageous (though a commercial hit in its time) was *Goodbye, Columbus* (Larry Peerce, 1969). Hungry to find material that could be presented in the form of a "youth-grooving flick" (as such items were now called), producers seized on an acclaimed 1959 novella by Philip Roth (1933–). Set in 1955, the narrative dealt with East Coast American Jews, some working-class, others nouveau-riche. A major problem for Neil Klugman (Richard Benjamin), stuck in a dead-end job, and Brenda Patimkin (Ali MacGraw) of Radcliffe, is the issue of sex-before-marriage: Whether or not to "do it." Had the movie been mounted as a period piece, illustrating the way we were, it might have been masterful. Instead, the issue was presented as contemporary, facing young people as the 1970s approached. An irony, apparently lost on director Peerce, rendered ridiculous the Old Thinking values of ultra-modern kids who apparently had never heard of Woodstock. Music by The Association, a mid-1960s soft-rock group, only made the 1950s mindset more absurd in context.

The film further revealed the inability of the old studios to deal with a Future Shock world in which things changed so rapidly that styles and sensibilities came in and out of fashion before anyone could adjust.[17] A traditional Hollywood movie takes well over a year to reach the screen, usually longer. *Goodbye, Columbus* was a Paramount release. Other films, turned out quickly by indie companies, offered youthful audiences more timely portraits of themselves. *For Singles Only* (Arthur Dreifuss, 1968) featured John Saxon, Mary Ann Mobley, and Lana Wood in a comedy-drama about newly instituted apartment buildings catering to young "swingin'" professionals, its assumption that all girls in residence were on the pill. *Chastity* (Alessio de Paola, 1969) dealt with a promiscuous wanderer (Cher in her first solo-starring role) who sleeps with men of all ages to compensate for the sexual molestation visited on her as a child. One of the first X-rated films (the equivalent of an R-rated movie of today), *All the Loving Couples* (Max Bing, 1969), became a top earner that year despite its shoe-string budget production values.

(a) (b)

(c) (d)

(e) (f)

SCENES FROM THE SEXUAL REVOLUTION, WAVE TWO: (a) Non-virginal yet 'good girls' of the post-Pill era inhabit a swinging apartment-house in *For Singles Only* (courtesy: Four-Leaf Prods./Columbia); (b) a recent college grad (Dustin Hoffman) becomes embroiled with an older woman (Anne Bancroft) in *The Graduate* (courtesy: Lawrence Turman/Embassy); (c) middle-aged/youth-obsessed adults (Dyan Cannon, Robert Culp, Natalie Wood, Elliott Gould) opt for an orgy in *Bob & Carol & Ted & Alice* (courtesy: Frankovich Prods./Columbia); (d) the hot tub becomes synonymous with casual sex in *Beyond the Valley of the Dolls* (courtesy: 20th Century-Fox); (e) an no-longer youthful couple (Ann-Margret, Jack Nicholson) must decide between their swinging-singles lifestyle or opting for marriage in *Carnal Knowledge* (courtesy: AVCO Embassy Pics.); (f) a bored wife (Catherine Deneuve) experiments with adultery, bondage included, in *Belle de Jour* (courtesy: Paris Film Prods./Hakim/Valoria).

More often than not, audiences for what were called Now Films wanted to
see fresh stars in such stories. During the following decade, this did not bode
well for performers who had appealed to the previous generation of youth-
audiences, even when such a star tried to change her image. *Doctor, You've
Got to Be Kidding!* (Peter Tewksbury, 1967) begins with Sandra Dee's character
rushed to a hospital to deliver her baby. Any of three young men she's casually
slept with (Dick Kallman, Dwayne Hickman, Bill Bixby) might be the father.
Each hopes she'll marry him, whether or not he's the biological dad. George
Hamilton, as a playboy not unlike the one he incarnated at decade's beginning, also wishes to marry her. Even this stock character has altered. And with
good reason; the tide had turned. In AIP's *Three in the Attic* (Richard Wilson,
1968), a superficial playboy finds himself kidnapped and tortured by the three
women (Yvette Mimieux, Judy Pace, Maggie Thrett) he'd been sleeping with
until they learn of one another and opt for a sisterhood of revenge.

As to Dee's film, *Doctor* conveyed a unique meaning owing to its casting:
Sandra Dee, up to then the last holdout (onscreen, at least) from the Sexual
Revolution, had at last "given in." The tragedy for that actress, and her career,
was that no one cared enough anymore to buy a ticket. The public had moved
on. Several other early 1960s youth stars did manage to revive fading careers
by hooking up with emergent writer-directors then in the process of revo-
lutionizing American commercial cinema. No more striking example exists
than Natalie Wood, wise enough to appear in *Bob & Carol & Ted & Alice*
(1969) for a first-time director.

Paul Mazursky was a onetime youth actor (*Blackboard Jungle*). Mazursky
sensed that the only solution to the problem of films doomed by the new
order of things was to overhaul the manner in which Hollywood product was
created. A new generation must conceive, write and direct a film in less than
half the time this process previously consumed. Co-written by Larry Tucker,
B&C&T&A drew on Mazursky's work with Chicago's Second City live-
comedy troupe and stints as a writer for such shows as *The Monkees* (1966–
1968). As critic Pauline Kael noted, the young auteur (a filmmaker with a
personal vision just then coming into fashion in the U.S.) had "developed
a style from satiric improvisational revue theatre . . . and from TV situation
comedy"[18] which lent itself well to the emergent motion-picture form. Other
then-current examples included *M*A*S*H* (Robert Altman, 1969). These
two breakthrough comedies (neither escapist fluff, both commercial as well
as critical hits) premiered as Hollywood closed down its sound stages. More

often than not, the New American Cinema would be shot on location for a heightened sense of reality.

As to *B&C&T&A*, the film focuses on upscale suburbanites living in a posh L.A. neighborhood. In their early thirties, the foursome (Wood and Robert Culp; Gould and Dyan Cannon) embody those teens who entered junior high school back in 1955. Now finished with college, they've experienced nearly fifteen years of constant culture shock, hoping to cling to Bob Dylan's dictum and remain "forever young." To achieve this, they attend Esalen consciousness-raising sessions, leading to awkward attempts at extra-marital affairs. Still, they remain products of the 1950s; guilt and jealousy plague these attractive friends when they do end up in bed together. They, like members of the audience who saw themselves reflected (and romanticized) in the onscreen characters, were caught in a bind: the first eager veterans of the Sexual Revolution somehow managed to also be among its final confused victims.

No greater contrast could possibly exist between this successful piece of work from the New Hollywood than a thudding disaster from the Old: *Prudence and the Pill* (Fielder Cook, 1968), based on a once-prescient novel by Hugh Mills. The book might have made for a timely comedy had it appeared on screen half a decade earlier. A married woman (Deborah Kerr), who has just begun taking the pill, is shocked to learn that she's pregnant by her husband (David Niven). Her teenage niece (Judy Geeson), assumed to be a virgin, stole the pills for her own use and replaced them with aspirins. Ensuing horror—the girl is not "pure"—came across as ridiculous. What might have made for a relevant social comedy in 1963 seemed antiquated after *Prudence* finally made it through the old development system. At once, studio assembly-line moviemaking halted.

Clearly, a new day had dawned. Not only for sexuality in America but popular cinema as fashioned by a necessarily altered Hollywood. The logical next step would be to portray more three-dimensional women who were liberated not only as to their bodies but in mind and spirit as well.

· 8 ·

FORMULATING A FEMININE MYSTIQUE

The Emergent American Woman on Film

"You don't own me,
I'm not just one of your many toys . . .
And please, when I go out with you
Don't put me on display, 'Cause
You don't own me."

—John Madara and David White, songwriters/
Leslie Gore, original performer, 1963

On November 10, 1966, *Penelope* (Arthur Hiller), starring Natalie Wood as the title character, premiered. Wood played an upscale young woman who apparently has it all: married to the handsome man of her dreams (Ian Bannen), now manager of a prestigious bank. But there's a problem: Penelope is miserable. She doesn't suffer abuse. If anything, her husband places Penelope on a pedestal, worshipping her as the perfect woman: beautiful, smart, funny and, best of all (from his point of view), the ideal housewife. Bored to tears, Penelope develops an odd obsession. She'll become a robber. Her target will be her husband's bank. When she tells her psychiatrist (Dick Shawn), he attempts to get Penelope to offer some viable motive for such anti-social behavior. No matter how hard she tries, Penelope cannot answer that question.

In fact, the answer had been presented three years earlier. In *The Feminine Mystique*, Betty Friedan (1921–2006) interviewed middle-to-upper-middle-class housewives, discovering that, behind smiling Faces, many suffered from severe frustration, even depression, despite achieving what they'd been told, when young, they most desired. "I want something *more*"[1] became the refrain, most citing a meaningful career as the missing ingredient. Rejecting everyone from Sigmund Freud (his theory that such women suffered from penis envy) and anthropologist Margaret Mead (who had argued that social functionalism for the race's survival necessitated women fulfilling a bio-logical child-bearing role), Friedan drew on *The Second Sex* (1949) by France's Simone de Beauvoir, which chronicled the "history of women's oppression."[2] Friedan would shortly serve as first president of the National Organization for Women, which set out to draw women "into the mainstream of American society (in order to achieve) equal partnership with men."[3] In this light, the seemingly innocuous comedy *Penelope* rated as the first commercial film to illustrate such points in mainstream entertainment.

*

The changeover can be seen in two films shot back to back by the same direc-tor and featuring the same star. Warner Bros. had been so pleased with the box-office success of *A Summer Place* they commissioned Delmer Daves to make similar movies starring teen heart-throb Troy Donahue. *Parrish* (1961), adapted from a novel by Mildred Savage, concerned a teenager, employed on a tobacco plantation, attempting to find himself. He becomes involved with three girls: Diane McBain as a spoiled child of wealth; Sharon Hugueny as an naive virgin; Connie Stevens as a working class woman, previously involved with several men. At the end, the title character rejects the rich bitch to marry the demure "nice" girl. She, despite her decency, appears less suited to him than the more experienced female. Six months later, *Susan Slade* reunited Troy and Connie for yet another teen-oriented soaper. Again, Stevens played the good-girl-gone-wrong, getting pregnant by a likable mountain climber (Grant Williams) who dies before he can marry her. Susan has to decide whether or not to tell her new beau (Donahue) the truth. She does and, in a turnabout from the earlier film, Troy accepts this, adopting the child as his own. If *Parrish* played as a throwback to the previous decade, *Susan Slade* looked forward to an era in which a woman's character, not the state of her maiden head, defines her.

Two other films, directed by Jean Negulesco for 20th Century Fox, serve as book-ends in grasping rapid changes women underwent as to status in a male-dominated world. In each, three young females, all from 'out of town,' agree to share a New York City apartment in hopes of achieving their life's desires. Scripted by Nunnally Johnson, from several pre-existing plays by female writers (Zoe Akins, Katherine Albert), *How to Marry a Millionaire* (1953) introduced bright, sophisticated Schatze (Lauren Bacall), the less-intelligent but determined Loco (Betty Grable), and scatter-head blonde bombshell Pola (Marilyn Monroe). The three share a common cause, stated outright in the title. However varied, all are gold-diggers—out to marry, and marry rich. None has career ambitions; work will only be considered when they're flat broke and in need of cash. The question addressing each is whether she would be willing to marry a man she doesn't love if he were wealthy; the major problem is spotting phonies (men who pretend to be rich but aren't) while clinging to a hardline attitude for success: no man will hitch up permanently with a woman who has "put out" during dating. In the end, all three come to an important decision: marrying for love rather than money. Schatze is amazed to discover that her own beloved regular guy (Cameron Mitchell) is a millionaire. This, according to tenets of the time, had her supposedly achieving the best of everything.

A little more than five years later, Negulesco's film of that title would indicate the degrees to which American women had altered, as well as ways in which they remained the same. Based on a bestselling-novel by Rona Jaffe (1931–2005), a graduate of prestigious Radcliffe College who following graduation had headed for Manhattan to conquer the publishing world, *The Best of Everything* exists in contrast to *Millionaire*. That had been a romantic comedy; here is romantic drama. Yet an eerie parallel dominates: Hope Lange is Caroline, an autobiographical character; Suzy Parker plays Gregg, the most seemingly sophisticated; Diane Baker is go-getter April. All are committed to finding the right man. But what a difference a half-decade makes! Though they often date older men, including wealthy ones, these are hardly fortune-hunters. To find a man who appreciates and understands her as a person is each young woman's objective, not that any would *mind* marrying a millionaire. Only, though, if she sincerely loves him. *And* if he would respect her right to continue with her career.

In this, they look forward to the goals of an ever larger number of young women in the upcoming decade. All three are serious not only about their daily jobs but also about their desired *professions*. Caroline yearns to become an executive, achieving that owing to her considerable abilities. April has no such ambitions, or for that matter talent. Yet she wants to be the best secretary possible. While Gregg takes a stenographer's job to pay her bills (none of these women, like the earlier three, perceives men as prey to pick up meal-tabs), Gregg is devoted to becoming a Broadway actress. While marriage is attractive (none wants to end up a sad career woman, like the editor played by Joan Crawford), each is defined by her desire to make it in the working world. At the end, when Caroline achieves her dream job as editor and connects with the endearing fellow-exec played by Stephen Boyd, she has achieved what the title describes. The best of everything is not some impossible dream, 1953 style, of a White Knight riding to her rescue with a large wallet.

*

What a contrast to *The Tender Trap* less than five years earlier! Reynolds' character might be thought of as a hardened and, as such, less vulnerable forerunner of Gregg. She achieves the accolades onstage Gregg would kill for, nevertheless insisting acting is a temporary ambition:

> A career is fine, but it is no substitute for marriage. A woman isn't a *real* woman until she's married and has children. Then, she's *fulfilled* . . . Marriage? *That's* what I want. (My) plan? Old-fashioned marriage with the house, kids, and a life that makes *sense*.[4]

Apparently, what she wants most is the situation Betty Friedan's interviewees railed against. In comparison, other onscreen women proved more forward-looking. In *Loving You*, Elvis Presley as Deke Rivers found himself torn between a man-eating female manager (Lizabeth Scott) and a demure, lady-like girl (Dolores Hart). A career woman, in that film's retro triangle, is wicked; the one who wants only to create a home, a "good girl." In the *Jailhouse Rock* script by Guy Trosper, Peggy Van Alden (Judy Tyler) collapses those extremes into a single character. Ex-con Vince Everett plays a minor gig at a run-of-the mill club and is spotted by aspiring talent manager Peggy, a teenager in years, a young woman in terms of maturity. She's ambitious, but not unscrupulously so; she would like to marry in time, but puts that on the back-burner. In Vince, she sees a potential gold mine but will not exploit him, taking only a fair share of profits. Peggy persuades Vince, after being ripped off by a record company, to form an indie firm with her. Once they date, Vince assumes Peggy "belongs to him." She makes clear that's not the case.

As Lesley Gore would sing five years later:

You don't own me.
Don't say I can't go out with other guys.[5]

Peggy would like to be in a serious relationship with Vince and will consider the possibility of, in time, marriage. For now, career comes first, hers *and* his. They are equals in a joint venture. Though Vince momentarily gets sidelined by a superficial movie star (Jennifer Holden), he realizes a trophy woman will no longer satisfy him. Peggy is the real deal; eventually he wants her as a partner in business and life.

Overnight, the onscreen image of who and what a young woman should and could be was challenged, even in a film as modest (as to budget) as *Let's Rock*. Pop-singer Tony Adane (Julius La Rosa) feels shunned when teen girls mob Paul Anka but not him. Except for one: Kathy Abbott (Phyllis Newman). Why, she wants to know, didn't he also perform his record's flip side on an Ed Sullivan-like show? Kathy reveals herself as a Brill Building girl, a fresh face among young talent then making waves at the imposing structure at 1619 Broadway where The Great White Way intersects with 49th Street. Initially viewed as a late-arrival extension of Tin Pan Alley (downtown at 28th and Sixth Avenue, home of the Music Biz from the cakewalk era through rag, blues, swing and Big Band), The Brill began to displace its predecessor in the early 1950s. Aging musical avatars had lost touch with current styles; Brill's younger talents embraced rhythm 'n' blues, Big Beat, and Rock 'n' Roll which were as open to the eager, ambitious females as they were to hungry young men. Neil Sedaka, Bobby Darin and Paul Simon shared studio space with singer/songwriters Lesley Gore, Carole King, and Laura Nyro.

Whatever its limitations, *Let's Rock* offers a surprisingly accurate depiction of such a woman. Kathy appears not much older than screaming-giggling female fans and is initially mistaken for one. Yet she's out to make a name for herself in contemporary music, gutsy enough to go out and ask a question rather than sulk when the cut that she penned isn't played. Marriage? She states: "It's about the last thing in the world I want right now." She means it, asserting this when Tony asks about the possibility of becoming 'involved.' She won't rule out romance: "I don't see why a man and a woman can't have a casual relationship, without getting 'serious.'" The implication is that sex is possible, *if* she decides he's worthy. She plans to initiate this if and when she decides that would feel 'right'—for *her*! When Tony kisses Kathy, she enjoys it. Kathy is younger enough than Tony to giggle when he's shocked that any female—the modern female—can enjoy the sensation yet not, like women of previous generations, insist this must lead to something more serious.

Once Tony and Kathy have become something of a couple, she stands by her man during times of trouble. But there's a key difference between Kathy and Tammy Tyree. Tammy sincerely supported her man and shared the hard work yet added nothing to Steve's farming endeavors other than her strength of arms and character. Not once did she suggest an idea of her own as to farming, nodding in agreement with his revolutionary scientific approaches. Kathy proves to be less a cheerleader than team captain. She devises the strategy by which they'll succeed, as Peggy did for Vince. Not only does her inner strength rise high when his will fails, but also her nimble mind and singular vision see them through. Before meeting Tony, Kathy was willing to work a full day's job in some menial position, then rush off to her closet-office, hoping to pen a recordable song. She understands the significance of rock 'n' roll:

TONY: You should be writing motion picture songs. *Important* music.
KATHY: Rock 'n' roll *is* important music! The kids listen to it, dance to it . . .
             live to it!

Kathy represents the ability of the era's bright young women to see beyond the new music's obvious topicality. She alone grasps the shape of things to come: Rock 'n' roll truly *is* here to stay.

(a) (b)

(c) (d)

EVOLUTION OF THE AMERICAN WOMAN: (a) In the early 1960s, Sandra Dee as Tammy encapsulated the retro 1950s ideal of a marriage-minded virgin; (courtesy: Universal); (b) Ann-Margret insists that uber-male Elvis pursue her instead of the other way around in *Viva Las Vegas* (courtesy: Jack Cummings Prods./MGM); (d) Natalie Wood opts for single-motherhood after becoming pregnant by Steve McQueen in *Love with the Proper Stranger* (courtesy: Pakula-Mulligan/Paramount); (e) Wood plays a pampered wife who, like one of Betty Friedan's interview subjects, desperately needs "something more" than upscale domesticity in *Penelope* (courtesy: MGM).

Other youth films focused on more 'normal' girls, living in the suburbs. After Judy in *Rebel*, the first representative girl was Dori Graham in *Rock Rock Rock*. Intriguingly, Dori collapses two top talents into a single character;

Tuesday Weld, the Carol Lombard of teen flicks, portrays her, Dori's singing
voice was provided by Connie Francis. Dori appears a pastiche of all the aver-
age, ordinary teen girls of the time. Significantly she—unlike *Rebel's* Judy—is
well-adjusted, in no way a juvenile delinquent. Nor does she hang with a
bad crowd. Dori stays at home on weeknights, watching TV with her parents, who do spend a lot of time with the kids. Dori's problem is talking her
father into a) giving her an advance on the weekly allowance so she can buy
a fashionable gown for the upcoming prom, and b) convincing him to allow
her to wear a strapless model. When her father insists Dori go out and earn
half the money herself, an idea she doesn't object to, we view a typical family
situation, that of the majority of kids rather than *Rebel's* troubled minority.
Dori does just what she's asked to, even if her awkward attempt at becoming
a businesswoman by loaning money to friends at an exorbitant rate reveals
her naivete about life.

Important too is that Dori isn't a sexual rebel. As Tuesday Weld opens her
lips, the voice of Connie Francis croons:

> I never had a sweetheart.
> No lovers' lane for me![6]

If a tad goofy, Dori serves as a role model of conventionality yet offers a surprisingly strong image of the New Woman (though a mere 15 years old) who
likes the idea of making money on her own, then spending it precisely as she
wishes to.

To the contrary, if any star's career represented the opposite of liberation,
it was the small oeuvre of Connie Francis. Following *Where the Boys Are*, in
which she played the shy girl, subsequent vehicles offered ever less successful variations on that film's title. The first, *Follow the Boys* (Richard Thorpe,
1963), had Connie and three female friends (one played by *Boys* co-star Paula
Prentiss) driving around Europe, attempting to catch up with a ship on which
their sailor husbands and boyfriends serve. There is no sense that they have,
or could consider, life choices, much less a career, other than dutifully doing
what the title suggests. *When the Boys Meet the Girls* (Alvin Ganzer, 1965)
casts Connie as Ginger, a postal worker who learns her father's compulsive
gambling has landed them in debt. Rather than solve the situation, as spunky
girls of that decade's first half might do, she throws her troubles on the shoul-
ders of her latest boyfriend (Harve Presnell). In between, Francis starred in

Looking for Love (Don Weis, 1964). Libby Caruso attempts to make a go of a singing career, yet the old-fashioned girl forsakes professional commitment in favor of convenience: When things don't work out as hoped for within a month, Libby quits Show Biz, taking a menial job to support her search for a man (Jim Hutton) to support her ever after.

The commercial failure of these films may have to do with a female audience's rejection during the early 1960s of the sort of 'catch a man and keep him no matter what' sensibility that played well during the previous decade. Francis would shortly be replaced by another singer-actress, Ann-Margret, who caught the tenor of these times effectively.

*

The first significant onscreen appearance of Ann-Margret occurred in *State Fair* (1962). Ellie, though young in years, is a seasoned midway performer who attracts the attention of a naïve farm boy (Pat Boone). In her song-and-dance number, Ellie opens the routine as a caricature of the old-fashioned goodie-two-shoes, dressed in a gaudy Raggedy-Ann inspired outfit. In midnumber, the chorus tears away her outer clothing to reveal a jet-black, skintight skirt beneath. Her feigned innocence disappears like a whiff of smoke; now, the fiery redhead knocks everyone, including the smitten Boone, for a loop. The sequence, however commercial (even crass) in intent, foreshadows many of the women Ann-Margret would play. Beneath her seemingly angelic good girls, there's a naughty female just itching to get out. Inside every one of Ann-Margret's bad girls (*Kitten With a Whip*; Douglas Heyes, 1964), we encounter a misunderstood good girl, longing to be understood. This 1960s star challenged the then in-place dichotomization of women into good and/ or bad girls.

In *State Fair*, she leads her latest conquest to her room, making clear he realizes "your friend Ellie has seen a *lot* of state fairs!" He reacts according to the old morality: "You're a bad girl?" Meaning a non-virgin. The audience knows more than he: Considering such forthrightness, Ellie is a good girl in every way *but* that. Ellie realizes she's ahead of her time. Though the handsome farmer gives her an engagement ring, she returns it when the fair concludes. Having overheard his parents talk about the fear of their son marrying "trash," she accepts this as her lot in life, leaving with other performers.

Before Elvis, John Lennon stated, there was nothing.[7] Nothing, that is, to capture the fervor and spirit of young people, the manners, morals, and music that defined those original teenagers. In truth, even after Presley, there existed no female counterpart, in song or onscreen, in mainstream movies (Mamie Van Doren did what she could in junk cinema)—until the emergence of Ann-Margret. If Elvis liberated male attitudes in the late 1950s, Ann-Margret did that for girls in the early 1960s. The two co-starred in *Viva Las Vegas* (George Sidney, 1964). Until then, rock 'n' roll might be thought of as sexist; less that it degraded women, only that there was no place for a woman who dared do the things Elvis did, say the words he said and, most important, dance with the unprecedented abandon that so shocked the nation back in 1955. To fully appreciate *Viva Las Vegas*, particularly its portrait of women, this film must be seen in contrast to its predecessor, *Fun in Acapulco* (Richard Thorpe, 1963). There, Elvis's good-natured expatriate romances three females: Teri Hope as an underage nympho-maniac teenager; Elsa Cárdenas as a female bullfighter who brings her talents into the bedroom as a dominatrix; and Ursula Andress as an overage beach bunny in a Bikini. The three females compete for the prize that is Elvis. Not surprisingly, he rejects the bad brat *and* the career-driven man-eater in favor of the Amazonian if demure, difficult-to-get Andress. She succumbs to Elvis only after making him work for it.

    Viva Las Vegas introduces an alternative paradigm, obvious in the credits. This was the first time a female won equal (if second) billing to Elvis. Such suggested equality is forwarded by the story. As Lucky, Elvis arrives in Vegas to compete in a Grand Prix. For once, he doesn't encounter a trio of lovelies eager to cat-fight over him. Attractive women abound; he focuses on Rusty, a swimming instructor. She does not, like Andress's assistant social coordinator at a similar establishment, view her work as a mere job but approaches her position as a professional. She has no plans of quitting once she meets the right guy. Initially, she's none too impressed with Lucky, despite his good looks. Elvis never came off less kingly: She's the Queen, pursued by other men including a European count (Cesare Danova). Only when Lucky proves more genuine and sincere does Rusty pick him over his elegant competition, despite that man's manners and money. Years later, Ann-Margret reflected on "a need in 'The Industry' for a female Elvis Presley."[8] Her gyrations concerned cultural conservatives; Pauline Kael gasped that her dancing could serve to "incite gang rape."[9] That comment, considered clever then, embodies the offensive/ outdated notion that any girl who dares dance as wild and free as a contemporary male is "asking for it."

Importantly, Ann-Margret's character is as virginal as Sandra Dee playing Tammy, true of Ann-Margret's role in *Bye Bye Birdie*. The main thrust of the Ann-Margret image reflects the reality of young women of her era: No longer could or should anyone, male or female, assume that a girl's desire to release inner energies on the dance floor implied lack of character. Shortly, though, that still-existing parallel between the two—character and virginity—would be challenged. Like several early-to-mid-Sixties *Playboy* centerfold girls who insisted they were virgins[10] despite posing in the nude, female liberation partly had to do with the announcement that any girl's acceptance, rather than repression, of her sexual identity didn't necessarily correlate to a personal history of sexual experience. Enjoying status as a sex symbol ought not, as was the case when Marilyn Monroe defined that role, to reduce a woman to the status of sexual object. The notion of Monroe's nameless 'Girl' from *The Seven Year Itch* (Billy Wilder, 1955), a creation of the 1950s, would be rejected by Ann-Margret's 1960s characters.

As Cindy Lauper would put it two decades later, "Girls just want to have fun"—as guys *always* have. Ann-Margret's greatest contribution was to announce onscreen that male (or female!) assumptions about a woman based on her dress and dancing were invalid. If a judgment had to be made (which would also in time be challenged), let it be based on her actual behavior.

That theme would crystalize in *The Swinger* (George Sidney, 1966), ridiculed at the time as a work of crass exploitation, but in retrospect the most significant of all Ann-Margret's vehicles. The film announces its self-conscious vulgarity by having the narrator (Robert Coote) speak his opening lines about the Los Angeles mid-Sixties scene while assorted off-screen slobs belch. The story presents an extended allegory for the manner in which women who, in the early 1960s, dared to bare it all (including in *Playboy*) came to grasp, during the decade's second half, that covering themselves back up again offered an alternative liberation, as Third Wave feminists were now forwarding.[11] Beautiful (and, again, virginal) Kelly Olsson (Ann-Margret) heads to the offices of a slick publication known for its female pictorials. No sooner does the Hefner-like editor (Tony Franciosa) glance in her direction than he offers her a Playmate-type layout. To his shock, she's there to sell him one of her stories. Kelly downplays her beauty; her desire is to be taken seriously for brains and talent. Like other Playboy males before him, Franciosa (embodying a final significant screen incarnation of that fast-fading male role model, soon to become a cautionary-fable figure) cannot at this point move past dichotomization. Women are, in his simplistic view, beautiful *or* brainy. By the end, he learns that a single female can have it all, setting the pace for post-feminism in the 21st century.

Building on the knowledge that director Sidney, following *Bye Bye Birdie* and and *Viva Las Vegas*, had set himself up as a Svengali to Ann-Margret's Trilby, Liz Smith noted that the director's "climactic porny fantasy about his star (concerns) a good girl, sort of, pretending to be bad . . . photographed from every comprehensive suggestive angle, and her own performance style tipped the material into areas that were slightly disturbing."[12] Sidney engages in simultaneous exploitation/ exploration of what would in time come to be called the male gaze. To convince the editor she's "experienced" enough to write mature stories, Kelly stages an elaborate faux-orgy at the hippie commune where she lives and works, including a near-nude body painting sequence that tested the fast-fading Production Code. The audience watching (primarily male) is openly invited to share in the visual pleasure of her writh-ing about, apparently wearing nothing but oil paints; also, though, induced to laugh *at* the taken-in editor (and that aspect of him that exists in male viewers of this film), dismissing his prurience and voyeurism. When he finally grasps that Kelly insists on being accepted as a person with brains first, a woman of beauty second, so did the male audience begin to understand their need to reject any dichotomization of women into virgins/vamps; good girls/bad girls/ beautiful or brainy.

Each woman, like every man, is an individual. However much that goes without saying today, it needed to be said (and visually 'said' by the movies) in the mid-Sixties. Intriguingly, Drive In fare like *The Swinger* tended to artic-ulate in entertainment such a statement before the middle-brow movies got around to doing that necessary job.

Soon, the issue of virginity will be sidestepped for Ann-Margret's char-acters. As to *R.P.M.* (Stanley Kramer, 1970), in which she plays a motor-cycle riding (see Ch. 12) sexy feminist and grad student—openly sleeping with her former teacher, he now promoted to school president— Roger Ebert noted: "Her quandary: Should she still shack up with Anthony Quinn after he stops being a radical professor and becomes a moderate administrator?"[13] Hollywood had begun to 'get it'; moral issues are all-important to this young woman but the state or lack of her maidenhead has nothing whatsoever to do with morality. Intellectual values/political loyalties dominate in a post-Sexual Revolution era. In *Carnal Knowledge* (Mike Nichols, 1971), Ann-Margret set role-model visions of the New Woman aside to vividly embody (and win an Oscar nomination for) her striking portrayal of the previous generation's girls-to-women: hanging on to her virginity in the early Sixties in hopes of winning a man's hand in marriage; surrendering at mid-decade when the Sexual Revolution suggested this might achieve her ends; now, as middle-age approaches, literally begging a guy she's sleeping with (Jack Nicholson) to marry her. Finally, when he capitulates, divorcing him in revenge for his not having courted her properly, as she was, when young, told she had a right to expect.

*

Ann-Margret's contributions aside, more than any other actress of her generation, Jane Fonda (1937–)—by conscious effort, blind luck, or remarkable serendipity—came to represent the contemporary young woman. Fonda would be cast in successive roles that embodied a generalized idea of American femaleness as it rapidly altered. Her screen debut in *Tall Story* (Joshua Logan, 1960) set the pace. Adapted from a 1959 stage play by Howard Lindsay and Russel Crouse, the female lead, June Ryder, is a slightly older, significantly taller version of Kim MacAfrey in *Bye Bye Birdie*—had Kim dumped Hugo Peabody and gone on to college. June majors in Home Economics but makes clear to everyone a career holds no interest for her. She's at school for one reason: to nab a husband, specifically the Big Man on Campus in every sense of that term. He's played by Anthony Perkins, who has as much in common with Hugo as June with Kim. Insecure, awkward, appealing, he's a top basketball player, also a fine student; i.e., he's excellent "husband material." Another late-1950s/early-1960s virgin, June reveals herself to be calculating and cynical. She sets out to catch him and does, her strategy celebrated rather than criticized by the film's shallow context.

FONDA AND FRIENDS: Jane not only played the best roles for women in the 1960s but turned down several others: (a) in *Tall Story* (courtesy: Mansfield Prods./Warner Bros.) she's a college co-ed, devoted to cheerleading today, marriage tomorrow; (b) Jane's recently-married college-grad in *Barefoot in the Park* (courtesy: Hal Wallis/Paramount) wonders if she might need "something more"; (c) subbing for Jane, Faye Dunaway's tag-along gun-moll in *Bonnie and Clyde* (courtesy: Tatira-Hiller Prods./Warner Bros.), transforms into the gang's leader; (d) Mia Farrow's bride in *Rosemary's Baby* (courtesy: William Castle Prods./Paramount) fights back against a manipulative/exploitive husband; (e) reversing the old 'rescue myth' of a man saving the woman, Sharon Tate rescues Tony Curtis from the surf in *Don't Make Waves*); (f) a desperate wife (Julie Christie) gives birth to her lover's child as her only means of social-protest in *Petulia* (courtesy: Warner Bros.-Seven Arts/Petersham Prods.)

Three years later, Fonda would play another virgin (of body if not mind) in still another Broadway adaptation. The 1961 play *Sunday in New York* was written by Norman Krasna who, a decade earlier, delighted his audiences while enraging guardians of popular morality with *The Moon Is Blue* in which a virgin rejects the attentions of an experienced older man. In *Sunday*, Eileen Tyler (Fonda) is a college grad whose fiancé (Robert Culp) pressures Eileen to sleep with him before their upcoming marriage. She has a serious career as a journalist, a notable change from June in Fonda's previous romantic comedy. Eileen takes the train from Albany, New York to Manhattan to confer with her older brother (Cliff Robertson) and discuss her problem. She's stunned to learn he's become one more embodiment of Sinatra's playboy from *The Tender Trap*. The irony is that when Eileen heads out on Sunday afternoon to find an attractive man and seduce him, abandoning old-fashioned ways to join la dolce vita, her target (Rod Taylor), initially eager for casual sex, refuses upon learning she is "the last 22-year-old virgin in America." No question that the Sexual Revolution had become a lifestyle for many young people. The problem now was achieving a sense of equality between women and men despite the continuing male fear/respect/desire for female virginity.

At this time, Broadway was still considered more sophisticated than Hollywood, movies consistently tagging along behind by several years. In The Big Apple, *Sunday in New York* was soon gone and forgotten, the once-contemporary comedy about early 1960s mores giving way to a timelier piece: *Any Wednesday* by Muriel Resnick. This would finally reach the screen in 1966 (Robert Ellis Miller). As had been the case with Sandy Dennis on Broadway, Fonda's Ellen emerges as a sweet, charming female. In that, she's not unlike earlier all-American girls in 1960s Hollywood films, if with one key distinction—not only is she not a virgin; Ellen is the mistress of a wealthy older married man (Jason Robards). The piece doesn't condemn her, nor does an eligible young man (Dean Jones) who accidentally enters Ellen's life. In earlier sex comedies, the plot may well have revolved around frantic attempts on her part to keep this guy from learning 'the truth.' Here she never considers the notion of hiding reality. Blatantly honest about who she is, casual as to the life she's living, Ellen must decide whether or not to take him up on his proposal. However radical elements of the play and film may be, it's important to note one major convention remains intact: this being a happy-ending Hollywood movie, she agrees to marriage. The only question: Which man?

Two Fonda films, each opening with a young couple's wedding, reveal the drastic sudden shift in attitudes about women and men in such serious relationships. In *Period of Adjustment* (1962), from the only sitcom by dramatist Tennessee Williams, Fonda is Isabel, a nurse who impulsively marries an enamored patient (Jim Hutton). Though the cars and costumes suggest the early 1960s, the movie's 1950s retro-mentality is revealed when George is identified as a Korean War vet. Following the ceremony, problems set in, deriving from each person's lack of experience—with others, or one another. George suffers from performance anxiety; Isabel, with no love affairs to her credit, has no idea how to help him overcome his problem. Here was a glimpse, in entertaining form, of many young American marrieds who, by trying to follow the rules of proper sexual etiquette before the boy placed a ring on the girl's finger, realized that when the time came to dim the lights and slip into bed, neither had a clue as to what they were supposed to do.

Six years later, *Barefoot in the Park* (Gene Saks, 1967) opens as yet another nice honeymoon couple is enjoying a horse-drawn carriage ride around New York City. Later they retire to their suite at the Plaza. In this adaptation of Neil Simon's 1963 play, Corrie (Fonda) proves to be a man-eater on the wedding night; she and husband Paul (Robert Redford) have clearly been diligently 'practicing' all along. Sex before marriage is now accepted as the status quo—not only for men but, at long last, women. No sooner are they ensconced in a Greenwich Village apartment than the Betty Friedan syndrome sets in: Corrie wishes she, like her husband, had a serious career. As close to ideal as their marriage may be (he's handsome, successful, and adores her) in an early-1960s definition of that term, these are the *late* 1960s, that moment when the feminist agenda questioned whether marriage in and of itself could be enough to satisfy a modern-thinking female. It's altogether possible to consider *Penelope* with Natalie Wood, in theatres one year earlier, as a prequel.

In fact, in 1963, Wood starred in a film that forwarded the girls-to-women movement. In *Love with the Proper Stranger* (Robert Mulligan, 1963), she plays a nice young woman who gets 'knocked up' during a one-night stand with a sexy jazz musician (Steve McQueen). When, pregnant, she approaches him, he becomes desperate, believing she will make him marry her. In fact, she only wants half the money it will cost for a (then-still-illegal) abortion. Initially, he's happy to oblige but, like previous couples in both *Blue Denim* (Philip Dunne, 1959) and *A Summer Place*, they can't go through with it. Believing himself to be a grand fellow, he offers to marry her. To his shock, she flatly refuses. She does, however, allow him to date and court her. She will marry him, but only if he's able to completely convince her that he wants to marry *her*—this specific *person*, this individual *woman*—because he's fallen in love with her, not only doing her "a favor." When he finally sets aside any old-male mentality (she's not worthy owing to being a non-virgin, even though he was the culprit), he does realize what a terrific human being she is. Here, the Sexual Revolution and a New Morality converge onscreen.

Now, not only could a young woman—the very woman of the 1960s who saw herself reflected on screen in Wood or Fonda—be comfortable with sex before marriage with potential mates for life. She might well take lovers casually, no longer suggesting she's a 'bad girl.' Though a sci-fi/ fantasy and foreign-lensed, *Barbarella* (Roger Vadim, 1969) might be seen as an allegory for the previous limited form of liberation (sexual) while completing Fonda's 1960s journey on film as in life. In the famed opening striptease, the title character (Fonda, bringing to life a French comic book heroine created by Jean-Claude Forest, Barbarella based on Bardot) reveals her potential for sensuality though she remains a virgin. During the narrative, she's initiated into sexual awareness by a gentle brute, seduces a quasi-angel, grows so sophisticated at (and accepting of) sex that she destroys the Orgasmatron which was supposed to sex her to death, and becomes the mistress of a futuristic Robin Hood-like rebel. At the conclusion, she appears ready to enjoy a lesbian experience with the Great Tyrant (Anita Pallenberg). That female is indeed a 'bad girl,' not owing to her sexual promiscuity but because she's cruel. Barbarella is good because she's kind, sexuality no longer having anything to do with one's morality. Having completed a cinematic crash course on the joys of sex, Fonda had in life (she was briefly married to Vadim) only one place to go. During the 1970s and beyond, Fonda portrayed modern women who become intellectually, spiritually, and emotionally liberated, sexual liberation having occurred before the film began.

*

Two roles Fonda passed on might have neatly fit into her amassing body of work. *Bonnie and Clyde* (Arthur Penn, 1967) features Warren Beatty and Faye Dunaway as the rural 1930s bank-robbing duo (Barrow and Parker). Viewers (particularly the young) perceived their onscreen experiences on the run as a period piece parallel to their own sense of outlawry during the difficult late 1960s. Notable too is the manner in which Bonnie emerges as a truly dynamic character, Clyde remaining relatively static. Early on, the small-town girl is overwhelmed by his tough-guy image and wants to be Clyde's gun-moll. In time, Bonnie realizes that he is all quicksilver-show, unable to pull off a robbery or perform properly in bed. Rather than leave, Bonnie seizes control of their professional and personal lives. *She* runs the gang, also nurturing Clyde in the bedroom. Later, she composes pulp poetry that will define their legend. *Bonnie and Clyde* offers a paradigm for the manner in which a strong woman might not only remain in a disappointing relationship but correct any problems.

Fonda also turned down Rosemary Woodhouse in *Rosemary's Baby* (Roman Polanski, 1968), from Ira Levin's bestseller. The title character, an intelligent if innocent bride, moves into The Bramford with her new husband Guy (John Cassavetes). (Whether they slept together before the ceremony is now a non-issue.) An old Manhattan apartment house, her home exists within a cocoon-like demi-monde characterized by fading elegance as to the building's appearance, also its elderly residents. Shortly after becoming pregnant, Rosemary suffers from dreams suggesting Guy, an aspiring actor, sold his soul to the Devil in exchange for professional success. Rosemary has been impregnated with the anti-Christ but, when she attempts to find help, is considered crazy. Most impressive at the time of release was the manner in which this film altered Hollywood movies in general, horror films specifically. Drawing on elements from his earlier work, including *Knife in the Water* (1962) and *Repulsion* (1965) Polanski re-invented a genre by banishing Gothic conventions and timeworn clichés. The horror occurs in real-world situations, paving the way for both *The Exorcist* (William Friedkin, 1973) and *The Omen* (Richard Donner, 1976).

In retrospect, *Rosemary's Baby* can be read as a parable for the syndrome Friedan first brought to the public's attention: (some/many) men perceive marriage as a status issue, acquiring a trophy wife who will be allowed no input into her husband's affairs, therefore unequal. She has no profession while he is ambitious at her expense. Even motherhood has no potential fulfillment for her, transferred by his unholy arrangement with the devil into one more means by which the male gains power. The woman must biologically carry the child; it is immediately taken away from her by others with her husband's okay to serve his greater purpose. She is denied even that old-fashioned female joy of motherhood.

*

At decade's end, a single film summed up what feminists perceived as the long-existent quandary for women. *Petulia* (Richard Lester, 1968), with a screenplay by Lawrence B. Marcus adapted from a timely novel by John Haase, focuses on a true arch-kook (Julie Christie). Young when the Sixties began, as that era rushes toward its conclusion, Petulia is mildly shocked to discover she's entering early middle-age. Presumably a child of great privilege who dropped out and entered the Haight-Ashbury Hippie scene, Petulia soon straightened out, marrying a handsome upscale man (Richard Chamberlain). Shortly, she (like Penelope several years earlier) became bored with his conventional ways. And, despite his fashionable long hair, his offensively chauvinistic retro-attitudes. In addition to showing her off as a trophy at glamorous events, he's abusive when the two are alone. Seemingly at random, Petulia picks a middle-aged doctor, Archie (George C. Scott), for her first affair. But what initially appears to be free *sex* turns out to be free *love*: Petulia is dazzled by this man's willingness to care for poverty-stricken people rather than attend to rich clients. If pretty boys were once Petulia's prey, now she longs for altruism and maturity. Yet escaping what Betty Friedan defined as the upper-middle-class trap isn't easy.

At the conclusion, she strikes a blow for personal freedom in the only way open to her: Giving birth to their love-child, convincing her husband the baby is his. Lester's directorial approach, meanwhile, qualifies this as a time capsule, with visual lyricism worthy of a New Wave classic by Truffaut. Stream-of-consciousness takes the place of traditional linear narrative, rivaling the experimentation of *Persona* (Ingmar Bergman, 1966). With this film's release, commercial Hollywood allowed itself to be fully conjoined with what previously had been confined to international art-house fare. In point of fact, however, that changeover began back in 1964, when this English director helped to set in place the British invasion.

· 9 ·

"THE BRITISH ARE COMING!"

When Bob Dylan Met the Beatles

> "A plausible mission of artists is to make people appreciate
> the world at least a little bit. The Beatles did (that)."
>
> —Kurt Vonnegut, 1971

On February 9, 1964, the Beatles made their first appearance on CBS's Sunday evening institution *The Ed Sullivan Show*. For months, radio stations across the U.S. had played songs from their album. On that Monday following, the British Invasion began in earnest. The previous evening, those viewers old enough to recall the Presley phenomenon experienced *deja-vu* at the exuberance of this next set of teens, notably the girls lucky enough to be in Sullivan's audience. For people who had constituted the First Wave of American teenagers, now young adults attending college or part of the work force, the Beatles likewise provided a Big Chill: sudden realization that their era of youth was, as of this moment, over. To a degree, they'd sensed this as early as 1961, while exiting high-school en masse. As to music, a significant number had become enamored of the growing folk phenomenon in its commercial stage (The Kingston Trio, 1961–62), followed by a compromise between that and something more authentic (Peter, Paul & Mary, 1962–1963), finally true walkin'/talkin' blues (early Bob Dylan, 1963–1964).

Meanwhile, the Second Wave of teens attending junior- and senior- high schools had grown increasingly impatient for their own equivalent of Elvis. In the past four years, record sales, which had soared between 1955–1960, plummeted—particularly discs marketed to The Young.[1] Rare exceptions included the bestselling Twist numbers by Chubby Checker and Joey Dee, which boasted a huge adult-crossover appeal. Phil Spector (1939–) introduced his "Wall of Sound," ushering in a wave of girl-groups (e.g., The Ronettes) as edgy and individualistic as the original rock 'n' rolls guys. Overall, this turned out to be a lackluster period. Nondescript performers like Bobby Vee ("Rubber Ball") and Bobby Vinton ("Blue Velvet") offered bland, M.O.R. pop-rock. As to major talents, Bobby Darin more resembled Frank Sinatra than Little Richard; Elvis had shifted to an easy-listening sound ("It's Now or Never") similar to Dean Martin. Any notion that Elvis once represented a "voodoo of frustration and defiance"[2] was long gone. Once, Presley played devil's advocate to Pat Boone. Now, they were indistinguishable in music and movies. On rare occasion, a throwback to the great tradition of greaser-rock hit the charts (Dion; "The Wanderer," 1962). Mostly, though, rock 'n' roll, if not dead, hibernated along with Jerry Lee Lewis who had headed back to the boondocks after his career-destroying child-bride scandal.[3]

Suddenly, there they were: John Lennon, Paul McCartney, George Harrison, and 'Ringo' Starr (aka, Richard Starkey). Earlier attempts to bring top Brit rockers to America—the Eddie Cochran-like Tommy Steele, who starred in *Rock Around the World* (Gerard Bryant, 1957); Presley-ish dreamboat Cliff Richard (*The Young Ones* (Sidney J. Furie, 1961)—failed miserably. They appeared nothing more than carbon copies of those American originals. Not so the Beatles, with their shaggy heads and bizarre grins, an iconography more goofy than threatening. Also, the Beatles were undeniably *cute*: charmingly cheeky, having more in common with precocious children than rebellious teens. Giddy girls bought diverse items—lunch-boxes, over-sized pins, wall-posters, bubble-gum cards, rings, embossed plastic wallets and the like. As a craze commenced, a number of young males grew their hair longer, sporting the neat mop-top style. Rare complaints from fuddy-duddies were registered, though the early Beatle look was clean-cut enough that no serious controversy erupted. Most important, young people—these kids but also a surprising number of those who had passed the age of 21, wanting to remain forever young, as Bob Dylan put it, in spirit if not years—bought the records: 45 rpm singles and 33 1/3 long-playing albums. Rock, at that precise moment in its history, became trans-generational.

Still, the hugest impact was on those truly young enough to embrace The Beatles ecstatically. Among them was Susan J. Douglas. In retrospect, she noted that the phenomenon could never have occurred, at least with such impact, had social history not again paved the way for another tidal wave in popular-culture: "The sense of possibility, of optimism, inevitable progress had been so buoying in the first three years of the 1960s that the youth of America took Kennedy's death especially hard."[4] Those who had entered junior-high in 1960 could not cope with the shock, felt wronged by forces beyond their control. "It was as if optimism itself had been gunned down in Dealey Plaza."[5] Adulation of the Beatles allowed teenagers "to fill this emotional and spiritual void, this deep grieving."[6] The Fab Four arrived when most needed. "Through the Beatles, some of us began to believe again that things were going to be all right."[7] A generalized ecstasy, earlier directed at classy JFK, was overnight transferred to four working-class kids from Liverpool. What mattered most was what these two entities had in common for a public craving youth and optimism; they offered hope.

Tragically, such joyful noise would not last long. Events of 1968, notably the assassinations of Dr. Martin Luther King (4/4/1968) and Sen. Robert Kennedy (6/6/1968), would annihilate any sense that altruism could yet win out. This led to what Sen. Eugene J. McCarthy, an obscure Democrat from Minnesota who would become the peace candidate by opposing the Vietnam War, described as a "hopeless"[8] period. Still, that remained four years off. In early 1964, most citizens were all but unaware of America's ongoing engagement in Southeast Asia. When the Beatles swept in, followed by other Brit groups, rock music and youth movies—in existence for ten years—would continue to blend into a larger youth culture dependent on their inseparable relationship. Already, the soundtrack of rock films had stretched beyond anything existing in more conventional ('adult') cinema. There, music was experienced in a theatre, perhaps popping up again via some hit single on record and radio, people sometimes humming the tune. Rock movie music remained with teenagers always. They listened to rock radio stations while driving from the theater to a newly-completed mall, where that music played over a sound system. Every afternoon, Dick Clark would feature this music on TV; each evening, they'd head up to their rooms and listen via radio or records. Then it was back to the movie a.s.a.p. to catch it again, for here was the onset of what would come to be called a "repeat viewing market."

As Jerry Garcia of the Grateful Dead would years later recall, *A Hard Day's Night* "had more impact on me and everybody I knew than (early Beatle) music did."[9] Indeed, if the music transformed the Beatles into overnight youth idols, that movie would establish them as lasting, highly influential pop-culture icons. And not only with the young.

*

Initially to have been titled "Beatlemania," A *Hard Day's Night* in its origi-nal conception was to be an inexpensive exploitation item. Its journey from minor-league entertainment to influential cinematic art, included today on many lists of the greatest films,[10] had to do with an unpredictable combina-tion of talent unexpectedly merging. For those who accept the auteur theory, with its insistence that a movie is ultimately only as good as its director,[11] the success is credited to Richard Lester (1932–). American-born though London-based, he was the first choice of all four Beatles to direct; Lennon was particularly excited when he noticed Lester's name on the list of potential candidates.[12] If Americans like Chuck Berry, Little Richard, Jerry Lee Lewis and others had, via their musical influence, led to the early Beatle sound, Lester unconsciously created their personalities (or at least public personas). With collaborators Spike Milligan and Harry Secombe, he was one of the zany geniuses behind *The Goon Show*, a 1950s BBC radio project that finally reached TV as *The Idiot Weekly*. Compared to the droll, dark Brit comedies from the Ealing Studio—*Kind Hearts and Coronets* (Robert Harner, 1949), *The Lavender Hill Mob* (Charles Crichton, 1951)—or those broadly-silly Benny Hill (1924–1992) vehicles and lowbrow *Carry On . . .* shenanigans, The Goons were avant-garde—surrealists who created, for the radio, sounds never before experienced in the real world or mass media. Lennon watched the TV incarnation and their emergent superstar, Peter Sellers, "religiously,"[13] fascinated by their combination of unrestrained goofiness with a smart, edgy attitude. In time, such English comedic institutions as *Monty Python's Flying Circus* and, in the U.S., *The Firesign Theatre*, *Laugh-In*, and *Saturday Night Live* all drew heavily on The Goons' puckish approach for their own sensibilities.

As to the Beatles, a sardonic yet lighthearted attitude toward their grow-ing legend, contrasting with an intense commitment to musical craftsmanship, had been evident in early live performances. Original drummer Pete Best's inability to leave his sultry Elvis/1950s image behind to join in such a Sixties' romp sensibility had more to do with his abandonment shortly before inter-national stardom than Best's musical gifts.[14] 'Intellectual clowns' serves as an apt description for the now-jelled Fab Four; like The Goons, the Beatles were aware of The Marx Bros. and their giddy approach to deflating pretension, particularly in *Duck Soup* (Leo McCarey, 1933), a favorite of Lennon and Lester.[15] The latter's feature-film directorial debut, *The Running Jumping and Standing Still Film* (1960) with Sellers, cinched him as their first/only choice. Given the official nod, Lester suggested Alun Owen (1925–1994), a gifted TV writer, to devise a screenplay. Lennon and his colleagues had adored "No Trams to Lime Street" (1959), a teleplay by fellow Liverpudlian Owen that, in their estimation, encapsulated the singular personality of their home-city. Lester and Owen developed a scenario in which the Beatles, now famous, leave Liverpool by train and head for London to appear on a TV show. From day one, with The Beatles' support, the director-writer team set about capturing what fans believed to be The Beatles' essence. Gilbert Taylor's black-and-white cinematography allowed for a documentary look as to individual images in the film shot on location.

Yet all involved were aware that the result would be more mythic than realistic. The complexity of relationships between band members, often strained, would not be acknowledged. Nor would their difficult dealings with the financial arena of show business. To suggest a fanciful departure from reality, Lester employed his earlier Goon approach—surreal sounds set against actual settings; bouncing bowler hats and fake beards that may have been intended as homages to Hans Richter's *Ghosts Before Breakfast* (1928), an early avant-garde classic. Also, Lester constantly references the daring new styles that had just come into being in England and Europe. Young filmmakers in Paris (Jean-Luc Godard, Francois Truffaut) employed hand-held cameras to free their visuals from the old tripod for what came to be called a Cinema Verite effect. In *Breathless* (1960) and *Jules and Jim* (1962) respectively, these young Turks featured bizarre editing tropes to fracture any time-space continuum and hand-held camera movements to suggest their characters' own hunger for personal freedom. While these experiments would not have yet been allowed in any major studio film, English or American, the Beatle movie was perceived as such a minor affair that executives-in-charge cared little as to what Lester did, so long as he had the film ready for a summer release.

(a)

(b)

THE (MUSICAL) TIMES, THEY ARE A-CHANGIN': (a) With the advent of the
Beatles and A *Hard Day's Night* (courtesy: Proscenium Films/Maljack Prods/Walter Stenson/
UA), rock 'n' roll was taken seriously as an art form for the first time; (b) shortly, Bob Dylan—
known for his 'pure' folk recordings—invented folk-rock, touring England in *Dont* (sic) *Look
Back* (courtesy: Leacock Pennebaker/Docurama/Warners Home Video).

If there is an underlying theme, it is a genial representation of the Generation Gap. In addition to offering living-cartoon extensions of The Beatles, here the foursome signifies the era's New Youth. They and adoring (mostly female) fans are set against caricatures of up-tight adults: a stuffy gent (Richard Vernon) who boards the train, Paul's "dirty old man" grandfather (Wilfrid Brambell), constantly insisting he's "clean"; a mannered London TV producer (Victor Spinetti); an over-bearing manager (Norman Rossington). The distinction between the film's created world and the Beatles' daily reality is obvious. Their actual manager (Brian Epstein; 1934–1967) was, as Lennon described him, "The Fifth Beatle,"[16] a loyal friend and sympathetic ear. Portraying that existent situation, however, wouldn't have allowed for needed comedic tension. Though widely accepted as an accurate portrait of the Beatles this was an artistic construct.

That term—"construct"—would prove all-important, particularly when considering A Hard Day's Night in comparison to a later (and decidedly non-Lester) film, The Magical Mystery Tour (Bernard Knowles; The Beatles, 1967). A Hard Day's Night went before the cameras on March 2, continuing for about six weeks, mostly shot in sequential order. Watching, a viewer's sensation is of being allowed a peek on the unrestrained fun that appears to be pure innovation every step of the way. However convincing, this audience-impact is entirely illusory.[17] Before writing, Owen spent time with the Beatles, noting not only the way they generally conversed but also specific phrases, these soon entering the script. Meanwhile Lester jotted down sight-gags, added alongside Owen's dialogue. A Hard Day's Night may play as pure romp and innovation, everything devised on the spot. The genius of the piece is the manner in which a film that had been planned to the nth degree could appear as so flamboyantly off-the-cuff. Lennon would recall that the collaborators were determined to show the Beatles as participants in their own overnight-legend status yet prisoners of it.[18] One moment that conveys such an ideology through an enjoyable anecdote, with no need to halt the fun and verbally state this message, has Ringo rushing through the London streets, attempting to escape lovely girls pursuing him. They do so because he's a Beatle; he runs not from them per se, rather to escape their desire to latch onto a celebrity, this a dehumanizing process that objectifies him. Any Beatle would do! Moments after, Ringo notes another pretty woman passing by, she unaware of who he might be. Intrigued by the notion of obscurity in her eyes, Ringo approaches but is told in no uncertain terms, "piss off." He dejectedly does. Like his pals, Ringo is caught in a paradox. As a Beatle, he can have virtually any girl he meets. As a person, he'll be rejected, the case before achieving fame.

*

That it would score at the box-office was a foregone conclusion. What had not been expected was the virtually unanimous praise garnered from the press. *Time's* anonymous reviewer called it "One of the smoothest, freshest, funniest films ever made for purposes of exploitation."[19] Embedded in that phrase was an issue which would dominate criticism from this moment on: Did/should a work's initial inception (in this case, merely to make money) be considered in assessing its aesthetic value? More important was a review from Bosley Crowther (1905–1981), then the grand old man of the *New York Times*. Ordinarily, Crowther would not deign to write about "minor" movies, leaving this to his colleague Howard Thompson while concentrating on major Hollywood productions and 'serious' international imports. The fact that he attended *A Hard Day's Night* suggests Crowther sensed something important in the air. Equally notable, this critic, known for his objective tone, waxed rhapsodically subjective. Uncharacteristically, he began:

> This is going to surprise you—it may knock you right off your chair—but the new film with those incredible chaps, the Beatles, is a whale of a comedy. I wouldn't believe it either, if I hadn't seen it with my own astonished eyes. . .[20]

Perhaps for the first time, a spokesperson for the *Times* had openly admitted that every critic, aware or not, approaches every new work with prejudices. Not those, of course, associated with social evil (racial, religious, gender); rather, prejudices that have been thought of as worthy, even necessary for a sophisticated viewpoint. There exists commercial junk, which can be summarily dismissed; there is art, which begs analysis. Yet voices ranging from Susan Sontag in letters to Andy Warhol on the graphic-scene were questioning this long-held approach. Was it possible that garish Sunday comic strips, mass-manufactured tomato soup cans, and films with titles like *The Little Shop of Horrors* were worthy of close consideration? Such radical ideas, now working their way into highbrow enclaves, embraced, even adored, lowbrow culture, from blue jeans to black leather. Perhaps a comic book was not some moronic child's reading venue of choice but a legitimate narrative form that ought to be referred to as The Graphic Novel. Maybe even rock 'n' roll could, should be taken seriously, as well as those movies that contain it. . .

The undeniable truth: suburbanites, at least those who were teenagers during the Youth Culture's First Wave, now lined up at mainstream theatres along with the Second Wave to see a film that, exploitation ambitions aside, included in its style an art-house sensibility, which as a result had now been introduced to virtually everyone. As Crowther continued, here was

> a fine combination of madcap clowning in the old Marx Brothers' style, and it is done with such a dazzling use of the camera that it tickles the intellect. . .[21]

The music also altered everything. In their own medium, the Beatles were true artists, not merely entertainers. Lennon and McCartney wrote most of the material; all sang the poems that, while delighting kids, also conveyed a philosophy on life: *their* philosophy. The manner of performance could not be separated from the material; here was a visual expression of the music and lyrics. The Beatles were an entity unto themselves; not, like most singers at the time, interpreters, therefore entertainers; perhaps talented enough, though hardly artists. By their existence, the foursome established rock 'n' roll as a legitimate art form. In truth, though, they partook of a tradition, never before properly acknowledged, that reached back to acoustics in the early 20th century folk era, notably Woody Guthrie (1912–1967), with his songs of political protest. Hank Williams (1923–1953), whose own guitar of choice was electric during the postwar era, proved that personal problems (specifically forlorn romance) could provide as strong a choice for material as social issues. Charles "Buddy" Holly (1936–1959) brought that concept into the rock era.

The emergence of Bob Dylan (Robert Zimmerman, 1941–) as a mainstream performer as well as behind-the-scenes writer coincided with the arrival of the Beatles. Purists who believed folk constituted a higher order of music than rock initially preferred Dylan owing to the type of genre prejudice discussed above. Such attitudes were challenged on July 25, 1965. On that day, a cult of diehard fans arrived, as they had for years, at the Newport Folk Festival. Pete Seeger (1919–2014), of the legendary Weavers, along with friends, admirers, and fellow practitioners of the form, celebrated what had become their alternative to currently popular music, Beatles' rock. Seeger was shocked, then, when Dylan (their bright young hope) proceeded to play an electric guitar. According to many who were there, Seeger swore "If I'd had an axe, I'd (have) cut the cable."[22] Dylan was branded a betrayer, sell-out, turn-coat; a traitor to the cause.

Actually, he had his own individual 'cause,' which did not conform to that of the folk community. His style was certainly influenced by Guthrie. This had been most notable during Dylan's formative years—a period when, like most artists in any medium, Dylan imitated idols while searching for his own singular style. Still, Dylan's "poems" weren't written about The Great Depression or the Dust Bowl but Civil Rights and anti-war/anti-Nuke issues, essential to this era. To stick with a tradition from the past might be perceived less as "pure" than "faux." Guthrie in the 1930s employed the most state-of-the-art acoustic guitar he could get his hands on. Sociologist Howard Odum has argued that, by clinging to what we perceive (perhaps incorrectly) to be pure forms, we inadvertently transform them into some-thing phony.[23] Even as earlier folkways were absolutely of their era, in style as in substance, so too then should the protest music of the 1960s be by, for, and of the Sixties. The Beatles, as England's premiere artists, might then be thought of as folkies for this era as much as rock 'n' roll performers. Lonnie Donegan (1931–2002), who combined old-fashioned Skiffle (employing home-made instruments devised from farming devices including wash-boards with the Big Beat) stated: "I always thought I was singing American folk music" despite any modification for his own era.[24] With this in mind, Dylan, as America's leading 1960s folkie, ought to sound more like the Beatles than the Weavers. "Popular culture," Marshall Fishwick noted, "is rooted in folk culture."[25] Properly understood, it *is* folk-culture—if only acknowledged as such on reflection, after the fact.

Shortly, posters of the Beatles and/or Dylan graced the bedroom walls of high-schoolers, who perceived them as sexy pop stars. Also, in college dorms where students received them as icons of a new, timely art form. Many of the latter would be surprised when, visiting a literature or music professor's office, they discovered a similar poster mounted there. The times, as Dylan put it, were a-changin'—and doing so at a Future Shock pace. What had in the past been a series of separate audiences, based on age and to a degree social-standing, now collapsed into larger base, their tastes dictated by the young. As a result, genre distinctions ceased to mean much. Rhythm 'n' blues, jazz, pop, and all other forms ceased to exist within strict barriers. Comingling freely, they in the process became an all-encompassing music for the Youth Culture, this soon far-reaching and constituting the reconfigured mainstream. Rock progressively became the umbrella that contained all previous musical forms; was, in fact, precisely what it had in reality been from the very beginning, this at last clear in the consciousness of a large portion of the public.

It made sense, then, that Dylan would return the Beatles favor (their American tours in 1964/1965/1966) by playing England in April–May 1965; and that, as with the Beatles, there would be a Dylan film, likewise created to further his growing musical-legend status. During that tour, filmmaker D.A. Pennebaker (1925–) accompanied Dylan. As with Lester directing A *Hard Day's Night*, this hardly rated as an arbitrary choice. An innovative documentarian always, Pennebaker's notable 1953 short, *Daybreak Express*, offered a mood-drenched view of New York's Third Avenue elevated subway moments before its demolition. These images were accompanied by mournful jazz, performed by Duke Ellington. Pennebaker's employment of popular music to influence the viewer's perception of his visuals set the pace for many filmmakers to come, as yet another once-profound distinction—between factual and fictional films—diminished. As much a slam-dunk for Dylan as Lester for the Beatles, the two collaborated on *Dont* (sic) *Look Back*, a 1966 release that like A *Hard Day's Night* focuses on mythologization of a popular music star caught between conflicting demands of a commercial industry and artistic integrity. By 1967, these two films were playing double-bills at college coffeehouses across the country. The audiences, mostly 21 or over, now wore their hair as long as high-schoolers as the concept of Teenagehood transformed from a firm twixt-twelve-and-twenty age demarcation into a rapidly expanding melding of mind, spirit, and attitude.

An early sequence featuring Dylan performing ("Subterranean Homesick Blues"), like several moments in the Beatle movie, served as a predecessor of the music video. Though this was one of the last sequences filmed, its introductory function allows us to understand that Pennebaker wanted his work to convey a reality all his own, not simply a mirror of actual events. When Dylan and Baez gently sing Hank Williams songs, they collapse folk and folk-rock with country, country rock experiencing its inception. Adding to the onscreen mix is John Mayall (blues), Ginger Baker (rock), Marianne Faithfull (her unique work influenced by rock, jazz *and* folk), all happily contained within this portrait of an expanding youth culture. Also, Allen Ginsberg, the one poet from the then fast-fading Beat Generation to make a happy transition into the still in-embryo hippie movement. (See Ch. 12.)

*

LONDON SWINGS: (a) In *Darling*, Julie Christie epitomized Andy Warhol's dictum that in our time everyone will be famous for fifteen minutes (courtesy: Anglo-Amalgamated) (b) a Mod photographer (David Hemmings) all but rapes his model (Veruschka) with the camera in *Blow-up* (courtesy: Bridge Films/MGM); (c) two 'birds' (Rita Tushingham, Lynn Redgrave) arrive in Piccadilly hoping to achieve fame and fortune in *Smashing Time* (courtesy: Partisan/Paramount); (d) a playboy (Michael Caine, left) must deal with the all-too-real pregnancy of a casual bed-mate (Vivien Merchant) in *Alfie* (courtesy; Paramount).

By the time that *Dont* (sic) *Look Back* reached American screens, the second Beatle film had been released. One song, "You've Got to Hide Your Love

Away" by Lennon, as he openly admitted, had been influenced by Dylan's approach to writing and performing.[26] This cinched their connection as well as the ever broadening horizons of a new music. Though *Help!* re-united them with Lester, this would be a different sort of motion picture. Dazzlingly bright colors create a hallucinatory rainbow, providing a forerunner to psychedelia while hastening its crossover from hippie culture into the mainstream. Rather than seeming stuffed into identical dark suits, the Fab Four recall London's Teddy Boys' self-mocking attitude, embracing anything Edwardian as those rough working-class teenagers become self-styled poseurs.[27] Instead of a fictionalized documentary, here was a broad spoof on James Bond fantasy-spy films, popular after the unexpected success of *Goldfinger* (Guy Hamilton, 1964). Though in truth none of the Beatles cared for the results,[28] *Help!* set the pace for everything from *What's New Pussycat?* (Clive Donner, 1965), a frenetic screen-comedy conjoining broad Burlesque gags with state-of-the-art post-Sexual Revolution humor, based on a script by Woody Allen; *Batman* on TV (1966), making everything old new again via its winking attitude to Bob Kane's (relatively) straight comic; and *The Monkees* (1966–1968), bringing a Beatles-like group (synthetically collected) to NBC-TV, proving America's most reactionary entertainment medium finally hoped to reach teens.

As to the film, *Help!*'s purposefully silly plot had a deadly Eastern cult attempting to procure a ring from Starr's hand. Though hardly noticed then, by today's standards such an exaggerated (mostly negative) depiction of India must be considered racially offensive. As to its music, *Help!* establishes the Beatles' ever greater sophistication with such stand-outs as McCartney's "Yesterday." The film furthers the inclusionary attitude toward all musical forms, with orchestrated compositions by Beethoven, Tchaikovsky, and Mozart; these are presented as harmonious with the Beatles' original work. In 1968, the instrumental "Classical Gas" by Mason Williams consolidated this approach, again belying *Blackboard Jungle*'s false myth that the new youth hoped to destroy all music existing previous to its own. The Cultural Revolution proved the opposite: a love of great music—classical, jazz, what have you. Anyone of any age who had been listening closely knew this for a fact. Between 1957–1960, Dion (DiMucci) and the Belmonts had, in addition to their youth anthem "Teenager in Love," topped the charts with their renderings of "That's My Desire" (Helmy Kresa and Carroll Loveday, 1931), "Where or When" (Richard Rogers and Lorenz Hart, 1937), and "When You Wish Upon a Star" (Leigh Harline, Ned Washington, 1940). R. Zimmerman's borrowing of Welsh poet Dylan Thomas's (1914–1953) first name revealed his adoration of the literary tradition, particularly its more flamboyant and romantic practitioners. Properly understood, rock 'n' roll doesn't refer to "a song" so much as a way of performing one. Back in the fifties, when Little Richard sang "Tutti Fruiti," it was a rock anthem; when Pat Boone performed it, the same number became pop. Rock is less some type of music than an attitude taken toward music, old or new. And toward life.

Such a reaching back into the past extended to long-ago fashions. Second Wave Youth embraced 1800s style granny glasses, retro-dresses for young women, bell-bottom pants for men. *Help!* projected the Beatles, and the society they had helped to create as well as reflected, in 1965, change occurring at the whirlwind speed of a roller-coaster. Though at this moment a Beatle movie could not fail at the box office, Leslie Halliwell correctly notes that *Help!* grew "exhausting . . . it looks good but becomes too tiresome to entertain."[29] Lennon would recall: "We were snorting marijuana for breakfast . . . Nobody could communicate with us. It was all glazed eyes and giggling all the time. In our own world."[30] Well on their way to the hallucinatory if unsatisfying (for fans and reviewers alike) indulgences of *The Magical Mystery Tour*, *Help!* offered a musical movie testament to the fast fading innocence associated with the early Beatle era. This was fitting, perhaps even necessary, as the war in Vietnam widened in extent and media coverage, the Civil Rights movement took on a more violent tone with annual summer ghetto burnings, and drugs (hard and soft) made ever greater in-roads into our society. (See Ch. 10.)

In-between the Lester films, other groups appeared in movies that aped such an aura of innocence, soon depleting any initial interest on the part of consumers. First into theatres (if most difficult to locate today) was *Ferry Cross the Mersey* (Jeremy Summers), detailing the attempts of a minor if likable group, Jerry (Marsden) and the Pacemakers, to break out into the big time. The film's modest appeal derives in part from its being produced by Brian Epstein, the music overseen by Beatles' producer-arranger George Martin (1926–). One film, *Seaside Swingers* (James Hill, 1965) with Freddie and the Dreamers, proved to be nothing more than a Beach Party clone reset on the English coast. Not to be outdone, Hollywood co-opted the Brit Invasion flick. Sam Katzman and Robert E. Kent, the producing/writing team that all but created the youth-exploitation genre, revved up their assembly-line for *Hold On!* (Arthur Lubin, 1966). Starring Herman Noone and his Hermits, the film drew on *A Hard Day's Night* with its depiction of teen-girl frenzy for any British boys with long hair and record contracts. Its best sight-gag, imitative of Ringo's key moment in A Hard Day's Night, features a girl who would kill to get close to Herman but rejects him while he's unrecognizable in non-Hermit garb. Also drawing from the Beatles (a real-life rather than film incident) has an over-age starlet (Sue Anne Langdon) hoping to revive her career by associating with a Brit band; this was the case with Jayne Mansfield during the Beatles' first American tour.[31] In the ultimate appropriation of Brit Invasion flicks into already existing American Youth Cinema, a Beach Party sequence is included. Bikini-star Shelley Fabares plays Peter's love interest. Other self-conscious campy nostalgia shenanigans (Noone riding a white horse like an Arthurian knight) look forward to The Monkees. A belated follow-up, Mrs. Brown, You've Got a Lovely Daughter (Saul Swimmer, 1968) continued the young/innocent band-on-the-run-in-London motif. By the time of its release, the craze was over. A year earlier, Smashing Time (Desmond Davis, 1967) depicted this demise as two girls (Rita Tushingham, Lynn Redgrave) travel from northern England to London in hopes of getting in on the action, arriving too late. The film's title, to put it mildly, proves ironic.

*

However short-lived, the Invasion's influence proved long-lasting. Back in the late 1950s, adoring of Elvis and his ilk, "The British had taken an American musical idiom and then made it their own."[32] The Brits had renewed and recreated what had always been best about early/honest/primitive rock: daring harmonies, unexpected but appealing changes in chord, ghostly echo chamber-effects producing notes that sounded fractured in context, a pace that could only be referred to as frantic. Also, manic accompanying movements proved infectious to fans who were desperately hungry to release teenage emotions (and anxieties) through some acceptable venue. Here was Old and New, England and America bundled together: wild mountain-music from the hillbilly hinterlands filtered through state-of-the-art engineering in technologically sophisticated studios. Though there is truth to the claim that "music was central to the experience and consciousness of many young people in the sixties,"[33] from the moment the Beatles arrived, everything and anything British hit home. Such a trend began before the Beatles, who profited from an already-in-progress syndrome. Walt Disney's Pollyanna (David Swift, 1960) starred England's Hayley Mills as an all-American girl. The international triumph Lawrence of Arabia (David Lean 1962) was directed by and had an Englishman (Peter O'Toole) in a role that only a few years earlier would likely have gone to Charlton Heston. Tom Jones (Tony Richardson, 1963), from a

1749 novel by Henry Fielding, recreated that youthful hero (Albert Finney) as a prototype of contemporary Teddy boys, gleefully getting in trouble with the Establishment while bedding one 'bird' after another. Richard Burton (1925–1984), a mid-level Hollywood star, overnight became a superstar, in part owing to his notorious romance with Elizabeth Taylor. Twiggy and Jean Shrimpton were soon the international models of choice. Tom Jones and Engelbert Humperdinck knocked Andy Williams and Perry Como off U.S. charts as to M.O.R. pop. On American TV, *The Avengers* and *The Prisoner* won large audiences. In swift succession, two Brit actresses—old-fashioned Julie Andrews (Disney's *Mary Poppins*; Robert Stevenson, 1964) and trendy Julie Christie (*Darling*; John Schlesinger, 1965)—won Hollywood's Best Actress Oscar.

The latter film proved particularly important. A voice-over establishes that what will unfold onscreen (recollections by Diana Scott, a celebrity) is being related to a documentarian (an off-screen Schlesinger, earlier cutting his directorial teeth in such a capacity). Her ascension to fame began (if anything Diana says is to be believed) when this child of the working class (as such social kin to the Beatles) happened to be in the right place at the right time. A BBC team, interviewing young people on the street about their new generation, picked Diana for one reason: *She's beautiful*. What Diana says off-the-cuff is superficial and self-absorbed, like the 20-year-old herself. Once broadcast, her incoherent ramblings take on significance. People take seriously what they see and hear on the Telly. This is, after all, the BBC; 'they' wouldn't have chosen this girl if she didn't know what she was talking about, would they? The appearance leads to a modeling gig, Diana soon embodying "the spirit of her era"; next, a stint as a movie star (looking beautiful in black lingerie while screaming in some silly horror film); and, finally, marriage to a European aristocrat. Diana becomes one of the era's leading international luminaries, illustrating everything Andy Warhol (1928–1987) then said in America about 'The Face' as key to celebrity in our media-mad Op/Pop world at mid-decade.[34]

Schlesinger reveals his approach in the title sequence. Pre-existing posters on buildings feature the tragic faces of malnourished children. These images had been presented to make passers-by aware of a crusade against world hunger. They are now in the process of being replaced by new posters featuring Diana's intoxicating features and vacant eyes. Schlesinger and screenwriter Frederic Raphael wordlessly announce the society they here depict is one in which serious causes make way for shallow concerns. Ideas introduced by Fellini in *La Dolce Vita* (1960), which had at the decade's cusp presented the paparazzi madly chasing a similar shallow beauty (Anita Ekberg) through Rome, are further developed: The hedonistic embrace of a Sweet Life, without signs of concern that our world appeared on the edge of oblivion. Only a year earlier, Stanley Kubrick's *Dr. Strangelove*, a spoof of earlier/deadly-serious atomic oblivion movies, and starring British invader Peter Sellers, had been subtitled *How I Learned to Stop Worrying and Love the Bomb*. In an age that giddily accepted rather than crawled under its collective seat in fear of utter absurdity, the cult of instantaneous if fleeting celebrity took hold. Beautiful People—"famous for being famous"[35] rather than any significant accomplishments—reigned supreme. Here was an era in which any girl who happened to have been born with features that the camera loved could become famous at least for fifteen minutes.

In context, 'Darling' refers less to the central character than the term with which Diana, and everyone in her charmed circle, refers to one another by. A world in which everyone calls everyone else (especially one's enemies) 'darling' is a world in which a once selective term, employed for intimates, has been rendered devoid of meaning along with everything else, as Jim Stark (and with him all of us) learned a decade earlier during the *Rebel Without a Cause*'s observatory sequence. The word has been reconfigured for a generalized mid-Sixties lifestyle based on immediate gratification and self-absorption—that very world which the Beatles try to run away from in *A Hard Day's Night*. As Lennon would recall, the second film's title song served as a plea for escape from this very pop/Op nightmare. The boys were desperate for a return to meaningful relationships ("Help! I Need Somebody. . .")

Darling's August release was preceded by *Having a Wild Weekend* (aka, *Catch Us If You Can*), distributed in April, a musical that in retrospect appears a footnote to Schlesinger's more ambitious film. This film's Diana is Dinah, an identical top fashion model played by Barbara Ferris, a Julie Christie looka-like. On impulse, Dinah runs away from her latest shoot (Diana does something similar in *Darling*) with a handsome stuntman (Dave Clark, initially surrounded by his Five). If their hope is to escape the plastic world and return to nature, the twosome is sorely disappointed. "The real world" turns out to be a dump, ugly rather than pastoral; their corporate employers use the weekend runaway as a publicity stunt, exploiting the young people even further. Simply, there is no getaway—a dark ideology, surely, for a supposed youth flick!

Like a *Hard Day's Night*, *Darling* impacted on commercial as well as artistic aspects of film. Initially, it played on America's art-house circuit, appealing mainly to an intellectual elite eager for intriguing imports. Then, the unexpected happened: Mainstream viewers lined up to purchase tickets. *Darling's* distributors moved the film over from small venues into larger theatres. Perhaps, as with *La Dolce Vita,* the masses were less interested in what truly did constitute innovative cinema than the more titillating aspects, including daring bedroom encounters in which Christie appeared on display in the near-nude. All the same, commercial success is what it is. Hollywood's power-elite, desperate to keep up with the proclivities of viewers, particularly young or young-in-mind people who were now the primary ticket-buyers, at once adapted *Darling's* stylistic sensibility into their own product.

As a result, movies, music, and popular culture in general would— *could!*—never again be quite the same.

· 1 0 ·

GO ASK ALICE

The Drug Culture on Film

"Tune in, turn on, drop out."
—Dr. Timothy Leary, 1966

The Beatles recorded *The Magical Mystery Tour* album from April through November 1967. Between September 11–25, they spent two weeks improvising an eponymously titled 52-minute TV film, directing much of the material themselves. With touring terminated, the movie franchise finished, "we wanted something to replace them," Lennon noted; "Television was the obvious answer."[1] Though Paul is often cited as this project's avatar, particularly the idea of non-scripted anecdotes to accompany the music,[2] John devised the array of eclectic visuals, Also, Lennon was aware of author Ken Kesey (1935–2001) and The Merry Pranksters. Marginalized intellectuals, they in the summer of 1964 embarked on a rainbow-painted bus tour, their ostensible aim, as chronicled by New Journalist Tom Wolfe (1931–) in *The Electric Kool-Aid Acid Test* (1966), to dump L.S.D. (Lysergic Acid Diethylamide) into drinking water of the American communities they passed through.[3] Such actions remained a largely mythic aspect of their journey, though the idea of a psychedelic-painted-bus 'trip' that turns normals into seers, able to envision "Lucy in the Sky With Diamonds," appealed to Lennon.[4]

"Intersubjectivity,"[5] a mute meeting of parallel psyches that connects diverse people on a level beyond the limits of language, was described in *The Psychedelic Experience (1965)* by Dr. Timothy Leary (1920–1996), which Lennon avidly read. Fascinated by any transcendental means of communication, Lennon experimented with LSD while contributing to *The Magical Mystery Tour.*[6] The film, though shot in gaudy color, aired as a black-and-white broadcast by the BBC on December 26, 1966. A two-disc album was released in the U.K., a single-disc version already available in America. That album succeeded commercially, remaining at the Number One Spot on U.S. charts for eight weeks.[7] Nonetheless, the film wasn't circulated in America owing to its disastrous reception in England. The general consensus held this to be a Vanity project: Obvious geniuses who had grown so sure of themselves, even smug, that they had come believe anything they threw together, however self-absorbed or incoherent, would be devoured by fans. Instead, such extreme anger was expressed toward the drug-fueled phantasmagoria that, humbled, the Beatles offered a public apology via a BBC appearance.[8]

Despite its cataclysmic failure, *The Magical Mystery Tour* (later to become a cult film) initiated late 1960s Drug Cinema. One of Lennon's favorite British poets, William Blake (1757–1827, had divided his work into the categories "Songs of Innocence" and "Songs of Experience." The former might, in our context, be thought of as an equivalent to such early 1960s movies as the Beach musicals and *A Hard Day's Night.* But by 1965, the world came to appear ever less fanciful to young creative minds. Drawing on elements from Blake—his open admiration of political revolutions and free-love, a willingness to take drugs that inspired strange visions he would creatively chronicle—popular cinema of the late 1960s might be thought of as our Youth Culture's "Songs of Experience."

*

Always, there had been movies that dealt with drugs. In pre-code Hollywood, filmmakers were relatively free to handle most any subject. Charlie Chaplin played a decent cop who rescues a slum girl from an evil dealer in *Easy Street* (Chaplin, 1917). Nearly two decades later, his Little Tramp becomes high after mistakenly ingesting cocaine in *Modern Times* (1936). Meanwhile, *The Drug Trade* (Irving Cummings, 1923) and *Human Wreckage* (John Griffith Way, 1923) typified silent movies that depicted the ravaged lives of addicts. The freedom of the screen that allowed for graphic portrayals of the Jazz Age lifestyle, including wild parties (sex and drugs prevalent), and highly publicized drug-related deaths of stars Lupe Velez, Wallace Reid, and Barbara La Marr, incited nationwide anger that caused Hollywood honchos to, in 1930, establish the Hays (later Breen) office: i.e., self-censorship to avoid what studio bosses most feared, outsiders policing their product. From then until 1969, The Code dictated that any film intended to play at respectable theatres couldn't depict anything that might offend anyone. As a result, forbidden subjects became the province of Poverty Row outfits. These supplied a steady stream of seamy product for a disreputable grindhouse circuit.

Cocaine Fields (aka *The Pace That Kills*; William A. O'Connor, 1935), *Reefer Madness* (Louis J. Gasnier, 1936), and *Assassin of Youth* (aka *Marihuana*, Elmer Clifton, 1937) all warned against the dangers of youth becoming hooked. Such virulently anti-drug projects forwarded a conservative view; so much so that, in the heydays of 1960s Drug Culture, they were shown "in italics" to hipsters who passed a joint around while watching. While World War II raged, even exploitation filmmakers turned to propaganda films. With the great conflict over, things returned to normal (a new normal, of course). On September 1, 1948 Robert Mitchum (1917–1997), who had recently become an offbeat film-noir lead (*Crossfire* (Edward Dmytryk, 1947) and blonde starlet Lila Leeds (1928–1999) were busted while smoking marijuana. Mitchum's career, which everyone assumed doomed, survived, making clear how quickly values had changed. Leeds, unable to recover, received an offer from quickie-flick filmmaker Sam Newfield to star in a movie designed to capitalize on lurid headlines.

The result, *"She Shoulda Said 'No!'"* (1949), proved so shoddy that director Newfield employed the pseudonym 'Sherman Scott.' The storyline follows nice girl Alice who, at college, puffs on a joint to join an in-crowd only to become hooked. Though fictional, the film was retitled *The Lila Leeds Story* to exploit the scandal, also *Wild Weed* and *Devil's Weed*. The incident's notoriety caused this no-budget item to, surprisingly, be a moneymaker. When mainstream theatre owners decided it was time to get in on such fast bucks, they presented the film without advance publicity. Instead, word-of-mouth spread among the "decent" folk, hungry for a peek but too "respectable" to visit some sordid grindhouse during daylight hours. Such showings always took place very late; some film historians believe this was how the term 'midnight movies' emerged.[9]

During the postwar era, as a liberalizing of the Hollywood product commenced and the Production Code necessarily adjusted, drug use returned to mainstream films. Most famous among them was *The Man with the Golden Arm* (Otto Preminger, 1955) starring Frank Sinatra as a heroin addict in a drama based on the novel by Nelson Algren. Though bolstered by strong reviews, the film was denied an MPAA Seal of Approval owing to horrific depictions of the character's withdrawal symptoms. Thanks to the box-office intake at posh movie-houses, the Code had to be altered. Still, the next such film, *Monkey on My Back* (Andre de Toth, 1957), was released without benefit of a Seal, likewise playing respectable venues, without controversy. When *A Hatful of Rain* (Fred Zinnemann, 1957) opened later that year and was acclaimed as one of the decade's finest films, drug depiction became as open a subject as, say, alcohol abuse.

   This subject swiftly entered into the emergent Youth Culture, if always (for the time being) portrayed negatively. *Teenage Devil Dolls* (aka *One Way Ticket to Hell*; D.B. Lawrence Price, Jr., 1954) had been filmed three years earlier by the one-time auteur to complete a Master's Degree at UCLA film school. Intended as a satire on grindhouse drug exposes, the movie received commercial release as a serious Youth Market cautionary fable. *Blackboard Jungle* included a drug reference during the final classroom confrontation when a student warns teacher Dadier that Artie West's outrageous behavior is a result of his being "hopped up on drugs." The first true Youth Cult Drug Movie would soon follow. *High School Confidential!* (Jack Arnold, 1958) initially appears one more J.D. exploitation item. Jerry Lee Lewis appears as himself, singing the title tune while students stream into a "typical" high school. All the genre clichés are present, including Russ Tamblyn as a new arrival planning to take over everything, Jan Sterling as yet another dream girl female teacher. As this was an Albert Zugsmith opus, there's a role for Mamie Van Doren as Tamblyn's promiscuous aunt. The "Buzz" character, in black-leather jacket, is played by John Drew Barrymore (aka John Barrymore Jr.).

   Then, everything changes; he's a marijuana dealer, hooking nice girls (Diane Jergens, Jody Fair) on pot he acquires from adult pushers (Ray Anthony, Jackie Coogan). In an effective reversal, Tamblyn is revealed to be a cop, gone undercover; Robert Blees based his screenplay on an incident from his career in law enforcement.[10] The ice broken, Youth Films were now free to depict drug abuse if only in a negative manner. *The Cool and the Crazy* (William Witney, 1958) featured an inverse of *High School Confidential's* paradigm: The new kid (Scott Marlowe) is the pusher. Though the script by Richard Sarafian oversells its premise that marijuana isn't only dangerous but deadly, on-location shooting in Kansas City allows for a vivid sense of juvenile noir. Next, the low budget *High School Big Shot* (Joel Rapp, 1959) had its teen-nerd character (Tom Pittman) try to impress a girl (Virginia Aldridge) by becoming involved in a drug-deal.

Even period-pictures, when designed for the youth-audience, offered anti-drug diatribes. *The Gene Krupa Story* (Don Weis, 1959) brought teens into theatres for this tale of a famed 1930s/1940s Big Band drummer via its cast of Youth favorites: Sal Mineo as Krupa, Susan Kohner as his girlfriend, Yvonne Craig as a 1950s style bad-girl, James Darren as a trusted friend. The film offered a harrowing vision of Krupa's descent from Swing-superstar to unemployable druggie. In a tragic irony, Mineo, sometimes a drummer, succumbed to the same trap. The following year, James Darren played the lead in *Let No Man Write My Epitaph* (Philip Leacock, 1960). Derived from Willard Motley's novel about Chicago tenements, Darren's street tough is reprimanded by his desperate mother (Shelley Winters) to not allow his father's fate—death in the electric chair—rule out his chance for a decent life. In a powerful turnabout, the teenager confronts her with a terrible truth: His poor attitude derives from her drug addiction. Expensive movies from big studios like MGM pulled their punches. *All the Fine Young Cannibals* (Michael Anderson, 1960) a drama about life on the edge, depicted the addictions of central characters based on jazz greats—Robert Wagner a Chet Baker type, Pearl Bailey re-imagining Billie Holiday. The filmmakers copped out on Rosamond Marshall's novel by having legal alcohol, not illegal drugs, cause their downfall.

It's worth noting that LSD, still legal, received its first film treatment at this point. William Castle (1914–1977) was already well-known for publicity stunts to hype his youth-oriented horror films. In *The Tingler* (1959), his plot included a faux parasite that exists on the edge of every human's spine and causes fear, then death, beginning with a a tingling sensation. The only way to overcome it is to scream. Castle rigged up vibrating devices on selected theatre seats that caused kids, while watching, to believe their own inner-tinglers had become active, like the onscreen characters screaming out loud. Screenwriter Robb White (1909–1990) had become fascinated with LSD as a result of his friendship with author Aldous Huxley. So Vincent Price, as a mad scientist, here reads a book about LSD, then takes the drug, and is soon hallucinating.

*

In many regards, *Synanon* (Richard Quine, 1965) rates as the last old-fashioned anti-drug movie. Set at that rehabilitation house for addicts, Alex Cord plays a heroin addict hoping to win back his life. The documentary-like approach

was undermined by unsubtly stated messages in the midst of over-ripe melodrama. The following year, A.I.P. released its first biker flick (see Ch. 12),
The Wild Angels (Roger Corman, 1966), also the initial film to portray drugs
from a non-moralistic perspective. The Hell's Angels, depicted here, feast on
a smorgasbord of drugs, legal and illegal, before heading out to rape and pil-
lage. If the film never condones such behavior, onscreen antics are presented
in a celebratory manner, the tone amoral. In a syndrome that would come to
be called para-cinema,[11] the lofty art house like the declasse Drive In showcased films that presented casual drug use, inter-related with free sex. The film
was *Blow-Up* (aka *Blow-up*; Michelangelo Antonioni, 1966). In summation,
the plot sounds similar to a Hitchcock thriller, most notably *Rear Window*
(1954), re-set in the Swingin' London. David (David Hemmings, incar-
nating real-life photographer David Bailey), drifts back and forth between
Old London's dreary factories, where he captures grim workdays of zombie-
like adults, and New London's Mod haunts, immortalizing beautiful 'birds'
(another Hitchcock reference) in Carnaby Street fashions. When he photographs a top model (Veruschka), David figuratively rapes her with his camera.
To momentarily escape encroaching madness owing to this dual-life David
slips off to a park to be at one with nature. While there, he spots a woman
(Vanessa Redgrave) seemingly kissing a man and photographs their tryst. As
he attempts to leave, she hurries after him, desperate. Believing he may have
inadvertently documented some silly extra-marital affair him, David brushes
her off. Later, she shows up at his studio, again demanding the film. Intrigued,
David plies her with marijuana (she apparently has not toked before) and they
engage in sex. She leaves, sure she now has the film, though he slipped her
a different roll. Curious, David develops the roll, noticing something is not
right. In a wordless sequence, David magnifies blow-up after blow-up of ever
smaller details, until finally he realizies the truth (or so it momentarily seems):
the woman did not kiss, but rather killed, that man.

CAN'T STOP THE MUSIC: (a) by the time the Beatles shot *Help!* they had embraced drugs, allowing such substances to motor the style and substance of their songs (courtesy: Subafilms/U.A.); (b) a hallucinogenic aura pervaded *Yellow Submarine*, an animated 'trip' the Beatles had little to do with but approved of (courtesy: Apple Films/U.A.); (c) despite a slew of problems, the Woodstock concert emerged in the popular imagination (and on film) as a rallying point for the Youth Movement (courtesy: W.B.); (d) later that year, The Rolling Stones' Altamont event sounded the death knell for any lasting hopes of love and peace among youth. (courtesy: Maysles Films/20th Century Fox).

When David returns to the park, he discovers the body. When he heads back to the studio, presumably to bring the blow-ups (photographic proof) to authorities as proof of what occurred, the images are gone. David visits a posh party, but everyone there is so high they believe his bizarre story to be a drug-induced hallucination. David encounters an ultra-high Veruschka, who earlier said she would fly off that afternoon.

DAVID: I thought you were in Paris?
MODEL: I *am* in Paris.

More than a smart gag, the line sums up this film's sensibility: we live in the mind, not the body, particularly while experiencing a drug 'trip.' David heads back to the park only to find the body gone. Was it removed, or did he previously see what he wanted to, not what was there? Without evidence, actual or photographed, he has no way of discerning whether anything that happened was real or imagined, In the mid-Sixties, in cinema as in life, reality and fantasy merge, drugs the catalyst. Life itself becomes something of an extended LSD trip.

Director Antonioni (1912–2007), famous for such previous classics of Existential ennui as *L'Aventura* (1960) and *La Notte* (1962), here proved that classic narratives from Hollywood's golden age could be revived in a new, relevant manner. While mixing and matching style and substance, other 'collapses' become apparent. Italian Antonioni shot the film in London. *Blow-Up* was a co-production of international movie-mogul Carlo Ponti and Hollywood's MGM. Music was provided by both jazz great Herbie Hancock and Jimmy Page and Jeff Beck. Richard Corliss, commenting on the sex and drugs, noted *Blow-Up's* commercial success "helped liberate Hollywood from its puritanical" adherence to the MPAA Code,[12] shortly gone. An international cinema, devoid of boundaries, coalesced; one that could raise intellectual issues via astounding visuals, long thought of as part of the minute art house's domain. Daringly explicit materials, for decades available at the grindhouse, had never before been seen in such an aesthetically and philosophically ambitious work. Yet like a Hitchcock thriller, *Blow-Up* satisfied as a genre entry. Here was a radical form of filmmaking that destroyed all previous demarcations: middle-of-the-road movie, cinema art, vulgar exploitation, para-cinema now coalescing.

*

By 1966, the public was aware that drug addiction could no longer be written off as a problem for society's marginalized few. Readers learned this from Jacqueline Susann's 1966 bestseller *Valley of the Dolls*. The film was helmed by Mark Robson, who a decade earlier brought *Peyton Place* to the screen. New young talent—Patty Duke as an aspiring Broadway actress, Sharon Tate as a would-be Tinseltown sex symbol, Barbara Parkins as a hopeful fashion model—portrayed ambitious girls hooked on "dolls": dolophine downers such as Nembutal. This marked an attempt by high-style Hollywood schlock-meisters to broaden the appeal of earlier glitzy-trash melodramas by targeting ever younger female ticket-buyers. The movie proved popular, if not a critical hit, in 1967, the year when absolutely everything altered. As a result of the success of *Bonnie and Clyde* and *The Graduate*, old standards self-destructed. Naturally, exploitation filmmakers with an eye toward the teen audience rushed to cash in. Columbia's B-movie maven from the 1940s and 1950s, Sam Katzman, saw a possibility in the "curfew riots" in Los Angeles during the summer of 1966 after adults passed an ordinance severely restricting the area's young people, then coming to be called "hippies" (see Ch. 11), from visiting their favorite clubs. Katzman oversaw the swift script-to-feature process of *Riot on Sunset Strip* (Arthur Dreifus). The movie includes actual footage of the turbulence to capture reality while reducing the budget by eliminating a need for reconstruction of those events. Arkoff and Nicholson at A.I.P. struck a distribution deal. Within months, the film played nationwide, largely to teens at Drive Ins.

Any daring on the filmmakers' part had limitations. The hero is not some young rebel but an older police chief (Aldo Ray) attempting to halt violence without harming any kids, many from privileged families. Tim (son of Mickey) Rooney plays the most prominent, an obnoxious spoiled brat; the film, like 1950s predecessors, exploited not only the material but teen-age ticket-buyers, promising a celebration of youthful freedom, putting such a notion down in context. Mimsy Farmer plays an innocent girl who arrives on 'the scene' in a wrong place/wrong time situation. Seemingly nice, actually dangerous longhairs force her to take LSD, then gang-rape the girl. *Maryjane* (Maury Dexter, 1968) shifted the focus to a small town, where another spoiled rich brat (Kevin Coughlin) turns fellow teens on to pot. Fabian, a pop idol from a decade earlier, plays a teacher who makes the mistake of admitting to the administration he tried pot in college and that there's nothing much to worry about. He becomes a pariah, not only with adults who perceive him as an apologizer for the kids but also to the kids, for drawing attention to their secret hobby.

If relatively new to high schools, pot had long existed as a fringe element on college campuses. Meanwhile, LSD became well-known, this semi-synthetic concoction having existed since 1938. University awareness is traced to Dr. Timothy Leary (1920–1996) who in 1960 traveled to Cuernavaca, Mexico to sample "the Mazatec mushrooms," believed to enhance and alter perceptions of native people wishing to achieve spiritual heights. Upon return, Leary and assistant Richard Alpert convinced superiors at Harvard to allow them to experiment with scientifically created equivalents such as LSD and psilocybin, a compound produced by mushrooms, hoping to reduce criminal tendencies among hard-case prisoners. Gradually, this idealistic mission transformed into something else entirely. Seminary students were given LSD in hopes of stimulating a sense of Nirvana: achieving a one-ness (and at peace with) the cosmos. When newspapers reported on Leary's "work," such important figures as poet Allen Ginsberg, media-maven Marshall McLuhan, and novelist Ken Kesey (whose drug-influenced 1962 book *One Flew Over the Cuckoo's Nest* had become an underground bestseller) supported Leary.[13]

Harvard, fearing that what they had sponsored was degenerating into recreational drug use (though LSD was not yet illegal), dismissed Leary. He wrote *The Psychedelic Experience*; when John Lennon admitted to reading it, the nation's youth picked it up. Folkways, the company which had released early Joan Baez albums, in 1966 distributed a disc with Leary reading from his works. LSD's appeal was solidified when he embarked on a series of university lectures, employing McLuhan-like mixed media—psychedelic imagery and "groovy" sounds to impress young listeners as to the perception-altering possibilities of a sugar cube drenched with LSD. Always anxious to jump on the next big thing, the media—newspapers, magazines, TV—allowed Leary a broad platform, doing so within a stated or implied put-down. At least one mainstream film (if a minor one) featured what appears to be a bad LSD trip. In *The Young Lovers* (Samuel Goldwyn, Jr., 1964), a college student (Nick Adams) freaks out on drugs.

Exploitation moviemakers sensed this could provide a late 1960s money-machine. Herschell Gordon Lewis, earlier nicknamed The Wizard of Gore for such graphically violent items as *Two Thousand Maniacs* (1964) and *Color Me Blood Red* (1965), set early-splatter aside to shoot an LSD trip for *Something Weird* (1967). During the early sixties, Roger Corman at A.I.P. had overseen a successful series of Edgar Allan Poe adaptations. In some cases, these handsome items cost as much as $250,000; as with the Beach films, such investments paid off. Cashing in on the British invasion, Corman shot two in England. *The Masque of Red Death* (Corman, 1964) featured Jane Asher, long-time girlfriend of Paul McCartney. A gifted newcomer Nicholas Roeg served as cinematographer. With a script by lauded horror/sci-fi writer Charles Beaumont, the film netted impressive reviews. Young Roger Towne (later to write *Chinatown*; Roman Polanski, 1974) devised a memorable script from several Poe works for the next, *Tomb of Ligeia* (Corman, 1964). Howard Thompson of the *New York Times* noted that the director created "a compelling sense of heady atmosphere" in large part due to his "arresting color shots."[14] Though the term "psychedelic" hadn't yet entered our popular idiom, employment of the term 'heady' proved telling when this movie, with its phantasmagoric sense of a meta-reality, became a favorite of "head audiences." Drug-cinema cognoscenti now shared a small list of favorite films to watch while stoned, including several Disney family films—*Fantasia* (Joe Grant, Dick Huemer, 1940, notably the dancing mushrooms), *Dumbo* (Samuel Armstrong, Norman Ferguson, 1941, specifically the "Pink Elephants on Parade"), and *Alice in Wonderland* (Clyde Geronimi, 1951)—all high (pun intended) on the list. When released in 1967, *2001: A Space Odyssey* (Stanley Kubrick) was immediately added. As one college student of the time said, "It's a great film even if you *aren't* stoned."

The Trip went into pre-production late in 1966. Several young talents worked on the script, Jack Nicholson (1937–) ultimately credited with the screenplay. He had recently endured a painful divorce from wife Sandra Harrison, his co-star in A.I.P.'s *The Terror* (Corman, 1963). To cope, Jack took LSD, diverting his experience into the screenplay. Originally, he hoped to play Paul Groves, who allows a pair of friends (Bruce Dern, Dennis Hopper) to talk him into employing drugs to relieve heartbreak after losing his wife (Susan Strasberg). A.I.P wanted Peter Fonda, something of a star owing to the success of *The Wild Angels*. "Turn off your mind, relax, and float downstream . . ." is the advice Dern's mentor gives Paul as he travels down an invisible rabbit hole. That line was appropriated from a Beatles song, "Tomorrow Never Knows": *Revolver*, 1966), verifying Nicholson's fascination with the group. Nicholson employed a variation on that statement for Fonda's final line as well. The music ranged from Gram Parsons and the International Submarine Band (more seen than heard) to Mike Bloomfield and the Electric Flag with the Strawberry Alarm Clock and The Seeds also present. Not since the late 1950s did youth music and youth movies so vividly conjoin.

Several sequences were shot on the Sunset Strip, Corman employing a hand-held camera, then in post-production opting for daring editing tropes borrowed from European art-house cinema. For Paul's (the character's name may be a Beatles reference) bad-trip fantasies, Corman borrowed the white-face appearance of Death from Ingmar Bergman's *The Seventh Seal* (1957); the carnival atmosphere in fluorescent color is lifted from Federico Fellini's *Juliet of the Spirits* (1965). Once more, esteemed art house and rural Drive In, a short while earlier seeming opposites, coalesce. The best (most memorable)

sequences are the least sensational. Paul wanders into a late-night laundro-
mat, trying to communicate with an ordinary woman; he sneaks into an
unlocked house, becoming involved in a memorably weird discussion with
a little girl. Always, the film reveals its exploitation origins, opening with
one of those Voice of God warnings that LSD has insidiously invaded every
American community, this "of great concern to all!" Though Paul experiences
horrific moments, at one point perceiving a chair as a public menace, most
footage features Salli Sachse, a holdover from Beach movies, in her bikini, if
this time wearing body paint, as the camera crunches her Go-Go dancing into
a kaleidoscopic effect while strobe lights flash.

Whatever the intended message, teenagers saw a hallucinatory festival
of female flesh. It was their turn to experience deja-vu as Corman recycled
sets left over from his Poe films. The film, which cost a whopping $450,000
(a huge budget for for A.I.P.), brought in over $10 million internationally.
Success engenders imitation; Youth Drug Films flourished. Nicholson's follow-up, *Psych-Out* (Richard Rush, 1968) emerged as less a drug expose than
a study of San Francisco's emergent counter-culture. (See Ch. 11.) Still, the
drug-expose approach is apparent. An artist (Henry Jaglom), who has taken
LSD for inspiration, becomes obsessed with his right hand, which he believes
possessed by an evil force, threatening to cut it off with a chainsaw. Female
lead Susan Strasberg, as the runaway teenager Jill, inadvertently takes S.T.P.,
experiencing menacing hallucinations. For girls of her age who caught this
film, here is a non-subtle warning to stay put, wherever you are, and as to
drugs just say 'no!'

*

The next step was for the hallucinogenic style to stretch into genres that
didn't focus on drugs or Hippies. The first such item rates as a masterpiece:
Point Blank (John Boorman, 1967). Lee Marvin plays Walker, an Alcatraz
escapee determined to retrieve money he stole while enacting revenge on
former partners who betrayed him. A fan of *Having a Wild Weekend*, particularly its dream-like aura, Marvin picked Boorman to direct. The storyline,
from a novel by Donald E. Westlake, offered classic noir of the type Marvin
appeared in during the 1950s. But the visuals are strikingly contemporary,
suggesting this last old-time gangster has wandered into the Pop/op world
of today. Continuing the transference of art-house devices such as stream-
of-consciousness via purposefully disorienting montage, the film rates as
the first neo-noir: Proof a supposedly long-retired genre could be revived if

re-approached from a state-of-the-art sensibility. *Point Blank's* "message": If the LSD trip resembles anything pre-existing this drug, it is The Movies— which transport a willing voyager from what Timothy Leary would call their "setting" (where the person is) if one's "set" (or mind-set) remains 'open,' into other worlds—strange, seductive, threatening phantasmagorias the psyche inhabits even as the body remains in place.[15] This abruptly ends when the trip—from a ticket-stub or sugar cube—has concluded.

During the following year, 1968, LSD-influenced cinema hit its peak, dominating middle-of-the-road product. *Skidoo* (Otto Preminger) offered an ambitious attempt by the fast-fading Hollywood studio system to assimilate the style and substance of the late 1960s, notably drugs, into a general-audience comedy. Jackie Gleason plays a retired mob hit-man, concerned about his flower-child daughter (Alexandra Hay), who is in love with a hippie (John Phillip Law). Though the film is too confused in intent and confusing in impact for any easy analysis of what it's supposedly saying, this does come across as Hollywood's initial defense of LSD. When Gleason inadvertently trips, his dark-side diminishes, thus fulfilling LSD's therapeutic rationale back when Dr. Leary originally hoped to help criminals. During the course of events as devised by screenwriter Paul Krassner (1932–), one of Kesey's Merry Pranksters and founder of the counter-cultural magazine *The Realist*, diverse characters who embark on LSD trips are positively enhanced. A prison guard (singer/songwriter Harry Nilsson) finds himself inspired to perform, all ballads written by Nilsson while on an LSD trip. This was also the year of *Candy* with Ewa Aulin. The teenager becomes a Tripper while at school, this loosening her inhibitions (some might say morals). And *Barbarella*, whose amorous adventures in deep-space are augmented (and her pleasure heightened) by drug-like substances. Amoral was the tone taken toward drugs, the case also in *I Love You, Alice B. Toklas* (Hy Averback), the best Hollywood film about the counter-culture (see Ch. 11). A hippie girl (Leigh Taylor-Young) seduces a businessman (Peter Sellers) via a pot-brownie recipe dating back to the film's namesake, with no apparent harm to either.

(a)   (b)

(c)   (d)

(e)   (f)

HELTER SKELTER: (a) the over-ripe soap opera *Valley of the Dolls* with Patty Duke rates as the first Hollywood film to depict the penetration of drugs into contemporary mainstream America (courtesy: 20th Century-Fox); (b) *The Trip* with Peter Fonda and Salli Sachse scored with audiences by portraying upscale L.A. types who had turned to LSD (courtesy: A.I.P.); (c) psychedelic drug imagery penetrated long-standing genres like noir, beginning with *Point Blank* (courtesy: M.G.M.); (d) Dennis Hopper (center) informs Peter Fonda (right, reclining) that his acid trip has gone 'bad' in *Easy Rider* (courtesy: Raybert/Columbia); (e) an all-girl band hits the big time but crashes via drug addiction in *Beyond the Valley of the Dolls* (courtesy: 20th Century-Fox); (f) rock star Mick Jagger enjoyed his best screen role to date in Nicholas Roeg's bizarre drug-inspired masterpiece *Performance* with Anita Pallenberg (courtesy: Goodtimes Enterprises/W.B.).

LSD appeared in several conventional genre films. The French-Italian comic-book-inspired thriller *Danger: Diabolik* (Mario Bava, 1968) featured casual drug use between the two super-villain leads (John Phillip Law, Marisa Mell), in its original uncut version. Most notable was *Yellow Submarine* (George Dunning, 1968). This animated fable about The Beatles (who did not supply their speaking voices) on a mission to save Pepperland from the Blue Meanies recalled a Disney charmer from that studio's golden era. Yet the cartoon style, similar to that of then-wildly popular Peter Max (who claimed to have worked on the movie but apparently did not)[16] was pure psychedelia. Here, essentially, was a 'trip' that could be taken by children of all ages. Still, exploitation filmmakers prevailed. *Mantis in Lace* (William Rotsler, 1968) picked up on the post-1967 trends for female nudity and graphic violence in the sordid tale of Lila (Susan Stewart), a wild Sunset Strip Go-Go dancer, who turns serial killer after ingesting a sugar cube.

Rounding out the year was *Head* (Bob Rafelson, Jack Nicholson), an American equivalent to the Beatles' *Magical Mystery Tour* as to concept and reception. Here, the subject was The Monkees (Davy Jones, Michael Nesmith, Peter Tork, Mickey Dolenz), a bubble-gum TV answer to the Beatles which Rafelson (1933–) helped create two years earlier for NBC. The script was supposedly concocted by the six-some while ingesting marijuana; the results, sans narrative, recall an LSD trip. The idea, apparently, was less to provide a sequel to the show than blow-up the wholesome Monkees myth, destroying it via a counter-cultural film with a pop-art approach and an eclectic cast including intellectual rocker Frank Zappa, Samson-like 1940s movie star Victor Mature, legendary stripper Carol Doda, boxing great Sonny Liston, and girl-next-door Annette Funicello. Audiences stayed away in droves.

*

In truth, the tide was beginning to turn back against drugs. If a biker film starring Peter Fonda had in 1966 initiated the onscreen amoral depiction of hallucinogens, another belonging to (though fully transcending) that genre, also with Fonda, signaled the end of the road. In *Easy Rider* (Dennis Hopper, 1969), two outlaw bikers (Fonda and Hopper) make plans to travel from the west coast to the southeast on an odyssey "in search of America," as the ads put it. This time, the fable appears to condemn hard, if not soft, drugs. Wyatt and Billy finance their journey through a cocaine sale, smuggled into L.A. from Mexico, to a pusher (music producer Phil Spector). The sequence proves so unpleasant, even threatening, that audiences sense, without being told, this quest for truth is doomed to fail, financed by an immoral act. Though a scene in which they and George (Jack Nicholson), a liberal square, smoke pot in the woods at night is played as pastoral, when Wyatt, Billy, and several prostitutes later take LSD at the Mardi Gras, their 'trip' is a notably bad one. When they are shot by rural rednecks at the finale, there's a strong sense this is not simply a realistic resolution but a final act of fate, set in place during the opening—their end pre-determined.

Even more emphatically anti-drug was *Performance* (Donald Cammell, Nicholas Roeg, 1970). While working on the script, Cammell allowed himself to be influenced by the writings of Argentinian Jorge Luis Borges (1899–1986), who argued that what we think of as reality is actually a fantasy, also France's Antonin Artaud (1896–1940). The latter's Theatre of Cruelty did not imply sado-masochism, rather the shattering of an audience's illusions. Doubling as cinematographer, Roeg brought the same phantasmagoric elements to this project he'd earlier employed for Corman's *The Masque of Red Death*. Initially, the story appears to be a defense of Leary's theory that hallucinogens might reduce the violent tendencies of career criminals. A London gangster (James Fox) on the lam hides with a burned-out rocker (Mick Jagger) and his female friend (Anita Pallenberg). They in the narrative, like Leary in actuality, convince the killer to try the mushroom Amanita Muscaria. Initially, he does appear calmer, at peace with the world. Then, the criminal reverts to his old ways—if considerably worse—shooting Jagger's character, turning Pallenberg's life into a bad trip. Leary was wrong, this mind-bending film seems to be telling us; drugs are in the end dangerous, not liberating.

*

Two 1970 documentaries provided the final onscreen suggestion that drugs could provide a righteous route to peace and love and a revived cautionary-fable warning that the United States was about to degenerate into a hopeless drug-addicted nation. *Woodstock* (1970) chronicled the August 15–18, 1969 musical concert at Max Yasgur's 600 acre farm in New York's Catskill Mountains. This was supposed to have been a commercial venture, attended by at most 50,000 people. But 400,000 who had heard about the event drove or hitchhiked to the rural site, most arriving without tickets. Artie Kornfeld and others in charge decided to allow 'the people' (mostly but not all young) to transform what had been a businessman's dream (now a nightmare, at least on that level) into a makeshift free concert. Drugs (hard as heroin, light as marijuana) were shared, rain poured down, and a variety of acts—1950s rock 'n' roll revivalists Sha-Na-Na (they do not appear in the eventual film), folk-balladeer Richie Havens, pop-star Melanie (also not in the film), Jimi Hendrix and The Experience—offering a psychedelic update of "The Star-spangled Banner"–performed. A make-shift community survived what might have been a disaster, emerging happy if bedraggled. At least two people died (non-violently) but this was kept quiet; births of children were widely publicized.

Woodstock, objectively studied, could have been portrayed as either a disaster or a pivotal moment in the now-fifteen-year-old history of the Youth Culture. The latter would prevail. First, *Life* went with a cover story. Singer-songwriter Joni Mitchell wrote an inspiring ballad. Young people and youth-wanna-bes who hadn't been there wished they had. That might not have been the case were they able to actually see the extent of filth and excrement. Such negative aspects were excised from the 1970 film during the editing process so that a seemingly realistic recording of an event would be romanticized by the omission of what had been left on the cutting room floor. Earlier, when Michael Wadleigh (1939–) was hired, no one could have guessed that *Woodstock* would emerge as anything other than another of the numerous rock concerts then being recorded since D.A. Pennebaker filmed a 1967 rock, folk, jazz, blues concert featuring Otis Redding, The Jefferson Airplane, and Simon and Garfunkel. That movie was released in 1968 *as Monterey Pop.* On the basis of its success, Kornfeld and his colleagues convinced Warner Bros. to invest $100,000 in a Woodstock film. Wisely, Wadleigh grasped that something unique was occurring. Beyond music or drugs, Woodstock constituted, in the 1960s term, a *happening:* a spontaneous explosion of Hippie attitudes. Afterwards, Wadleigh (some attribute this decision to editors Martin Scorsese and Thelma Schoonmaker) shifted the focus from stars onstage to comedy and drama among the concert-goers.

During the year between the concert and the film's release, many came to view Woodstock as a non-violent shot heard round the world. Here was a signal, announcing the birth of a new U.S. in which peace and love prevailed, rock music the starting point. True or mythic, the film enshrined just such a vision. And, of course, seeing is believing—even if what one sees has been manipulated to shape a pre-existing thesis. Any such sweet dream would be shattered less than four months later, at the Altamont Speedway in Northern California, Dec. 6, 1969. Here was where the Rolling Stones would play the final gig of their U.S. tour. As numerous fans had complained about the high ticket price, Jagger and the band-members decided that, to depart with warm feelings, they would offer up a free concert. Pre-publicity hyped this as Woodstock West. Various Woodstock stars—the Jefferson Airplane and Santana among them—generously offered to join. The emerging idea was that this latest happening would prove that the three days of peace, love and music (all free) in upstate New York had not been an aberration but an indication of the shape of things to come: a wonderful new world in which the young, and young at heart, could celebrate the dawning of the age of Aquarius.

That this would not be the case became evident immediately. Moments after arriving, Jagger was attacked rather than embraced by one of the 300,000 concert-goers, most having already embarked on bad drug trips. The Grateful Dead, grasping that nastiness rather than good-vibes would dominate, left without playing a note. Believing (unwisely, as it turned out) that a now-solidified Youth Culture could police itself, planners hired members of the Hell's Angels motorcycle gang to keep the peace. Self-confessed outlaw youth had begun referring to law enforcement officers as "The Pigs" at least since a police riot at the Democratic convention during the summer of 1968. Supposedly, hippies and bikers were all now a part of the same new order of things, the Youth Culture. As Sly of the Family Stone would so charmingly put it, "We are family!"

Nothing could have been further from the truth. The Hell's Angels set about brutalizing concert-goers, killing one (Meredith Hunter). "I'd have preferred the cops," Jagger is rumored to have commented. Desperately attempting to turn things around, performer Grace Slick shouted: "You gotta keep your bodies off each other unless you intend love." Sadly, that was then (Woodstock); this, now (Altamont). *Rolling Stone*, the journal of new music and youth culture, admitted that, with four people dead, this was "Rock and roll's all-time worst day."[17] They might have added that Altamont proved the precise opposite of what it was supposed to have established: that young people on drugs could be trusted to behave non-violently. As evidenced in the film *Gimme Shelter* by the Maysles Bros., circulated in 1970, Altamont (or at least this rendering of the event as cinematic art) presented Woodstock's dark doppelganger.

As to any nation-wide, large-scale movement in which longhairs handed out flowers to squares in hopes of bringing about an end to the old order, an ongoing war-machine sustained by the military-industrial complex, that abruptly ended. By 1971, no one on any campus wore love beads, bell-bottom jeans, or granny glasses. The new order, as it turned out, had been a passing fancy. Ultimately, the double tragedy of that single day's ugliness, Altamont opened the doors fully for an ever more widespread and violent drug culture while writing an obit for everything sweet and sincere about the Hippies.

· 1 1 ·

REVOLUTION FOR THE SELL OF IT

The Beat Generation and the Hippie Movement

"If you're going to San Francisco
Be sure to wear some flowers in your hair.
For if you're going to San Francisco
You're going to meet some gentle people there."

—John Phillips, Scott McKenzie; 1967

Before the Hippie Movement, there was the Beat Generation. Or was there? "Three people do not make a generation,"[1] Gregory Corso (1930–2001), whose "Bomb" was the first published anti-nuke poem, commented. Gary Snyder (1930–), Pulitzer-prize winner and original poet laureate of the ecology movement, asserted that they were at most a small circle of friends which briefly attracted immense media attention.[2] Jack Kerouac (1922–1969), who coined the term, borrowed 'beat' from jazz: People who had been beaten down by the nouveau conformity (white-bread suburbia) in postwar America and possibility of total destruction (The Bomb); engaged in a search for Beatitude, spiritual salvation with its potential to relieve human suffering.[3] By 'generation' Kerouac likely referred not to his era but a dozen or so philosophers and poets who met in and around Columbia University, then moved downtown to Manhattan's Greenwich Village during the 1940s.

Most straights were dumbfounded if fascinated (but not threatened, owing to the Beats' insularity) by what might have better been described as The Beat Phenomenon or Sub-culture. Most prominent were Jack Kerouac, author of *On The Road* (1957), a best-selling novel that spread the Beat gospel; Neal Cassady (1926–1968), charismatic con-man and compulsive car-thief who inspired several naïve poets to romanticize him as the final old-west outlaw; Allen Ginsberg (1926–1997), a gentle genius whose "Howl" (1955) perfectly expressed the group's sensibility and whose congeniality brought together an odd combination of diverse figures; William Burroughs (1914–1997), an older drug-addicted mentor (also a Harvard grad hailing from a moneyed family) whose neat ties and conventional suits caused this soft-spoken radical to appear a combination of Kafka's K and Dostoevsky's Underground Man, and whose *Naked Lunch* (1959) brought surrealism to the mainstream. Also on the West Coast spiritual cousin Lawrence Ferlinghetti (1919–), inventor of modern-phantasmagoric poetry with *A Coney Island of the Mind* (1958), co-founder of San Francisco's City Lights bookstore. Too varied to share a single constraining viewpoint, all Beats did react against Eisenhower-era normalcy, sharing Kerouac's view that:

> The only people for me are the mad ones, the ones who are mad to live, mad to talk, mad to be saved, desirous of everything at the same time, the ones who . . . burn, burn, burn, like fabulous roman candles exploding . . . across the stars.[4]

Mainstream Hollywood, unable to comprehend the Beats, ignored them. A rare exception was *Funny Face* (Stanley Donen, 1957), adapted from a 1927 Broadway musical with songs by George and Ira Gershwin. Its dated book was replaced by a new story about a high-fashion photographer (Fred Astaire, referencing Richard Avedon) who, bored with the middle-of-the-road 1950s 'look,' visits Greenwich Village to discover if one of those Beat girls might inspire him. Jo (Audrey Hepburn), a free spirit, scoffs at haute-couture but agrees to model after realizing this will net her enough money to fly to Paris. There, she can study with an Existential philosopher not unlike Jean-Paul Sartre, whose writings greatly impacted on America's Beats.[5] *Funny Face* merely scrapes the surface of Beatdom, but the glimpse is admiring and respectful, also finding humor in their arch-seriousness about impending doom.

At one point, Jo dances, becoming the Beats' Terpsichore, much influenced by the earlier work of Isadora Duncan (1877–1927) if re-interpreted for the 1950s. Several years later, such a dance style would again be appealingly rendered in *Visit to a Small Planet* (Norman Taurog, 1960), from a Gore Vidal (1925–2012) play; he was briefly a member of the Beats. Vidal's stage-version satirized everything that characterized the decade. The 1960 film starring Jerry Lewis as an oafish alien introduced him to a typical suburban situation, in which the Kreton is at a loss as to how to behave. When he discovers a subterranean (cellar) club frequented by Beats, he's at home. Lewis's over-the-top physical humor is paired off against Barbara Lawson (aka Barbara Bostock) in the requisite black leotard, intensely dancing in the Underground manner. The film's UFO approach hints that the Beats were indeed 'out of this world,' though inhabiting planet earth. That may explain why journalist Herb Caen described them as Beat-niks,[6] fusing Beat with Russia's first space-craft, Sputnik (1957).

*

Only one Beat film clicked at the box-office: *Bell, Book and Candle* (Richard Quine, 1958), a romantic comedy. James Stewart plays a suburban straight who wanders into a Greenwich Village bookstore and falls under the spell of its proprietress (Kim Novak), a witch. Only once did a major studio take a stab at the original Beats. *The Subterraneans* (1960), based on Kerouac's 1958 novella, offered a roman à clef: George Peppard (Jack), Roddy McDowell (Corso), Jim Hutton (Ginsberg) and Arte Johnson (Vidal) presented (or as those writers insisted misrepresented) via noms de plume. M-G-M backed away from the book's central issue—interracial love, which focused on Kerouac's romance with an African American woman. In the film, the female becomes a Frenchwoman (Leslie Caron), removing any impact and ideas. The Beats come off as insufferably self-important, justifying hedonism with intellectual pretensions. The movie's single claim to greatness is its soundtrack, featuring Shelly Manne, Gerry Mulligan, and Carmen McRae, among many other jazz greats.

Here is a hint of what The Beat Generation was actually *about*—why rebellious young whites, mostly from the middle class, became Dharma Bums. Their hunger to sleep with women of color could not be separated from their love of music with roots in the African American experience; the once-dangerous soundtrack of the Roaring Twenties finally achieved a modicum of respectability now that rock 'n' roll had become pop-music's Whipping Boy. No one nailed this aspect of Beatdom so effectively as Norman Mailer in "The White Negro."[7] By joining the Beats, Anglo hipsters announced a desire to *be* black. Such a failure of courage would return in *Paris Blues* (Martin Ritt, 1961), from Harold Fender's novel. Two musicians, one black (Sidney Poitier), the other white (Paul Newman) are expatriates owing to a mutual hatred of race restrictions in America. Equals, they play French cellar clubs side by side, bigotry a non-issue. The film's cop-out occurs early on. These friends encounter a pair of pretty tourists, one white (Joanne Woodward), the other black (Diahann Carroll). Newman has asserted[8] that originally this was to have been a daring depiction of two mixed-race couples. Hollywood was not yet ready for such a volatile premise.

Instead, we watch two conventional match-ups: Poitier and Carroll; Newman and Woodward. Effective, though, in defining the Beat sensibility is the final scene. Newman's character loves Woodward's, yet refuses to return to the U.S. That would dictate becoming a suburbanite. As a Beat, he must be loyal to his great love—jazz. Not until 1967 would a U.S. film dare suggest that a black musician and a white woman might love one another. In *Sweet Love, Bitter* (Herbert Danska), an adaptation of John A. Williams' 1964 novel *Night Song,* Godfrey Cambridge plays a variation of Charlie "Bird" Parker (1920–1955), Diane Varsi the female lead. No major distributor would touch the material, so this excellent indie barely received distribution. The British proved more daring. *All Night Long* (Basil Deardon, 1962), a reworking of Shakespeare's *Othello* (1603), concerns a black jazz-genius (Paul Harris) and a white songstress (Maria Velasco) who fall in love. The film's attitude is so enlightened that no one ever mentions, much less criticizes, the relationship. When the Iago figure (Patrick McGoohan) attempts to break the two up, his scheme has nothing to do with racial prejudice, only that he wants the lady to sing the blues in his new band whereas she plans to retire after marriage. The moody noir carries its integrationist theme further when black blues great Charlie Mingus and Jewish intellectual-innovator Dave Brubeck groove together, proving jazz knows no ethnic boundaries.

Depictions of London's Beat scene, particularly its roots in jazz, can be traced back to London's West End stage-musical *Expresso Bongo* and, a year later, Val Guest's screen adaptation. Proceeding much like an early Elvis musical—*Loving You, Jailhouse Rock, King Creole*—the film offers a savage satire on cynical adults in the music business, particularly their eagerness to exploit such young talent. The gifted youth is here played by Cliff Richard (1940–), hyped as The English Elvis. A bongo player in a Beat coffeehouse, this teenager is swept up by a jaded agent/manager (Laurence Harvey) promising fame and fortune though he cuts an illegal contract to rob most of the money. In an intriguing plot-turn, Harvey's villainous character veers the idealistic youth away from jazz, toward rock 'n' roll, simply because of its greater commercial potential. Here is the only screen depiction of the manner in which the Beats, who over intervening decades have come to be seen as second cousins to rockers, were more hostile to this new music than most main-streamers.

As to the rockers, they likewise despised Beats. A 1959 song, (I Belong to) "The Beat Generation," written by Bob McFadden and Rod McKuen, attacked the Beats' focus on intellectual philosophy over the Big Beat:

> Some people like to rock. Some people like to roll.
> But me, I like to sit around and satisfy my soul.[9]

As to *Beat Girl* (Edmond T. Gréville, 1962), the title proves a misnomer. This B-budget item has much in common with juvenile delinquent films from the U.S. Gillian Hills made a spectacular debut as a Lolita-like nymphet. The blonde bombshell organizes fellow teens in ever wilder rebelliousness for the sheer hell of it. As such, *Beat Girl* illustrates the attitude of conservative social-observer Norman Podhoretz who claimed that "the spirit of the Beat Generation strikes me as (identical to) that which animates the young savages in leather jackets who have been running amuck in the last few years with their switch-blades and zip guns."[10] In fact, few if any juvenile delinquents loved poetry and jazz or studied Eastern spirituality. However, many people accepted that faux point of view as gospel.

*

Surprisingly, the exploitation filmmakers who ordinarily rushed to cash in on anything new remained wary about the Beats. Over at A.I.P., director Corman and writer Charles Griffith did create a five-day-wonder for $50,000 called *A Bucket of Blood* (1959), about a clumsy busboy (Dick Miller) at a Beat haunt. After he accidentally kills a cat belonging to his landlady, the desperate youth covers it with clay; when the remains are discovered, he's hailed as a genius for his sculpture 'Dead Cat.' The film is pure camp and fun as such. Belatedly, Albert Zugsmith mounted *The Beat Generation* (Charles F. Haas, 1959), its screenplay co-written by a young Richard Matheson. Naturally, there was a ripe (and sleazy) role for Mamie Van Doren. The storyline has little to do with Beats. The project was to have been a lurid low-budget noir about a serial rapist (Ray Danton) and a determined if psychologically unbalanced detective (Steve Cochran) out to stop him. Zugsmith needed some hook to hang this on, so rather than have the villain visit a piano bar, the location was changed to a Beat café. Hipsters in burly sweaters, some sporting goatees, play bongo drums, recite pretentious poetry, and engage in truly bizarre dancing. Maila Nurmi (TV's horror-movie host Vampira), decked out in requisite black leotard, appears aloof. When the police-hero stakes out the joint, his partner asks what he thinks about The Scene. The lead character snarls that they're a bunch of "pseudo-intellectuals" and faux bohemians. His comment is offered without authorial qualification.[11]

The Beat Generation at least included characters who physically resembled Beats, or more correctly Beatniks (hangers-on and would-be Beats), however stereotypical. Not so *The Beatniks* (Paul Frees, 1960), about a violent street gang. Their leader (Tony Travis) is "discovered" while singing along to a record and marketed as a potential rock 'n' roll star. The film's title further reveals how little Hollywood, or for that matter the public, understood Beats, again employing the term to describe street thugs while also furthering the myth (see Ch. 2) that juvenile delinquency and rock music were interrelated. In a rare move, television—despite its identity as the most conservative entertainment medium—came closer to offering an honest portrait of, if not a Beat, then a Beatnik. *The Many Loves of Dobie Gillis* (1959–1963) rates as the first network series with a teen (Dwayne Hickman) as title character; previous sitcoms (*Father Knows Best*, *The Adventures of Ozzie and Harriet*) did feature teenagers in supporting roles. Dobie was the boy next door, clean-cut, as normal as apple pie, always in pursuit of elusive Thalia Menninger (Tuesday Weld), inevitably losing her to the local rich kid (Warren Beatty). Dobie cried his heart out to Maynard G. Krebs (Bob Denver), a misfit who had discovered a sense of identity by imitating Beats.

(a)   (b)

(c)   (d)

'SELL IT WITH SEX!': That age-old dictum held true for Counter-Culture movies; (a) a lurid exploitation flick, *The Beat Generation* was merely a recycled serial-killer saga (courtesy: MGM); (b) the first 'serious' film about Beats likewise employed a beautiful woman's body to sell tickets (courtesy: MGM); (c) one minor incident in *I Love You, Alice B. Toklas* became the centerpiece of the publicity, with *Kiss My Butterfly Tattoo!* the new name in many international markets (courtesy: Warner Bros./Seven Arts); (d) a mini-skirted teenage blonde was prominently placed in poster-art for this schlock flick about politicized Hippies (courtesy: A.I.P.)

Virtually every high school boasted such a Beatnik, assuming the superficial aspects—goatee, hipster phrasing, loose-fitting sweaters—if not the essentials of the real deal. Dobie and Maynard entered college at the beginning of the show's third season on NBC (1961), precisely when that first wave of American teenagers, arriving at junior-high schools in 1955, now in large numbers moved on to higher education. Immediately, the show's tone altered, particularly as to Maynard. With each episode, the Beat slang lessened. Sheila James, who played Zelda, a non-beautiful girl adoring of Dobie, has explained that the series had to adjust. These were the 1960s, precisely when Beats swiftly fell out of favor.[12] From that point on, Maynard more resembled Hippies then on the horizon of everyday life and pop culture. As to Beats, they had been born out of frustration with the Eisenhower era, with its elderly president and emphasis on a middlebrow mindset. Overnight, that was history. A New Frontier opened, as John F. Kennedy announced. The new president spoke of passing the torch to a new generation; young people no longer felt disenfranchised, rather the center of attention.

The Beats' raison d'etre no longer existed; shortly, neither did they. When the final Beat movie appeared, *Wild Seed* (Brian G. Hutton, 1965), Michael Parks playing a Kerouac-like dharma bum, this engaging indie seemed strangely dated: a curio from our collective past; an image of a rebel-hero that had been contemporary only a few years earlier but which now seemed distant, remote; something of an anachronism. The most interesting aspect of the film involves the teenage runaway he hooks up with (Celia Kaye) to go 'on the road.' In many ways, she might be thought of the first onscreen depiction of a Hippie.

*

The Beats and Hippies did share common interests: Marijuana, free love, and a generalized disrespect for the status quo. Mostly, they were different. The beats were darker, older; often in a state of depression; devoid of missionary zeal to win the mainstream over to their ways, more than satisfied to remain underground; devoted to jazz as the musical tie that binds like-souls into a small community. Hippies wore bright colors, were younger. Their "groovy" approach to life implied an upbeat approach. Flower children delighted in achieving converts, hoping Hippie-dom would spread globally. Mostly they paraded about in public parks, enjoying the sunshine. Their music of choice was rock 'n' roll. If true Beats numbered at most forty, with several thousand Beatnik imitators, there were four thousand hippies and more than forty thousand counting weekend-wannabes.[13] Beats adored or hated this new counterculture. Ginsberg, thrilled, was accepted as a mentor. Kerouac considered Hippies shallow, ridiculous. The transitional film was *Having a Wild Weekend*. While in London, Steve (Dave Clark) and Dinah (Barbara Ferris) are surrounded by Hippies. As the two tear off for that wild weekend, they pass one flower-child after another on the streets. When they reach a natural setting, boy and girl discover a deserted building full of sad people. These are Britain's last Beats; they've retreated here to die, along with the movement they were once a part of. The leads return to London where everyone—at least everyone young or trying to appear young—wants to have fun.

In America, the Movement coalesced in 1966 when some 10,000+ long-hairs called Haight-Ashbury home.[14] They were diverse: Long-time residents, younger newcomers, under-age runaways. Originally, the dream was to make every day a holiday. As Rare Earth would put it: "I just want to celebrate another day of living!"[15] A first glance of Hippiedom appeared in a near-future sci-fi genre piece. *Seconds* (John Frankenheimer, 1966), adapted by Lewis John Carlino from David Ely's cult novel, opens on the dreary East Coast. An aging banker (John Randolph) commutes between his home in Scarsdale and a Manhattan office. What the Beatles would tag a Nowhere Man, he's entirely aware of that. Secretly he makes arrangements with "The Company" that, for a considerable sum, promises to fake his death. Following plastic surgery, he emerges as a handsome younger fellow (Rock Hudson) and slips off to the West Coast. At Malibu Beach, this Second (as such are called) takes a mysterious woman (Salome Jens) as his lover, joining the hedonistic lifestyle. All of his new companions imitate the young Hippies via beach orgies by day and drug-fueled, free-sex parties at night.

Ahead of its time, *Seconds* provided a metaphor for plastic surgery as a (seeming) solution to growing old(er), solving an ancient problem: Once is not enough. As the anti-hero comes to despise his superficial existence and long for the substance of an actual home, *Seconds* transforms into a cautionary fable. Yet another old Hollywood hand, George Sidney, mounted the first mainstream project (if something of an inflated B flick) about actual Hippies. In *The Swinger,* a mature (in years) suited Establishment male (Tony Franciosa) develops a crush on a Hippie girl (Ann-Margret), who inhabits a commune. He turns voyeur to catch a glimpse of whatever "today's" young people do. Aware of his presence, the Hippies stage a fake orgy, treating the leering male to a reasonable facsimile of what he expected, including a lavish body-painting sequence. During the following year, 1967, Hippiedom peaked in life and on film. In *The Trip*, several scenes involve authentic street-people; while on the Sunset Strip, Fonda's Paul descends into a popular cellar club where acid-rock plays and strobe lights whir, marijuana is passed about. Mostly, this film (like *Seconds*) takes place in upscale environs. Extravagant homes where Fonda and others meet were shot on location in Laurel Canyon, the Hollywood Hills. Impressive art on view makes clear these are (relatively) young people with money. Some apparently get it from parents; others, like Paul, have high-paying careers. At one point, he shoots a commercial at Big Sur, a seaside paradise Kerouac rhapsodized about in a 1962 prose-poem. Everyone on screen wears expensive designer-variations of authentic Hippies' thrown-together wardrobes. Everyone (who was anyone), regardless of age, wanted to appear part of the Age of Aquarius. With Flower-Power 'in,' every-day people purchased mass-produced peace medallions; originals had been hand-crafted. Real Hippies tie-dyed their jeans, ripped from years of wear; part of a self-conscious poverty-chic, middle-class people bought pre-dyed, pre-ripped jeans at local K-Marts while Beautiful People spent considerably more on virtually the same thing at chi-chi Rodeo Drive boutiques.

Throughout *The Trip*, characters speak expected Hippie jargon—"groovy," "man," "far-out," etc.—until repetition becomes excessive, overdone, ludicrous. Yet the phoniness of these actors' delivery to a degree legitimizes the piece. These aren't Hippies but members of chic crowd coasting along on the edge of mainstream Hollywood, eager to hook onto the latest trend; the actors play characters playing at being Hippies. A.I.P. turned away from pseudo-Hippies to analyze the actual Scene in *Psych-Out* (Richard Rush, 1968). This time, Nicholson plays a role: Stoney, perfect nickname for a perennial Stoner. Though drugs are everywhere, they aren't the motor that drives this film. Rather it's the wider, broader counter-culture of the Haight. Highly impactful is cinematography by Laslo Kovacs (1933–2007) who would rise up and out of exploitation flicks to shoot *Five Easy Pieces* (Bob Rafelson, 1970), starring Nicholson, the first true classic of the following decade. Even in this low-budgeter, Kovacs reveals his great camera eye, capturing the street-scene while visually commenting on it, eliminating the need for mundane explanatory words.

The story deals with a teenage runaway, Jill (Susan Strasberg) searching for her brother (Dern) among the subculture. This allows her to become involved with area inhabitants including Nicholson's Stoney, an aspiring musician, and Dave (Dean Stockwell), a guru-like character who rarely leaves his lair. If Stoney's drug-use is casual and communal, passing joints around with fellow rockers (Adam Roarke, Max Julien), Dave's serves as a means to an end; every drug-high hopefully brings him closer to God, Truth, Nirvana. A turning point occurs when an agent offers representation for Stoney's band. Instead of elation, Dave expresses concern. Dave is a Hippie, dedicated to those values all speak of. Stoney, in contrast, gradually reveals himself to be a poseur, *The Trip*'s Paul in embryo. If Stoney can score bigger gigs, he'll abandon old friends to swiftly reach the top. *Psych-Out* posits the two as foils. It makes sense then that at the end, Dave dies while Stoney is on the verge of achieving success. Jill, meanwhile, is so devastated by her bad trip that she appears ready to run away from Hippie-dom, back home to the straight life.

*

Even at its peak, Hippie-Era Cinema warned about the dire consequences of such a seemingly sweet lifestyle. Just such a dual cautionary-fable—the dangers of drugs and a potential for seemingly sincere people to be corrupted—would be forwarded in *The Love Ins*. Over at Columbia, Sam Katzman still ran the exploitation unit, producing this cheap item (Arthur Dreifuss, 1967) which, lurid title aside, is an ambitious undertaking. The story has less to do with its title premise (free sex) than radical politics then evolving. This led to a Hippie sub-set. The Yippies (Youth International Party) constituted a far-left political wing led by such strident activists as Abbie Hoffman (1936–1989) and Jerry Rubin (1938–1994).[16] In the film, Larry (James MacArthur) and girlfriend Patricia (Susan Oliver) are expelled from a San Francisco college for publishing an Underground newspaper. In protest, Dr. Jonathan Barnett (Richard Todd) quits his job. Shortly, the three share a shabby, overcrowded apartment. As a result of his beau geste, Barnett (who like Timothy Leary advocates LSD as a positive mind-expanding experience) becomes a hero to local longhairs. At the movie's midpoint, everything alters. During a drug-experimentation session, Patricia experiences a bad trip, coming to believe she's Alice in Wonderland. Freaking, she has to be subdued by Larry. This causes the young man to do some soul-searching. While he never turns his back on freedom of speech or free love, Larry does decide that drugs are a mistake. But when he attempts to confront Dr. Barnett about this, the youth is rudely rejected.

Meanwhile, another seeming Hippie, Elliott (Mark Goddard), has negatively influenced the once altruistic if wrongheaded doctor. Speeches delivered for free in the park are now packaged, attendees needing to purchase tickets. Step by step, Elliott turns the onetime man of principle into a naïve dupe, later a cynic who craves power and adulation. As ever-more adults as well as teens are won over to his 'way' (which resembles the Hare Krishna movement) and Patricia abandons Larry to become this charismatic figure's mistress, Barnett believes less in the message he once honestly proposed, dedicated only to his self as superstar, with political ambitions on a national level. The film resembles, in theme if not in quality, *All the King's Men* (Robert Rossen, 1949) and *A Face in the Crowd* (Elia Kazan, 1957), depictions of home-grown demagogues who once cared about values and people. Larry assassinates Barnett at a rally only to realize that instead of ending this nightmare, he has forwarded it. Barnett will become a martyr, ever more romanticized in memory.

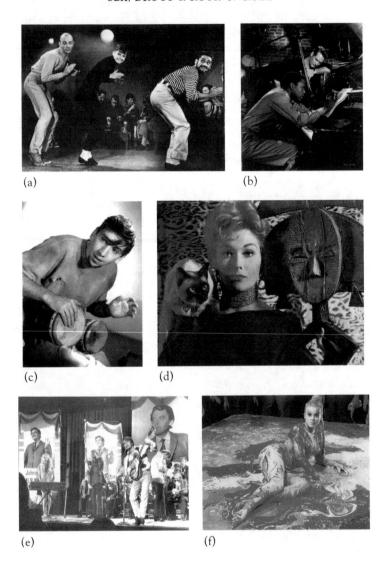

THE BEATS AND THE HIPPIES: (a) In a rare Hollywood A film about the counter-culture, Audrey Hepburn (center) becomes an Underground-style Terpsichore in *Funny Face* (courtesy: Paramount); (b) Sidney Poitier (lower left) and Paul Newman (upper right) play jazz musicians who head abroad to escape narrow-mindedness and racial prejudice at home in *Paris Blues* (courtesy: United Artists); (c) Bob Denver portrayed a high school 'Beatnik,' complete with goatee and bongo drums, on TV's *The Many Loves of Dobie Gillis* (courtesy: CBS); (d) In *Bell, Book, and Candle*, Kim Novak enacted Greenwich Village's most bewitching Beat (courtesy: Columbia); (e) a rock star (Chris Jones) is co-opted by a slick political leader in *Wild in the Streets* (courtesy: A.I.P.); (f) Ann-Margret indulges in a body-painting 'happening' at a Hippie commune in *The Swinger* (courtesy: Paramount).

The following year, A.I.P. released *Wild in the Streets* (Barry Shear), its narrative a projection of growing fears that Hippie-dom's emergent political agenda would re-ignite the Generation Gap. Max Frost (Christopher Jones), a charismatic rocker, is enlisted by a senatorial hopeful (Hal Holbrook) to campaign for him and bring in the youth vote. When this succeeds beyond anyone's expectations, Max runs for president, winning by a landslide once the voting age is lowered. In office, he goes power-mad and, living up to the mantra "never trust anyone over 30," insists everybody above that age be rounded up, kept in camps, and spoon-fed LSD. In a not-unexpected irony, Max is eventually taken down by ten-year-olds who believe the phrase ought to be altered to "never trust anyone over 20." An inverse of that concept had already been presented in the English art-house item *Privilege* (Peter Watkins, 1967). In it, a naïve singer (Paul Jones) is manipulated by church and state to win young people over to a right-wing agenda until a Hippie (Jean Shrimpton) helps him realize that he's been co-opted by the Establishment.

*

In fact, depictions of student protest (surprisingly positive in nature) had appeared early in the decade. In *The Explosive Generation* (Buzz Kulik, 1961), a well-intentioned teacher (William Shatner) is asked by a teenager (Patty McCormack) in his health class if they might discuss human sexuality. Hoping to be relevant, he agrees. When parents hear of the situation, they assume the worst, browbeating the administration into firing him. Aware they were responsible for this unexpected result, the kids form a massive protest. In Walt Disney's *A Tiger Walks* (Norman Toker, 1964), enlightened young people realize that the caging of wild animals in zoos is morally wrong. They form a protest movement to alter things, youthful altruism here depicted as positive for society. At mid-decade, the country bitterly divided over such issues as Civil Rights and the war in Vietnam. The split had less to do with age than attitude: liberal vs. conservative; peace symbol decals on cars compared to American flags, long-hair vs. short. For every rock anthem such as Buffalo Springfield's "Something's happenin' here . . .," there was a counter-revolutionary song like Merle Haggard's "Okie from Muskogee."

Paradoxically, by 1970 old Hollywood was attempting to be hip while exploitation moviemakers consistently put Hippies down. To update his 1965 Broadway musical (with Burton Lane) *On a Clear Day You Can See Forever* (Vincente Minnelli), about a woman (Barbra Streisand) with ESP, Alan Jay Lerner added the role of her Hippie stepbrother, played by Jack Nicholson in an early mainstream project. The other extreme appeared in a biker flick, *Satan's Sadists* (Al Adamson, 1970), in which Haight residents are shallow as to politics:

BOY HIPPIE: What are we protesting tonight?
GIRL HIPPIE: I don't know, but it should be fun!

Several films stand out for their integrity and perceptiveness. *I Love You, Alice B. Toklas* (Hy Averback, 1968) effectively portrayed the phenomenon from an outsider's point of view. Peter Sellers plays an ambulance chasing lawyer, replete with power-clothing and expensive car, also a dominating mother (Jo Van Fleet) worthy of *Portnoy's Complaint* and a desperate-for-marriage girlfriend (Joyce Van Patten). Circumstances bring him in contact with the Hippies he has, during the past year, been observing with curiosity. A gorgeous flower-child (Leigh Taylor-Young) even allows him to kiss the butterfly tattoo that adorns her left thigh. When he subsequently attempts to marry his fiancée, he can't go through with the ceremony and runs away. Shortly he's living with his Hippie-princess, now clothed in the proper regalia for a convert including Nehru jacket. Momentarily, he seems to inhabit heaven on earth, adopting the phrases his lover spouts. Absolutely everything is "groovy." Their honeymoon period doesn't last long. She opens their doors to dozens of street people who crash in the pad, causing him to fondly recall his privacy. The dream girl turns into a nightmare when she casually shares herself with other men. Worst, he realizes that by escaping conventional life he hasn't found true freedom, only an alternative conformity. Those in the Hippie sub-culture follow as strict a code of behavior as in the world-at-large. Here too he plays a role, rather than becoming his own true self. Hippiedom isn't better or worse than everyday existence, only its alternative-equal. Any social system imposes a mindset that squelches individuality.

The movie that most effectively captured authentic Hippies, as well as the Commune lifestyle, was *Alice's Restaurant* (Arthur Penn, 1969), its inspiration a walkin'-talkin' blues ballad by Arlo Guthrie (1947–). In the song, longhair Arlo, while avoiding the draft, shares a Thanksgiving dinner with friends Ray and Alice, afterwards dumping the garbage. He's soon arrested for that minor infraction of the law. When Arlo is finally dragged before the Draft Board, he's pronounced unfit to serve in the military owing to criminal status; i.e., he won't be allowed to kill people overseas having once littered at home. That's incorporated into the script by Guthrie, Penn, and Venable Herndon.

But Penn employs the anecdote as his starting point for a social epic about the counter-culture's origins. The deconsecrated church in Barrington, MA run by Alice (Pat Quinn) and Ray (James Broderick) to shelter lost Hippies, while grounded in reality, is combined with other such places as a signifier of the communal movement. Fictional characters allow greater verisimilitude.

In such a manner, Penn was able to include the Vietnam War protest movement, American youth going on the road via hitchhiking as a way of life, the fascination with motorcycles over autos (other than wildly colored hippie vans), the purposeful hassling of long-hairs by officials, and the absorption of drugs into everyday life. Also, the emergence of the Groupie as a chosen way for sexually-liberated girls. "I want to sleep with you," one tells Arlo, portraying himself, "'cause maybe you'll get to be an album someday." Penn balances this representation of the Movement with significant particulars from Arlo's own life, including his reunion with his bedridden father Woody (Joseph Boley), king of the 1930s protest singer-songwriters, and Pete Seeger as himself. Fortunately, Penn refuses to simplify; Hippies or no, these are people with clashing egos. Serious problems that infect straight society reappear in this supposed enlightened enclave. Ray beats his life-mate regularly. When not inflicting violence on her, he plays emotional mind games that destroy Alice's sense of self to cover his own vulnerabilities. Though Penn shot the film in the languid style of a French New Wave film, contrasting with the slick approach of Averback's project, the two films reach the same conclusion: People are people, no matter what lifestyle they choose, or what choices (fashions, drugs, etc.) they may make.

*

How quickly Hippie films fell out of favor, particularly those with left-leaning political messages, can be seen by the fates of two released in 1970. *The Strawberry Statement* (Stuart Hagmann), derived from a book by James Simon Kunen, dealt with the 1968 student take-over of Columbia University by campus radicals. Students were enraged after learning that their supposedly sacrosanct university was deeply involved with the government as to the Vietnam War; also an area on campus was segregated. When spokespersons requested a meeting, the university's president sarcastically replied that young people didn't know "strawberries" about anything.[17] Police were summoned to remove occupiers from administrative offices. The movie's setting was switched to the West Coast, eliminating any hope for a convincing docu-drama. Screenwriter Israel Horovitz dumped Kunen's complex analysis of the event in favor of a flat rendering of how one non-involved youth (Bruce Davison) transforms, through experience, into a committed radical, also allowing him a sappy romance with a cute co-ed (Kim Darby). Rather than the ragged-edged raw power of *Easy Rider*, this film seemed slick, not unlike TV shows (*Mannix; Mission: Impossible*) Hagmann had previously directed. Box-office was dismal.

One year earlier, *Time* had tagged *Easy Rider* as "the little film that killed the big film."[18] They could not have been more wrong. If *Easy Rider* ruled the box office late in 1969, by the summer of 1970, people of every age and political persuasion lined up to see *Airport* (George Seaton, 1970), a throwback to the kind of all-star extravaganza Ross Hunter had produced in the 1950s and early 1960s. For Universal, *Airport* represented a calculated risk. If, like other recent old-fashioned ventures that had tanked—*The Way West* (Andrew McLaglen, 1967) and *Star!* (Robert Wise, 1968)—*Airport's* $10 million budget might have sunk the studio. Instead, it netted over $100 million worldwide. Simultaneously, MGM released *Zabriskie Point*, an American film directed and co-written by Michelangelo Antonioni, the genius behind *Blow-up*. A non-political student (Mark Frechette), wrongly arrested during a sit-in, turns radical. In the title strip of desert, accompanied by a lovely free spirit (Daria Halprin), he engages in a sex orgy while planning to blow up the Establishment. Antonioni was a major artist, not like Hagmann a commercial hack. So while *The Strawberry Statement* can be dismissed as failed commercial junk, *Zabriskie Point* rates as a work of art, if also a failure. Partly this was due to the leads, non-actors who, though attractive, were without charisma, much less talent at performing.

Despite what MGM hoped would be the big draw—beautiful young bodies engaging in sex—nobody, young or old, cared. *Zabriskie Point* may have looked like an *Easy Rider* low-budgeter, yet it cost almost as much as *Airport*, the budget reaching $9 million. With a return of less than $900,000, this cataclysmic failure all but drove once lofty MGM into bankruptcy. Clearly, a Youth Film with a radical political Hippie/Yippie agenda had no future in Hollywood. A year later, Dennis Hopper's expensive follow-up to *Easy Rider*, *The Last Movie* (1971), shot in Peru with most of the cast and crew high on drugs, registered as yet another expensive flop. In an incredible irony, a tightly-budgeted film with a near-identical title, *The Last Picture Show* (Peter Bogdanovich, 1971), offered a soap opera about life in a small Texas town circa 1950. A kind of southwestern *Peyton Place*, this tightly-budgeted work scored as a critical and commercial hit. The film was shot in nostalgic black-and-white, recalling the glory days of John Ford and Howard Hawks. *The Last Picture Show* ushered in an early-1970s neo-conservatism to moviemaking. Also, Bogdanovich's success heralded the tip of an iceberg for a nostalgia craze, leading to other films about the good ol' days.

*

What killed the Hippie Movement and, with it, Hippie Movies? A swift series of events sounded the death-knell. Between August 8–9, 1969, a group of long-hairs led by Charles Manson entered the Benedict Canyon home of filmmaker Roman Polanski (he was in Europe at the time), murdering his wife, actress Sharon Tate (8 ½ months pregnant) and four others. From this moment "gentle people" could no longer describe all (or even most) Hippies. When, on February 17, 1970, Jeffrey MacDonald killed his wife and two children, the doctor/Green Beret officer initially appeared likely to get away with the crimes by insisting a Manson-like cult had invaded their North Carolina home, chanting "Kill the pigs!" He had attempted to win sympathy by playing off the now widespread hatred of Hippies among mainstream Americans. As to political radicalism, on May 4, 1970, four students were killed by National Guardsmen on the Kent State campus during a protest. The number of young people willing to continue with such activities dropped off precipitously. Meanwhile, Richard Nixon proved true to a 1968 promise that as president he would eliminate the draft in favor of an all-volunteer military. Though college students had a few years earlier posited themselves as idealists, opposing what they called "an immoral and illegal war," truth-be-told the vast majority were realists (some might even say cynics) who didn't want to fight and die in some faraway and remote conflict. With any such threat removed, the vast majority of students abandoned street protests and quietly returned to classes, parties, and sporting events. One aspect of the Hippie culture they did not abandon: drugs, soft and hard.

Important, too, is that the catch-phrase "live fast, die young!" proved all too real. Many youth idols passed at a notably young age: Jimi Hendrix (1942–1970), Janis Joplin (1943–1971), Edie Sedgwick (1943–1971). As the title of one 1970s film suggested, maybe getting straight was the key to survival for those who preferred to go on living. Ultimately, Hippie-dom—however wider its temporary appeal in comparison to Beat-dom—was as confined to its era as that earlier alternative. When John Lennon cut his hair shorter, insisting if everyone wore theirs long, then long-hair no longer meant anything, so did millions of fans.[19] Like the Kennedy years, Hippiedom might best be thought of as a Camelot: One brief, shining moment when, for true believers in peace and love, good vibrations truly were heard.

Rare films released in 1970 that included Hippiedom and which succeeded at the box office were more critical than celebratory, as such capturing
the tenor of their times. *Beyond the Valley of the Dolls* (Russ Meyer) told the
lurid tale of three Hippies (Dolly Read, Cynthia Meyer, Marcia McBroon)
who form an all-girl band and hit the big time, thanks to a Phil Spector-
like manipulating-manager (John LaZar). He turns out to be a murderer, pre-
dicting the real-life counterpart's eventual killing of Lana Clarkson in 2003.
Written with tongue firmly in cheek by Pulitzer-prize winning film critic
Roger Ebert (1942–2013), the movie emerged less as a sequel to the tacky
Jacqueline Susann hit than a satire, even burlesque, of it. Ebert expressed
surprise that "some critics didn't know whether the movie 'knew' it was a
comedy,"[20] implying this was self-conscious rather than naïve camp. Meyer
had always treated supposedly serious subjects (sex, violence) with a broad/
bizarre sense of humor. For the first time, Meyer worked with an A-movie
budget (close to a million dollars). The resultant product, its lowbrow sensibility aside, played at older respectable theatres and newly popular suburban
mall multiplexes. When the edgy film returned profits amounting to more
than ten times its investment, the reality dawned on all that an X-rated film
could attract the mainstream public. The following year, a more ambitious
X-rated movie, *Midnight Cowboy* (John Schlesinger), would win the Oscar for
Best Picture.

*

While most Hippie-era movies disappeared without a trace, *Easy Rider* remains
a classic. The leads are often described as Hippies, though that was not the case.
Wyatt (Fonda) and Billy (Hopper) are outlaw-bikers/drug-dealers, Hippies
employed as a foil for such self-serving characters. At one point, the bikers
visit a commune and are amazed by the generosity they encounter. "We're
eating their food, Billy," Wyatt marvels. This sweet-spirited sequence, albeit
brief, remains the most enduring image of Hippies on film. Shortly, Fonda and
Hopper take off on their motorcycles, traveling down the highways and roads
less taken. In so doing, they offer an appropriate late 1960s variation on one of
the most original, essential, revealing of all American syndromes: The desire
to get up and go, see what exists over the next hill, light out for new territories,
and explore the unknown. It's not for nothing the first Beat Generation novel
by John Clellon Holmes had been titled *Go* (1952). Or that, in *The Wild One*,
Brando's Johnny claimed: "We don't 'go' nowhere. We just *go*."

· 1 2 ·

LONESOME HIGHWAYS

Of Car Culture and Motorcycle Mania

"Well, I'm the type of guy
Who'll never settle down.
I roam from town to town . . .
They call me the wanderer,
Yeah, the wanderer.
I roam around, around, around."
—Ernie Maresca, Dion di Mucci (1961)

As stated earlier, 1967 was the year in which everything changed, in American life and The Movies which, if in a romanticized way, reflect the world around us. The country had become more divided than at any time since the Civil War. Now, however, the rift had less to do with geography (though that did figure in with Blue State/Red State divisions ever more evident) than attitudinal. America entered into the Culture Wars.[1] One sector of the audience, if it went to The Movies at all, lined up to see *The Green Berets* (John Wayne, 1968), a rare defense of our involvement in Southeast Asia. The other half skipped that in favor of *I Love You, Alice B. Toklas*. Gone, seemingly forever (though that was *not* the case), was any equivalent to the Andy Hardy family films of the pre-war years that once brought all sectors of the potential audience together.

Two significant films released that year reveal the extremes of commercial moviemaking at this key juncture. The 35-year-old Production Code vanished, allowing for a virtual Anything Goes approach so long as moviemakers were willing to accept an R, or harsher X, demarcation. Each movie, in its unique manner, offered a variation on one key theme that has always defined our national sensibility. A previously cited song of that year conveyed this essential American syndrome: "People in motion . . ."[2] No entertainment form was better suited to capture this syndrome than the visual art-form of Cinema.

*

Two for the Road (Stanley Donen, 1967) concerns an attractive couple, Joanna (Audrey Hepburn), presumably American, and Mark (Albert Finney), British. This chronicle of among other things their youthful romance does not conclude with a typical Hollywood happy ending. Their 'meeting-cute' in the south of France (he originally favors another girl, played by Jacqueline Bisset) is but one of four tales. All focus on road trips through this picturesque countryside. Twelve years are covered, not as linear narrative; their complex relationship emerges via anecdotes drawn from differing journeys. From Hippie back-packers to young marrieds traveling with another couple, to truly miserable middle-aged people to mature parents, acceptant of their spouses, warts and all, the plot is presented in a stream-of-consciousness style, which would have been a no-no for commercial cinema a decade earlier. Director Donen (1924–) cut his teeth by making marvelous musicals at MGM including *Singin' in the Rain* (1952) with Gene Kelly. John Baxter appears correct in arguing that the "essence of a (Rock) Hudson/(Doris) Day" type of brittle romantic-comedy-drama is revisited here.[3] Baxter points out that, unlike *Pillow Talk* (Michael Gordon, 1959), this film is "commendably free of sentiment."[4] The script is by Frederic Raphael (1931–), who wrote *Darling*. In *Two for the Road* appealing aspects of conventional movies—beautiful people, gorgeous settings, intriguing romance—were now contextualized within a sophisticated, intellectual framework.

As with other films of this era, a long-held myth is shattered. *Two for the Road* insists there are no such things as happy endings, at least not where marriage is concerned. Always, it's a daily struggle once the honeymoon is over, youthful idealism giving way to disappointment, then cynicism, and finally (for those who survive as a couple) a reasoned, realistic relationship. One marvelous bit sums it all up. In story Number One, the couple can't stop talking while enjoying dinner at a chateau. Seated across from them is a middle-aged pair. They eat silently; the youngsters wonder how any couple could end up so pitifully, vowing to never become like that. A cut-away takes us ten years forward in time. *They* are now the silent middle-aged couple.

In the final exchange between Jo and Mark, they are forgiving yet critical. They face one another in a luxurious Mercedes; earlier, they hitchhiked. Wise, tolerant smiles cross seasoned faces, replacing the giddy laughter of their first joint venture on the road as in life.

> "Bitch," he sighs.
> "Bastard," she responds.

Here a unique story of two singularly realized people also conveys universality. No didactic speeches are needed to announce that this is not only about their lives, but ours.

A totally different approach was taken in *Bonnie and Clyde*. If Hepburn's star-moniker allowed *Two for the Road* bookings at mainstream theatres, *Bonnie and Clyde* roared onto the Drive In circuit, bringing art-house approaches to the masses. A film that vividly recreates a past period (the 1930s) is consistently informed with the sensibility of that era during which it was made. Beatty hired two young and, at the time, inexperienced screen-writers, then a team. David Newman (1937–2003) would, during the next decade, co-author such projects as the retro-screwball-comedy *What's Up, Doc?* (Peter Bogdanovich, 1972) and two *Superman* films (Richard Lester, Richard Donner, 1978/1980). Robert Benton, who would go on to direct, won Oscars for his screenplays for *Kramer vs. Kramer* (Benton, 1979) and *Places in the Heart* (Benton, 1984). Beatty initially hoped to lure either of France's greatest New Wave directors, Francois Truffaut (1932–1984) or Jean-Luc Godard (1930–). Ultimately, he picked Arthur Penn (1922–2010), whose outlaw saga *The Left-Handed Gun* (1958) starring Paul Newman as Billy the Kid had contained the needed balance of giddy comedy and sudden violence. In some ways obeying crime-genre rules, *Bonnie and Clyde* went out of its way to fly in the face of convention. This included the notion that a film's style ought to be consistent. Here, the contrast between a Keystone Cops type sequence in which car-oriented action is speeded up during a getaway (to the goofy tune of a bluegrass banjo) purposefully goes against the grain of slow-motion for the characters' death. This conclusion would be described by numerous critics as a "ballet of blood."[5]

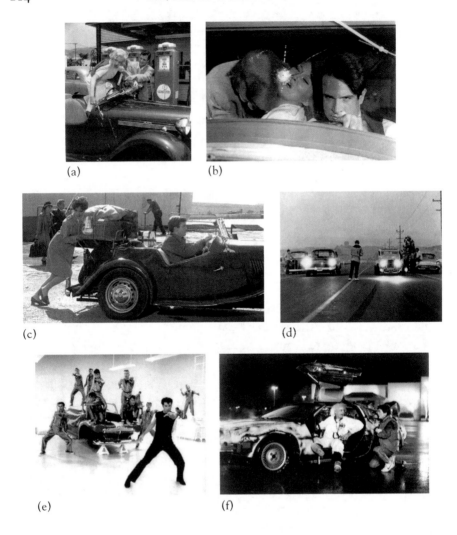

ON THE ROAD: Like movies and rock 'n' roll, car culture represented the burgeoning Youth Movement: (a) actor Richard Long (right) gives Mamie Van Doren (left) a driving lesson in a mid-1950s publicity still (courtesy: Universal-International); (b) in the seminal 1967 paradigm-buster *Bonnie and Clyde*, historical 1930s criminals (Michael J. Pollard, Faye Dunaway, Warren Beatty)—re-imagined as cinematic surrogates for Sixties' outlaw youth—live and die in their car (courtesy: Warner Bros./Seven Arts); (c) from teenage lovers to middle-class marrieds, a couple (Audrey Hepburn, Albert Finney) reveal their relationship via varied trips in *Two for the Road* (courtesy: 20th Century Fox); (d) kids engage in an early-morning drag race in *American Graffiti* (courtesy: Lucasfilm/The Coppola Company/Universal); (e) in a garish tribute to Fifties' car culture, John Travolta and fellow gang members extoll their Wheels in *Grease* (courtesy: Paramount); (f) Doc Brown (Christopher Lloyd) and Marty McFly (Michael J. Fox) head forward to the past in *Back To the Future* (courtesy: Amblin Ent./Universal).

Bosley Crowther, grand old man of the *New York Times*, offered a devastating review that proved only how out of touch he had become. When *Bonnie and Clyde* became a hit despite his objections, Crowther followed the critique with two more scathing articles; by 1970, he was forced to retire. *Time* initially offered a characteristically glib put-down only to, in a landmark decision, take it back. A cover story (12/8/1967), featuring an evocative painting by Robert Rauschenberg, included a full apology, along with the claim that no other film so fully represented the changeover taking place as the old studio system ground to a halt. At the heart of the film's success is car culture. No sequence more beautifully realized this ongoing concern of American cinema than that in which a middle-class couple (Gene Wilder and Evans Evans), in their conventional auto, try to escape from the pursuing outlaws, driven by one of the guys. The middle-class girl is at the wheel in the other coup, and her sad-eyed boyfriend can only urge her to go a little faster: "Step on it, Velma!"

*

The early 20th-century's chief innovations in transportation and entertainment developed simultaneously if independently but inter-acted immediately. When Canadian-born Mack Sennett (1880–1960) moved his small company west to what is now Echo Park, Sennett carved his own niche by inventing slapstick comedy. His Keystone Cops and daring Bathing Beauties looked like so many cartoons come to life as they rushed about at high-speed, this augmented by an under-cranking of the pre-electric camera.[6] Pie-in-the-face became a specialty, if with precedents in Vaudeville. What emerged as The Fun Factory's other great feature was the car chase, in which flivvers roared down L.A. streets or across rural roads. No one had seen anything like it, this unique and natural convergence of movies and motor-cars, both then still new. Many such short-subjects contained sequences in which relatively young people in cars whiz by older folks walking or riding in horse-drawn vehicles. As Mark S. Foster noted, "the automobile symbolized the youthful vitality of the economy, as well as freedom and independence"[7] for an ever enlarging number of Americans.

Kids with cars, including those who wished to race, didn't strike adults of the early 20th century as a menace, merely engaging as a timely hobby. Shortly after joining Sennett's car-crazy team, British-born genius Chaplin initially adapted his Little Tramp guise in *Kid Auto Races in Venice* (Henry Lehman, 1914), Charlie observing the Junior Vanderbilt cup competitions.

Even during the Depression, other than for rural gangsters in life and occasionally on the screen, youth's attraction to cars didn't appear a cause for adult concern. Boys next door worked hard to purchase old cars, souping them up as hot-rods. A prime example was provided by Mickey Rooney in *Love Finds Andy Hardy* (George B. Seitz, 1938). His girlfriends, Anne Rutherford and Lana Turner, don clothing designed for a drive. "One does not enter an automobile in a crinoline or bustle or encaged in such unyielding fabric that sitting, not to mention enduring bumps, is a medical hazard," Helen Frye noted.[8] Victorian clothing (along with its concurrent morality) was abandoned since

> the standard of beauty will change to accommodate desirable objects of everyday use . . .
> Gradually the car began to dictate styling specific to its own unique character . . .
> the two-cylinder Reo was not the cleanest machine to climb into with yards of skirt.
> Skirts obligingly shortened.[9]

Everything in society is synergistic: Jazz, short skirts, flapper dance styles, the thrill of illegal alcohol, and fast cars jelled into the Jazz Age. When the Depression hit, cars and trucks became a necessity for Okies, groups of displaced farmers who hit the road in a desperate search for work. This syndrome was vividly depicted in John Steinbeck's 1939 novel *The Grapes of Wrath* and the 1940 John Ford film. During the war years, when many young people married soon after meeting so girls could go to bed with guys about to be shipped overseas while clinging to the notion that a woman ought to be a virgin until legally hitched, autos were often employed to escape from the madding crowd. "Cars fulfilled a romantic function from the dawn of the auto age," David L. Lewis argues. "They permitted couples to go much farther away from front porch swings, parlor sofas, hovering mothers, and pesky siblings than ever before."[10] If adults expressed concern, there was yet no open hostility.

The Big Wheel (Edward Ludwig, 1949), produced before the public became preoccupied with juvenile delinquency, might be thought of as the last old-time youth car-racing film. Rooney, still playing a kid at age 30, sets out to win the Indianapolis 500. His older mentor (Thomas Mitchell) perceives no generation gap, car-racing being the link that cuts across age divisions. Earlier, the shape of things to come was presented in *The Devil on Wheels* (Crane Wilbur, 1947), the first film to deal with the sudden development of illegal, unsupervised street-racing. The approach taken is a cautionary fable in which the teen-lead (Darryl Hickman) forsakes safety to compete with a rough crowd, in time paying the price. In the first such film produced during the 1950s, *Hot Rod* (Lewis D. Collins), Jimmy Lydon learns the same lesson.

Now, however, a Generation Gap theme is introduced. The boy's father (Art Baker), like Andy Hardy's dad a judge, is disappointed to realize his son disobeys orders not to engage in illegal racing owing to peer pressure. Just such a situation was immortalized in song by Charles Ryan (1955):

> My Pappy said, 'Son—,
> You're gonna drive me to drinkin'
> If you don't stop racin'
> That hot-rod Lincoln.[11]

Several filmmakers attempted to show the other side of the story. In *The Cool Hot Rod* (Sid Davis, 1953), a wise-guy troublemaker arrives in Inglewood, CA, trying to bait local teens into illegal races. To a boy, they refuse; the city fathers have created a controlled drag-strip. There, under adult supervision, kids more safely race. Still, most movies emphasized the negative to exploit interest in thrills 'n' spills. Even if young people obeyed the rules, merely owning a hot-rod or sports car could spell grief. In one of Roger Corman's early efforts, *The Fast and the Furious* (John Ireland, Edward(s) Sampson, 1954), a pretty girl (Dorothy Malone) driving such a vehicle finds herself kidnapped by a prison escapee (Ireland) in need of a swift means of reaching the Mexican border. When J.D. films hit big (1956–1958), often connecting bad behavior to rock 'n' roll, hot-rod hooligans replaced safe-driving kids on screen—so much so that anyone who caught such films might believe that a virtual epidemic had spread nationwide. The truth was something else; only one in a hundred kids who drove got into trouble.[12] One would never have guessed that from The Movies.

Two 1957 films convey the prevailing attitude. In *Hot Rod Rumble* (Leslie H. Martinson) a teenage-rebel (Richard Hurtunian) attempts to conform to local rules but is blamed for the daredevil driving antics of another youth (Wright King). At A.I.P., Russoff and Arkoff revamped their Bad Girls Go to Hell formula for the hot-rod template. In *Dragstrip Girl* (Edward L. Cahn), Fay Spain played a naughty Nymphet who competes with black-leather-boys. Furthering the J.D./rock/hot-rod collapsing, Frank Gorshin performs a Big Beat number in homage to the title character in which curves associated with cars and females merge:

> She's my drag-strip girl
> With a streamlined chasis.
> Got a set of pipes

And a grille that's classy.
Dragstrip baby!
Flip a switch and she's got to go!
Her motor starts a sparkin'
And she won't say 'no.'[13]

One prominent psychiatrist argued that "The more immature the male, the more his sexuality is apt to be linked to . . . cars."[14] By 1958, it was all but impossible to make a Youth Movie that didn't include hot-rodding, *High School Confidential!* a case in point. During the film's first half, a boy played by Michael Landon offers what seems a foil to Russ Tamblyn's troublemaker. He's the class president, always well-mannered. Then comes a sequence in which the kids assemble for an illegal race. Surprisingly, Landon's character shows up. More amazingly, he soon proves to be the wildest driver in the group. The message, apparently, is that hot-rods are, like (or so moviemakers would have had us believe) rock, able to cause good kids to go bad. No film more fully illustrated this than *Hot Rod Gang* (Lew Landers, 1958), in which a would-be drag-racer (John Ashley) pays for his hot-rod by performing rock 'n' roll when not engaged in fist-fights. In *Hot Car Girl* (Bernard Kowalski, 1958), the perennial no-good Nymphet Jana Lund enacts the title charac-ter. She ruins the life of a tough teen (Richard Bakalyan, a genre staple) by winning him away from his more decent/demure regular girl (June Kenney).

The cycle continued with such lesser items as *Hot Rod Girl* (Leslie H. Martinson, 1956), *Dragstrip Riot* (David Bradley, 1958), *Road Racers* (Arthur Swerdloff, 1958), *Speed Crazy* and *The Ghost of Dragstrip Hollow* (William Hole, Jr., 1959), and *T-Bird Gang* (Richard Harbinger, 1959). By the time *The Wild Ride* (Harvey Berman, 1960) arrived, most teens had lost interest, despite the presence of young Jack Nicholson. Like many other late 1950s Youth Culture Sub-Genres, hot-rod movies all but disappeared at the dawn of a new decade. They had not breathed their last. Over at A.I.P., *Fireball 500* (William Asher, 1966) featured an attempt to keep their fast-fading Beach cycle alive by segueing into hot-rodding of the legal variety; a romantic trian-gle was provided by Frankie Avalon, Annette Funicello, and Fabian. The film was successful enough that Fabian (Forte) and Annette re-teamed the follow-ing year for *Thunder Alley* (Richard Rush). James Darren and Pamela Tiffin, the 'stars' of the antiseptic big-budget beach film *For Those Who Think Young*, were reunited for *The Lively Set* (Martinson, 1964), a similar subdued studio misconception of what kids wanted to see. At about the same time, Elvis

Presley, now a mainstream star, balanced beaches with legal racing in *Viva Las Vegas*, *Spinout* (Norman Taurog, 1966), *Clambake* (Arthur H. Nadel, 1967), and *Speedway* (Taurog, 1968). As with rock, hot-rodding had been reclaimed from its negative associations to become good, clean fun—more so as the era of nasty Motorcycle Movies began.

*

Once, when a TV interviewer asked Hell's Angel head honcho Sonny Barger (1938–) to name his favorite movie, the biker claimed it had been *The Wild One*. Further questioned as to whom he saw as a representative of himself, Barger scoffed at Brando's Johnny, insisting Marvin's Chino was the Hell's Angels role model.[15] The organization, originally formed as a weekend club by former military men who had served in that unit,[16] took on darker aspects after the California incident that in time led to *The Wild One*. (See Ch. 1.) Such an idea might have been unthinkable at the fin-de-siecle, when cars and cycles were introduced, then mainstreamed. This impacted on the American psyche. Such 1800s mass-transit innovations as buses and railroads tended to make citizens more communal, sharing tight spaces with one another. With motor-cars, people could travel with relatives and friends. Or alone. A car allowed personal control in a manner that mass transit denied, fostering a sense of individuality, rugged if/when one broke speeding laws. Power, ego, and a sense of self-reliance emerged. Even more than cars, the motorcycle led to libertarianism[17]: One could drive as fast as one chose, the speeding ticket soon a possible just-dessert, this causing a mainstream citizen to feel like something of an outlaw. If early cycles were equipped with side-cars for the wife and kids, such an orientation soon fell by the wayside. Bikes emerged as the preferred vehicle of men, young in years or attitude, who wanted to be by themselves or with a motorcycle Momma hanging on tight, if tellingly behind the man, notably without control.

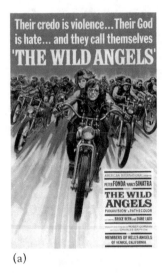 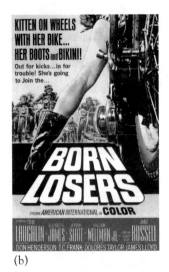

(a)   (b)

(c)   (d)

BETTY FRIEDAN MEETS THE BIKER FLICK: As the Women's Movement achieved ever greater visibility, its ideology appeared in even the least likely of genres. (a) females on backseats are trophy-girlfriends of powerful guys in pre-feminist films like *The Wild Angels* (Roger Corman, 1966; courtesy AIP); (b) a would-be feminist riding her own bike is molested by a gang, then rescued by a good guy, in *Born Losers* (T.C. Frank (aka Tom Laughlin, 1967; courtesy: Fanfare/Otis/AIP); (c) abused by bikers, a strong woman empowers herself rather than allowing a man to save her in *Bury Me an Angel* (Barbara Peeters, 1972; courtesy: Meier and Murray/New World); (d) a female finally achieves full power (and sisterhood) by becoming the leader of an all-female outlaw biker gang in *Hell's Belles* (Maury Dexter, 1969; courtesy: AIP).

What Warren Belasco wrote about early automobile travel and camping was enhanced by the proliferation of motorcycles: An "individualistic sport with rebellious, antiestablishment implications," also marked by sensations of "self-reliance and independence" as well as "spontaneity and mobility."[18] An element of "nostalgia"[19] emerged, owing to a contemporary person's sensation that frontier values were reasserted. It's not for nothing that in *Easy Rider*, the two biker-anti-heroes are called Wyatt (Earp) and Billy the Kid/Bonney/Antrim), or that the latter wears a cowboy hat and fringed buckskin jacket. The result of this "new primitivism" was to foster "a hedonistic focus on immediate experience and gratification that contrasted sharply with the older (American) production ethic of thrift, sobriety, and postponed satisfaction."[20] Live fast, die young. While it would be ridiculous to claim that the auto-car or motorcycle was responsible for such a shift in values, it's clear those objects were part and parcel of an ongoing alteration in the fabric of everyday life. During the 1960s, at least in the U.S., cycles were associated with that class of society then generally reviled as Poor White Trash. Abroad, and particularly in France, such elements of lowbrow American pop culture were revered—Paris, a city where lowly genre films, comic books, and Burlesque/striptease were taken seriously. In 1963, cult author André Pieyre de Mandiargues published *The Motorcycle* in which a well-to-do young married woman leaves a conventional husband to join her illicit lover by donning a black-leather jumpsuit and traveling on a motorcycle the latter bought for her. This story did not reach the screen until 1968 (Jack Cardiff). Under the titles *Girl on a Motorcycle* and *Naked Under Leather*, Marianne Faithfull, a Brit rocker and Mod actress, starred. The delay had to do with a desire to cast Brigitte Bardot, pop culture's original good-bad girl, in the lead role, in part because the book was written with Bebe in mind.

That French sex kitten, who had popularized the bikini, had taken to wearing skimpy black-leather outfits, posing alongside motorcycles. There was a feminist as well as feminine aspect to this. Bardot proved the female of the species could, like a man, follow the advice of Johnny and "Just go!" Here was an early case of a relatively highborn Beautiful Person choosing Poverty Chic by making an element of American White Trash lifestyle a part of the international Jet Set scene. Face-piercing, denim worn in respectable company, even tattoos would all follow suit.

*

Perhaps surprisingly, *The Wild One* had not spawned a cycle of biker films. One reason was economic: Harleys are expensive. Exploitation filmmakers were at a loss to provide a fleet of cycles for a low-budget item. A.I.P. did take one tentative stab with *Motorcycle Gang* (Edward L. Cahn, 1957), a rip-off featuring Steve Terrell as the Johnny-esque good biker, John Ashley as a Chino-like baddie. The leads were so inferior, the attack on a town so paltry that *Motorcycle Gang* failed to click with the kids. One MGM B flick did include bikes: *Key Witness* (Phil Karlson, 1960), about an ordinary citizen (Jeff Hunter) menaced by gang members after witnessing a murder. Dennis Hopper tore around Los Angeles on a chopper long before *Easy Rider*. Motorcycles also played a prominent role in one Z-budgeter starring Arch Hall, Jr. (1943–), whose over-the-top approach to teen-rebel roles caused him to appear like a Tex Avery cartoon of James Dean. Hall's miniscule oeuvre, mostly produced by his father Arch Hall Sr. and directed by Ray Dennis Steckler, proved so beyond the fringe that most of their movies were rejected by Drive Ins, though they did elicit an underground following. Despite its title, *The Choppers* (Leigh Johnson, 1961) featured hot-rods, not motorcycles. A hog was central to *Wild Guitar* (Steckler, 1962).[21] In it, Hall manically rides into Hollywood, there scaling the heights of the music Biz by performing Swamp Blues—a seamy sub-genre of Rockabilly that crossed traditional Cajun tunes and Creole melodies with the Big Beat sound.

During the early 1960s, so far as mainstream movies were concerned, the most iconic image of a cycle appeared in *The Great Escape* (John Sturges, 1963), a World War II yarn. Even in such a period piece, it's worth mentioning the bike was ridden by Steve McQueen, whose image always suggested an outlaw, not James Garner, a steady Establishment type. The most significant early 1960s film about bikers is *Scorpio Rising* (Kenneth Anger, 1963). Bruce Byron plays a contemporary outlaw who models himself on Brando and Dean, keeping their 1950s icons alive into the Sixties. That's precisely what Anger (1927–) hoped to achieve[22]. This indie was the first 1960s film to include nostalgia for the previous decade. The narrative (what little there is) offers stream-of-consciousness and as such, qualifies this as among the first American movies to fuse an art-house approach with grindhouse subject matter. The film leaps without explanation from documentary-like realism, as bikers roar down a highway, to elements that are supernatural, in some cases occult. This alternative movie received bookings in several legitimate theatres owing to support from many key critics, who sensed that a New American Cinema was about to emerge and wanted to acknowledge this by supporting an early example.

Anger includes close-ups of genitalia and violence. Yet these are, in a playfully perverse manner, presented subliminally—each on screen for less than a second. Anger's purpose appears to have been to merge ultra-macho biker regalia, including fetishistic elements (black leather and Nazi symbols) with homosexuality. This did not endear this edgy auteur to outlaw gangs. Defying genres, a viewer can't discern where the documentary footage ends and rehearsed sequences begin. Inclusion of a rock score influenced the eventual work of Martin Scorsese and Quentin Tarantino. Meanwhile, a dream-like quality impressed David Lynch, even as the kitsch sensibility had an impact on John Waters. Though largely forgotten today, Anger's experimental biker-flick was among the most influential movies of its era. It offered an early glimmer of the manner in which the underground would, in less than a decade, surface.[23]

Earlier, a commercial British film explored an anti-genre concept of segueing from realism to science fiction, with motorcycles serving as the common denominator. Directed by Joseph Losey (1909–1984), a one-time Hollywood filmmaker blacklisted during the McCarthy era, now working in England, The Damned concerns a U.S. tourist (MacDonald Carey) vacationing in a seaside village. He is robbed and beaten by motorcycle-riding Teddy Boys, the inverse of upscale juvenile delinquents who self-consciously wore redneck garb in Rebel Without a Cause. Teddy Boys are working-class British youths who affect the aristocratic mien of the Edwardian Age.[24] Led by an amoral overgrown brute (Oliver Reed) these giddy, violent-prone thugs set the pace for Alex and his Droogs in the Anthony Burgess novel A Clockwork Orange (1962) and Stanley Kubrick's 1971 film. During the second half, the victim stumbles upon a military institution where children are transformed into mutants by government sponsored scientific experimentation. Though the convincingly nightmarish film never turns didactic, the implied meaning is that this specific case of adult insensitivity to children at the facility is indirectly related to, and indicative of, the manner in which adults have socially abused teenagers who as a result become motor-psycho Teddy Boys in everyday life.

In the U.S., Motorpsycho (Russ Meyer, 1965) presents three bikers who assault several women, who then seek revenge. Meyer was (as always) more interested in the bust-size of his actresses than in hogs ridden by outlaws.[25] Many of Meyer's future films would deal with the issue of rape from a female victim's point of view, causing his body of work to present difficulties for feminist analysis: Should members of the late 1960s Women's Movement celebrate this auteur for condemning male violence against women or criticize him for his onscreen display of the female form? Significant too is the idea (a first for American cinema) of a deranged Vietnam veteran bringing that war's insane violence back home.

*

Intriguingly, what kick-started the outlaw-biker genre was all but identical to what had caused *The Wild One* to be produced a dozen years earlier. *Life*, recalling the sellout success of their earlier (and faux) Biker Riot cover, wanted to learn whether lightning might strike twice. This time, the magazine featured a cover-story about a biker funeral that caught the public's interest. A.I.P. executives, ever on the lookout for anything intriguing to exploit, assigned Roger Corman to swiftly produce a movie. Several drafts from Charles Griffith and Peter Bogdanovich were rejected, then consolidated into a script and *The Wild Angels* (1966) went before the cameras. Second-generation Hollywood stars Peter Fonda (as "Heavenly Blues") and Nancy Sinatra (his biker-babe Mike) rode a Harley Davidson, followed by a mass of bikers including several members of the Venice (CA) Hell's Angels chapter. The film concluded with a recreation of that biker burial (Bruce Dern as Loser) though any narrative leading up to it proved the least important element onscreen. A thin plot existed to display bikers riding, partying, taking drugs, attacking women, fighting (with each other and normals), also challenging one another to daredevil stunts. A breakthrough for commercial cinema appeared in the amoral tone, never condemning the bikers and, if anything, seeming to celebrate their antics as a last bastion of freedom in an overly organized America. Here, though, there are a few gestures at decency that would disappear in the coming cycle. Blues recalls Brando/Johnny as he (like a gentleman) stops the harassment of a nurse by fellow bikers. Para-cinema might be thought to begin when this Drive In flick was chosen to open the prestigious Venice Film Festival. On what A.I.P. had considered a risky $350,0000+ investment, *The Wild Angels* netted over $15 million internationally.[26] No question a sequel, then a series, would follow.

A.I.P.'s first, *Devil's Angels* (Burt Topper, 1967), offered a recycling of *The Wild Angels* as to script, though stunt-action sequences were more successfully staged. Likewise, John Cassavetes made a more convincing chopper-king than the slim Fonda. Also, in *The Glory Stompers* (Anthony M. Lanza, 1968), Dennis Hopper brought a sense of all-out madness to Chino, the character's name a reference to Lee Marvin's role in *The Wild One*. Most telling in these two otherwise routine biker romps is that the onetime supporting-villain now assumes the lead. Mean motorcyclists were no longer marginalized, emerging as outlaw anti-heroes during the decade's second half. Later in 1967, two A.I.P. projects were paired and released on a double-bill, the company already fearful that a single such flick could no longer pull in audiences. Significantly, the package was released not only in the usual venues (Drive Ins or fading downtown theatres) but, in many markets, to more respectable venues. The films in tandem reveal strengths and weaknesses inherent in the genre.

Hell's Angels on Wheels (Richard Rush) features Jack Nicholson as a loner-biker who attempts to fit in with a gang led by Adam Roarke only to realize, after plenty of on-the-road action and off-the-choppers romance with biker-babe Sabrina Scharf, that he was better off riding solo. There is no plot and little in the way of characterization. Yet the film casts a hypnotic spell, thanks to Laszlo Kovacs's glorious cinematography in combination with Rush's dynamo-charged direction. A viewer loses any sense of watching this passively, rather experiencing a sense of transportation on a drug-induced dream that violates all notions of time and space in a way that Corman's *The Trip*, released that same year, failed to achieve. Hallucinatory in impact, this Movie-Movie's mesmerizing style makes one wish a better script had been employed, leading to a genre masterpiece. In truth, such a piece of writing did exist in the poorly-directed film *Hell's Angels* was paired with. *Born Losers* ('T.C. Frank,' aka star/co-writer Tom Laughlin) offered the most ambitious vision of society in a biker-flick since *The Wild One*. Set in the southwest, a Johnny Chino type conflict is at once established between the good-loner biker Billy Jack (Laughlin), a part-Native American and former Green Beret silent-hero throwback to Gary Cooper and, earlier still, William S. Hart, and the crazed ringleader (Jeremy Slate) of a vicious gang. Dropped into their ongoing conflict is Vicky (Elizabeth James, credited as co-scenarist), a well-to-do girl in a private school, neglected by her ever-absent father.

In a state of emotional despair, the bikini-clad girl takes off on her mini-bike only to run afoul of (and in time be raped by) the outlaw cyclists but afterwards rescued by Billy Jack. The script's sensitivity to Vicky's plight transforms what initially seems a generic biker-flick into a bold feminist statement. As in *The Wild One* there's also an exploration of why so many good girls in nearby towns would be attracted to the bad boys who invade rural communities, the young-female response a result of the unsatisfying quality of life in this de-energized mainstream America. Corruption by local officials and law enforcement's deep-seated fear of confronting a truly dangerous gang (hassling a non-troublemaking biker like Billy Jack is easier and less threatening) adds to the sense that this movie is *about* something. Yet the visual approach is so lackluster and conventional that *Born Losers* fails to create the necessary visceral excitement. Its penultimate image, however, remains indelible. When Laughlin finally shoots Slate, the bad-biker's body flies backward in slow-motion, up against the apartment's inner-wall. There, a poster of James Dean has been tacked up. As the dead body slowly eases toward the floor, it's revealed that blood, from where the shot pierced through his back, has left a vertical red line on the black-and-white blow-up of Dean's face, blood appearing to drip down from the icon's lips.

*

Carbon copies of The Wild Angels could not long sustain a genre; other tropes had to be introduced. As, simultaneously, the feminist movement made itself felt, several films focused on all-girl gangs, as violent (that is, equal in evil) as their male counterparts: She Devils on Wheels (Herschel Gordon Lewis, 1968), Hell's Belles (Maury Dexter, 1968), The Hellcats (Robert F. Slatzer, 1968) and The Mini-Skirt Mob (Dexter, 1968). Other movies offered something other than the formula plot: Run, Angel, Run! (Jack Starrett, 1969) cast William Smith as a biker with literary aspirations who sells an inside story about his gang to a magazine only to be tracked down as a traitor by former friends. Wild Wheels (Kent Osborne, 1969) set bikers against beach boys in dune buggies. Rebel Rousers (Martin B. Cohan, 1969) remains memorable if only for the most madcap of all portrayals of a beyond-belief biker courtesy of Jack Nicholson in impossibly over-large striped pants.[27] Attempts to keep the cycle alive became ever more daring and, in some cases, desperate. C.C. and Company (Seymour Robbie, 1970) offered the offbeat casting of gridiron-great Joe Namath aboard a hog and the first-onscreen (albeit brief) nude scene for sex-symbol Ann-Margret. Hell's Bloody Devils (Al Adamson, 1970) took the idea of offbeat casting a giant step further by allowing the Kentucky Fried Chicken Franchise's Col. Harlan Sanders his only onscreen role. The Losers (Starrett, 1970) combined the outlaw-biker genre with conventional action-adventure as five hard-riders head to Nam and put the Cong in their place. Angels Die Hard! (Richard Compton, 1970) turned the genre inside-out by having several decent bikers framed for crimes they didn't commit by a corrupt police force. Angel Unchained (Lee Madden, 1970) featured a conscience-stricken biker (Don Stroud) who drops out of the scene to hang with peaceful Hippies and Native Americans. The Hard Ride (Burt Topper, 1970) pitted a combat-weary marine (Robert Fuller), home from his tour of duty, alternately finding himself attracted to and repulsed by the biker subculture. Bury Me an Angel (Barbara Peeters, 1971), the first biker film to be directed by a woman, features Dixie Peabody as a "white-trash Amazon"[28] who takes on the not-so-tough bad bikers who killed her brother.

(a)

(b)

(c)

(d)

(e)

(f)

OF PROTOTYPES AND PARADIGMS: On film as in life, history repeats itself; (a) Lee Marvin's outlaw biker Chino in *The Wild One* led to (b) Jack Nicholson's self-conscious homage fifteen years later; (c) Brigitte Bardot's once-daring pose in black leather with a huge bike paved the way for (d) Marianne Faithfull a decade hence; (e) Marlon Brando's less threatening biker Johnny set the pace for (f) Henry Winkler as The Fonz on ABC-TV's *Happy Days*.

No possible variation would be overlooked. Whereas *Black Angels* (Laurence Merrick, 1970) had featured the first all-African American onscreen biker gang, *The Pink Angels* (Lawrence Brown, 1971) offered a group of gay riders. *Chrome and Hot Leather* (Lee Frost, 1971) featured a battle to the death between outlaw bikers and patriotic Green Berets. The end of the cinematic highway for conventional biker flicks, however, was evident in *Werewolves on Wheels* (Michel Levesque, 1971) a less-than-satisfying combination of the biker and horror genres.

In truth, the biker flick as a generic item was doomed from the moment *Easy Rider* appeared. This film, a contemporary American odyssey, became as Roger Ebert would note, "one of the rallying points of the late '60s."[29] Such an impact resulted not only from qualities in the film but also serendipity as to timing for the release, as well as several events that occurred during its production schedule. A.I.P, for instance, turned Fonda and Hopper down flat when the two pitched their idea. Sam Arkoff may have believed the cycle was all but over, though it's more likely he distrusted the ambitious script, co-authored by cult novelist Terry Southern. Had A.I.P. taken on the project, much of its power may have been lost in that company's attempt to reduce this to something more generic. On release, Richard Schickel of *Life* and other critics noted that, choppers aside, here was a film that "transcended" the genre to become a one-of-a-kind work.[30] Executives at Columbia spotted the possibilities here and gave Fonda and Hopper a green light. However, the budget was so tight that a traditional music score, always intended, wasn't affordable. At a screening for studio executives, the filmmaking team slipped rock classics onto the soundtrack, promising to eliminate them as soon as they were allowed to hire a composer. In a rare reversal of expectations, old-time studio men-in-suits insisted they loved the rock soundtrack and demanded it remain in place.[31]

While shooting, Hopper fell behind schedule, at which point Rip Torn, cast in the role of alcoholic Southern lawyer George, had to leave owing to previous commitments. His high-status as a much-admired actor had been calculated to lift this project up and out of the ordinary so the loss initially appeared disastrous. In a moment of inspiration Hopper cast Jack Nicholson. However excellent Torn might have been, Nicholson's performance allows the film to achieve greatness thanks to precisely the right actor in a role he clearly was born for. Nicholson received a Best Supporting Actor Oscar nomination and became the perfect superstar for the next decade when, in films like *Five Easy Pieces* and *Carnal Knowledge* (Mike Nichols, 1971) he created a new kind of A list star for an industry that, on the verge of dying, survived and flourished once marginalized moviemakers became a reconfigured mainstream. Another such figure was Laszlo Kovacs. While many of the dramatic elements fail to hold up, particularly the pretentiously pseudo-philosophic ramblings by Fonda's Captain America, the cinematography offers us what Ebert hailed as a visual "time capsule."[32] The initially easy, later hard ride passes through big cities and small towns, farms and ranches, super-highways and bygone back-roads, a Hippie commune and a middle-American parade and, in New Orleans, the Mardi Gras, a brothel, and a cemetery. For Kovacs, *Easy Rider* served as a transitional piece from B films like *Psych-Out* (see Ch. 11) to the new order of things. One year later, a road movie starring Nicholson (*Five Easy Pieces*), which previously would have been confined to Drive Ins (or perhaps the art house) played at M.O.R. mall theatres.

Todd Gitlin rightly asked, "What was marginal anymore, where was the mainstream anyway?" when, as Beth Bailey added, "the Beatles were singing 'Why Don't We Do It in the Road?'"[33] such songs no longer confined to so-called Underground FM radio stations, but now part of the AM Top 40s format. All the same, had *Easy Rider* appeared half a year earlier (before Woodstock) or half a year later (after Altamont) public reception might have been less ecstatic. Owing to mass publicity (much of it over-romanticized) about Woodstock, millions of Americans, young in years or young in spirit, felt they'd missed the great generational moment for having not 'been there.' The documentary film of that event wouldn't be released for another year. Still, they wanted "in": catching *Easy Rider* allowed for such a sensation. They felt stymied by our government's dragging its heels as to ending the Vietnam war or making hoped-for strides as to Civil Rights. This played into the picture's potential as a hit for, as Pauline Kael put it, *Easy Rider's* "sentimental paranoia obviously rang true to a large, young audience's vision"[34] of themselves. Appearing halfway between *Bonnie and Clyde* and *The Wild Bunch* (Sam Peckinpah, 1969), here was yet another vision of on-the-edge outlaws rubbed out by the cold Establishment; Wyatt and Billy are shot down by Southern rednecks. As Robert M. Pirsig noted about journeys in general, those on motorcycles in particular: "Sometimes it's better to travel than arrive."[35] For multiple reasons, here was the right film for this moment. If released after the Altamont disaster, signaling a gradual pulling away from the Hippie-as-hero syndrome, it might have fizzled.

More than any other of its considerable qualities, *Easy Rider* did capture the age-old American lure of the open road in the unique manner that this could only be experienced via motorcycle, an experience that rivaled the dharma inherent in surfing. No one has ever captured the distinction between driving in an automobile and riding on a motorcycle so vividly as Pirsig did in *Zen and the Art of Motorcycle Maintenance:*

> In a car, you're always in a compartment, and . . . through that car window, everything you see is just more TV. You're a passive observer . . . On a cycle, the frame is gone. You're continually in contact with it all. You're in the scene, not just watching.[36]

The motorcycle provided a happy answer to those who perceived that life in the 20th century was becoming ever more passive, including most jobs at the modern workplace. Here was an opportunity be active again, if only—as Johnny admits in *The Wild One*—on weekends, when he and others of his ilk escape their blue-collar traps to achieve momentary freedom. As Ebert observed, *Easy Rider* was less a biker flick, despite those incredible choppers, than "a road picture . . . celebrating sex, drugs, rock 'n' roll, and the freedom of the open road."[37] Even after America and Hollywood entered the 1970s, when drug use would become a subject for social and cinematic criticism, those other elements—sex and rock 'n' roll—would remain central to the experiences of life. Also, watching what Aristotle, two and a half millennia earlier, called 'imitations of life': in his time, drama. In ours? The Movies.

Epilogue

LET THE GOOD TIMES ROLL

Once Upon a Time in the Late 1950s/Early 1960s

"Just take the old records off the shelf
I'll sit and listen to them by myself
Today's music ain't got the same soul
I love that old time rock 'n' roll."
—Bob Seger, 1978

One evening in late winter of 1969, a 26-year-old gradstudent at a major university, and his wife, two years younger, invited a top student and the fellow's current girlfriend over to their place for coffee and conversation. The young man's hair was long, scraggly, like that of most every other boy on campus. His date, not surprisingly, wore granny glasses and love beads. The two were virtual Poster Children for the then-current Hippie Era. Not wanting to appear un-hip, the grad-student, who in 1955 had been among that first wave of American teenagers, revealed his collection of the latest 33 1/3 L.P. albums: *Stand* (Sly and the Family Stone), *Abbey Road* (The Beatles), *Let It Bleed* (The Rolling Stones), *Tommy* (The Who), and eponymously titled discs by Led Zeppelin, The Velvet Underground and Crosby, Stills & Nash.

While flipping through these possibilities for something to listen to, the younger couple happened on something unexpected: a worn album (cardboard cover frayed at the edges, the circular wax item inside scratched) with the unlikely title A *Million or More*. No need to concern yourselves with *that*, the grad-student chuckled. It was a relic, an antique. A throwback to his younger days. An old album collecting dust that featured million-selling early rock 'n' roll numbers he'd enjoyed in his own youth.

Put it on! The Hippie-ish kids begged. *We want to hear it.*

While giddy jump-numbers and slow ballads played, the gradstudent and his wife were implored to tell all about how it was, so long ago and far away. Well, let's see: girls were expected to be virgins until they married, at least *nice* girls. Guys saved their small change, hoping to in time afford a hot rod so they could take their dates to a Drive In. Parties with the lights turned low for the last dance (no later than eleven p.m.) were allowed. Still, as these were good kids, adult chaperones hovered close.

Gee, the co-ed sighed, knowing she and her boyfriend would shortly head back to his apartment to smoke grass, listen to the Kinks, and engage in casual sex. *If only I'd lived back then . . . it all sounds so* wonderful *. . .*

*

George Lucas's decision to not only include car-culture but make this element central to *American Graffiti* had much to do with that film's unexpected success. The 1973 release takes place on an end-of-summer evening in 1962, in and around the small California town of Modesto. Recently graduated from high school, members of the First Wave of 1950s teens make ready to search for jobs or leave for college, while younger members of The Second Wave prepare to segue from junior- to senior-high. The two mix and match at a sock-hop during which the torch of youth is symbolically passed from one generation to the next. All dance to Oldies and Goldies from rock's original era. Any sense their favorite songs were ever controversial is long gone. Now, such music constitutes a semi-conscious soundtrack to a time-period and corresponding mindset that (if no one realizes this yet) is about to pass into history—and the parallel realm of popular culture which, beginning in the postwar years if not before, takes on the function of our modern mythology.

*

(a)   (b)

BACK IN BLACK (LEATHER, THAT IS): What in 1958 had seemed radical and threatening now appeared charmingly retro in context of the revolutionary spirit of 1968: (a) Elvis struts his stuff (though now "in italics") for the famed Comeback Special (courtesy: Binder/ Howe Prods./NBC); (b) Brigitte Bardot shows a lot of skin while winking at her post-modern audience—on network TV, no less! (courtesy: Les Films du Quadrangle/NBC).

If nostalgia for that era first exploded with the release of *American Graffiti*, a few predecessors appeared much earlier. One might argue that the point of germination had been December 3, 1968, when at 9 p.m. (Eastern) NBC broadcast what has come to be called "The Elvis Comeback Special." Col. Tom Parker had thought the hour might consist of Elvis performing Christmas songs, ushering in the holiday season while creating renewed interest in his simultaneous album. During planning and production, the show transformed into something more inclusive. A key motive was to bring Presley back into the center of attention for those twenty-five-year-olds who had, back in 1954–1955, unofficially crowned him the King of their evolving Youth Culture, as well as for younger kids of early 1960s who had enjoyed Presley's Beach Movies. And too for the Third Wave; those reaching teen-hood in

'65, referred to as Hippies. Movies could no longer perform that function as the disastrous box-office failure of two recent Presley vehicles, *Double Trouble* (1967) and *Live a Little, Love a Little* (1968, both Norman Tokar) had made abundantly clear to Hollywood producers.

With musical-movies no longer viable, Parker decided to bring Elvis full circle by returning him to the medium in which he'd originally achieved stardom. The resultant TV show earned great ratings (expected), also strong reviews (less so). Likely the latter wouldn't have been the case had Elvis merely stepped onstage and offered a redo of what he'd presented ten years ago. Instead, the performer, who way back then had seemed utterly unaware of himself and his impact, was now supremely self-conscious—of his own body and its image; of the response to his movements, grandiose and slight, had on an audience. And, too, of the time that had elapsed since last he'd appeared before the live TV cameras. Finally, Elvis also seemed aware of the way in which pretty much everything in America had, over the past decade, changed—except for him. If anything appeared different about Elvis, that had to be his new-found ability to wink at an audience while still delivering the goods.

Strutting about in a dazzling black-leather jumpsuit, he over-exaggerated earlier gyrations to the glee of fans, some of whom had forgotten him but fell in love with Elvis all over again. Him, and what Presley now represented about their own former selves. He giggled at their delight, gently/smartly kidding his earlier persona without betraying it via outright burlesque. What might have been a sad attempt to recapture glory days of yore instead revealed a reconfiguration of the past that took into account everything that he, and we, had been through. Not only did Elvis at that moment initiate the Nostalgia Movement; far more significantly, he introduced post-modernism to the public-at-large, whether or not most people outside of academia would ever even hear that term.

Perhaps Elvis would have been enough. Yet there was more to come. Elvis's surly grin communicated "in italics" for the first time segued into Brigitte Bardot's infamous pout. Here now was that other (and, in her time, notorious) force from 1957: Bebe, the female Elvis. Apparently naked under some sort of wrappings (she an early-arriving Christmas present), Bardot cooed into the camera: "How'd you like to spend the night with me?" Executives at NBC, having decided to take this risk, held their collective breath. Behind-the-scenes, all were fearful the network might, the following morning, be inundated by angry phone-calls: How dare you put something so sexy on network TV? Nothing of the sort occurred. Brigitte Bardot, like Elvis, had long since been contextualized by our rapidly-altering times as well as a change in values such Future Shocks necessitated. Her sense of Sexual Liberation, like Presley's, now paled in comparison to what was currently going on in life and its media-distorted reflections. What had seemed so shocking to the Establishment in 1957–1958 came across, in a 1968 context, as charmingly old-fashioned.

"What's the matter with kids today?" actor Paul Lynde had wailed in both the Broadway and Hollywood versions of *Bye Bye Birdie* about teenagers who worshipped Elvis-type stars—and, by implication, Bardot-like Sex Symbols. "What's the matter with Sammy Kaye?" (Or Betty Grable?) Millions of middle-Americans nodded their head in agreement. "What's the matter with kids today?" millions of young adults (those who had over the past ten years slipped into that very suburbia their parents once inhabited and which, in their youth, they'd condemned as too conformist) wondered when, in the late 1960s, youth turned on to Jim Morrison in music and, shortly thereafter, Linda Lovelace, the first nationally-heralded hardcore porn star.

What's wrong with Elvis? Or, for that matter, Bebe?

*

Such a process of mythologization could not be initiated during the 1950s—not when Halberstam's "mean time" had always been in evidence. The most mundane elements of every-day life (a small minority of citizens actually feared that Lucille Ball's red hair, though broadcast in black-and-white on CBS, might be some secret signifier of communism) caused anxiety and suspicion to always exist just below the Eisenhower era's calm surface. A gradual sentimentalizing of what, for those who lived through such gray days were the worst of times, can only begin once they are gone. In England during the fifth century, crude and filthy huts, rampant/omnipresent disease, and a wholesale bloodletting of the common people didn't lead to legends of bold Arthur, beautiful Guenivere, idealistic knights devoted to a chivalric code, and the grand concept of Camelot: A storybook Utopia high on a hill. Glorious idylls of king and countrymen were penned by Alfred, Lord Tennyson between 1859 and 1885. In the New World, Owen Wister mythologized the desolate American frontier, which as the historian Frederick Jackson Turner noted came to an end in 1900, after this concept passed into memory in his 1902 novel *The Virginian*. In the 1950s, marginalization of rock 'n' roll and those teenagers who adored it had led to notably *un*-happy days.

Until they were over and done. Then, the nouveau-present proved so unpleasant that what had preceded it could be recalled as a brief, shining moment of innocence and enchantment that, sadly, slipped through our fingers and was sorely missed.

People create mythology because something deep, primitive, and essential in the human psyche demands it. Adults, teenagers, and small children alike during the 1950s found their mythology—a "nostalgia for a vanished past"[1] which has little to do with the history of hard, boring days—in the old West. Horse Operas dominated movie and TV screens beginning early in the 20th Century, continuing until the early 1960s. In appealing configurations, lone white-knights (Shane in theatres, Cheyenne in one's living-room) rode into a tough town, cleaned it up, romanced the prettiest local gal, and then headed off into the sunset in search of more adventure. Once, it had been that way. Everybody knew this to be true since seeing is believing. Most people accept such fantasies as gospel, particularly when they have been vividly realized by Hollywood's top craftsmen. Such a mythology, however far removed from any once-existent reality, sustains a people through the unpleasant current day. That is the function of mythology—always has been; likely always will be just so long as long as humankind exists.

Mythology assures people that a Golden Age once existed. If that is so, it may just come around again. If not, at least we can draw sustenance from its long-lingering beauty.

In in the words of Northrop Frye this embodies

> The wish fulfillment element in romance . . . (as such) recreation of (days gone by) brings us into a present where past and future are gathered . . . a pastoral, paradisal, and radically simplified form of life obviously takes on a new kind of urgency in an age of pollution and energy crisis.[2]

Mythologization of the old West dissipated even as JFK's New Frontier dawned. That hardly seems coincidental. Between 1960–1963, few people needed to rely on *any* imagined past. The then-abiding myth was that rarest of rarities, the impossible dream: a contemporaneous mythology. *Camelot* the musical play had premiered on Broadway while a modern version existed (or so the media announced, and an adoring public believed) in the White House. Who needs a gloried past when the present itself assumes that function? Then, suddenly, on one dark day in Dallas 1963, all that abruptly ended. There would be no retreat in the grim present which followed to the old West. Revisionism had begun; ever more people became ever more aware of the devastation of nature and the land, as well as racism toward pre-existing peoples, that characterized the real West.

Perhaps Thomas Wolfe had been right; maybe you can't go home again— at least not to a mythology that once served its purpose but no longer func- tions. On the other hand, you (we; a people) can create other/alternative mythologies to displace those that cease to work. Beginning in 1965, one key source would be science fiction: *Star Trek* on TV; *Planet of the Apes*, *2001: A Space Odyssey*, and in due time *Star Wars* in theatres, continuing on up to the present day. When Gene Rodenberry (1921–1991) pitched *Star Trek*, he described his show as "Wagon Train to the Stars."[3] His new series premiered shortly after the earlier one was finally cancelled. Rodenberry suggested at this key juncture that the space fantasy would replace the horse opera, the two genres one and the same other than a switch from past to present. And even that would not always be the case; Lucas set *Star Wars* in a galaxy not only far, far away but long, long ago, high-tech gunfighters shooting it out in fantastical cantinas that echoed old West saloons. The future is telescoped into the past for present-day entertainments that function as contemporary variations on humankind's timeless heroic legends.

Another approach was to find some other past period to mythologize. None so well fits such a bill as what has just disappeared. During the immediate postwar era, Hollywood movies such as Irving Berlin's *White Christmas* (Michael Curtiz, 1954) posited the bloodthirsty Battle of Bulge as a wonderful moment in the lives of those who had been there: Starving, freezing, being shot at. With our American Camelot evaporating in late 1963, the Fifties took on such an aura by contrasting with an ever uglier present. At once, Eric Von Zipper and his black leather biker-gang roared onto brightly-lit West Coast beaches. Toward decade's end came an intense sense of wistful melancholy: In *Out of It*, a final Gidget-like late-night beach party occurs. Now, though, the boys make ready to head not back to school but Vietnam, where many will die.

*

"I don't believe in heroes anymore,"[4] Dennis Hopper (who had on many occasions during the late 1950s and 1960s appeared on screen alongside traditional cowboy stars John Wayne, Kirk Douglas, and Burt Lancaster) announced during the 1969 release of his obviously anti-heroic *Easy Rider*. Undoubtedly, a notably unheroic-age had been ushered in as the soaring sensation that was Woodstock swiftly gave way to the youth-culture thud at the Altamont Speedway. Beginning with *Joe* (John Avildsen, 1970) and *Midnight Cowboy*, these led to a near-future dystopian vision in *A Clockwork Orange* (Stanley Kubrick, 1971), a call for ordinary citizens to turn vigilante and kill off recidivistic primitives (*Death Wish*; Michael Winner, 1974), finally a full vision of New York City as hell on earth (*Taxi Driver*, Martin Scorsese, 1976). Westerns (*The Wild Bunch*; Sam Peckinpah, 1969), romance-drama (*Carnal Knowledge*;

Mike Nichols, 1971), and large-scale studio musicals (*Cabaret*; Bob Fosse, 1972) survived by becoming as nasty and cynical (if often brilliantly so) as Old Hollywood predecessors had been engagingly crowd-pleasing.

At its best, The New American Cinema (as it was hailed) did offer serious work—more intelligent and ambitious than anything that preceded it during The Golden Age of Hollywood. Nicholson, a marginalized youth-star of the 1960s, played the lead in such remarkable projects as *Five Easy Pieces* and *One Flew Over the Cuckoo's Nest* (Milos Forman, 1975). Like Jack, many talented writers and directors working in early 1970s mainstream films had in the previous decade paid their dues by laboring on Roger Corman's B movies: Scorsese, Monte Hellman, Francis Ford Coppola, Bob Rafelson and Hal Ashby among them. Importantly, they didn't leave their B movie roots behind. In *The Godfather* (Coppola, 1972), old-fashioned consummate craftsmanship as to period-piece production values was successfully merged with a more honest (and knowing) approach to the world. Fittingly, the onetime young turk, now the 'mature' Marlon Brando, worked in tandem with such up-and-coming talents as Al Pacino and, in *The Godfather, Part Two* (1974), Robert De Niro—each actor hailed as a potential 'new Brando.' It's not for nothing that Coppola cast mentor Corman in a key role for the sequel. Those films proved that the gangster-genre could be reinvented; *Chinatown* (Roman Polanski, 1974) did the same for film noir, with Nicholson cast as a Humphrey Bogart-type private-eye. Brilliantly, the period piece about corrupt land sales in Southern California from a half-century earlier featured a contemporary spin. "Watergate," more than one critic noted, "with real water."[5]

Movie Brats, as they were called,[6] set out to Phoenix-like recreate what had always been best about Hollywood films. Shortly, such ultra-serious-minded talents as Coppola and Scorsese would be joined by the more lighthearted George Lucas and Steven Spielberg. During the decade's second half, they reinvented the dimly-remembered Popcorn Film, which after *Easy Rider* had briefly been considered irrelevant. How could Flash Gordon or Buck Rogers exist in a world (and cinema) that no longer believed in heroes? Even Lucas was bitten by the "I want to be taken seriously as an artist" syndrome. His first project had been the intense/intellectualized sci-fi film *THX 1138* (1971), a cold-hearted *1984/Brave New World* clone produced by Coppola. While shooting it (and including a brief Buck Rogers clip at the beginning as a foil for the serious stuff to follow) Lucas fantasized about how much more fun it would have been to do a remake of Flash Gordon, that 1930s serial he'd fallen in love with while watching TV in the 1950s. Less than five years later, Lucas was more or less doing that with *Star Wars* (1977). He and Spielberg thereafter collaborated on *Raiders of the Lost Ark* (1981), an old-Hollywood/Studio era high-adventure yarn if now featuring a post-modern wink to a knowing audience.

(a) (b)

(c) (d)

THE MORE THINGS CHANGE, THE MORE THEY STAY THE SAME: (a) Mickey Rooney and Judy Garland sip a soda together during the 1930s in *Babes in Arms* (courtesy: MGM); (b) in the 1950s, Dwayne Hickman and Tuesday Weld share a malt in *The Many Loves of Dobie Gillis* (courtesy: CBS-TV); (c) Jana Lund and her partner enjoy bopping to the beat in the 'revolutionary' 1950s film *Don't Knock the Rock* (courtesy: Clover/Columbia); (d) Olivia Newton-John and John Travolta revive that now retro-style in the 1970s film *Grease* (courtesy: Paramount).

*

In the Indiana Jones trilogy, Harrison Ford collapsed John Wayne from A movies with Ronald Reagan from B films. Significantly, the public—older, middle-aged, and young people—responded with enormous enthusiasm. After a more than five-year-absence, the old-fashioned hero (now given a contemporary glibness) was back in style. In an incredible turnaround, Hopper—the former late 1960s radical incarnate or so he'd seemed—endorsed conservative Ronald Reagan for the presidency in 1979. Simply, a nation needs its mythology; Reagan provided that by campaigning before the Alamo, wearing a Stetson. Elect me, the unspoken implication was, and Davy Crockett, that hero of the mid-1950s whom Reagan at one point had hoped to portray,[7] would come riding back into our lives. Jimmy Carter, his notable intelligence aside, couldn't compete with that. Reagan's victory was less one of Republicans over Democrats, conservative beating liberal, than of myth, with its simple answers to everything, reasserting itself and its enormous appeal, however dubious when compared to the real world, with all its depressing complexities. And, not surprisingly, the Western made something of a comeback following Reagan's victory: *The Long Riders* (Walter Hill), *Bronco Billy* (Clint Eastwood), *The Mountain Men* (Richard Lang), *Urban Cowboy* (James Bridges), and the much-maligned *Heaven's Gate* (Michael Cimino). In truth, though, people now preferred their cowboys in a distant galaxy. The former star of *How the West Was Won* (1962) George Peppard played Space Cowboy in the Corman-produced *Battle Beyond the Stars* (Jimmy T. Murakami).

And, of course, there were the now-mythologized 1950s: Lest we forget, Ford played a Stetson-wearing contemporary cowboy driving a hot-rod rather than riding a horse in Lucas's *American Graffiti*. In the wake of that seminal film, Hollywood (and the Brit film industry) hoped to recapture its once certain pulse on the public's tastes by churning out endless nostalgia items. The under-seen *Out of It* (1969) and over-rated *Last Picture Show* (1971) would be followed by *Let the Good Times Roll* (Sid Levin, Robert Abel, 1973); *That'll Be the Day* (Claude Watham, 1973); *Stardust* (Michael Apted, 1974); *The Lords of Flatbush* (Stephen Verona, 1974), *Sparkle* (Sam O'Steen, 1975); *American Hot Wax* (Floyd Mutrux, 1976); *The Buddy Holly Story* (Steve Rash, 1978); *I Wanna Hold Your Hand* (Robert Zemeckis, 1978); *National Lampoon's Animal House* (John Landis, 1978), *The Kids Are Alright* (Jeff Stein, 1979); *Elvis* (John Carpenter, TV 1979); *Quadrophenia* (Franc Roddam, Martin Stellman, 1979), and *The Wanderers* (Phil Kaufman, 1979). In some cases, nostalgia stretched further back, to the war years (*Summer of '42*; Robert Mulligan, 1971) or even the turn of the century (*The Sting*; George Roy Hill, 1973). This trend did not diminish as time went by: *Porky's* (Bob Clark, 1982), *The Outsiders* (Francis Coppola, 1983), *Chuck Berry: Hail! Hail! Rock 'n' Roll* (Taylor Hackford, 1987), *La Bamba* (Luis Valdez, 1987); *Dirty Dancing* (Emile Ardolino, 1987),

Heartbreak Hotel (Chris Columbus, 1988), *Hairspray* (John Waters, 1988), *Great Balls of Fire* (Jim McBride, 1989), *Cry Baby* (John Waters, 1990), *Ed Wood* (Tim Burton, 1994), *Forrest Gump* (Robert Zemeckis, 1994), *L.A. Confidential* (Curtis Hanson, 1997). Fascination (some might say obsession) with the late 1950s/early 1960s continues unabated in the 21st century: *The Majestic* (Frank Darabont, 2001), *Mona Lisa Smile* (Mike Newell, 2003), *Beyond the Sea* (Kevin Spacey, 2004), *Hollywoodland* (Allen Coulter, 2006); *Hairspray* (Adam Shankman, 2007), *Revolutionary Road* (Sam Mendes, 2008), *The Help* (Tate Taylor, 2009), *X-Men: First Class* (Matthew Vaughn, 2011), *Hitchcock* (Sacha Gervais, 2012), *On the Road* (Walter Salles, 2012), *Saving Mr. Banks* (John Lee Hancock, 2013), *42* (Brian Helgeland, 2013), *Jersey Boys* (Clint Eastwood, 2014), *Get on Up* (Tate Taylor, 2014), and TV's *Mad Men* (2007–2015).

*

However surprisingly, this nostalgia craze began to creep into contemporary culture at the height of Hippiedom. Lest we forget, at Woodstock, Sha-Na-Na, most famous of the old-time rock 'n' roll revival bands, performed. When the movie (aimed at a long-hair audience) emerged, they were nowhere to be seen. Perhaps if the film's release had been delayed, Bowser and his boys might have made an appearance. The stage musical *Grease* premiered in 1971 in Chicago, where the story is set. An unanticipated enthusiasm for the show caused it to move to Off-Broadway in 1972. Long lines of ticket-buyers caused a swift shift-over to the Great White Way. Not coincidentally, this occurred even as another musical, *Hair,* closed its doors.

That "tribal-rock" show had debuted off-Broadway in 1967, moving uptown the following year, where it ran for 1,750 performances. Its appeal was never to Hippies (members of the counter-culture couldn't afford the admission price) but middle-aged people, men arriving in suit and tie, expensive new dresses for out-of-town Midwestern tourist ladies. They came to sneak a peek at what was then thought of as controversial: interracial casting and mild female nudity. The original book by James Rado and George Ragni, never very good, was watered-down considerably for a target audience of those over thirty. The play's greatest asset was its music, including ("Age of Aquarius") by Galt MacDermot. Though *Hair*'s run must be considered successful, note too that the show closed precisely when the Hippie Era ceased to exist. A smart motion picture appeared in 1979, directed by the gifted Milos Forman; the movie died at the box office. One year earlier, the disappointing film version of *Grease,* helmed by the dreadful director Randal Kleiser, became a commercial sensation despite weak reviews. The distinction: while the era depicted in *Hair* had come to be seen as a momentary aberration, the Fabulous Fifties enshrined by *Grease* had sprung back to meaningful life.

In its original incarnation, *Grease* had been, if anything, anti-mythic. The original play opens as several nice kids attend the tenth anniversary of their high-school graduation, musing about whatever happened to the Greaser element, which failed to show for this polite reunion. The scene shifts back, over the years, to those marginal teens, more satirized than sentimentalized. Here was a case of the public demanding that a play change its tone as it moved to New York and Hollywood. With each rendering, the nastiness and in some cases brutality of the characters was reduced, Danny Zucko transformed from one of *Blackboard Jungle*'s "Young Savages" to a singing-redo of TV's Fonz. Henry Winkler's character had on ABC's *Happy Days* become what cowboy-heroes of yore were in those once-beloved Westerns. Like Paul Le Mat's West Coast greaser in *American Graffiti*, Winkler's clean-cut delinquent (clearly a contradiction in terms) rode to the rescue of the weak. In such a sanitized recreation, Fonzie's motorcycle appeared no more menacing than Wyatt Earp's trusted steed in the earlier American mythology of the Western.

These were, after all, the downbeat 1970s. A crippling oil shortage, an economic recession, and the arrival of Disco caused everyone to want to revisit what had, presumably, been better times . . . happier days.

As to the *Grease* movie, young people were among the most avid ticket-buyers. Partly, that had to do with current teen-idols, John Travolta and Olivia Newton-John, as the black-jacket boy and his Sandra Dee-like girlfriend. The inclusion of car-culture didn't hurt. In one of the most memorable sequences (stage and film), Danny and fellow greasers dance around their souped-up hot-rod, Greased Lightning. The *Grease* film returned $394,955,690.00 on an investment of $6 million. Seven years later, another (superior) film, also starring a current teen-idol (Michael J. Fox), featured a mix of car-culture, old-time 1950s rock 'n' roll, and one additional element—sci-fi time-travel on the order of that great late 1950s/early 1960s TV show, *The Twilight Zone. Back to the Future* (Robert Zemeckis, 1985) was produced by Spielberg, with visual-effects courtesy George Lucas's Industrial Light & Magic. The Movie Brats knew what they were doing. Shot for $19 million, this lighthearted comedy-drama-romance-fantasy-adventure-nostalgia-brought in well over $389 million during its initial year of release.[8]

Again, the young as well as young-at-heart flocked to catch it. In an all-important early decision, many of the streets on view during the modern (1985) tale were shot at existing locales in California. For those sequences set in the small town of Hill Valley, 1955, the company moved to the Courthouse Square on the Universal back-lot. Its artificiality proved perfect—necessary for this film's sensibility. After all, what Marty McFly returns to is not the real 1950s but the myth, this charmingly rendered in obviously faux sets. Between the releases of *Grease* and *Back to the Future*, *Hair* had opened and closed. The late 1960s never did became the good old days. The early Sixties? Now, *there* was a time . . .! In *Back to the Beach* (Lyndall Hobbs, 1987) Frankie and Annette return to the scene of their glory days as a middle-aged married couple; their offspring wishes current times could be as much fun as things (supposedly) were back then.

As mentioned, *Hair* played on Broadway for four years, but was long gone before the movie opened and then quickly closed. *Grease* was going strong onstage when the 1978 film premiered, not closing until 1980. The play ran for a remarkable 3,388 performances, a record at that time. Before New York revivals in 1994 and 2007, touring companies, regional productions, even high-school Senior Play mountings kept *Grease* alive and kicking.

With each, the lyrics became more mainstream, ever less edgy—less honest to the Fifties historically if more in tune with the massive mythology now surrounding that era. By the time of the film's release, the end of any Generation Gap, so far as movies were concerned, had occurred. Young and old alike hungered for retro entertainment.

Everything old was new again.

Not everyone approved. Pauline Kael of The *New Yorker* complained that Lucas and Spielberg's return to bold heroes painted in broad strokes, with hissable villains for their foils, led to the "infantalization of the culture."[9] Whether or not one agrees with her value judgment—i.e., this was a bad thing—there could be no question the American public had chosen simplicity over sophistication in pop culture as in politics. Sociological critics argued that Indiana Jones was one and the same with "Brass" Bancroft, a Nazi-fighter played by Ronald Reagan in similar (if low-budgeted) films back in 1940. Electing one to the White House while choosing to watch the other in action at theatres might be inter-related, since social issues and patterns in entertainment continuously converge.

As to reboots of such beloved 1950s figures as Superman and Batman, or their 1960s counter-parts the *Enterprise* crew and denizens of that planet of apes, pretty much everyone in the country—young and old, liberal and conservative, Blue State/Red State—hungered for such stuff. For a few hours, Americans could once again converge into a community, setting aside the lonely crowd mentality that had appeared at the onset of our postwar world. Everyone could escape an unpleasant present and revisit the past. Not, of course, the historic past—the way we were—which few wanted to be reminded of. Rather, a mythic past: The way we wish we'd been and now choose to believe had been real. With its capacity for rendering mass fantasies in momentarily believable visuals, the cinema effectively accomplished that.

*

"Where were you in '62?" ads for *American Graffiti* asked in 1973. In radio-spots, popular D.J. Wolfman Jack (1938–1995), who played himself in the film, voiced those words. The implication: If what we think of as the '50s did not begin until 1955 this did not end until 1962: The twilight of our American innocence before the JFK assassination plunged everyone into an ongoing and apparently endless nightmare. Lucas's film focuses on four boys—a budding writer (Richard Dreyfuss), an all-American type (Ron Howard), a greaser/car-nut (Paul Le Mat), and an agreeable nerd (Charles Martin Smith)—as well as the varied girls they are already, or soon become, involved with. Each is a well-realized individual, thanks to the rich Gloria Katz/ Willard Huyck script. Still, a 1973 viewer sensed these were, if not (thankfully!) stereotypes, than surely archetypes. Each youth embodies some distinct aspect of teen-hood. However specific the setting, this story proved universal in implication.

As to that effective come-on line: the tightly-budgeted movie, with its echoes of the first Youth Culture flicks from a decade and a half earlier, had been designed to appeal to those who likewise were young at that key junc-ture, when Lucas's movie is set. Such people were just now turning thirty, the very age that during the late 1960s a radicalized youth declared was the cut-off point for trustworthiness. Yet such citizens, now young adults, didn't perceive themselves as such. Having experienced the Songs of Experience, realizing they didn't much care for them, they now hungered to return to the Songs of Innocence, then wallow in glorious simplicity forever. More nostalgic than realistic, however many precise details of that time and that place were correctly displayed, *American Graffiti* allowed for just such a conception. A more authentic film about four boys wandering around that same year played simultaneously. *American Graffiti*, shot for $770,000, raked in tens of millions;

Mean Streets (Martin Scorsese, 1973), shot for little more than $500,000, satisfied its backers by netting a modest $3 million. Like Lucas, Scorsese (1942–) employed music from the period as his soundtrack for an ensemble piece/coming of age project.

Why, then, the notable distinction in profits?

As Scorsese's title implies, this may have had to do with its substantially different tone. *Mean Streets* presents a nasty—mean, as Halberstam put it—time. Here is an East Coast, big city, ethnic (Little Italy) terrain. Cars are of only marginal importance while forces of adult evil—La Cosa Nostra—are never far from youth's activities. *Mean Streets* came far closer to the truth; in comparison, *American Graffiti* might be tagged the Disney version. (Lucas and Spielberg have often acknowledged the huge impact of that movie mythmaker on their work). The choice between these movies, each high in quality, might be structured as a preference for realism or romanticism. Americans revealed their national preference at the box office—and the world, by now thoroughly Americanized, shortly followed suit.

In some cases, fifteen-year-olds went to see *American Graffiti* with their thirty-year-old parents. On the way home, kids asked: Was it *really* like that back then? Did everybody have fun all the time? And, *hey!* Why isn't it like that anymore? Most adults lied—to themselves as well as to the kids: Yes! *Once upon a time . . . we all of us lived in . . . happier days.*

Hollywood has rarely been about telling the truth. Its primary function, harking back to the Andy Hardy family films, was to present audiences with a vision of our better selves—the people we ought to strive to be, if all-too-often fail to become. Such an enduring legacy had dissipated in the late 1960s and early 1970s, when post-*Easy Rider* movies set out in search of 'the real America,' whatever that might be. After one glance at the first such film, audiences turned away in droves. Did anyone in America purchase a ticket to see Jon Voight in *The Revolutionary* (Paul Williams, 1970)?

Still, Walt Disney was gone. John Ford, Howard Hawks, and Frank Capra had retired. At which point Lucas, Spielberg, and company, raised on those masters but harboring youthful visions more in tune with their own times, stepped in to fill the void. In a bestselling book about Disney, first published the same year that the Elvis/Bebe "comeback specials" aired, Richard Schickel attempted to determine the root of that entertainer's appeal. Disney, Schickel concluded, was neither an easy to tag liberal or conservative. Properly understood, his had been "the politics of nostalgia."[10] This speaks to a national desire to return to "an imagined past"[11] which informed "much of the new

popular culture."[12] During the actual 1950s, those stuck in unsatisfying suburbia could relive what had never been by strolling along Main Street, U.S.A.
in the Disneyland park.

Such nostalgia was not only confined to Disney, the most easily accessible
of all family entertainers. If anyone then on TV might have been thought of
as Disney's dark doppelganger, it was Rod Serling (1924–1975). *The Twilight
Zone* provided as many nightmares as Disney's TV-hour did sweet dreams. Still,
here the politics of nostalgia was also in evidence. Serling's personal favorites
among episodes he personally wrote were "Walking Distance" (10/30/1959)
and "A Stop at Willoughby" (5/6/1960). In each, a harried upper-middle-
class business executive, traveling from his high-paying/intellectually empty
Madison Avenue job to a gorgeous if emotionally stifling home in nearby
Connecticut, desperately wants to revisit (in the former) the village in which
he was raised or (in the latter) a peaceful hamlet where Huckleberry Finn and
Tom Sawyer fish on the big river, and band concerts always play . . . even as
they do on the avenue all visitors to The Magic Kingdom must pass through.
Main Street U.S.A., not Tomorrowland, was Rod Serling's favorite place to
spend time in California's Disneyland.[13]

Back in the Fifties, the supposed conventional entertainer Disney and
signifier of intellectual stimulation Serling seemed cultural, perhaps political, opposites. Today, they comfortably collapse: "The Twilight Zone Tower of
Terror" rates as one of the most popular rides at Disney parks. Another favorite spot is The Disney Drive In. There, visitors slip into scaled-down retro
automobiles, enjoying old black-and-white horror flicks on a big screen while
car-hops whiz up on roller-skates to take orders for burgers and fries while old-
time rock 'n' roll endlessly plays. It's Mel's Diner from *American Graffiti* with
werewolves on view in glorious black-and-white to round things off.

If beginning in 1955 Disneyland allowed then-modern people to escape
unsatisfying suburbia and mean times around them, now that *Happy Days* era
is where our sentimental journey leads. The Fifties forever, as people of all
ages like to say entering a Johnny Rockets retro-diner at any mall. And, after,
stopping by some boutique where icons of Elvis, Marilyn Monroe, James Dean
and the Beatles are always on sale. The late 1950s/early 1960s Youth Culture,
once marginalized, gradually became the dominant American culture. And
not only in sweet-spirited films. The nasty/sexy couple (John Travolta and
Uma Thurman) in Quentin Tarantino's *Pulp Fiction* (Tony Scott 1994) head
for a 1950s café where blonde hostesses resemble Marilyn, Jayne Mansfield,

and Mamie Van Doren. Which is to say we continuously live out another Disney favorite, *Peter Pan*: "I *won't* grow up . . ."

*

Those two couples who had shared coffee, conversation, and an album of late 1950s/early 1960s Oldies/Goldies in 1969, then slipped out of contact, bumped into each other again five years later. This occurred at a theatre where *American Graffiti* was showing. The older couple, like many people of their age (now thirty), made it a point to dress and style their hair in a flattering manner that defied any easy identification as to age. The younger, bereft of bell-bottoms now and having matured over the past half-decade, looked almost identical to their somewhat older friends. Few in the crowd could have guessed they were anything but contemporaries. The four entered and sat together, enjoying a film that enshrined the very music they had together listened to once upon a time in the now-bygone Hippie era.

Intriguingly, the counter-culture seemed considerably further away than the fabled Fifties and early Sixties they now watched and listened to, in recreated form, on the screen.

At the first sight of Mel's Diner and initial notes of "Rock Around the Clock," the former grad-student (now a full-time college prof) suddenly felt old. That was, perhaps, to be expected. Less so (and he marveled at this) was that, noticing people of all ages, like him and his friends wearing denim while grooving to the music and enjoying all onscreen antics, any sense of age swiftly diminished. Within minutes, he felt like a teenager again—once more enjoying music that, when he'd been young, was scoffed at by parents, teachers, and other adults as nothing but momentary madness, a passing phase. They'd get over it when they grew up. The kids knew better. Rock 'n' roll was not only the music of the hour. As Danny and the Juniors had announced, it was here to stay.

Two hours later, senior citizens, mature suburbanites, young marrieds, dating couples, teenagers, and even small kids exited. Everybody carried the enchantment of *American Graffiti*, and all that the movie and its music stood for, with them.

Like all post-1970 people, they wanted to remain, as Neil Diamond so aptly put it, forever in blue jeans.

Or, as Bob Dylan had earlier stated, forever young.

LAST STOP ON LIFE'S LONESOME HIGHWAY: At *American Graffiti*'s end, a Fifties style greaser (Paul Le Mat) who in 1962 remains loyal to that era's bygone styles finally wins a big race, only to drive off into the sunrise and (as we learn from the final credits) die shortly thereafter; this dramatic fiction beautifully encapsulated the coming conclusion of the First Wave of Youth culture, which itself passed shortly after the 1963 assassination of President Kennedy. (courtesy: Lucasfilm/The Coppola Company/Universal).

NOTES

Prologue

1. For further reading, see Anderson, Karen. *Wartime Women: Sex Roles, Family Relationships, and the Status of Women During World War II*. Westport CT: Praeger, 1981; also, Weatherford, Doris: *American Women and World War II*. Onehunga, NZ: Castle Books, 2009; and Winkler, Allan M. *Home Front U.S.A.: America During World War II*. Wheeling, IL: Harlan Davidson, 2000.
2. For the complete story of this syndrome in a broad and all-inclusive context, see Mondale, Sarah. *School: The Story of American Education*. Boston MA: Beacon Press, 2002; and, for additional material focusing on the major issues raised in this book's study of 1955–1970: Pulliam, John D. and Van Patten, James J. *History of Education in America*. Upper Saddle River, NJ: Pearson, 2006.
3. Bryant, J. Alison. *The Children's Television Community*. Abingdon, UK: Routledge, 2006; pp. 23–37.
4. For further reading, see Marling, Karal Ann. *As Seen on TV: The Visual Culture of Everyday Life in the 1950s*. Cambridge, MA: Harvard University Press, 1996; also, Sewell, Philip W. *Television in the Age of Radio: Modernity, Imagination, and the Making of a Medium*. New Brunswick, NJ: Rutgers University Press, 2014.
5. Fure-Slocum, Eric. *Contesting the Postwar City: Working Class and Growth Politics in 1940s Milwaukee*. New York: Cambridge University Press, 2013, particularly pp. 51–73; also, Cohen, Lizabeth. *A Consumer's Republic: The Politics of Mass Consumption in Postwar America*. New York: Vintage, 2003.

6. The manner in which this entertainment form came into being is nowhere so effectively chronicled as in Alba, Ben and Leno, Jay. *Inventing Late Night: Steve Allen and the Original Tonight Show.* Amherst, NY: Prometheus Books, 2005.

7. Gordon, Berry, and Asamen, Joy K. (eds.) *Children and Television: Images in a Changing Socio-Cultural World.* Thousand Oaks, CA: Sage Publications, 1991; pp. 49–53.

8. Anderson, Paul F. *The Davy Crockett Craze: A Look at the 1950s Phenomenon and Davy Crockett Collectibles.* Darien, CT: R&G Productions, 1996; pp. 21–37.

9. Recommended for further reading, see Conway, Mike. *The Origins of Television News in America: The Visualizers at CBS in the 1940s.* New York: Peter Lang, 2012; and Fielding, Raymond. *The American Newsreel: 1911–1967.* Norman: University of Oklahoma Press, 1972.

10. Lecie, Robert. *Conflict: The History of the Korean War (1950–1953).* Boston: Da Capo Press, 1996; also Kaufman, Burton. *The Korean Conflict.* Westport, CT: Greenwood, 1999; pp. 39–52, 61–68.

11. Osgood, Kenneth. *The Cold War at Home: Eisenhower's Secret Propaganda Battle at Home and Abroad.* Lawrence: University Press of Kansas, 2006; particularly pp. 111–137.

12. Svehla, Susan and Svehla, Gary J. *Atom Age Cinema: The Offbeat, the Classic and the Obscure.* Baltimore, MD: Midnight Marquee Press, 2014; pp. 32–38.

13. Halberstam, David. *The Fifties.* New York: Random House, 1993; p. 9.

14. Taylor, John Russell. *Hitch: The Life and Times of Alfred Hitchcock.* Boston: Da Capo Press, 1996; pp. 121–147.

15. Hitchcock, Alfred, and Wilder, Thornton (Hitchcock, Anna, uncredited) *Shadow of a Doubt.* The original screenplay housed at Universal Studios, California; 1941–1942.

16. Eisenhower, Dwight D. *Crusade in Europe: A Personal Account of World War II.* New York: Doubleday & Company, 1948.

17. Schepp, Brad, and Schepp, Debra. *TV Wonderland: The Enchantment of Early Television.* Portland, OR: Collectors Press, 2005; pp. 52–58.

18. "It Had to Be Murder," 1942; included in the retrospective *The Cornell Woolrich Omnibus.* New York: Penguin Group, 1997. For further reading, see Sharff, Stefan. *The Art of Looking in Hitchcock's Rear Window.* Pompton Plains, NJ: Limelight Editions, 2004; pp. 17–32.

19. Riesman, David, Glazer, Nathan, and Denney, Revel. *The Lonely Crowd: A Study of the Changing American Character.* New Haven, CT: Yale University Press (reissue), 2001; most specifically, pp. 104–107.

20. This quote has often been attributed to Jones, supposedly offered during the numerous press conferences for his novel *The Thin Red Line* (1962); others insist Jones was quoting some earlier author. The phrase does sound similar to, if notably different in attitude from, a statement by Benjamin Franklin from the 1770s: "There was never a good war or a bad peace." For further reading, see MacShane, Frank. *Into Eternity: The Life of James Jones: American Writer.* Boston: Houghton Mifflin, 1985.

21. The entirety of this massive undertaking is explained thoroughly in MacGregor, Morris. *Integration of the Armed Forces, 1940–1965.* Amazon Digital Services, 2012.

22. Howard-Pitney, David. *Martin Luther King Jr., Malcolm X, and the Civil Rights Struggle of the 1950s and 1960s: A Brief History.* New York: Bedford/St. Martin's, 2004; pp. 81–126.

23. Holt, Irvin. *Cold War Kids: Politics and Childhood in Postwar America (1945–1960)*. Lawrence: University Press of Kansas, 2011; pp. 44–61.

24. For a detailed account, with precise dates as to the various steps in this project's troubled development, see Ferrer, Margaret Lundrigan and Navanna, Tova. *Levittown: The First 50 Years*. Mount Pleasant, SC: Arcadia, 1997; pp. 11–27.

25. Kusher, David. *Levittown: Two Families, One Tycoon, and the Fight for Civil Rights in America's Legendary Suburb*. New York: Walker & Company, 2009; particularly pp. 121–227.

26. Halberstam, p. 133.

27. Goldberger, Paul. *Up from Zero: Politics, Architecture, and the Rebuilding of New York*. New York: Random House, 2005; pp. 101–197.

28. Halberstam, 134.

29. Reynolds, Malvina. *Malvina Reynolds Songbook*. Paducah, KY: Schroeder, 1984; p. 28.

30. See: Boone, Pat. *Twixt Twelve and Twenty*. New York: Dell Publishing, 1960.

31. See Lorber, Richard, and Fladell, Ernest. *The Gap*. New York: McGraw-Hill, 1968.

32. Binder, Arnold, Geis, Gilbert, Bruce, Dickson D. *Juvenile Delinquency: Historical, Cultural and Legal Perspectives*. Cincinnati: Anderson Publishing, 2000; pp. 39–51.

33. Myers, John E.B. *Child Protection in America: Past, Present, and Future*. New York: Oxford University Press, 2006; pp. 187–221.

34. Maier, Thomas. *Dr. Spock: An American Life*. Boston: Houghton Mifflin Harcourt, 1998; pp. 421–473.

35. Mayer, Martin. *MADISON AVENUE, U.S.A.: The Inside Story of American Advertising*. New York: Penguin, 1961; pp. 32–58.

36. For the most complete study of how advertising on television has impacted the cereal preferences of young viewers since the 1950s, and "experiments" like the Maypo sales approach, See Sugumar, V. Raji, and Chrysolyte, S. Jasmina. *Impact of TV Viewing Behaviour on the Cereal Food Choices of Children*. Chandler, AZ: Academic Publishing, 2013.

37. Slade, Giles. *Made to Break: Technology and Obsolescence in America*. Cambridge, MA: Harvard University Press, 2007; pp. 53–67.

38. Schlosser, Eric. *Fast Food Nation: The Dark Side of the All-American Meal*. Boston: Houghton Mifflin Harcourt, 2001 (reprint); pp. 73–84.

39. Witzel, Michael Karl. *The American Motel*. Minneapolis, MN: Motorbooks International, 2000; pp. 33–54.

40. Farrell, J. *One Nation Under Goods: Malls and the Seduction of American Hopping*. Washington, D.C.: Smithsonian, 2003; pp. 62–69.

41. The subject is delineated with a rare combination of sensitivity toward minorities and objective reporting of social trends in Wilkerson, Isabel. *The Warmth of Other Suns*. New York: Vintage, 2011 (reprint); most specifically, see pp. 23–29.

42. Halberstadt, Hans. *Combines and Harvesters: Motorbooks International Farm Tractor Color History*. Minneapolis, MN: Motorbooks International, pp. 6–9.

43. Lemann, Nicholas. *The Promised Land: The Great Black Migration and How It Changed America*. New York: Vintage, 1992, pp. 51–63.

44. For a full understanding, see Meisler, Richard J. *Black Ghetto: Promised Land or Colony?* Lexington, MA: Heath, 1972.

45. Halberstam, p. 28.

46. Cannon, Poppy, quoted in Halberstam, p. 495.

47. For a lighthearted look, see Ferry, Kathryn. *The 1950s Kitchen*. Colchester, UK: Shire Library, 2007. For a more analytical approach, see Rees, Jonathan. *Refrigeration Nation: A History of Ice, Appliances, and Enterprise in America*. Baltimore, MD: Johns Hopkins University Press, 2013.

48. Hine, Thomas. *Populuxe: The Look and Life of America in the '50s And 60s, From Tailfins and TV Dinners to Barbie Dolls and Fallout Shelters*. New York: Knopf, 1986; pp. 33–46.

49. For an introductory study, see Sapiro, Virginia. *Women in American Society: An Introduction to Women's Studies*. New York: McGraw-Hill, 2003.

50. "(The) Ballad of Davy Crockett" by George Bruns (music) and Thomas W. Blackburn (lyrics) caught on after the song was introduced late in October 1954 on an early Disneyland broadcast and increased in popularity after the Crockett shows began airing in December of that year. *Billboard* records that the most popular version, sung by Bill Hayes, reached Number One on the charts March 26 and remained there until April 23, though the song—also performed by Fess Parker for Disney and Tennessee Ernie Ford among others—entered the Top Ten before that and remained on that list long after. All told, ten million copies of the various recordings were sold.

51. Smith, Norman R. *Transistor Radios (1954–1968)*. Atglen, PA: Schiffer, 1998. Also, for the manner in which the transistor radio was quickly taken over by Japanese manufacturers and marketed at a lower price in America, see Handy, Erbe, and Blackham, Antonier. *Made in Japan: Transistor Radios of the 1950s and 1960s*. San Francisco: Chronicle Books, 1993; pp. 12–43.

52. For a finely-tuned telling of the song's evolution from the original composition to various recorded versions to inclusion in movies and finally the impact on Youth Music in general, see Dawson, J. *Rock Around the Clock: The Record That Started the Rock Revolution!* Montclair, NJ: Backbeat Books, 2005.

53. The full story of the emergence of this form, including its country-music antecedents and impact on rock music to come, is vividly related in Dregni, Michael, Burgess, Sonny, et al. *Rockabilly: The Twang Heard 'Round the World*. Minneapolis, MN: Voyageur Press, 2011.

54. Millard, Andre. *The Electric Guitar: A History of an American Icon*. Baltimore: Johns Hopkins University Press, 2004; pp. 121–154.

55. Haslam, Gerald W. *Workin' Man's Blues: Country Music in California*. Los Angeles: University of California Press, 1999; pp. 170–171.

56. Huber, Patrick; Goodson, Steve; Anderson, David (eds.) *The Hank Williams Reader*. New York: Oxford University Press, 2014. A virtual omnibus of the best ever written about Hank Sr., scholarly and lighter-weight articles alike, many dealing with roadhouse-country music's impact on early rock.

57. Altschuler, Glenn C. *All Shook Up: How Rock 'n' Roll Changed America*. New York: Oxford University Press, 2004. Early chapters explore not only the raw aesthetics of rhythm 'n' blues music but the reaction to such electronic age hillbilly music entering the discourse on American music.

58. Ward, Brian E. *Radio and the Struggle for Civil Rights in the South*. Gainesville: University Press of South Florida, 2006; pp. 98–121.

59. Halberstam, p. 463.

60. Jackson, John A. *Big Beat Heat: Alan Freed and the Early Years of Rock 'n' Roll*. New York: Schirmer Books, 1995; pp. 55–73.

61. Escott, Colin; Hawkins, Martin. *Good Rockin' Tonight: Sun Records and the Birth of Rock 'n' Roll*. New York: St. Martin's Griffin, 1992; pp. 47–61.

62. Kazan, Elia. *Elia Kazan: A Life*. Boston: Da Capo Press, 1997, pp. 248–249.

63. Halberstam, p. 480.

64. Personal interview between author and Dennis Hopper; 1990.

65. *Daily Mail. Elvis: The Illustrated Biography*. London: Transatlantic Press, 2011; p. 31.

*

Chapter One

1. For a brief but accurate and telling summary, see Knight, Arthur. *The Liveliest Art: A Panoramic History of the Movies*. New York: Mentor Books/New American Library, 1957; pp. 110–112. A fuller, richer history of this material can be found in Jeff, Leonard J., Simmos, Jerald L. *The Dame in the Kimono: Hollywood, Censorship, and the Production Code*. Lexington: The University of Kentucky Press, 2001.

2. Wood, Michael. *America in the Movies*. New York: Delta/Basic Books, 1975; p. 23.

3. The always liberal, often didactic filmmaker tells his own story with surprising good-humor and appreciated humility in Kramer, Stanley, and Coffey, Thomas M. *A Mad, Mad, Mad, Mad World: A Life in Hollywood*. New York: Harcourt, 1997.

4. The best-ever summation of the concept hails from the person often credited with inventing the form, Wolfe, Tom. *The New Journalism*. London: Pan Macmillan UK: Picador Books, 1975.

5. No better (or more entertaining) view of the early Beatles, with inclusion of all the various stories that have derived from their formative years is available than Kramer, Larry. *When They Were Boys: The True Story of the Beatles' Rise to the Top*. Philadelphia, PA: Running Press, 2013.

6. J. Ronald Oakley. *God's Country: America in the Fifties*. New York: Dembner Books, 1986; pp. 42–55, 219–223, 348–354.

7. Garry Wills. *John Wayne's America*. New York: Touchstone/Simon & Schuster, 1988; pp. 273–274.

8. Bell-Metereau, Rebecca. "1953: Movies and our secret lives" (pp. 89–10) in Pomerance, Murray. *American Cinema of the 1950s*. New Brunswick, NJ: Rutgers University Press, 2005.

9. Peter Manso. *Brando: The Biography*. New York: Hyperion, 1994; pp. 129–143.

10. The unique chemistry of participants at the famed school, with emphasis on Brando's contributions, appears in Garfield, David. *A Player's Piece: The Story of the Actor's Studio*. New York: Macmillan, 1980.

11. For a short if effective run-down on ever-changing sensibility in Hollywood's vision of our country, see Lewis, Jon. *American Film: A History*. New York: W.W. Norton & Co., 2007.

12. Kean, Leslie. *UFOS: Generals, Pilots, and Government Officials Go on the Record*. New York: Three Rivers Press, 2011; pp. 37–58.

13. Kreidl, John. *Nicholas Ray*. Woodbridge, CT: Twayne Publishers/G.K. Hall and Company, 1977; pp. 25–28.

14. Mulvey, Laura, "Visual Pleasure in Narrative Cinema" (written 1973, originally published in *Screen*, 1975); since widely re-published. During the latter 20th century Mulvey's article was widely considered to be the seminal ice-breaker of a new form of criticism that collapsed key elements of auteurism, semiotics, psychoanalysis, and feminist theory, while introducing the term "the male gaze." In the early 21st century, many critics (female and male, straight and gay) have repudiated the narrowness of Mulvey's approach by insisting that women as well as men enjoy the act of 'gazing' at sensual objects (male or female) on the screen, and that this is indeed a key source of The Movies' appeal to people in general, not some patriarchal paradigm.

15. The complexity of Ladd, including the emotional and sexual underpinnings of his brief life, are best chronicled in *Ladd: The Life, the Legend, the Legacy*. Linet, Beverly. New York: Arbor House/Putnam, 1979.

16. Doherty, Thomas. *Teenagers and Teenpics: The Juvenilization of American Movies in the 1950s*. Philadelphia: Temple University Press, 2002; pp. 58–82.

17. Personal discussions between the author and Nicholas Ray over the five-year period from 1970–1975 in preparation for a planned book that never materialized.

18. Personal discussions between the author and Dennis Hopper, held in 1979 and 1988 for the above-mentioned book on Ray.

19. Dawson, Jim. *Rock Around the Clock: The Record That Started the Rock Revolution!* San Francisco: Backbeat Books/CMP, 2005; pp. 113–128.

20. However dated it may be considered today, for a fascinating study of the juvenile delinquent mind and the manner in which an inclination toward street crime may be detected in such a young person's vocabulary and phrasing, see Bennett, James. *Oral History and Delinquency: The Rhetoric of Criminology*. Chicago: University of Chicago Press, 1988.

21. Bogle, Donald. *Toms, Coons, Mulattoes, Mammies, & Bucks: An Interpretive History of Blacks in American Films*. New York: Continuum, 2001 (Fourth edition); pp. 157–199.

*

Chapter Two

1. Doherty, p. 60.

2. Dawson, pp. 27–36.

3. Fine, Benjamin. *1,000,000 Delinquents*. New York: The World Publishing Company, 1955; pp. 23–27.

4. Tropiano, Stephen. *Rebels and Chicks: A History of the Hollywood Teen Movie*. New York: Back Stage Books, 2006; p. 45.

5. "Doctor Urges Comic Book Ban." *New York Times*, 4 September 1948, p. 6.

6. United States Congress, Records of the Subcommittee to Investigate Juvenile Delinquency (Washington D.C., *The Congressional Record*).

7. United States Congress, Records of the Subcommittee to Investigate Sex and Violence in Motion Pictures and their Social Impact on the Impressionable Young (on file: Washington D.C., *The Congressional Record*).

8. To view The Comic Book Code of the late 1950s in its entirety, see www.comics.dm.net/codetext.html.

9. Dale, Alan. *The Spider and the Marionettes*. New York: Lyle Stuart, 1965.

10. Savage, Kerry. *Payola in the Music Industry: A History, 1880–1991*. Jefferson, NC: McFarland, 2013.

11. Halberstam, p. 466

12. For a complete history of this syndrome, including the 1950s though tracing the situation back even further and continuing the exploration into the present, see Freund, David M. *Colored Property: State Policy and White Racial Relations in Suburban America*. Chicago: University of Chicago Press, 2010.

13. Shaw, Arnold. *Rockin' 50s*. New York: Hawthorne Books, 1974; p. 154.

14. Quoted by Kamin, Jonathan, "The Social Reaction to Jazz and Rock" in *Journal of Jazz Studies 2* (1974): 99.

15. Oakley, p. 283.

16. For an insightful depiction of the meteoric rise and just as swift fall, see Jackson, John A. *The Alan Freed Story- The Early Years of Rock 'n' Roll*. Jefferson, NC: Collectibles Press, 2007.

17. Crenshaw, Marshall Crenshaw, *Hollywood Rock: A Guide to Rock 'n' Roll in the Movies*. New York: HarperPerennial/Agincourt, 1994; p. 189.

18. Brode, Douglas. *Elvis Cinema and Popular Culture*. Jefferson, NC: McFarland, 2006; pp. 45–47.

19. Guralnick, Peter. *Last Train to Memphis: The Rise of Elvis Presley*. Boston: Little Brown, 1994; pp. 411–412.

20. Adams, who apparently took his own life in 1968, left behind a journal of his friendship with Elvis that was found some thirty years later by his daughter and published: Adams, Nick, & Adams, Allyson. *The Rebel and the King*. N.P.: WaterDancer Press, 2002.

21. Sigall, Martha. *The Boys of Tente Terrace: Tales from the Golden Age of Animation*. Columbia, MO: University Press of Missouri, p. 71.

22. de Seife, Ethan. *Tashlinesque: The Hollywood Comedies of Frank Tashlin*. Middletown, CT: Wesleyan University Press, 2012.

23. The man who apparently invented late-night TV recalls his career, including his shift from political liberal to cultural conservative, in Allen, Steve. *Reflections*. Amherst, NY: Promethus Books, 1994.

24. For an excellent study of the syndrome, see Spencer, John Michael. *The Rhythms of Black Folk: Race, Religion, Pan-Africanism*. Trenton, NJ: African World Press, 1995. For an equally impressive study of Jordan's revolutionary approach, see Chilton, John. *The Story of Louis Jordan and His Music*. Ann Arbor: University of Michigan Press, 1994.

25. The term here is employed in the manner first suggested by McLuhan, Marshall. *The Extensions of Man*. McGraw-Hill, 1964.

*

Chapter Three

1. Graham, Don. *No Name on the Bullet: A Biography of Audie Murphy*. New York: Viking, 1989; Audie's early experiences as a dirt farmer are chronicled in pages 26–52.
2. Marsh, Dave. *Elvis*. New York: Barnes & Noble/Smithmark, 1997; See in particular, pages 58–121 for Elvis's early fascination with Hollywood movies, far in excess of his interest in music.
3. Morales, Julio. *Puerto Rican Poverty and Migration: We Just Had to Try Elsewhere*. Westport, CT: Praeger, 1986.
4. Fine, Benjamin. *1,000,000 Delinquents*. New York: The Word Press, 1956.
5. Tropiano, pp. 45–47.
6. Tropiano, p. 44.
7. Tropiano, p. 46.
8. Tropiano, pp. 44–48.
9. Tropiano, p. 45.

*

Chapter Four

1. Sanders, Don, and Susan. *The American Drive-In Theatre*. New York: Cresline, 2013; pp. 9–13.
2. Sanders, pp. 10–14.
3. Mast, Gerald. *A Short History of the Movies* (Third edition). Indianapolis: Bobbs-Merrill Educational Publishing, 1981; pp. 93–97.
4. For an analysis of the manner in which sudden population changes altered the political, social, and cultural attitudes of the U.S. public, see Miller, Nathan. *New World Coming: The 1920s and the Making of Modern America*. Boston: Da Capo Press, 2004.
5. Luce himself employed that phrase for a February 17, 1941, *Life* story urging America's entrance into World War II, though clearly he was drawing on an emergent ideology that others had posited during the century's opening decades and, perhaps, earlier still; for a full understanding of the concept and its application to the nation's evolving vision of itself, see Evans, Harold. *The American Century*. Knopf, 1998.
6. Sanders, p. 10.
7. Sanders, p. 8.
8. Sloan, Alfred P. *My Years With General Motors*. New York: Crown Business, 1990; particularly pp. 350–401, in which the firm's postwar vision of itself in the American auto industry, and Sloan's own contributions to changes, are detailed.
9. No more comprehensive (or entertaining) retelling of this B movie mini-kingdom exists than in Smith, Gary A. *American International Pictures: The Golden Years*. Albany, GA: BearManor Media, 2013.
10. "Shock Theatre" and its encouragement of life accompaniments is analyzed in Watson, Elena M. *Television Horror Movie Hosts: 68 Vampires, Mad Scientists and Other Denizens of the Late-Night Airwaves*. Jefferson, NC: McFarland & Co., 2000.

11. Biskind, Peter. *Seeing Is Believing: How Hollywood Taught Us to Stop Worrying and Love the Fifties.* New York: Pantheon Books, 1983; pp. 217–223.

12. Guylas, Aaron John. *Extraterrestrials and the American Zeitgeist: Alien Contact Tales Since the 1940s.* Jefferson, NC: McFarland, 2013; see, in particular, pp. 89–104.

13. Stam, Robert. *Reflexivity in Film and Literature: From* Don Quixote *to Jean-Luc Godard.* New York: Columbia University Press, 1992.

14. Norris, Christopher. *Deconstruction: Theory and Practice.* Routledge, 2002.

15. Rhodes, Guy Don. *Edgar G. Ulmer: Detour on Poverty Row.* Boston: Lexington Books, 2008; p. 242.

16. Corman, Roger. *How I Made a Hundred Movies in Hollywood and Never Lost a Dime.* Boston: Da Capo, 1998; see, specifically, pp. 141–157 to grasp the auteur's unique techniques for achieving quality (or at least a certain sort of artistic sensibility) on a nearly nonexistent budget.

17. Havis, Allan. *Cult Films: Taboo and Transgression.* Lanham, MD: University Press of America, 2007.

18. Svehla, Gary J. *Guilty Pleasures of the Horror Film.* Baltimore: Midnight Marquee Press, 1996.

19. The original essay was most recently included in Rieff, David (Ed.). *Susan Sontag: Essays of the 1960s and 70s.* New York: Library of America, 2013.

20. Compton, Michael. *Pop Art.* Paris: Hamlyn, 1970; pp. 21–47.

*

Chapter Five

1. Allen, Woody. *Sleeper:* Original screenplay, 1973.

2. The phrase is usually credited to Marjorie Rosen, who first employed "Mammary Madness" as a means of explaining the sudden emphasis on a woman's bustline following the early appearances of Jane Russell during the late 1940s and then, in the 1950s, Monroe, Mansfield, and Mamie Van Doren. See *Popcorn Venus.* New York: Avon Books, 1974.

3. Koper, Richard. *Fifties Blondes: Sexbombs, Sirens, Bad Girls and Teen Queens.* Duncan, OK: BearManor Books, 2010; p. 319.

4. Thomas, Bob. "Sex Goddess Lives to Tell Her Story." *Times Daily/* Associated Press (12/2/1997).

5. Van Doren, Mamie. *Playing the Field.* New York: Putnam (Adult), 1987; pp. 122–124.

6. Van Doren, p. 126.

7. Mamie's dissatisfaction with Universal and the manner in which they attempted to shape her career was first reported by Bob Thomas: "Mamie Van Doren Wants to Stop Shadowing Monroe" (1/22/1954), Associated Press story in the *Tuskaloosa News.* Her reflections on how and why this occurred were featured in Wilson, Earl: "Kitty Loses Voice, Finds Religion" (8/7/1962), his long-syndicated national column.

8. That question was posed by Bettie in 1998, when several *Playboy* reporters tracked her down to the simple Southwestern home where she frugally lived. One year earlier, Page's attitude about her belated super-stardom served as the starting point for: Foster, Richard.

The Real Bettie Page: The Truth About the Queen of the Pinups. New York: Carol Publishing/ Birch Lane Press, 1997.

9. Truman Capote ostensibly made this statement, probably not in print (at least not originally) but during an informal gathering of literati, possibly in a New York bar. The statement was later analyzed in the *New York Times* (10/25/1992).

10. For the best analysis of the non-studio B movie as it emerged during the 1950s, including but not limited to Zugsmith's career and his shifting company loyalties, as well as his indie output in conjunction with the Powers That Be (or were), see Clark, Randall. *At a Theatre Near You: The History, Culture, and Politics of the American Exploitation Film*. London: Routledge, 2013.

11. Van Doren, p. 148.

12. For a thorough and entertaining analysis of how the Queen B moniker emerged, beginning with Mamie and continuing until the early 21st century, see Keeyes, Jon. *Attack of the B Queens*. Opelousas, LA: Luminary Press/Midnight Marquee Press, 2003, particularly pp. 1–37.

13. The superstar's repulsion for anything perceived as sleazy in popular culture was presented as a foil to the actual woman who existed behind the Doris Day image, as explained in smart and unsentimental tones by McDonald, Tamar Jeffers. *Doris Day Confidential: Hollywood, Sex, and Stardom*. London: I.B. Taurus, 2013.

14. Officially, the quotation did not appear until Walt Kelly (1913–1973) employed it for an Earth Day poster in 1970; fans of his long-running *Pogo* comic-strip insist that they recall reading it way back in the mid-fifties.

15. Sullivan, Steve. *Va Va Voom!: Bombshells, Pin-Ups, Sexpots and Glamour Girls*. Los Angeles: Rhino/General Publishing Group, 1995. For further reading, see Fusco, Joseph. *The Films of Mamie Van Doren*. Duncan, OK: BearManor Media, 2010.

16. Maltin, Leonard. *Leonard Maltin's Movie Guide (2008)*. New York: Signet, 2007.

17. The phrase has variously been attributed to Una Stannard, Andrea Dworkin, Shulamith Firestone, and Kate Millet, among others who identified themselves as radical feminists, either in their writings or at university lectures. No mainstream Second Wave feminists have ever been credited with originating the phrase, nor has any stepped up to take credit for it.

18. No academic study more beautifully captures the acceptance of post-feminist thinking of various Hollywood sex symbols who were patently (and unfairly) rejected by Second Wave feminists than Munford, Rebecca, and Waters, Melanie. *Feminism and Popular Culture: The Post-Feminist Mystique*. New Brunswick, NJ: Rutgers University Press, 2014.

19. Ricci, Mark, and Conway, Mark. *The Films of Marilyn Monroe*. New York: Cadillac Publishing, 1964; pp. 22–24.

20. Founded in 1952, *Confidential* founded a base readership of several million people by taking the new postwar-freedom gleefully to the sort of stories which the *New York Times* would have considered un-fit to print. The sordid publication was marketed almost exclusively to right-wing types who condemned the kind of illicit affairs that appeared in its pages while taking a kind of bizarre pornographic pleasure in them. Not only such low-brow types as Mamie and Jayne were all but vivisected here; more supposedly upscale Hollywood women like Lana Turner and Ava Gardner also had their secret lives presented to the public—or, at least, a certain part of them.

21. See: www.mamievandoren.com; "Bedtime Stories"

22. Sullivan, pp. 79–80.

23. The ongoing relationship between Mamie and Jayne, leading up to their eventual meet-ing and this supposedly true comment, is well chronicled in Betrock, Alan (Ed.), *Jayne Mansfield vs. Mamie Van Doren: Battle of the Blondes*. N.p.: Shake Books, 1993.

24. Saxton, Martha. *Jayne Mansfield and the American Fifties*. Boston: Houghton Mifflin Company, 1975; p. 201.

25. Saxton, p. xiii.

26. Saxton, p. 34.

27. The concept is explored by various feminist authors in Gornick, Vivian, and Moran, Barbara K. *Women in a Sexist Society: Studies in Power and Powerlessness*. New York: Basic books, 1971.

28. Saxton, p. 201.

29. Saxton, p. xix.

30. Saxton, p. xi.

31. Mailer, Norman. *Marilyn: A Biography*. New York: Grosset & Dunlap, 1973; pp. 72–97.

32. Virtually no stone is left uncovered, though what emerges does seem to be presented in a cynically salacious manner in Strait, Raymond. *The Tragic Secret Life of Jayne Mansfield*. Washington, DC: Regnery, 1974.

*

Chapter Six

1. Lencek, Lena & Bosker, Gideon. *Making Waves: Swimsuits and the Undressing of America*. San Francisco: Chronicle Books, 1989; p. 90.

2. Bensimon, Kelly Killoren. *The Bikini Book*. New York: Assouline, 2006; pp. 22–26.

3. Evans, Mike. *The Bikini Book*. New York: Universe Publishing, 1996; p. 15.

4. Evans, p. 10.

5. Evans, ibid.

6. Albright, Mary Ann; "Real-life 'Gidget' Recalls Life at OSU," an interview with Kathy Kohner (Zuckerman), *Corvllis-Gazette-Times* (1/23/2007).

7. Lisanti, Thomas. *Hollywood Surf and Beach Movies: The First Wave, 1959–1969*; p. 29.

8. Lisanti, pp. 29–30.

9. Lisanti, p. 30.

10. Lisanti, pp. 35–36.

11. Nash, Graham. Though the song has long been considered an anthem of the Woodstock Generation following its premiere on the *Déjà Vu* album (recorded, 1969; released, 1970) by Crosby, Stills, Nash & Young, Nash actually wrote the piece while still performing with the Hollies (which he'd helped form in 1962) though never recorded by that group.

12. Funicello, Annette. *A Dream Is a Wish Your Heart Makes: My Story*. New York: Hyperion, 1994; pp. 154–159. Also, Lisanti, pp. 72, 77.

13. Lisanti, p. 83.

14. Lisanti, ibid.

15. Lisanti, Ibid. For more on this subject, see Arkoff, Samuel Z. *Flying Through Hollywood by the Seat of My Pants: From the Man Who Brought You "I Was a Teenage Werewolf" and "Muscle Beach Party."* Secaucus, NJ: Carol Publishing, 1992.

16. American International Pictures; financial archives.

17. The precise manner in which Mary Pickford, Mae Marsh, and their friends the Gish sisters were picked as role models for the all-American girl-next-door type is sensitively portrayed in Gish, Lillian. *Dorothy and Lillian Gish.* New York: Charles Scribner's Sons, 1973; pp. 4–39. Also see Rotha, Paul. *The Film Till Now.* Middlesex, UK: Hamlyn (updated edition), 1967; pp. 172–178.

18. The issue of narcissism, as well as the question of whether bodybuilding ought to qualify as a legitimate sport, is treated in Todd, Jan. "Bodybuilding" in *St. James Encyclopedia of Pop Culture*, Independence, KY: Gale Group, 1999.

19. For a revealing study laced with welcome dry/wry wit, see Clum, John M. *"He's All Man!" Learning Masculinity, Gayness, and Love from American Movies.* Basingstoke, UK: Palgrave Macmillan, 2002.

20. Apparently, this statement was first employed during the Berkeley Free Speech Movement (1964–1965) and may have been uttered by Jack Weinberg, a graduate student who was taking part in the demonstrations. However much this became a universal youth mantra during the late 1960s, here is one more case of a specific phrase being taken out of context as Weinberg later insisted he only said it (off the cuff, not as a political position) to get rid of an annoying older journalist.

21. Lisanti, Tom. *Drive-In Dream Girls.* Jefferson, NC: McFarland & Company, 2003; p. 234.

22. McNulty, Patrick (interviewer); Bruce Brown quote in *The Los Angeles Times*, 1966.

23. Brown, Bruce; *Variety* interview (1966), quoted by Lisanti, p. 279.

*

Chapter Seven

1. Grisez, Germain & Shaw, Russell. *Beyond the New Morality: The Responsibility of Freedom.* Notre Dame: University of Notre Dame Press, 1988; pp. 25–39.

2. Halberstam, p. 273.

3. Pomeroy, Wardell B.; Martin, Clyde E.; Gebhard, Paul H & Kinsey, Alfred C. *Sexual Behavior in the Human Female.* Philadelphia, PA: W.B. Saunders, 1953.

4. For the most complete study of the Comstock Laws and other attempts by society to restrict freedom of expression as to film and other examples of 20th-century popular entertainment, see Strub, Whitney. *Obscenity Rules: Roth vs. United States and the Long Struggle over Sexual Expression.* Lawrence, KS: University of Kansas Press, 2013, particularly pp. 100–143.

5. Much of the information contained in the opening paragraphs of this chapter is drawn from Eig, Jonathan. *The Birth of the Pill: How Four Crusaders Reinvented Sex and Law.* New York: W.W. Norton, 2014.

6. Doherty, Thomas. *Teenagers and Teenpics: The Juvenilization of American Movies in the 1950s.* Philadelphia: Temple University Press, 2002; p. 127.

7. By far, for the best treatment of this subject and how it was enshrined by pre-Women's Movement Hollywood, see Haskell, Molly. *From Reverence to Rape: The Treatment of Women in Movies*. Chicago: University of Chicago Press, 1987.

8. The complexity of Doris Day, the real woman and the imagined role model that she not only agreed to play but helped shape and mold is best revealed in Kaufman, David. *The Untold Story of the Girl Next Door*. London: Virgin Books, 2010.

9. Universal Studio Archives; Box-Office receipts, 1957.

10. Rosen, Marjorie. *Popcorn Venus: Women, Movies, and the American Dream*. New York: Avon Library, 1974; p. 311.

11. Kazan, Elia. *Elia Kazan: A Life*. Boston: Da Capo Press, 1997; pp. 279–291.

12. *Time* Magazine "Cinema, New Pictures"; December 24, 1956.

13. Wallach, Eli. Personal interview with the author, October 1965 at the Actors Studio.

14. Though Jacques Lacan (1901–1981) appears to have originated the contemporary use of the term 'gaze' in psychological situations in life and art, while Michel Foucault (1926–1984) pioneered philosophical applications of this concept, the specific application of a 'gaze' in relationship to the process of watching movies dates to Mulvey, Laura. "Visual Pleasure and Narrative Cinema" (article).

15. Music and lyrics from the original play, which premiered on April 14, 1960, at the Martin Beck Theatre on Broadway, would (at least for this song) remain the same in the movie; the difference is in the context of performance, owing to notably different actresses and their diametrically opposite approaches.

16. Scanlon, Jennifer. *Bad Girls Go Everywhere: The Life of Helen Gurley Brown, the Woman Behind* Cosmopolitan *Magazine*. New York: Penguin (Reprint), 2010.

17. Toffler, Alvin. *Future Shock*. New York: Random House, 1970.

18. Kael, Pauline. *The New York*, Current Cinema, December 1969.

*

Chapter Eight

1. Friedan, Betty. *The Feminine Mystique*, originally published 1963. For today's readers, the most highly recommended 50th anniversary text is Fermaglich, Kirsten, and Fine, Lisa (Eds.); New York: Norton Critical Editions, 2012.

2. de Beauvoir, Simone, originally published 1949. For today's readers, the most highly recommended reprint is *The Works of Simone de Beauvoir: The Second Sex and the Ethics of Ambiguity*. N.p.: CreateSpace Independent Publishing Platform, 2011. This double-barreled helping of de Beauvoir's writings allows for a full grasp of what has come to be called Existential Feminism.

3. Jacqueline, Herrmann. *The National Organization for Women and the Fight of the Equal Rights Amendment*. Santa Cruz, CA: GRIN Verlag GmbH; pp. 3–7, 11–17, and 22–23.

4. Shulman, Max, and Smith, Robert Paul. *The Tender Trap* (stage play, 1954; Broadway Theatre Archives) and *The Tender Trap* (screenplay, 1954–1955; Metro-Goldwyn-Mayer Archives.)

5. Madara, John, and White, David; 1963, Philadelphia. Though in the early 1970s Second Wave feminists loved to imply that 17-year-old Lesley Gore had written as well as performed this ode/anthem to young female emancipation, which reached Number Two on the *Billboard* Pop Charts, in truth both the music and lyrics were created by early examples of emancipated men.

6. Co-producer/co-scenarist Milton Subotsky (1921–1991) did triple duty here by composing the original songs with Frank Virtue and Ray Ellis; the commercial success of this minor project allowed Subotsky to form his own Amicus Prods. several years later.

7. "Elvis Is Everywhere"; *The New York Times* (8/16/2007); some sources suggest that this, or a similar statement, was made on August 28, 1965, after the Beatles met Elvis in person; see Davies, Hunter. *The Beatles: The Authorized Biography*. New York: McGraw-Hill, 1968; p. 19.

8. Gamson, Joshua. *Claim to Fame: Celebrity in Contemporary America*. Los Angeles: University of California Press, 1994, p. 57.

9. Kael, Pauline; quoted by Liz Smith, "The Swinger." wowowow.com. (1/08/2013).

10. One hallmark of *Playboy* during the fifteen-year period covered in this study was the insistence on eliminating the long-standing dichotomization between 'good' (virginal) and 'bad' (sensuous) women. In addition to portraying 'nice' girl-next-door types in the nude, editor Hugh Hefner happily published proclamations by various Centerfold subjects as to their physical state of innocence so as to educate a male reader about the misconception of drawing conclusions about any female owing to her attitude toward physical display. See Edgren, Gretchen. *The Playboy Book: Fifty Years*. Hong Kong: Tashen, 2007.

11. For the fullest spectrum of attitudes, see Gillis, Stacy; Howie, Gillian, and Munford, Rebecca (Eds.) *Third Wave Feminism: A Critical Exploration*. Basingstoke, UK: Palgrave Macmillan, 2004.

12. Smith, Liz; ibid.

13. Ebert, Roger. "R.P.M." review (10/24/1971).

*

Chapter Nine

1. Steve Chapple and Reebee Garofalo, *Rock 'n' Roll Is Here to Pay* Chicago: Nelson-Hall, 1977, p. 60.

2. ———. *Rolling Stone (Illustrated) History of Rock and Roll: The Definitive History of the Most Important Artists and Their Music*. New York: Random House, 1992; p. 92.

3. Tosches, Nick, and Marcus, Greil. *Hellfire: The Jerry Lee Lewis Story*. New York: Grove Press, 1998; pp. 132–159.

4. Douglas, Susan J. *Where the Girls Are: Growing Up Female with the Mass Media*. New York: Random House/Times Books, p. 113.

5. Douglas, p. 113.

6. Douglas, p. 113

7. Douglas, p. 119.

8. McCarthy, Eugene J. Personal interview with the author, conducted at WHEN-AM Radio in Liverpool, NY; 1979.

9. Garcia, Jerry, quoted in Peter, Joseph. *Good Times: An Oral History of America in the Nineteen Sixties*. New York: Charterhouse, 1973; p. 188.

10. Corliss, Richard. "All Time 100 Movies" in *Time* (2/12/2005).

11. Sarris, Andrew. *The American Cinema: Directors and Directions 1929–1968*. Boston: Da Capo Press, 1968; pp. 1–37.

12. Yule, Andrew. *The Man Who "Framed" the Beatles: A Biography of Richard Lester*. New York: Donald I. Fine, 1994; pp. 40–92.

13. Lennon, John; personal interviews with the author, conducted during October 1971 at the St. Regis Hotel, New York.

14. Every history of the Beatles contains its own version of what happened, why, and who was 'really' to blame. For the most touching, persuasive, and memorable, see Best, Pete & Doncaster, Patrick. *Beatle! The Pete Best Story*. Medford, NJ: Plexus Publishing, 1994.

15. John Lennon, interview with the author.

16. Gelly, Devorah. *The Brian Epstein Story*. New York: Faber and Faber Ltd., 1999; p. 49. For further reading, see Tiwary, Vivek J., and Robinson, Andrew C. *The Fifth Beatle: The Brian Epstein Story*. New Orleans: M Press, 2013.

17. Yule, pp. 46–82.

18. Yule, pp. 71–79; also, Lennon, interviews with the author.

19. ———. "A Hard Day's Night Review" (unsigned) in *Time* (8/12/1964)

20. Crowther, Bosley. "A Hard Day's Night Review" in *The New York Times* (8/12/1964).

21. Crowther, ibid.

22. Marcus, Greil. *The Old, Weird America: The World of Bob Dylan's Basement Tapes* (New York: Holt, 2001); p. 12 (originally published in 1998 as *Invisible Republic: The Story of the Basement Tapes*.

23. Odum, Howard, p. 47.

24. Entertainment: "Skiffle King Donegan Dies"; *BBC News* (11/4/2002).

25. Fishwick, Marshall. *Parameters of Popular Culture*. Bowling Green, OH: Popular Press, 1974; p. 2.

26. Lennon, interviews with author.

27. Gelden, Ken & Thornton, Sarah (eds.) *The Subculture Reader*. New York: Routledge, p. 401.

28. Yule, pp. 94–109.

29. Halliwell, Leslie. *Film and Video Guide*. London: HarperCollins, 2008, p. 338.

30. Shelf, David. *All We Are Saying*. New York: St. Martin's, 2000; p. 176.

31. The meeting has alternately been reported as occurring on August 25 or 26th, 1964, at the Whiskey-a-Go-Go; to understand the state of mind that the 31-year-old actress was in at the time, see Saxton, Martha. *Jayne Mansfield and the American Fifties*. Boston: Houghton Mifflin, 1975; pp. 175–186.

32. Miles, Barry. *The British Invasion*. New York: Sterling, 2009; p. 15.

33. Gitlin, Todd. *The Sixties: Years of Hope, Days of Rage*. New York: Bantam, 1987; pp. 810–86, 200–203.

34. Warhol set about creating a vast collection of images, each focusing on some fascinating (celebrity) face during the early 1960s; he continued this trend through to the following

decade. Marilyn Monroe and Elizabeth Taylor were among them, but so was Elvis Presley, this one more early example of the manner in which the edgy/artsy elite had become fascinated with vestiges of mainstream popular culture, particularly those that had been marginalized as vulgar. For the best source of information on Warhol's motivations, see Warhol, Andy. *The Philosophy of Andy Warhol*. New York: Harvest, 1977.

35. Such quotes as "famous for fifteen minutes" and "famous for being famous" are usually attributed to Warhol at the opening of his show at Moderna Museet in Stockholm, 1968. For further explanation, see Warhol, Andy and Hackett, Pat. *POPism: The Warhol Sixties*. New York: Mariner Books, 2006.

*

Chapter Ten

1. Lennon, John ("Interview"). *The Beatles Anthology*. San Francisco: Chronicle Books, 2000; p. 272.
2. McCartney, Paul ("Interview"). Ibid; Paul explains that he had been involved with making elaborate home movies and that while watching them he and the other band members seized on the idea to create a more elaborate home movie about The Beatles that might provide similar enjoyment for their fans.
3. Wolfe, Tom. *The Electric Kool-Aid Acid Test*. New York: Farrar, Straus, Giroux, 1968. A remarkable piece of writing in the New Journalism style and a classic of that then-emergent genre in which the author's subjective attitudes toward events being discussed takes precedence over any notions that a reporter ought to remain entirely objective; such an impressionistic verbal portrait can be trusted more by readers as an honest presentation of what the situation meant to the writer than a factual delineation of what actually occurred, and this is absolutely the case here.
4. Norman, Philip. *John Lennon: A Life*. New York: Ecco/HarperCollins, 2009; pp. 243–281.
5. Gillespie, Alex, and Cornish, Flora. "Intersubjectivity: Towards a Dialogue Analysis." *Journal for the Theory of Social Behavior (40)*; pp. 19–46.
6. See: Goldman, Albert. *The Lives of John Lennon*. New York: William Morris & Co., 1968 (though this book provoked extreme controversy on publication, owing to its less-than-flattering depiction of the artist (specifically in terms of John's drug use), in fact most of what is reported here must be considered accurate.
7. Mausch, Dave, and Swenson, John. *The Rolling Stone Record Guide, 1st Edition*. New York: Random House/The Rolling Stone Press, 1979; p. 27.
8. Davies, Hunter. "Take a Ride Through the Beatles Magical Mystery Tour"; CBS Local Media resources.
9. Hoberman, J., and Rosenbaum, Jonathan. *Midnight Movies*. Cambridge, MA: Da Capo Press, 1991; pp. 17–31.
10. Robert Blees (1918–2015) became interested in writing while serving as a navigator during World War II for the U.S. Army Air Corps. In Hollywood, he contributed to nearly a dozen motion pictures; by all accounts, he had hoped that *High School Confidential!* would

be produced as a serious film about youthful crime, not the teen-exploitation epic that his piece eventually emerged as.

11. See: Hawkins, Joan. Cutting Edge: *Art-Horror and the Horrific Avant-Garde*. Minneapolis: University of Minnesota Press, 2000; here is perhaps the most exquisite analysis of the parastetcinema/Para-Cinema/Para Cinema concept yet offered.

12. Corliss, Richard. "When Antonioni Blew Up the Movies": *Time*, April 2007.

13. See Leary, Timothy. *Flashbacks*. New York: Tarcher/Penguin, 1997; also Parker, Scott F. *Conversations with Ken Kesey*. Jackson: University of Mississippi Press, 2004.

14. Thompson, Howard. "Tomb of Ligeia" reviewed in *The New York Times;* May 16, 1964.

15. Leary's ideas, including the "setting" and other aspects of his counter-cultural agenda from the university tours in the late1960s, are expounded upon in Leary, Timothy. *The Psychedelic Experience: A Manual Based on the Tibetan Book of the Dead*. New York: Citadel Underground, 2000; particularly, pp. 57–71.

16. Fans of Peter Max's artwork consider him the single genius who most effectively caught the spirit of the Hippie era in a way that communicated to the masses, a kind of Norman Rockwell with a contemporary edge; those who do not dismiss Max as a minor figure who momentarily dazzled the public with derivative and superficial renderings of what lesser known but more talented people had already initiated; an overview, including the ever-intriguing issue of his involvement with the animated Beatles movie, can be found in Riley, Charles A. Jr. *The Art of Peter Max*. New York: Harry N. Abrams, 2002.

17. Burks, John. "Rock and Roll's Worst Day" in *Rolling Stone* (2/7/1970); for a fascinating, detailed, and scrupulously accurate report, see: Kirkpatrick, Bob. *1969: The Year That Changed Everything*. New York: Skyhorse Publishing.

*

Chapter Eleven

1. Corso, Gregory, quoted in Morgan, Bill. *The Typewriter Is Holy: The Complete Uncensored History of the Beat Generation*. Berkeley CA: Counterpoint (Perseus), 2011; p. xxi.

2. Snyder, Gary, quoted in Charters, Ann. *Beat Down to Your Soul: What Was the Beat Generation?* New York: Penguin/Putnam, 2001; p. xv.

3. Herbert Huncke (1915–1996), an associate of Corso, Kerouac, and Co., may likely have been the person who first introduced them to that term as a pre-existing concept in the jazz community, and particularly among African American artists. The first instance in which this appeared in print may have been Holmes, John Clellon. "This Is the Beat Generation" in *The New York Times* (11/16/1952).

4. The phrase originally appeared in *On the Road* (New York: Scribner's, 1957) when, in Chapter One, Sal Paradise (Kerouac's alter-ego) announces his intention to seek individual freedom by going out into the world with Dean Moriarty (based on Neal Cassidy).

5. The philosophical work of Jean-Paul Sartre was well circulated among members of the Beat Generation during their formative years. Most notable was "Existentialism: A Clarification" (1944), in which Sartre argued that "man must create his own essence" by

"throwing himself into the world, suffering there, struggling there," a process by which "he gradually defines what man he is before he dies."

6. The term "Beatnik" (mildly condescending though clearly a comedic means of revealing how non-threatening this counter-culture was to mainstream people of the era, was introduced by Herb Caen (1916–1997) as part of his punditry column for the *San Francisco Chronicle*, probably initially employed late in 1957 or early in 1958.

7. "The White Negro" by Norman Mailer, originally published in *Dissent* (1957), was widely distributed as a pamphlet when published by San Francisco's City Lights bookstore. In it, Mailer argues that the fascination with African American jazz, beginning among a small, select circle of white hipsters in the early 20th century, went mainstream in the 1920s, then increasing with each passing decade. During the postwar era, this syndrome moved ever further up from the Underground into society at large. The article was re-published in *Advertisements for Myself* (New York: G.P. Putnam's Sons, 1959); this volume is now available from Harvard University Press.

8. Interviews conducted by the author with Paul Newman on his films for various magazine and newspaper articles between 1973–1984.

9. "Dor" is the pseudonym employed by Bob McFadden and Rod McKuen in 1959 for their two-sided novelty hit from Brunswick Records. Side One was "The Mummy," a take-off on the Youth Culture's absorption with Universal horror films from the 1930s and 1940s following their release to TV that year as the "Shock" package. Side Two mocked the Beats, furthering the goofy approach taken toward that very serious subculture which began with Herb Caen's employment of the term Beatnik.

10. Podhoretz, quoted in Morgan.

11. Intriguingly, the first use of 'The Beat Generation' as a term does not belong to Holmes, Huncke, Kerouac or any of the others associated with the group. Exploitation filmmaker Zugsmith, when readying his film of that title for release, checked and was surprised to realize that no one had yet thought to officially register it with the office and did so himself. Hence, he has always "owned" it.

12. "Interview with Sheila James Kuehl" (Digital); Archive of American Television, 2013.

13. Miles, Barry. *Hippie*. New York: Sterling Publishing, 2005; pp. 9–18.

14. McCleary, John Bassett. *Hippie Dictionary: A Cultural Encyclopedia of the 1960s and 1970s*. Berkeley, CA: Ten Speed Press, 2002; pp. xi–xiv, 227.

15. Written by Dino Fekaris and Nick Zessus, appearing on the *One World* album (1971) produced by Tom Baird as well as a Live in Concert Rare Earth album that same year.

16. Among several studies on organized student radicalism, by far the finest as to quality of writing, attention to specific detail, and objectivity of attitude is: Sale, Kirkpatrick. *SDS: The Rise and Development of Students for a Democratic Society*. New York: Random House, 1973.

17. The statement itself is ordinarily credited to Herbert Deane, an administrator of Columbia University at the time. As such, he was speaking both for himself and for his colleagues, all of them utterly unaware of how insensitive such phrasing would sound to a student body that had, for the most part, been orderly enough up until that moment. Deane has repeated said that his words were jumbled and taken entirely out of context though transcripts of

his interview with the campus radio station make clear that this was indeed the essence of his position and that of the administration itself.

18. Cocks, Jay, in *Time* (Spring 1970); quoted in Brode, Douglas. *The Films of the Sixties*. Secaucus, NJ: Citadel Press, 1990; p. 163.

19. Interviews conducted by the author with John Lennon in Fall, 1971 at the suite at New York's St. Regis Hotel where Lennon and Yoko Ono were living and editing their experimental films.

20. See: Roger Ebert's Film Festival (Website); this and other quotations by the late critic/screenwriter originally appeared in *Film Comment* (1980).

*

Chapter Twelve

1. Hunter, James Davison. *Culture Wars: The Struggle to Control the Family, Art, Education, Law, and Politics in America*. New York: Basic Books, 1992; pp. 56–59.

2. Original song written by John Phillips, recorded by Scott McKenzie, produced as a record by Lou Adler. Intriguingly, what was accepted by the public at large as an essentially improvisational ode to the Youth Movement had actually been carefully planned as a commercial for the upcoming Monterey International Music Festival (June 1967), thus offering one more example from the CounterCulture era of the manner in which schemes to make money, however effectively realized, were mis-perceived as open artistic contributions to the public.

3. Baxter, John. *Hollywood in the Sixties*. London: The Tantivy Press, 1972; p. 101.

4. Baxter, p. 101.

5. The phrase appeared in so many national and local reviews, ranging from positive to negative to undecided, that it is now impossible to pinpoint which critic was the first to employ this or a similar phrase; several important instances include Crowther, Bosley, *The New York Times* (8/14/1967); Ebert, Roger, *Chicago Sun Times* (9/25/1967); Cook, Page, *Films in Review 18*, no. 18 (October 1967); Johnson, Albert, *Film Quarterly 21*, no. 2 (Winter 1967–1968).

6. Sherk, Warren M. *The Films of Mack Sennett*. Metuchen, NJ: Scarecrow Press, 1997; pp. 17–28, 32–36.

7. Foster, Mark. "The Automobile and the City," in Lewis, David L., and Goldstein, Laurence (eds.). *The Automobile and American Culture*. Ann Arbor: The University of Michigan Press, 1980; p. 24.

8. Frye, Helen. "The Automobile and American Fashion, 1900–1930" in Lewis/Goldstein, p. 48.

9. Frye, p. 48.

10. Lewis, "Sex and the Automobile: From Rumble Seats to Rockin' Vans" in Lewis/Goldstein, p. 123.

11. Originally written in 1955 by Charles Ryan and recorded by him as 'Charley Ryan and the Livingston Brothers." Ryan re-recorded the song in 1959, when it reached the charts once again; it also charted in 1960 when Johnny Bond offered a cover. Perhaps the best known

268   SEX, DRUGS & ROCK 'N' ROLL

version is the 1972 hit by Commander Cody and His Lost Planet Airmen, which not surprisingly, considering its time period, offered a tongue-in-cheek/winking-at-the-audience
version of what had previously been performed straight.

12. Best, Amy L. *Fast Cars, Cool Rides: The Accelerating World of Youth and Their Cars.* New York: New York University Press, 2005; pp. 28–42, 51–65.
13. Reports vary but, according to several cast and crew members, the song, which offi-cially is credited to Ronald Stein, also had artistic contributions from Arkoff, Cahn, Rusoff, and Gorshin. For the best analysis of this particular film, see Smith, Gary A. *American International Pictures: The Golden Years.* Fort Worth: BearManor Media, 2013; p. 55.
14. Dr. Joyce Brothers, quoted by Lewis, p. 127.
15. Geraldo Rivera interview; ABC-TV, 1974.
16. Thompson, Hunter S. *Hell's Angels: A Strange and Terrible Saga.* New York: Ballantine Books, 1996; pp. 23–52.
17. Sanford, Charles L. "'Women's Place in American Car Culture," in Lewis/Goldstein, p. 137; also Smith, Julien. "A Runaway Match: The Automobile in American Film, 1900–1920," also in Lewis/Goldstein, p. 182.
18. Belasco, Warren. "Commercialized Nostalgia: The Origins of the Roadside Strip," in Lewis/Goldstein, p. 107.
19. Belasco, p. 108.
20. Belasco, p. 108.
21. Deming, Mark. "Biography: Arch Hall, Jr."; Allmusic.
22. Hutchison, Alice L. *Kenneth Anger.* London: Black Dog Publishing, 2011; pp. 43–47.
23. Biskind, Peter. *Easy Riders, Raging Bulls: How The Sex-Drugs-and-Rock 'n' Roll Generation Saved Hollywood.* New York: Simon & Schuster/Touchstone, 1999; pp. 243–246.
24. Smith, Richard and Steele-Perkins, Chris. *The Teds.* Stockport, Cheshire: Dewi Lewis Publishing, 2003; pp. 29–44.
25. McDonough, Jimmy. *Big Bosoms and Square Jaws: The Biography of Russ Meyer, King of the Sex Film.* New York: Three Rivers Press, 2006; pp. 132–136.
26. Box Office Domestic Rentals for 1966: *Variety* (archives).
27. Two excellent sources for tracking down both popular and little-known examples of the cycle cycle: Seate, Mike, *Two Wheels on Two Reels: A History of Biker Movies.* North Conway, NH: Whitehorse Press/Kennedy Associates, 2000; Wyatt, James. *Sleazy Riders: A Guide to the Sleaziest Biker Flicks Ever Made.* N.p.: Simple Studio, 2011.
28. Wooley, Joseph, and Price, Michael H. *The Big Book of Biker Flicks.* Tulsa, OK: Hawk Publishing, 2005; p. 131.
29. Ebert, Roger. "Easy Rider" (originally reviewed 1969), re-reviewed on October 24, 2004; GREAT MOVIES.
30. Shickel, Richard. "*Easy Rider* Review"; *Life* (9/1969).
31. See Hill, Lee. *Easy Rider.* London: British Film Institute, 1996.
32. Ebert, GREAT MOVIES/Website.
33. Gitlin, Todd; quoted by Bailey, Beth, "Sexual Revolution(s)" in Farber, David (Ed.) *The Sixties: From Memory to History.* Chapel Hill: The University of North Carolina Press, 1994; p. 257.

34. Kael, Pauline. *The New Yorker* review, quoted by Ebert, GREAT MOVIES/Website.
35. Pirsig, R(obert) M. *Zen and the Art of Motorcycle Maintenance*. New York: William Morrow, 1974; p. 52.
36. Pirsig, p. 79.
37. Ebert, GREAT MOVIES/Website.

*

Epilogue

1. Frye, Northrop. *The Secular Scripture: A Study of the Structures of Romance*. Cambridge, MA: Harvard University Press, 1976; p. 178
2. Frye, p. 179.
3. Geraghty, Lincoln. *Living With* Star Trek: *American Culture and the* Star Trek *Universe*. London: I.B. Taurus, 2007; p. 134.
4. This quotation was offered by Hopper to numerous members of the working press during fall 1969, at the time of *Easy Rider's* release. Hopper was responding to questions about why his film casts Peter Fonda as 'Wyatt,' a drug-dealing biker, and whether this decision was 'informed' by the fact that Fonda's father Henry played the upstanding and heroic marshal Wyatt (Earp) in My *Darling Clementine* (John Ford, 1946).
5. Zimmerman, Paul D. "Blood and Water" in *Newsweek*; July 1, 1974; p. 74.
6. Pye, Michael. *The Movie Brats: How the Film Generation Took Over Hollywood*. New York: Holt McDougall, 1979; pp. 37–59.
7. Numerous Reagan biographies deal with the actor/president's long-time friendship with Walt Disney; in particular, see Dinesh D'Souza, *Ronald Reagan: How an Ordinary Man Became an Extraordinary Leader*. Free Press/Touchstone.
8. Box Office Mojo/IMDB; Top Box Office Hits of 1985.
9. Kael, Pauline, quoted in Brode, Douglas. *The Films of Steven Spielberg*. New York: Citadel Press/Kensington, 1995; p. 25.
10. Shickel, Richard. *The Disney Version*. New York: Simon and Schuster, 1968; p. 23.
11. Shickel, pp. 24–25.
12. Shickel, p. 25.
13. The author's personal interviews with Rod Serling, conducted between 1971–1975. These are included in Brode, Douglas and Serling, Carol. *Rod Serling and the Twilight Zone*; Fort Lee, NJ: Barricade Books, 2009.

BIBLIOGRAPHY (SELECTED)

Adams, Nick & Adams, Allyson, *The Rebel and the King* (WaterDancer Press, 2002).

Alba, Ben and Leno, Jay, *Inventing Late Night: Steve Allen and the Original Tonight Show* (Amherst, NY: Prometheus Books, 2005).

Allen, Steve, *Reflections* (Amherst, NY: Promethus Books, 1994).

Altschuler, Glenn C., *All Shook up: How Rock 'n' Roll Changed America* (New York: Oxford University Press, 2004).

Anderson, Karen, *Wartime Women: Sex Roles, Family Relationships, and the Status of Women During World War II* (Westport, CT: Praeger, 1981).

Anderson, Paul F., *The Davy Crockett Craze: A Look at the 1950s Phenomenon and Davy Crockett Collectibes* (Darien, CT: R&G Productions, 1996).

Arkoff, Samuel Z., *Flying Through Hollywood by the Seat of My Pants: From the Man Who Brought You "I Was a Teenage Werewolf" and "Muscle Beach Party"* (Secaucus, NJ: Carol Publishing, 1992).

Baxter, John, *Hollywood in the Sixties* (London, UK: The Tantivy Press, 1972).

Bennett, James, *Oral History and Delinquency: The Rhetoric of Criminology* (Chicago, IL: University of Chicago Press, 1988).

Bensimon, Kelly Killoren, *The Bikini Book* (New York, NY: Assouline, 2006).

Best, Amy L., *Fast Cars, Cool Rides: The Accelerating World of Youth and Their Cars* (New York, NY: New York University Press, 2005).

Best, Pete & Doncaster, Patrick, *Beatle! The Pete Best Story* (Medford, NJ: Plexus Publishing, 1994).

Betrock, Alan (ed.), *Jayne Mansfield vs. Mamie Van Doren: Battle of the Blondes* Shake Books, 1993).

Binder, Arnold; Geis, Gilbert; Bruce, Dickson D., *Juvenile Delinquency: Historical, Cultural and Legal Perspectives* (Atlanta, GA: Anderson Publishing, 2000).

Biskind, Peter, *Easy Riders, Raging Bulls: How The Sex-Drugs- and-Rock 'n' Roll Generation Saved Hollywood* (New York: Simon & Schuster/Touchstone, 1999).

———. *Seeing Is Believing: How Hollywood Taught Us to Stop Worrying and Love the Fifties* (New York: Pantheon Books, 1983).

Bogle, Donald, *Toms, Coons, Mulattoes, Mammies, & Bucks: An Interpretive History of Blacks in American Films* (New York: Continuum, 2001 (Fourth Edition).

Boone, Pat, *Twixt Twelve and Twenty* (New York: Dell Publishing, 1960).

Brode, Douglas, *Elvis, Cinema and Popular Culture* (Jefferson, NC:) McFarland, 2006.

Brode, Douglas & Serling, Carol, *Rod Serling and the Twilight Zone* (Fort Lee, NJ: Barricade Books, 2009).

Bryant, J. Alison, *The Children's Television Community* (Abingdon, UK: Routledge, 2006).

Chapple, Steve & Garofalo, Reebee, *Rock 'n' Roll Is Here to Pay* (Chicago: Nelson-Hall, 1977).

Charters, Ann, *Beat Down to Your Soul: What Was the Beat Generation?* New York, NY: Penguin/ Putnam, 2001.

Chilton, John, *The Story of Louis Jordan and His Music* (Ann Arbor, MI: University of Michigan Press, 1994).

Clark, Randall, *At a Theatre Near You: The History, Culture, and Politics of the American Exploitation Film* (London, UK: Routledge, 2013).

Clum, John M, *"He's All Man!" Learning Masculinity, Gayness, and Love from American Movies* (Basingstoke, UK: Palgrave Macmillan, 2002).

Cohen, Lizabeth, *A Consumer's Republic: The Politics of Mass Consumption in Postwar America* (New York: Vintage, 2003).

Compton, Michael, *Pop Art.* (London, UK: Hamlyn, 1970).

Conway, Mike, *The Origins of Television News in America: The Visualizers at CBS in the 1940s* (New York: Peter Lang, 2012).

Corman, Roger, *How I Made a Hundred Movies in Hollywood and Never Lost a Dime* (Boston, MA: Da Capo, 1998).

Crenshaw, Marshall, *Hollywood Rock: A Guide to Rock 'n' Roll in the Movies* (New York, NY: HarperPerennial/Agincourt, 1994).

Dale, Alan, *The Spider and the Marionettes* (New York: Lyle Stuart, 1965).

Dawson, J., *Rock Around the Clock: The Record That Started the Rock Revolution!* (Montclair, NJ: Backbeat Books, 2005).

de Beauvoir, Simone, *The Works of Simone de Beauvoir: The Second Sex and the Ethics of Ambiguity* (CreateSpace Independent Publishing Platform, 2011).

Doherty, Thomas, *Teenagers and Teenpics: The Juvenilization of American Movies in the 1950s* (Philadelphia, PA: Temple University Press, 2002).

Douglas, Susan J., *Where the Girls Are: Growing Up Female with the Mass Media* (New York, NY: Random House/Times Book, 1994).

Edgren, Gretchen, *The Playboy Book: Fifty Years* (Berlin/Hong Kong; Taschen, 2007).

Eig, Jonathan, *The Birth of the Pill: How Four Crusaders Reinvented Sex and Law* (New York, NY: W.W. Norton, 2014).

Eisenhower, Dwight D., *Crusade in Europe: A Personal Account of World War II* (New York: Doubleday & Company, 1948).

Escott, Colin & Hawkins, Martin, *Good Rockin' Tonight: Sun Records and the Birth of Rock 'n' Roll* (New York, NY. St. Martin's Griffin, 1992.

Evans, Harold, *The American Century* (New York, NY; Knopf, 1998).

Evans, Mike, *The Bikini Book* (New York, NY: Universe Publishing, 1996).

Farber, David (ed.) *The Sixties: From Memory to History* (Chapel Hill, NC: The University of North Carolina Press, 1994).

Farrell, J., *One Nation Under Goods: Malls and the Seduction of American Shopping* (Washington, D.C.: Smithsonian, 2003).

Ferrer, Margaret Lundrigan & Navanna, Tova, *Levittown: The First 50 Years* (Mount Pleasant, SC: Arcadia, 1997).

Fine, Benjamin, *1,000,000 Delinquents* (New York; The World Publishing Company, 1955).

Fishwick, Marshall, *Parameters of Popular Culture* (Bowling Green, OH; Popular Press, 1974).

Freund, David M., *Colored Property: State Policy and White Racial Relations in Suburban America* (Chicago, IL: University of Chicago Press, 2010).

Friedan, Betty, *The Feminine Mystique* (New York: W.W. Norton & Co., 1963).

Frye, Northrop, *The Secular Scripture: A Study of the Structures of Romance* (Cambridge, MA. Harvard University Press, 1976).

Funicello, Annette, *A Dream Is a Wish Your Heart Makes: My Story* (New York, NY; Hyperion, 1994).

Fure-Slocum, Eric, *Contesting the Post War City: Working Class and Growth Politics in 1940s Milwaukee* (New York, NY: Cambridge University Press, 2013).

Fusco, Joseph, *The Films of Mamie Van Doren* (Albany, GA: BearManor Media, 2010).

Gamson, Joshua, *Claim to Fame: Celebrity in Contemporary America* (Oakland, CA: University of California Press, 1994).

Garfield, David, *A Player's Piece: The Story of the Actor's Studio* (New York: Macmillan, 1980).

Gelden, Ken & Thornton, Sarah (eds.), *The Subculture Reader* (New York, NY: Routledge, 2005) Second Edition.

Gelly, Devorah, *The Brian Epstein Story* (London, UK: Faber and Faber Ltd., 1999).

Geraghty, Lincoln, *Living With Star Trek: American Culture and the Star Trek Universe* (London, UK: I.B. Taurus, 2007).

Gitlin, Todd, *The Sixties: Years of Hope, Days of Rage* (New York, NY: Bantam, 1987).

Goldberger, Paul, *Up from Zero: Politics, Architecture, and the Rebuilding of New York* (New York: Random House, 2005).

Goldman, Albert, *The Lives of John Lennon* (New York: William Morris & Co., 1968).

Gordon, Berry & Asamen, Joy K. (eds.), *Children and Television: Images in a Changing Socio-Cultural World* (New York, NY: Sage Publications, 1991).

Gornick, Vivian & Moran, Barbara K., *Women in a Sexist Society: Studies in Power and Powerlessness* (New York, NY: Basic Books, 1971).

Graham, Don, *No Name on the Bullet: A Biography of Audie Murphy* (New York: Viking, 1989).

Grisez, Germain & Shaw, Russell, *Beyond the New Morality: The Responsibility of Freedom* (Notre Dame, IN: University of Notre Dame Press, 1988).

Guralnick, Peter, *Last Train to Memphis: The Rise of Elvis Presley* (Boston, MA: Little Brown, 1994).

Guylas, Aaron John, *Extraterrestrials and the American Zeitgeist: Alien Contact Tales Since the 1940s* (Jefferson, NC: McFarland, 2013).

Halberstadt, Hans. *Combines and Harvesters: Motorbooks International Farm Tractor Color History* (Minneapolis, MN: Motorbooks International, 1994).

Halberstam, David, *The Fifties* (New York, NY: Ballantine Books, 1994).

Halliwell, Leslie, *Film and Video Guide* (London: HarperCollins, 2012).

Handy, Erbe & Blackham, Antonier, *Made in Japan: Transistor Radios of the 1950s and 1960s* (San Francisco, CA: Chronicle Books, 1993).

Haskell, Molly, *From Reverence to Rape: The Treatment of Women in Movies* (Chicago, IL: University of Chicago Press, 1987).

Haslam, Gerald W, *Workin' Man's Blues: Country Music in California* (Los Angeles/Oakland; University of California Press, 1999).

Havis, Allan, *Cult Films: Taboo and Transgression* (Lanham, MD: Rowman & Littlefield: University Press of America, 2007).

Hawkins, Joan, *Cutting Edge: Art-Horror and the Horrific Avant-Garde* (Minneapolis, MN: University of Minnesota Press, 2000).

Hill, Lee. *Easy Rider* (London, UK: British Film Institute, 1996).

Hine, Thomas, *Populuxe: The Look and Life of America in the '50s and 60s, from Tailfins and TV Dinners to Barbie Dolls and Fallout Shelters* (New York, NY: Knopf, 1986).

Hoberman, J. & Rosenbaum, Jonathan, *Midnight Movies* (Cambridge, MA: Da Capo Press, 1991).

Holt, Irvin, *Cold War Kids: Politics and Childhood in Postwar America (1945–1960)* (Lawrence, KS: University Press of Kansas, 2011).

Howard-Pitney, David, *Martin Luther King Jr., Malcolm X, and the Civil Rights Struggle of the 1950s and 1960s: A Brief History* (New York, NY: Bedford/St. Martin's, 2004).

Huber, Patrick; Goodson, Steve; Anderson, David (eds.), *The Hank Williams Reader* (New York: Oxford University Press, 2014).

Hunter, James Davison, *Culture Wars: The Struggle to Control the Family, Art, Education, Law, and Politics in America* (New York, NY: Basic Books, 1992).

Hutchison, Alice L., *Kenneth Anger* (London, UK: Black Dog Publishing, 2011).

Jackson, John A., *The Alan Freed Story—The Early Years of Rock 'n' Roll* (Scottsdale, AZ: Collectibles Press, 2007).

Jackson, John A. *Big Beat Heat: Alan Freed and the Early Years of Rock 'n' Roll* (New York: McGraw-Hill; Schirmer Books, 1995).

Jeff, Leonard J., Simmos, Jerald L., *The Dame in the Kimono: Hollywood, Censorship, and the Production Code* (Lexington, KY: The University of Kentucky Press, 2001).

Kaufman, Burton, *The Korean Conflict* (Westport, CT: Greenwood Press, 1999).

Kaufman, David, *The Untold Story of the Girl Next Door* (London: Virgin Books, 2010).

Kazan, Elia, *Elia Kazan: A Life* (Boston, MA: Da Capo Press, 1997).

Kean, Leslie, *UFOS: Generals, Pilots, and Government Officials Go on the Record* (New York: Three Rivers Press, 2011).

Keeyes, Jon, *Attack of the B Queens* (Opelousas, LA: Luminary Press/Midnight Marquee Press, 2003).

Knight, Arthur, *The Liveliest Art: A Panoramic History of the Movies* (New York: Mentor Books/The New American Library, 1957).

Koper, Richard, *Fifties Blondes: Sexbombs, Sirens, Bad Girls and Teen Queens* (Albany, GA; BearManor Books, 2010).

Kramer, Larry, *When They Were Boys: The True Story of the Beatles' Rise to the Top* (Philadelphia, PA: Running Press, 2013).

Kramer, Stanley & Coffey, Thomas M. *A Mad, Mad, Mad, Mad World: A Life in Hollywood.* San Diego, CA: Harcourt, 1997.

Kreidl, John, *Nicholas Ray* (New York; Twayne Publishers/G.K. Hall and Company, 1977).

Kusher, David, *Levittown: Two Families, One Tycoon, and the Fight for Civil Rights in America's Legendary Suburb* (New York: Walker & Company, 2009).

Leary, Timothy. *Flashbacks* (New York: Tarcher/Penguin, 1997).

Lencek, Lena & Bosker, Gideon, *Making Waves: Swimsuits and the Undressing of America* (San Francisco, CA: Chronicle Books, 1989).

Leary, Dr. Timothy, *The Psychedelic Experience: A Manual Based on the Tibetan Book of the Dead* (New York, NY: Citadel Underground, 2000).

Lecie, Robert, *Conflict: The History of the Korean War (1950–1953)* (Boston, MA: Da Capo Press, 1996).

Lemann, Nicholas, *The Promised Land: The Great Black Migration and How It Changed America* (New York; Vintage, 1992).

Lewis, David L. & Goldstein, Laurence (eds.), *The Automobile and American Culture* (Ann Arbor, MI: The University of Michigan Press, 1980).

Lewis, Jon. *American Film: A History* (New York: W.W. Norton & Co., 2007).

Lisanti, Thomas, *Drive In Dream Girls* (Jefferson, NC: McFarland & Company, 2003).

———. *Hollywood Surf and Beach Movies: The First Wave, 1959–1969* (Jefferson, NC: McFarland, 2012).

Lorber, Richard & Fladell, Ernest, *The Gap.* (New York: McGraw. Hill, 1968).

Maier, Thomas, *Dr. Spock: An American Life* (Boston, MA; Houghton Mifflin Harcourt, 1998).

Mailer, Norman, *Marilyn: A Biography* (New York, NY: Grosset & Dunlap, 1973).

Manso, Peter, *Brando: The Biography* (New York: Hyperion, 1994).

Marcus, Greil; Gurdnick, Peter; Sante, Luc; Gordon, Robert, *Rockabilly: The Twang Heard 'Round the World* (Minneapolis, MN: Voyageur Press, 2011).

————. *The Old, Weird America: The World of Bob Dylan's Basement Tapes*. (New York, NY: Holt, 2001).

Marling, Karal Ann, *As Seen on TV: The Visual Culture of Everyday Life in the 1950s* (Cambridge MA: Harvard University Press, 1996).

Marsh, Dave. *Elvis* (New York: Barnes & Noble/Smithmark, 1997).

———— & Swenson, John. *The Rolling Stone Record Guide, 1ˢᵗ Edition* (New York: Random House/The Rolling Stone Press, 1979).

Mast, Gerald, *A Short History of the Movies* (Third Edition) (Indianapolis: Bobbs Merrill Educational Publishing, 1981).

Mayer, Martin, *MADISON AVENUE, U.S.A.: The Inside Story of American Advertising* (New York: Penguin, 1961).

McCleary, John Bassett. *Hippie Dictionary: A Cultural Encyclopedia of the 1960s and 1970s.* (Berkeley, CA: Ten Speed Press, 2002).

McDonald, Tamar Jeffers, *Doris Day Confidential: Hollywood, Sex, and Stardom* (London UK: I.B. Taurus, 2013).

McDonough, Jimmy, *Big Bosoms and Square Jaws: The Biography of Russ Meyer, King of the Sex Film* (New York: Three Rivers Press, 2006).

McLuhan, Marshall. *The Extensions of Man* (New York: McGraw-Hill, 1964).

Meisler, Richard J., *Black Ghetto: Promised Land or Colony?* (Lexington, MA: Heath, 1972).

Miles, Barry, *Hippie* (New York, NY; Sterling Publishing, 2005).

————. *The British Invasion* (New York NY: Sterling, 2009).

Millard, Andre, *The Electric Guitar: A History of an American Icon* (Baltimore, MD: Johns Hopkins University Press, 2004).

Miller, Nathan, *New World Coming: The 1920s and the Making of Modern America* (Boston, MA: Da Capo Press, 2004).

Mondale, Sarah, *School: The Story of American Education* (Boston, MA: Beacon Press, 2002).

Morales, Julio, *Puerto Rican Poverty and Migration: We Just Had to Try Elsewhere* (Westport, CT: Praeger, 1986).

Morgan, Bill, *The Typewriter Is Holy: The Complete Uncensored History of the Beat Generation* (Berkeley, CA: Counterpoint/Perseus, 2011).

Munford, Rebecca & Waters, Melanie, *Feminism and Popular Culture: The Post-Feminist Mystique* (New Brunswick, NJ; Rutgers University Press, 2014).

Myers, John E.B., *Child Protection in America: Past, Present, and Future* (New York, NY: Oxford University Press, 2006).

Norman, Philip, *John Lennon: A Life:* (New York, NY: Ecco/HarperCollins, 2009).

Norris, Christopher, *Deconstruction: Theory and Practice* (New York, NY: Routledge, 2002).

Oakley, J. Ronald, *God's Country: America in the Fifties* (New York, NY: Dembner Books, 1986).

Osgood, Kenneth. *The Cold War at Home: Eisenhower's Secret Propaganda Battle at Home and Abroad* (Lawrence, KS: University Press of Kansas, 2006).

Parker, Scott F., *Conversations with Ken Kesey* (Jackson: University of Mississippi Press, 2004).

Peter, Joseph, *Good Times: An Oral History of America in the Nineteen Sixties* (New York: Charterhouse, 1973).

Pirsig, Robert M., *Zen and the Art of Motorcycle Maintenance* (New York, NY; William Morrow, 1974).

Pomerance, Murray, *American Cinema of the 1950s* (New Brunswick, NJ; Rutgers University Press, 2005).

Pomeroy, Wardell B.; Martin, Clyde E.; Gebhard, Paul H & Kinsey, Alfred C., *Sexual Behavior in the Human Female* (Philadelphia: W.B. Saunders, 1953).

Pulliam, John D. and Van Patten, James J., *History of Education in America* (Upper Saddle River, NJ; Pearson, 2006).

Pye, Michael, *The Movie Brats: How the Film Generation Took Over Hollywood* (New York, NY: Holt McDougall, 1979).

Rees, Jonathan, *Refrigeration Nation: A History of Ice, Appliances, and Enterprise in America* (Baltimore, MD: Johns Hopkins University Press, 2013).

Reynolds, Malvina, *Malvina Reynolds Songbook* (Paducah, KY: Schroeder, 1984).

Rhodes, Guy Don, *Edgar G. Ulmer: Detour on Poverty Row* (Lanham, MD: Lexington Books, 2008).

Ricci, Mark & Conway, Mark, *The Films of Marilyn Monroe* (New York: Cadillac Publishing, 1964).

Rieff, David (ed.)., *Susan Sontag: Essays of the 1960s and 70s* (New York NY: Library of America, 2013).

Riesman, David; Glazer, Nathan; and Denney, Reyel, *The Lonely Crowd: A Study of the Changing America* (New Haven, CT: Yale University Press (reissue), 2001).

Riley, Charles A. Jr., *The Art of Peter Max* (New York: Harry N. Abrams, 2002).

Rosen, Marjorie, *Popcorn Venus: Women, Movies, and the American Dream* (New York, NY: Avon Library, 1974).

Rotha, Paul, *The Film Till Now* (Middlesex, UK: Hamlyn (updated edition), 1967).

Sale, Kirkpatrick, *SDS: The Rise and Development of Students for a Democratic Society* (New York, NY; Random House, 1973).

Sanders, Don and Susan, *The American Drive In Theatre* (New York, NY: Cresline, 2013).

Sarris, Andrew, *The American Cinema: Directors and Directions 1929–1968* (Boston; Da Capo Press, 1968).

Savage, Kerry, *Payola in the Music Industry: A History, 1880–1991* (Jefferson, NC; McFarland, 2013).

Saxton, Martha, *Jayne Mansfield and the American Fifties.* (Boston, MA; Houghton Mifflin Company, 1975).

Scanlon, Jennifer, *Bad Girls Go Everywhere: The Life of Helen Gurley Brown, the Woman Behind Cosmopolitan Magazine* (New York: Penguin (Reprint), 2010).

Schepp, Brad & Schepp, Debra, *TV Wonderland: The Enchantment of Early Television.* (The Collector's Press, 2005).

Schlosser, Eric, *Fast Food Nation: The Dark Side of the All-American Meal* (Boston: Houghton Mifflin Harcourt, 2001).

Seate, Mike, *Two Wheels on Two Reels: A History of Biker Movies* (North Conway, NH: Whitehorse Press/Kennedy Associates, 2000).

Sewell, Philip W., *Television in the Age of Radio: Modernity, Imagination, and the Making of a Medium* (New Brunswick, NJ: Rutgers University Press, 2014).

Shaw, Arnold, *Rockin' 50s* (New York, NY: Hawthorne Books, 1974).

Shelf, David. *All We Are Saying* (New York, NY: St. Martin's, 2000).

Sherk, Warren M, *The Films of Mack Sennett* (Metuchen, NJ: Scarecrow Press, 1997).

Shickel, Richard, *The Disney Version* (New York, NY: Simon and Schuster, 1968).

Slade, Giles, *Made to Break: Technology and Obsolescence in America* (Cambridge, MA: Harvard University Press, 2007).

Sloan, Alfred (P.), *My Years With General Motors* (New York, NY: Crown Business, 1990).

Smith, Gary A. *American International Pictures: The Golden Years* (Albany, GA: BearManor Media, 2013).

Smith, Norman R., *Transistor Radios (1954–1968)* (Afglen, PA: Schiffer Publications Ltd, 1998).

Smith, Richard & Steele-Perkins, Chris, *The Teds* (Stockport, Cheshire: Dewi Lewis Publishing, 2003).

Spencer, John Michael. *The Rhythms of Black Folk: Race, Religion, Pan-Africanism* (Trenton, NJ: African World Press, 1995).

Stam, Robert, *Reflexivity in Film and Literature: From* Don Quixote *to Jean-Luc Godard* (New York: Columbia University Press, 1992).

Strait, Raymond, *The Tragic Secret Life of Jayne Mansfield* (Washington, DC: Regnery, 1974).

Strub, Whitney, *Obscenity Rules: Roth vs. United States and the Long Struggle over Sexual Expression* (Lawrence, KS: University of Kansas Press, 2013).

Sugumar, V. Raji & Chrysolyte, S. Jasmina., *Impact of TV Viewing Behaviour on the Cereal Food Choices of Children* (Chandler, AZ: Academic Publishing, 2013).

Sullivan, Steve. *Va Va Voom!: Bombshells, Pin-Ups, Sexpots and Glamour Girls* (Los Angeles: Rhino/General Publishing Group, 1995).

Svehla, Gary J., *Guilty Pleasures of the Horror Film* (Baltimore, MD: Midnight Marquee Press, 1996).

——— & Svehla, Susan, *Atom Age Cinema: The Offbeat, the Classic and the Obscure* (Baltimore, MD: Midnight Marquee Press, 2014).

Taylor, John Russell, *Hitch: The Life and Times of Alfred Hitchcock* (Boston: Da Capo Press, 1996).

Thompson, Hunter S., *Hell's Angels: A Strange and Terrible Saga* (New York: Ballantine Books, 1996).

Tosches, Nick & Marcus, Greil, *Hellfire: The Jerry Lee Lewis Story* (New York, NY: Grove Press, 1998).

Tropiano, Stephen, *Rebels and Chicks: A History of the Hollywood Teen Movie* (New York, NY: Back Stage Books, 2006).

Van Doren, Mamie, *Playing the Field* (New York NY: Putnam (Adult), 1987).

Ward, Brian E., *Radio and the Struggle for Civil Rights in the South* (Gainesville: University Press of South Florida, 2006).

Warhol, Andy, *The Philosophy of Andy Warhol* (New York, NY: Harvest, 1977).

——— & Hackett, Pat, *POPism: The Warhol Sixties* (New York: Mariner Books, 2006).

Wilkerson, Isabel, *The Warmth of Other Suns* (New York: Vintage, 2011) (reprint).

Wills, Gary, *John Wayne's America* (New York, NY: Touchstone/Simon & Schuster, 1988).

Winkler, Allan M., *Home Front U.S.A. America During World War II* (Wheeling, IL: Harlan Davidson, 2000).

Witzel, Michael Karl, *The American Motel* (Minneapolis, MN: Motorbooks International, 2000).

Wolfe, Tom, *The Electric Kool-Aid Acid Test* (New York, NY: Farrar, Straus, Giroux, 1968).

Wood, Michael, *America in the Movies* (New York: Delta/Basic Books, 1975).

Wooley, Joseph & Price, Michael H, *The Big Book of Biker Flicks* (Tulsa: Hawk Publishing, 2005).

Wyatt, James, *Sleazy Riders: A Guide to the Sleaziest Biker Flicks Ever Made* (Simple Studio, 2011).

Yule, Andrew, *The Man Who "Framed" the Beatles: A Biography of Richard Lester* (New York, NY: Donald I Fine, 1994).

NEWSPAPER-JOURNAL ARTICLES/WEBSITES (SELECTED)

Albright, Mary Ann; "Real-life 'Gidget' Recalls Life at OSU," an interview with Kathy Kohner (Zuckerman); (*Corvallis-Gazette-Times*; 1/23/2007).

Burks, John. "Rock and Roll's Worst Day" in *Rolling Stone* (2/7/1970).

Cocks, Jay (*Time*, Spring 1970).

Corliss, Richard. "When Antonioni Blew Up the Movies": *Time*, April 2007.

Corliss, Richard. "All Time 100 Movies" in *Time* (2/12/2005).

Crowther, Bosley, "A Hard Day's Night Review" (*The New York Times*; 8/12/1964)

Deming, Mark. "Biography: Arch Hall, Jr."; *Allmusic*.

"Doctor Urges Comic Book Ban." *New York Times*, 4 September 1948, p. 6.

Ebert, Roger. "Easy Rider" (originally reviewed 1969), re-reviewed on October 24, 2004; Great Movies (Website).

——, Film Festival (Website).

——. "R.P.M." review (10/24/1971).

Gillespie, Alex & Cornish, Flora. "Intersubjectivity: Towards a Dialogue Analysis" (*Journal for the Theory of Social Behavior* (40), pp. 19–46).

Holmes, John Clellon, "This Is the Beat Generation" (*The New York Times*; 11/16/1952).

"Interview with Sheila James Kuehl" (Digital); Archive of American Television, 2013.

Kael, Pauline; quoted by Liz Smith, "The Swinger")Wowowow.com.; 1/08/2013).

Kamin, Jonathan, "The Social Reaction to Jazz and Rock" in *Journal of Jazz Studies* 2 (1974): 99.

Mailer, Norman. "The White Negro" (*Dissent*, 1957).

McNulty, Patrick (interviewer); Bruce Brown quote (*The Los Angeles Times*, 1966).

Mulvey, Laura, "Visual Pleasure in Narrative Cinema" (written 1973, originally published in *Screen*, 1975).

Schickel, Richard. "*Easy Rider* Review"; *Life* (9/1969).

Thomas, Bob. "Sex Goddess Lives to Tell Her Story." *Times Daily*/Associated Press (12/2/1997).

Thompson, Howard. "Tomb of Ligeia" review (*The New York Times*; May 16, 1964).

Wilson, Earl, "Kitty Loses Voice, Finds Religion" (8/7/1962), nationally syndicated news column.

Zimmerman, Paul D. "Blood and Water" in Newsweek; July 1, 1974; p. 74.

UNCLASSIFIED/DE-CLASSIFIED DOCUMENTS (SELECTED)

MacGregor, Morris. *Integration of the Armed Forces, 1940–1965*. Amazon Digital Services, 2012.

United States Congress, Records of the Subcommittee to Investigate Sex and Violence in Motion Pictures and Their Social Impact on the Impressionable Young (on file: Washington, D.C., The Congressional Records).

United States Congress, Records of the Subcommittee to Investigate Juvenile Delinquency (on file: Washington, D.C., The Congressional Records).

ABOUT THE AUTHOR

DOUGLAS BRODE is a screenwriter, playwright, novelist, graphic novelist, film historian, and multi-award-winning journalist. Born and raised on Long Island, he traveled upstate for his education. After completing undergraduate work at S.U.N.Y. Geneseo and graduate work in Shakespearean studies and creative writing at Syracuse University, Brode and his wife Sue (Johnson) remained in central New York and raised a family. Brode became a film critic for such local newspapers as the *Syracuse New Times* and *Post-Standard*, as well as daily commentator on WHEN-AM radio and a member of the TV news teams for the local ABC and CBS affiliates. Brode also appeared to great acclaim in a number of regional theatre stage productions. He then joined the faculty of Syracuse University, the Newhouse School of Public Communications, Department of TV, Film, and Digital Media to create and teach the Film Classics program.

Brode wrote the screenplay for the motion picture *Midnight Blue* (1996) starring Harry Dean Stanton and Dean Stockwell, as well as the novels *Sweet Prince: The Passion of Hamlet* (2004) and *"PATSY!": The Life and Times of Lee Harvey Oswald* (2013). The author of nearly forty books on movies and the mass media, his work includes *Films of the Fifties, Films of Steven Spielberg, Denzel Washington* (a biography), *Shakespeare in the Movies* (for Oxford University Press), two books on Walt Disney—*From Walt to Woodstock* (2004) and *Multiculturalism and the Mouse* (2006), both for University of Texas Press, Austin—and *Elvis Cinema and Popular Culture* (2007) for McFarland Press. His articles have appeared in such academic journals as *Cineaste* and *Television Quarterly* as well as commercial publications ranging from *Rolling Stone* to *TV Guide*.

A lifelong fan of Westerns, he is the author of *Shooting Stars of the Small Screen: An Encyclopedia of TV Cowboys* (University of Texas Press Austin), *Dream West: Politics and Religion in Cowboy Movies* (University of Texas Press Austin), and *John Wayne's Way: Life Lessons From the Duke* (twodot press) as well as the graphic novel *Yellow Rose of Texas: The Myth of Emily Morgan* (McFarland) in collaboration with illustrator Joe Orsak.

As to the science fiction genre, Brode and Carol (widow of Rod) Serling collaborated on *Rod Serling and* The Twilight Zone: *The Official 50th Anniversary Tribute* (2009). His science-fiction short-story "Ides of Texas" appears in the volume *More Stories from The Twilight Zone*, edited by Carol Serling. Also, Brode co-edited a two volume set of essays on *Star Wars* for Scarecrow Press and an upcoming similar pair of volumes on *Star Trek* for Rowman & Littlefield. Brode is the author of the soon-to-be released *Fantastic Planets, Forbidden Zones, and Lost Continents: The 100 Greatest Science-Fiction Films* (University of Texas Press, Austin).

As an educator, Brode created the Film Classics program for Syracuse University's Newhouse School of Public Communications. He taught Cinema Studies courses within the Department of TV-Film-Digital Media from 1990 until his recent retirement.

He is pictured above with John Lennon and Yoko Ono, visiting them at John's request to further their serious study of film history in the autumn of 1971 at their suite at New York's St. Regis Hotel. (Photo credit: Richard Brown)

GENERAL INDEX

(Boldface numbers indicate photos)

FILM TITLE INDEX

Toby Miller
General Editor

Popular Culture and Everyday Life (PC&EL) is the new space for critical books in cultural studies. The series innovates by stressing multiple theoretical, political, and methodological approaches to commodity culture and lived experience, borrowing from sociological, anthropological, and textual disciplines. Each PC&EL volume develops a critical understanding of a key topic in the area through a combination of a thorough literature review, original research, and a student-reader orientation. The series includes three types of books: single-authored monographs, readers of existing classic essays, and new companion volumes of papers on central topics. Likely fields covered are: fashion; sport; shopping; therapy; religion; food and drink; youth; music; cultural policy; popular literature; performance; education; queer theory; race; gender; class.

For additional information about this series or for the submission of manuscripts, please contact:

Toby Miller
Department of Media & Cultural Studies
Interdisciplinary Studies Building
University of California, Riverside
Riverside, CA 92521

To order other books in this series, please contact our Customer Service Department:

(800) 770-LANG (within the U.S.)
(212) 647-7706 (outside the U.S.)
(212) 647-7707 FAX

Or browse online by series: www.peterlang.com